DIGITAL SYSTEM DESIGN USING PROGRAMMABLE LOGIC DEVICES

DIGITAL SYSTEM DESIGN USING PROGRAMMABLE LOGIC DEVICES

Parag K. Lala
Department of Computer Science and Computer Engineering,
University of Arkansas, USA.

BSP BS Publications
A unit of **BSP Books Pvt., Ltd.**

4-4-309, Giriraj Lane, Sultan Bazar,
Hyderabad - 500 095 - A.P.
Phone : 040 - 23445605, 23445688

Indian Reprint 2003
Reprint 2015

This reprint of ***Digital System Design Using Programmable Logic Devices*** has been published by arrangement with the author **Parag K. Lala**.

The book was previously published by Pearson Education, Inc. under Prentice Hall Inc. New Jersey.

For sale in India, Pakistan, Bangladesh, Myanmar, Srilanka, Mauritias and Nepal only.

Published by :

BSP BS Publications
A unit of **BSP Books Pvt., Ltd.**

4-4-309, Giriraj Lane, Sultan Bazar,
Hyderabad - 500 095 - A.P.
Phone : 040 - 23445605, 23445688
e-mail : contactus@bspublications.net
www.bspublications.net

Printed at
Aditya Offset Process (I) Pvt. Ltd.
Hyderabad.

Price : Rs. 425.00
ISBN - (13) : 978-81-7800-039-8

To my wife Meena,
and children Nupur and Kunal

Contents

CHAPTER 6
New Generation of Programmable Logic Devices, 167

CHAPTER 7
Logic Cell Array, 242

Index, 281

Preface

The traditional approach to digital system implementation has been to use logic gates (e.g., NAND/NOR and flip-flops). This resulted in a design philosophy which emphasizes the use of a minimal number of gates to implement a system. Although this philosophy is still fundamentally sound, advances in integrated circuit technology have made it impractical. With modern complex chips, the cost of saving a single gate or flip-flop is almost insignificant. Although a minimal gate logic circuit design is still relevant (e.g., in chip design), the majority of the digital systems are designed using LSI/VLSI devices rather than optimized logic at the gate level.

In recent years, the programmable logic devices (PLD) have become extremely popular as building blocks for digital systems. PLD technology and design practice are rapidly replacing the traditional method of logic design.

This book covers and compares many different PLDs from different manufacturers and provides design examples to show their applications. The emphasis is on guiding the readers to learn how to implement logic systems from specifications using PLDs.

Chapter 1 deals with various options currently available for implementing digital systems, and compares their relative merits. The design methodology for implementing systems using programmable logic devices is presented and some popular software design packages are introduced. Chapter 2 discusses the earliest PLD (i.e., PROM) and its applications in logic design. This chapter also deals with PLE devices. Chapter 3 covers FPLA devices offered by Signetics, Inc. A number of design examples have been considered. Chapter 4 focuses on the architecture and applications of FPLS devices. Chapter 5 discusses PAL devices and their applications. Architectures of new generation PAL devices are also dealt with. Chapter 6 covers erasable PLDs as well as devices with fold-back architectures. It also discusses devices specifically designed for state machine implementation. Chapter 7 is devoted to the discussion of Logic Cell Array chips offered by Xilinx, Inc. Each chapter, except Chapter 1, is supplemented by a problem set.

The book is intended for both an academic and a professional audience. It can be used as a textbook for an advanced level course in logic design in a Computer Engineering curriculum. Practicing engineers will also find it suitable for self-study.

With the increased complexity of PLDs, the user requires access to design software for efficient translation of design ideas into device programs. Several such software packages (e.g., ABEL and CUPL) which support virtually every PLD on the market are available. As a part of the logic design courses using PLDs, the students should be familiarized with one of these software packages. In this text, the use of ABEL and PALASM2 has been illustrated with several examples.

A number of people have helped me write this book, but first and foremost my thanks go to my wife, Meena for her forbearance during the writing of the book, and for her assistance in editing and typing the manuscript. The reviewers have done an admirable job by providing a critical and constructive review of an earlier version of the manuscript. I would also like to thank several of my former students particularly Gary Morgan, Jim Chan, Akhtaruzzaman Ali, Vinod Narayanan, and Dali Tao.

Chapter 1

Introduction

Traditionally, digital systems have been implemented with fixed-function SSI/MSI devices. A considerable range of such devices has been proposed. Since they are produced in bulk, these devices are relatively inexpensive. Other advantages include relatively high reliability and several sources of supply. However, a digital system implemented with SSI/MSI devices requires large board space, which leads to a larger product and a higher manufacturing cost. Moreover, it is often difficult to find a ready-made device which matches the exact function to be implemented. One additional problem is that a large number of devices on a board leads to a large number of interconnections, which, in turn, increases the probability of failure due to wrong or missing connections. Failed solder joints are generally the leading cause of board failures; reduction of interconnections reduces the solder joints.

By reducing a system's component count, it is possible to improve its reliability and lower its power consumption. However, the most important benefit derived from component reduction is that the cost of printed-circuit manufacturing and system support is significantly reduced. Currently, three design approaches are available in order to compact a system into fewer packages:

1. Full custom;
2. Semicustom; and
3. Programmable logic devices.

1.1 FULL CUSTOM DESIGN

The **full custom design** approach allows the most efficient utilization of silicon in the implementation of a circuit. As a result, it not only offers the smallest possible chip area for a circuit, but the reliability of the circuit is significantly improved as well. The most time-consuming part of the full custom design approach is the layout. Since the major goal is to pack the maximum amount of logic in the minimum possible area, the layout often has to be done by hand. Extraordinary care has to be taken to avoid errors because, in such a tightly packed environment, the correction of errors is often extremely difficult and time consuming. The use of **computer aided design (CAD)** in the efficient area utilization has not yet met with great success. Thus, the full custom design significantly increases the development costs and stretches the turnaround time for new designs. However, the full custom design is practicable in high-volume productions since the initial design and development cost can be spread over the large number of chips being produced.

An alternative approach to full custom design is to use **silicon compilers.** Ideally, a silicon compiler should accept the specification of a circuit written in a hardware description language and produce a complete chip layout. The advantage of a silicon compiler is that the design time can be drastically reduced. However, the silicon compilers which are currently available do not generate layouts as efficient as those hand-crafted by experienced designers.

A custom chip, whether manually or automatically designed, has to be fully tested to ensure that it performs satisfactorily. Although various techniques for testing chips, and designing them for testability, have been proposed in recent years, the problem is still very much there. As design density increases, it is becoming increasingly more important to consider testability aspects at the early stages of the design.

1.2 SEMICUSTOM DESIGN

Semicustom design means that transistors inside a chip can be interconnected in different ways to customize different designs, rather than being specifically designed in accordance with a particular specification [1]. Currently, there are two different approaches to semicustom design:

1. Gate-arrays; and
2. Standard cells

A **gate-array** consists of a collection of blocks, each block being a fully functional logic unit. By specifying interconnections among the blocks, gate-arrays can be customized to individual circuits. There is a certain category of gate-arrays which do not have prefabricated functional blocks. This type of gate-arrays, known as **uncommitted logic arrays,** consists of a matrix of identical prefabricated transistors grouped into small cells. A particular design is customized by interconnecting the transistors within a cell, and then interconnecting the multiple cells.

Semicustom design using **standard cells** enable the designers to begin with predesigned functional modules at their disposal, rather than starting from scratch, as in full custom approach. The functional modules or cells are stored in a database. The customization of a circuit is performed by partitioning the circuit into functional modules corresponding to those available in the data base and then laying out the cells and interconnecting them.

Gate-arrays offer the quickest and the most inexpensive route to semicustom implementation. The major disadvantage of gate-arrays is that the final implementation may contain unused cells causing chip area to be wasted. The standard cell approach overcomes this disadvantage by using only desired modules on a chip. The resulting chip area is not as optimized as in the full custom approach, but there is a significant reduction in the design effort. Since gate-arrays offer the fastest turnaround time, they are preferred for the first prototype of chips to confirm functionality and performance. Then, standard cells or full custom pin-for-pin replacements may be selected for high-volume production in order to reduce costs.

1.3 PROGRAMMABLE LOGIC DEVICES

Programmable logic devices (PLDs) may be considered as a compromise between the standard products and custom or semicustom circuits. Figure 1.1 compares the relative merits of fixed function devices, programmable devices, along with semicustom and custom integrated circuits according to some important criteria in digital design. Programmable logic devices offer a general architecture which the user can customize by inducing permanent or reversible physical changes in selected parts. Thus, these devices incorporate the user-programmable feature of semicustom design. In addition, they are smaller and simpler to use, and have a faster production turnaround time than gate-arrays. Although programmable logic devices cannot match the full range of gate-array performance, rapid increases in device densities and speed in recent years, along with developments in CAD tools, have narrowed the gap. It has been predicted that these devices will account for $2.12 billion in sales in 1990 as compared to $240 million in 1984, with the additional sale coming out of the standard-products and gate-array market (see Figure 1.2) [2].

Most programmable logic devices consist of an AND array followed by an OR array. The inputs to the device enter the AND array through the

	Fixed Function Devices	*Programmable Logic Devices*	*Semicustom*	*Full Custom*
Unit cost	Low	Low to medium	Medium	High
Cost/equivalent gate	Medium	Medium	Low	Lowest
Development time	Weeks	Hours	Weeks	Months
Space efficiency	Low	Medium	Medium	High
Non-recurring engineering costs	Low	Low	Medium	High
Ease of design change	Good	Good	Poor	Poor
Application support	Good	Fair	Fair	Fair
Alternate sources	Multiple	Multiple	Usually one	One

FIGURE 1.1
Comparison of different design approaches

buffers which generate both the true and the complement of the input signals. Each gate in the AND array generates a **minterm** of the input variables; a minterm is known as a **product line** in the programmable logic device nomenclature. The device outputs are produced by summing the product terms in the array of OR gates.

The AND-OR structured programmable logic devices can be grouped into three basic types:

1. Programmable read only memory (PROM);
2. Field-programmable logic array (FPLA); and
3. Programmable array logic (PAL).

The simplified structure of each device type is shown in Figure 1.3. As can be seen from the individual diagram of the devices, in a PROM, the AND array is fixed and the OR array is programmable. In a FPLA, both arrays are programmable. A PAL device is the mirror image of the PROM; its AND array is programmable, while the OR array is fixed.

PROMs as **programmable logic elements (PLE)** have been around for many years. However, like all memory devices, the outputs of a PROM are indeterminate after any input changes until the end of the access time period. Thus, if a PROM output is connected to the clock input of a registered device, the device may be triggered erroneously due to glitches which appear at the PROM output prior to the completion of the access time.

Programmable logic arrays (PLAs) are often used to implement multiple input/multiple output combinational logic circuits. PLAs are manufactured in two different ways. In the first, every possible connection is made through a fuse at every crosspoint; a crosspoint is the intersection of an input line or an output line with a product line. The undesired connections can be removed later by blowing the appropriate fuses. This type of PLAs is known as **field-**

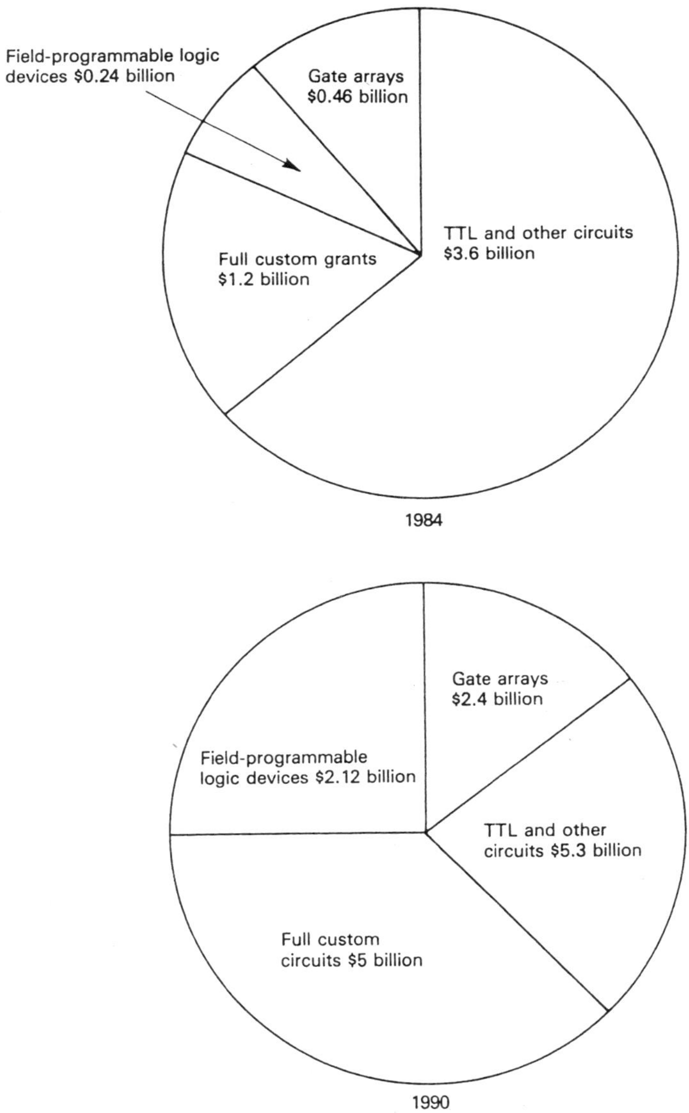

FIGURE 1.2
Increase in the consumption of field-programmable logic devices (Courtesy of Electronics International © 1986.)

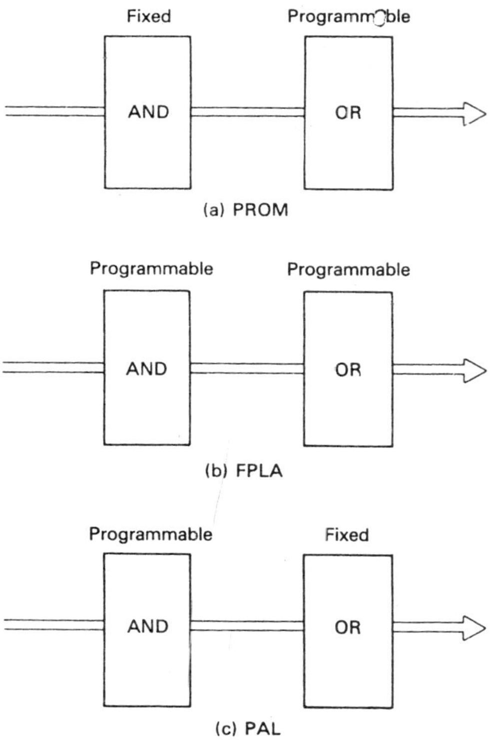

FIGURE 1.3
Structures of programmable logic devices

programmable logic arrays or **FPLAs.** Alternatively, the appropriate connections at the crosspoints can be made via transistors instead of fuses; such PLAs are mostly embedded in VLSI chips. In this book, we will deal with FPLA devices only.

The FPLA family was introduced by Signetics in the mid-1970s at about the same time the PAL family was marketed by Monolithic Memories. In general, FPLA devices are more flexible than PALs because they provide two programmable arrays rather than one. Thus, the same AND output can be sent to any number of OR gates. On the other hand, in a PAL, sets of AND outputs are permanently connected to an OR gate, making it impossible to share product terms among the outputs. If a product term is common to two different functions, then the product term has to be duplicated so that each output can use one. However, a FPLA device has fewer product terms than a PAL because two programmable arrays consume more space. The PAL devices are smaller than FPLA devices because they contain a single programmable array, and, for the same reason, they are easier to manufacture. PALs are actually implemented by placing a NAND array after the programmable OR array, creating an OR-NAND structure which, by DeMorgan's theorem, is equal to AND-OR with input variables implemented.

The basic AND-OR structure has been augmented in many programmable logic devices with registers and feedback options which allow implementation of state machines in addition to combinational logic. Furthermore, additional features such as tri-state outputs, security fuse, and flip-flop initialization have also been incorporated in many devices in order to enhance flexibility of applications. A **security fuse,** when blown, prevents the reading of the programmed pattern in a device; thus, proprietory design cannot be copied. The initialization of flip-flop is important for testing a state machine based on programmable logic devices. On power-up, if the state machine is in a known state, it is relatively easy to find a test sequence to check the proper state transitions in the machine. Some of the newer registered devices have a feature known as **preload,** which allows the loading of any desired initial state into the register; this considerably simplifies what is otherwise an extremely complicated task—the testing of state machines.

In recent years, CMOS technology is being used in implementing erasable logic devices. Such devices have erasable memory cells rather than fuses for connecting input lines to the product lines. The fuse-based devices are supplied by the manufacturer with all the fuses intact. A function is programmed by selectively blowing the fuses. In an erasable device, on the other hand, appropriate bits are stored in selected cells in order to make the connections required to implement a function. To date over fifteen companies offer programmable logic devices. Among those are the following:

- Actel Semiconductors
- AMD
- Altera
- Cypress Semiconductor
- Exel Microelectronics
- Fairchild
- Gould Semiconductors
- Intel
- International CMOS Technology
- Lattice Semiconductors
- National Semiconductor
- Signetics
- Seiko Semiconductors
- Texas Instruments
- VLSI Technology
- Xilinx

This list is not guaranteed to be complete or currently correct.

1.4 NOTATIONS FOR PROGRAMMABLE LOGIC DEVICES

In order to understand the AND-OR structures, which are different from conventional gates, a new logic notation has been developed. Figure 1.4 shows a four-input AND gate and its adopted notation. The four inputs are shown as vertical lines. The AND gate itself has a single input line, referred to as a **product line.** The vertical lines are connected to the product line through fuse links; an "X" at the intersection of the lines represents an intact fuse. If the "X" is not present at an intersection, then the corresponding input variable is not a part of the product term.

For example in Figure 1.4, if we delete "X" from the intersection of the input line B and the product line, this will indicate that the corresponding fuse has been blown (see Figure 1.5a). The product line now implements ACD as shown in Figure 1.5b.

A further extension of this convention is shown in Figure 1.6a which illustrates the input lines and buffers. The input lines are long lines running vertically through the array. Each input buffer has a true and an inverted output; the output lines of a buffer are permanently connected (shown as •) to an input line. Notice that an OR gate is added to the structure. All the fuses in the bottom AND gate are intact. This will result in the corresponding product line being at logic 0 since the true and the inverted inputs are being ANDed. Thus, the AND gate has no effect on the sumterm. The conventional logic representation of the function implemented in Figure 1.6a is shown in Figure 1.6b. When all the fuses on a product line are blown, the output of the corresponding AND gate becomes logic 1. Thus, the output of the programmed circuit shown in Figure 1.7 will be logic 1. Notice that the bottom AND gate has an "X" marked inside it. This indicates that all fuses in the product line are intact. Consequently, the output of this AND gate will be at logic 0.

As mentioned earlier, both the AND and the OR arrays in FPLA devices are programmable. Figure 1.8 shows the basic FPLA structure for a two input, two output logic segment. All the fuses in this segment are intact. In order to implement a NOR and a NAND function, the fuses have to be blown as shown in Figure 1.9a. Both functions require a programmable AND

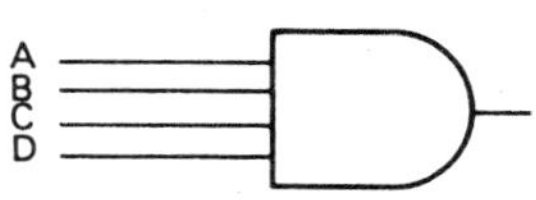

FIGURE 1.4a
A four-input AND gate

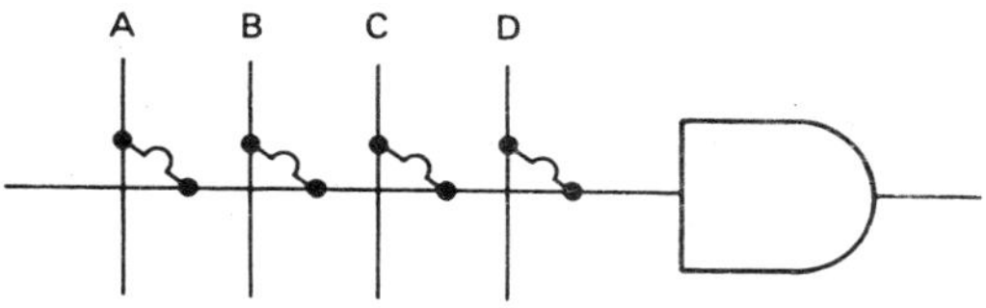

FIGURE 1.4b
Fusible input connections to the AND gate

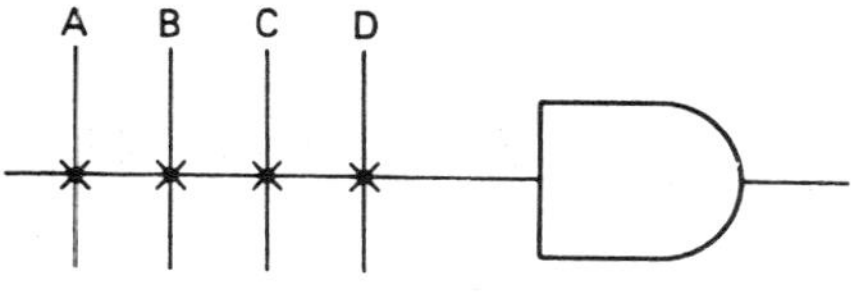

FIGURE 1.4c
Notation.

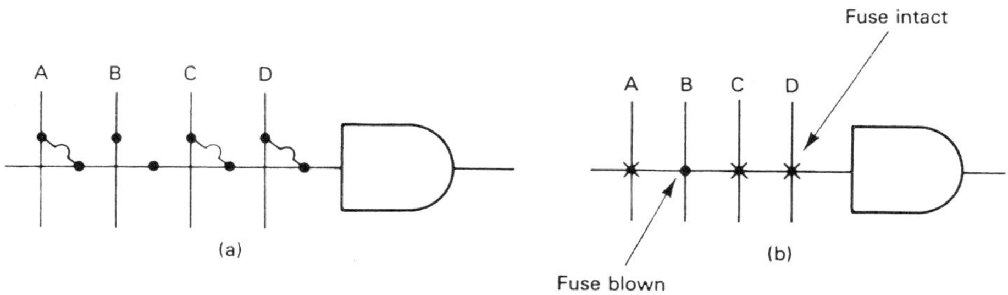

FIGURE 1.5
Product line implements ACD

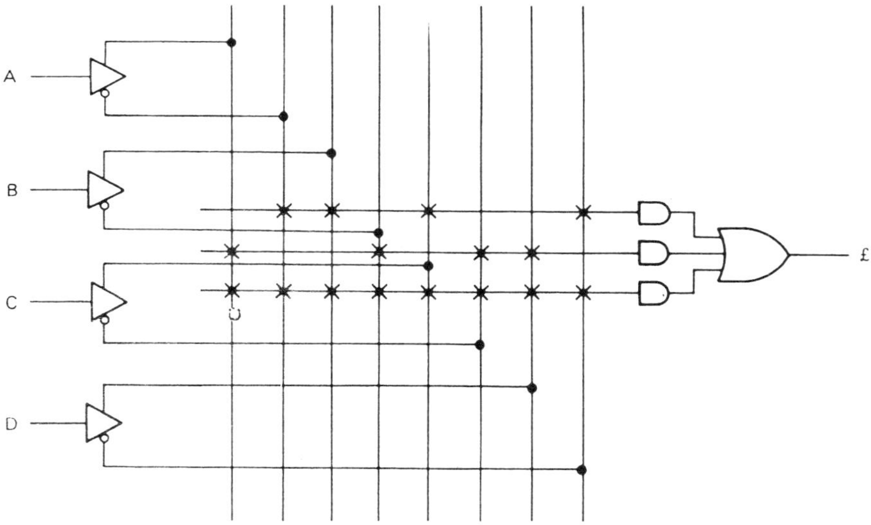

FIGURE 1.6a
Portion of the programmable logic array programmed to implement $f(A,B,C,D) = \overline{A}BC\overline{D} + A\overline{B}\overline{C}D$

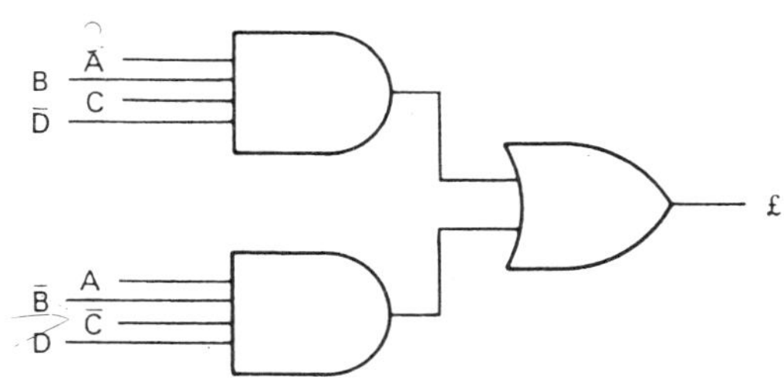

FIGURE 1.6b
Conventional logic representation of the same function

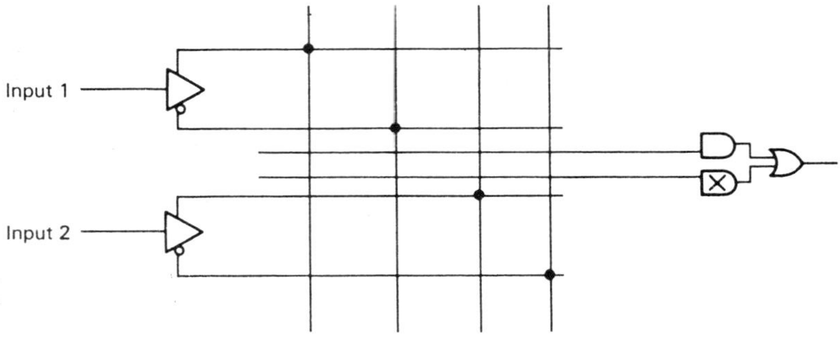

FIGURE 1.7
Product lines with all fuses blown and all fuses intact

and a programmable OR gate. Figure 1.9b illustrates the implementation of the EX-OR function which requires two AND gates and an OR gate, thus one output of the logic segment is not used. The status of fuses needed in order to implement a function in a FPLA device are recorded in the FPLA's program table. Figure 1.10 shows the appropriately coded program table for realizing the NOR, the NAND, and the EX-OR functions of Figure 1.9. Inputs I_1 and

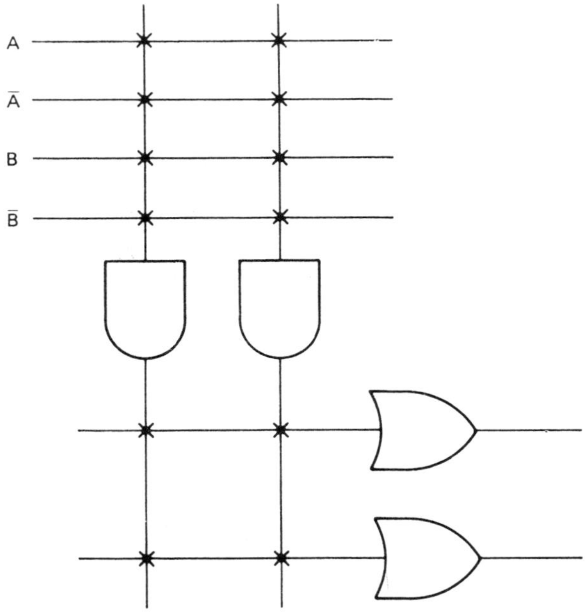

FIGURE 1.8
A FPLA segment

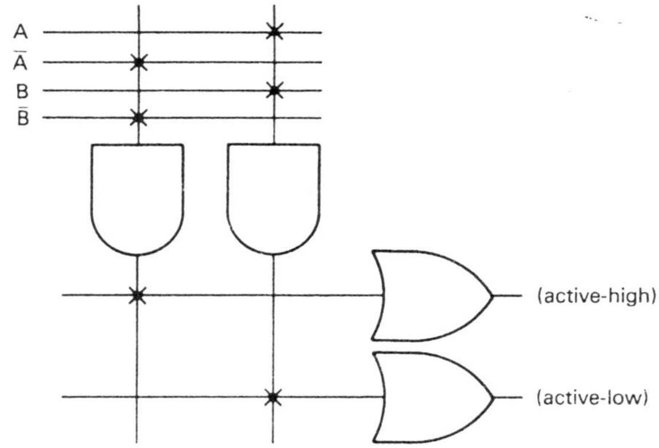

FIGURE 1.9a
NOR, NAND functions

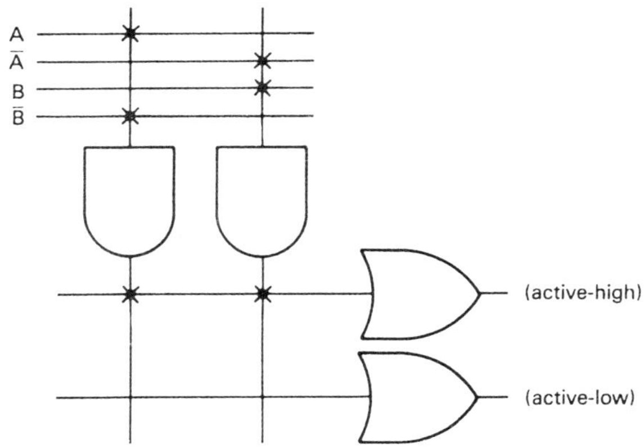

FIGURE 1.9b
EX-OR function

I_2 are assigned the variables A and B, respectively. Notice that in order to implement the NAND function, the polarity of the output from the second OR gate has to be inverted (i.e., made active-low). This is recorded as "L" in the polarity of this output. Each row in the AND part of the program table corresponds to a product term of a function. If a product term does not belong to "s" function, the corresponding output is **inactive** and a "•" is entered in the table.

Most of the programmable logic devices, FPLAs and PALs, allow user programmable output polarity. This is provided by incorporating an EX-OR gate at the output of each OR gate, as shown in Figure 1.11a. If the fuse is

			Polarity		
			L | H		
			OR		
Product term	Input (I_m)		Output (F_p)		
	2	1	2	1	
$\bar{B}$ $\bar{A}$	L	L	•	A	$F_1=\bar{A}\ \bar{B},\ F_2=\overline{A\ B}$
B A	H	H	A	•	
$\bar{B}$ A	L	H	•	A	
B $\bar{A}$	H	L	•	A	$F_1=\bar{A}\ B+A\ \bar{B}$
Variable name	B	A			

FIGURE 1.10
Coded program table corresponding to NOR, NAND, and EX-OR functions

intact as in Figure 1.11a, the output will be active-high; this is indicated as polarity "H" in Figure 1.10. On the other hand, if the fuse is blown as in Figure 1.11b, the input of the EX-OR gate becomes logic 1, and the EX-OR gate functions as an inverter; this is recorded as polarity "L" in Figure 1.10.

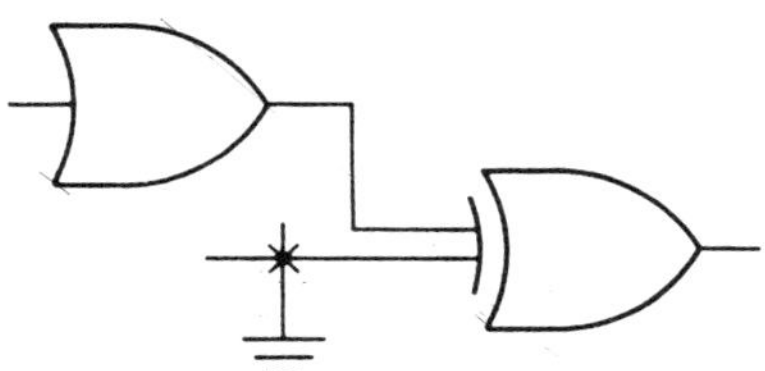

FIGURE 1.11a
Active-high output

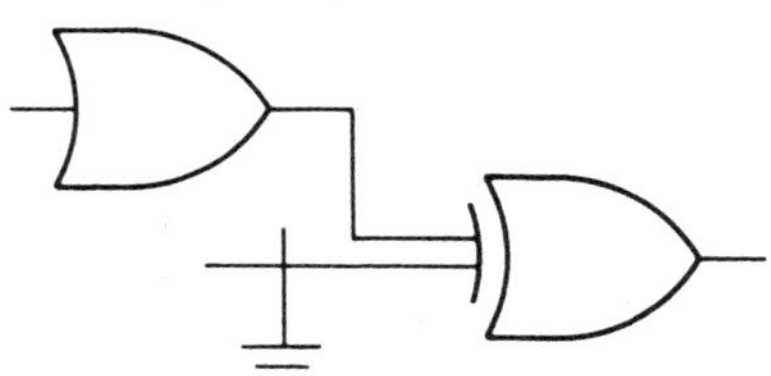

FIGURE 1.11b
Active-low output

The programmable output polarity often allows the complement of a Boolean function to be programmed into the device if the number of product terms in the original expression exceeds the number available in the device.

1.5 DESIGN METHODOLOGY USING PROGRAMMABLE LOGIC DEVICES

The design process using programmable logic devices requires the following distinct steps:

1. Specification of the function that the desired circuit should perform. State diagrams and truth tables are often most convenient. For many recently introduced PLDs, schematic entry is extremely popular.
2. Generation of Boolean equations required to implement the function.
3. Minimization of the Boolean equations; this step is necessary to ensure that the product terms are equal to or fewer than those available in the selected device.
4. Generation of a **fuse map** from the Boolean equations; a fuse map represents the states of cells or fuses in a device (e.g., the "1"s and "0"s represent blown (no connection) and intact (connection) fuses respectively.
5. Logic simulation. This step is extremely important for complex circuits, especially sequential circuits. The purpose of logic simulation is to verify that the design is correct before it is actually implemented using the programmable device. A function table records the expected input patterns to the device and the corresponding correct responses. The simulator compares each input/response pattern to check that the device performs exactly as the design specifies.
6. Programming the selected device. The binary fuse patterns generated in step 4 are stored onto the device.
7. Testing. The programmed device is tested to ensure that it functions according to the circuit specification. Currently the testing of a programmed device is based on verifying that the device gives correct responses to input patterns similar to those used to perform simulation. No formal techniques for testing programmed devices are currently available.

1.6 DESIGN SOFTWARE

Design aid software are provided by many manufacturers of programmable devices to develop and simulate designs based on their proprietary chips. In addition, several companies have marketed software packages to support all types of devices. Commercially available design packages can be classified into two categories: **assemblers** and **compilers.** Assembler-based packages allow the defining of input and output pins with their appropriate logic equations.

Compiler-based packages, on the other hand, need only either the truth table or the state diagram of a design. Examples of assembler-based PLD software are PALASM (AMD), PLAN (National Semiconductor), and AMAZE (Signetics). Available compiler-based software include CUPL (Logical Devices) and ABEL (Data I/O).

PALASM (PAL Assembler). PALASM was specifically designed to accept input files of Boolean equations, called **PAL design specification,** and to generate the fuse map of a selected PAL device in a **Joint Electronic Device Engineering Council (JDEC)** approved format. The most recent version of this software package, PALASM2, can easily define systems requiring up to 10 PAL devices, each implementing 10 to 100 Boolean equations. It can be used to customize most of the current 20- and 24-pin PALs, as well as the devices of much higher complexity. The PALASM2 is available free-of-charge, and runs on **VAXes** (under **UNIX™** and **VMS™**), **IBM-PC/XT/AT** (under **MS-DOS™**), and on DAISY workstation (under DNIX™ 5.1).

A design specification for a PAL involves defining the input and output pins of a selected device with their appropriate Boolean equations. The Boolean equations are composed of three parts: the pin name, which is the symbolic output name on the left side; the registered or non-registered symbol, := or =, respectively; and the logic expression on the right. The expression on the right side of the assignment symbol is written using the operators *(AND), +(OR), /(NOT), :+:(EX_OR). If an output polarity of a device has to be made active-low, the corresponding pin is prefaced with the / operator in the pin assignment list. Alternatively, an active-low polarity can be achieved by prefacing the output pin in the Boolean expression with the / operator. Similarly, active-high polarity can be obtained by using /pin in the pin list and /pin in the Boolean equation, or by not using / in the pin list and the corresponding Boolean equation.

PALASM2 can also be used to describe state machines. The description consists of three segments: **declaration, state,** and **conditions.** The declaration segment defines pin names and **string substitutions.** A string corresponds to a certain frequently used logic expression or part of it. To eliminate the repetition of a string, it may be substituted with a short name in the declaration segment. Then, instead of using the string, one can use the word to identify it. The state segment contains information such as the type of state machines (i.e., Mealy or Moore), transition and output equations, as well as the default outputs and state transitions. A state transition equation defines states in terms of conditions that determine transition to other states. An output equation specifies the conditions and the outputs from a present state. The condition segment contains equations, corresponding to the branching conditions used in the state segment, to determine state transitions and outputs.

ABEL (Advanced Boolean Expression Language). ABEL is a **universal** compiler in the sense that it supports all types of PLDs. Currently, it is widely used in the industry. A variety of input formats is accepted by ABEL (e.g., truth table, state diagrams, and Boolean equations). It is also possible to express a design in any combination of these input formats.

Four types of operators are used in ABEL: logical, arithmetic, relational, and assignment. The logical operators, !(invert), &(AND), #(OR), $(EX_OR) and !$(EX_NOR), are used in Boolean expressions. The arithmetic operators, −(2′ complement or subtraction), +(addition), * (multiplication), /(division), %(modulus, remainder from division), <<(shift left), and >>(shift right), define arithmetic operations. The relational operators, ==(equal), !=(not equal), <(less than), >(greater than), <=(less than or equal to), and >=(greater than or equal to) are used to compare two items in an expression. The assignment operators, =(unclocked assignment (i.e., combinational output)), := (clocked assignment or registered output) are used in Boolean equations. ABEL also allows the user to describe state machines using IF_THEN_ELSE, CASE, GO TO, and WITH_ENDWITH statements. Additional features of ABEL include a powerful minimizer for logic equation reduction, and a logic simulator for verifying the design before actually programming a device.

ABEL runs on VAX (under VMS or UNIX), IBM XT/AT/PS2 (and MS-DOS compatibles), as well as on workstations such as Sun, Daisy, Valid, and Apollo/Mentor.

Schematic Capture. Logic designs are often expressed as schematic diagrams. A schematic entry program (e.g., DASH, OrCAD, PCAD, or Schema II) allows logic design schematics to be directly drawn on the host computer's screen using primitive logic symbols or user-defined macros. The DASH-ABEL schematic capture program from Data I/O, uses the information in the DASH output file to generate the source file for ABEL, with Boolean equations replacing the logic circuit schematic.

To show a comparison of the three design tools (schematics, PALASM2, and ABEL), let us consider a schematic of a traffic light controller circuit at an intersection and implement PALASM2 file and ABEL file. Figure 1.12 shows the intersection. In the intersection, the lights controlling east and westbound traffic will have identical indications, as will the lights controlling north and southbound traffic. Sensors are installed that cause signals "e" and "w" to logic high if there is an eastbound or westbound vehicle at the intersection. In the absence of any eastbound or westbound vehicles, the north-south lights will remain green. However, if either sensor indicates the presence of a vehicle, the traffic lights will cycle through to allow the vehicle to pass.

A state diagram of the controller circuit is shown in Figure 1.13. The diagram identifies four possible states of the circuit and indicates the input

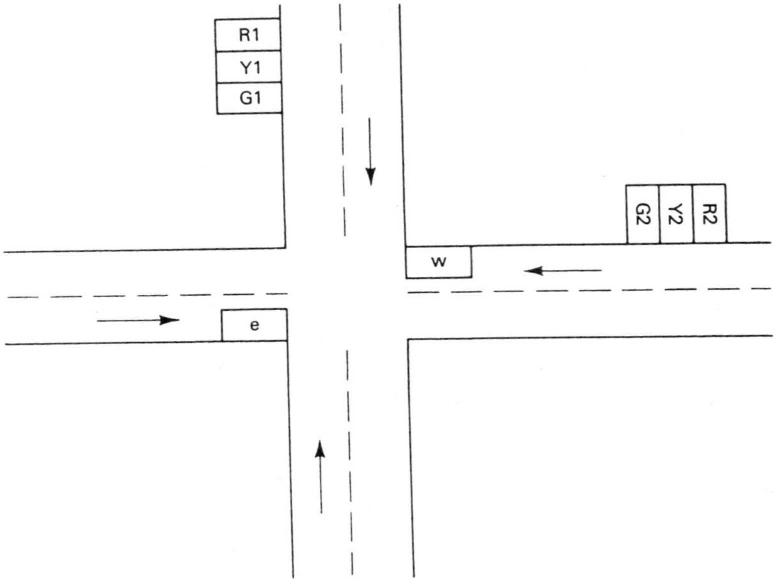

FIGURE 1.12
Traffic intersection

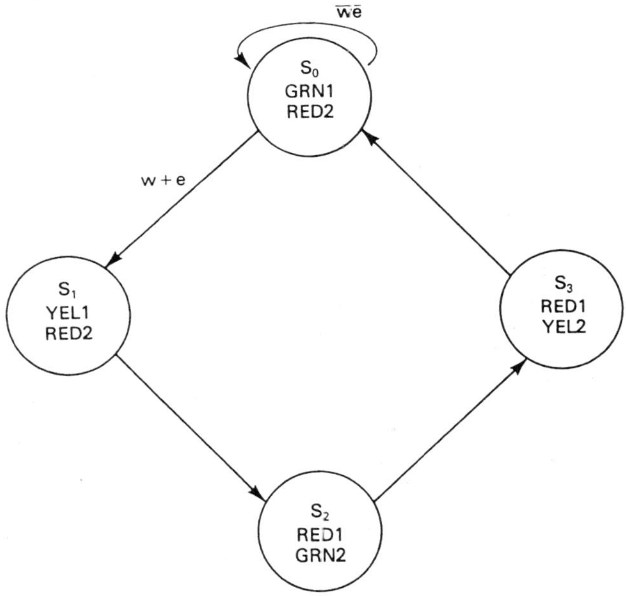

FIGURE 1.13
State diagram of the controller circuit

conditions that cause all possible state transitions, as well as the status of the lights as outputs at each state. The schematic diagram of the circuit is shown in Figure 1.14a. The circuit can be implemented with a single programmable logic device (e.g., PAL16R8 (see Chapter 5)). The ABEL or the PALASM2 source file for the circuit can be directly derived from its state diagram; they contain the information necessary for creating the JDEC file for PAL16R8. Figure 1.14b and c show the ABEL and the PALASM2 source file respectively.

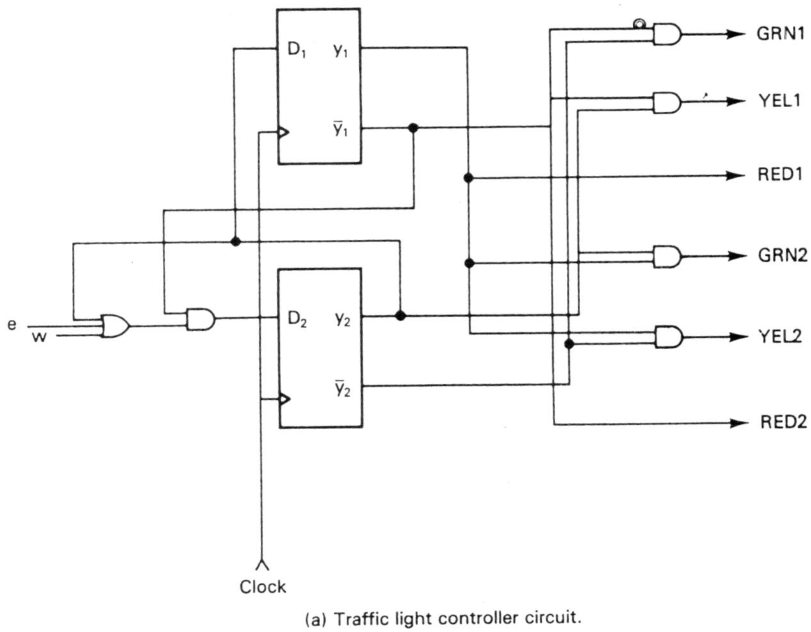

FIGURE 1.14a
Traffic light controller circuit

```
module          traffic_light
title       'traffic light
Parag K. Lala         May 7, 1989'

    d1          device 'p16R8';

    q1,q0                       pin 18,19;
    clock,e,w,enable            pin 1,2,3,11;
    red_1,yel_1,grn_1           pin 15,16,17;
    red_2,yel_2,grn_2           pin 12,13,14;
    sreg                         = [q1,q0];

    A = 0;    B = 1;    C = 3;    D = 2;        "state values

State_diagram sreg;
    State A:
        grn_1 = 1;
        yel_1 = 0;
        red_1 = 0;
        grn_2 = 0;
        yel_2 = 0;
        red_2 = 1;
        IF (e # w) THEN B;
        ELSE A;

    State B:
        grn_1 = 0;
        yel_1 = 1;
        red_1 = 0;
        grn_2 = 0;
        yel_2 = 0;
        red_2 = 1;
        GOTO C;

    State C:
        grn_1 = 0;
        yel_1 = 0;
        red_1 = 1;
        grn_2 = 1;
        yel_2 = 0;
        red_2 = 1;
        GOTO D

    State D:
        grn_1 = 0;
        yel_1 = 0;
        red_1 = 1;
        grn_2 = 0;
        yel_2 = 1;
        red_2 = 0;
        GOTO A;

end
```

FIGURE 1.14b
ABEL source file

```
TITLE       Traffic light controller
PATTERN     State Machine
AUTHOR      Parag K. Lala
DATE        May 5, 1989

CHIP              S_Machine         PAL16R8

;PINS   1    2   3   4    5    6    7    8    9    10
        CLK  E   W   NC   NC   NC   NC   NC   NC   GND

;PINS   11   12    13    14    15    16    17    18   19   20
        /OE  RED2  YEL2  GRN2  RED1  YELI  GRN1  Q1   Q0   VCC

STATE

    MOORE MACHINE

    ;state assignments

    A = /Q1 * /Q0; 0-0
    B = /Q1 *  Q0; 0-1
    C =  Q1 *  Q0; 1-1
    D =  Q1 * /Q0: 1-0

    ;state equations
    POWER_UP := VCC → A;
    A := C1 → B;
       + C2 → B;
       + C3 → B;
       +  ⟶ A;
    B := VCC → C;
    C := VCC → D;
    D := VCC → A;

    ;output equations

    A.OUTF := GRN1 * RED2;
    B.OUTF := YEL1 * RED2;
    C.OUTF := RED1 * GRN2;
    D.OUTF := RED1 * YEL2;
CONDITIONS

    C1 = E * W;
    C2 = E * /W;
    C3 = /E * W;

;(simulation is optional—not included here)
```

FIGURE 1.14c
PALASM2 source file

REFERENCES

1. E. E. Hollis, *Design of VLSI Gate Array ICs,* Prentice-Hall, Inc., 1987.
2. B. Cole, *Field-Programmable Logic: A New Market Force,* Electronics Int., June 27, 1986, pp. 25–31.
3. *PAL/PLE Device Programmable Logic Array Handbook,* Monolithic Memories, 1986.
4. *Programmable Logic Data Manual,* Signetics Corp., 1986.

Chapter 2

Programmable Read Only Memory (PROM)

A **memory** is a device in which information can be stored for future use. In general, a memory consists of several locations; each location being identified by a unique address. A memory location may be used to store one or more information bits. The process of entering information into memory locations is known as a **write** operation. The accessing of information from memory locations is known as a **read** operation. The maximum number of information bits that can be stored in a memory is specified as its **capacity.** For example, if a memory has 512 locations, each of which stores information bits of length 4, then the memory capacity is 2K (equal to 2,048 bits). Such a memory is referred to as 512 × 4 memory.

The time required for the content/s of a location to be available at the output of the memory (after the address of the location has been provided) is known as the **access time.** The time elapsed from the start of one memory operation (read or write) to the time another memory operation can be initiated, is called the **cycle time.**

Memories in general can be classified into two categories:

1. Sequential access memory; and
2. Random access memory.

In a **sequential access memory,** a piece of data may be accessed by sequentially searching all the information bits stored on the device until the desired data is found. On the other hand, in a **random access memory** (RAM), any of the locations may be accessed in any order with similar access time for each location. One of the most popular types of RAM is **read only memory (ROM).** In ROM, once the data is stored, it cannot be altered any further. There are four basic variations of read only memory:

1. Mask programmed ROM;
2. Programmable ROM or PROM;
3. Erasable PROM or EPROM; and
4. Electrically Erasable ROM or EEROM.

2.1 MASK PROGRAMMED ROM

Mask programmed ROMs are often referred to as **basic ROM.** They are programmed by the manufacturers to the user's specifications and cannot be altered after manufacturing. This type of ROM is economical only in large quantities, since the cost of custom programming is high. Figure 2.1 shows the

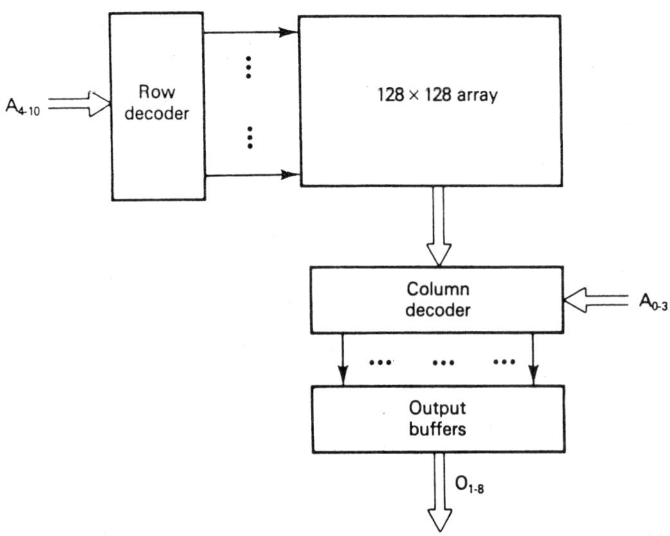

FIGURE 2.1
Block diagram of Am9218

block diagram of Am9218 mask programmable ROM. This is fabricated using n-channel MOS technology and organized as 2,048 words by 8 bit. The inputs and the outputs of the device are fully TTL compatible. It operates with a single + 5 V + 5% power supply and is fully static, requiring no clocks for operation. The three programmable chip selects may be defined by the user and are fixed during the masking process.

2.2 PROM

This type of read only memory is available with all conductive elements intact. The conductive elements, called **fuses,** are made from special alloy (e.g., nickel-chromium or titanium-tungsten) which break open when current flowing through them exceeds a certain limit. A blown fuse represents one binary state and an unblown fuse represents the other state.

The major drawback of the PROMs is that once programmed they cannot be altered further. Thus, if an error is made in programming, a PROM must be discarded.

Programmable logic devices in the form of PROMs have been around for many years. In fact, all programmable logic devices were manufactured using bipolar fuse technology until 1985.

2.3 EPROM

EPROMs were pioneered by Intel Corporation in 1970. They differ from PROMs in that they can be erased and reprogrammed again and again, whereas PROMs can be programmed only once. The data in an EPROM is erased by exposing the device to ultraviolet light; special windows are built into the device package to provide access to ultraviolet light. Typically, erasure times vary from 15 minutes to about one hour.

The major advantage of EPROMs is that they can be programmed with a certain content, used, and then reprogrammed with a different content. Thus, they are very useful in applications where data requirements change constantly. Once the data pattern for an EPROM is firm, the user can opt for a masked ROM in the final production. In general, it is possible to obtain a ROM that is pin compatible with any given EPROM. However, there are a few disadvantages associated with EPROMS:

1. They have to be removed from the circuit in order to be erased.
2. Only block erasure is possible (i.e., the entire contents of a device has to be erased; individual bytes cannot be erased).
3. Packages with a quartz window are expensive.

These disadvantages, however, are offset in many applications by EPROMs flexibility and low cost. Besides, several manufacturers are currently offering these devices with built-in registers. For example, the Cypress Semiconductors offer registered CMOS EPROMs in 512, 1K, 2K and 8K by 8 configurations. The EPROM technology has also been used to develop high-density programmable logic devices; the high density is possible because the EPROM cell is much smaller than fusible links in PROMs. Like the EPROMs, these programmable logic devices are also erasable, hence they are known as **EPLDs (erasable programmable logic devices).** Chapter 6 discusses the configurations and applications of the currently available EPLDs.

2.4 EEPROM

EEPROMs avoid many of the problems of EPROMs. They are similar to EPROMs, except that they are erased and programmed using electric pulses. This feature allows both erasing and programming to be done without disturbing the chips in the host system. Erasing can be accomplished by using a **byte erase mode** or a **block erase mode.** In the block erase mode, the entire chip is erased, whereas in the byte erase mode, the content of a single addressed location is erased.

The two most important characteristics of EEPROMs, as far as users are concerned, are **endurance** and **data retention** [1]. Endurance in an EPROM specification refers to the maximum number of times each cell in the memory can be erased and reliably rewritten. Several of the currently available EEPROMs (e.g., XL2865A (8K × 8 bit) offered by Exel Microelectronics, Inc.) are designed for applications requiring up to 10,000 rewrites per EEPROM byte. The data retention is the ability of an EEPROM cell to retain charge over long periods of time. For example, the XL2865 is specified for a data retention of 10 years.

In recent years, several manufacturers have the CMOS EEPROM technology to design programmable logic devices (e.g., ISPGAL (In-system Programmable General Array Logic) of Lattice Semiconductors, ERASIC (Electrically Reprogrammable Application Specific IC) of Exel Microelectronics, Inc., and PEEL (Programmable Electrically Erasable Logic Devices)) of International CMOS Technology, Inc. These devices are considered in detail in Chapter 6.

2.5 PROGRAMMABLE LOGIC ELEMENT (PLE)

Traditionally, PROMs have been used to store software in microprocessor-based systems. However, they can also be used to implement logic functions. The concept that a PROM can be used as a logic element has led to the development of PLE devices. A PLE is essentially a PROM with a programmable OR array being driven by a fixed AND array. Currently 15 such devices are marketed by Advanced Micro Devices, Inc. These include both **combinational** and **registered units.** The combinational group consists of eleven devices:

PLE5P8/A	PLE10P4
PLE8P4	PLE10P8
PLE8P8	PLE11P4
PLE9P4	PLE11P8
PLE9P8	PLE12P4
	PLE12P8

The numbers preceding and succeeding "P" in a device specify the number of inputs and outputs, respectively. The letter "P" denotes that the output of the device is non-registered. Figure 2.2 shows the block diagram of

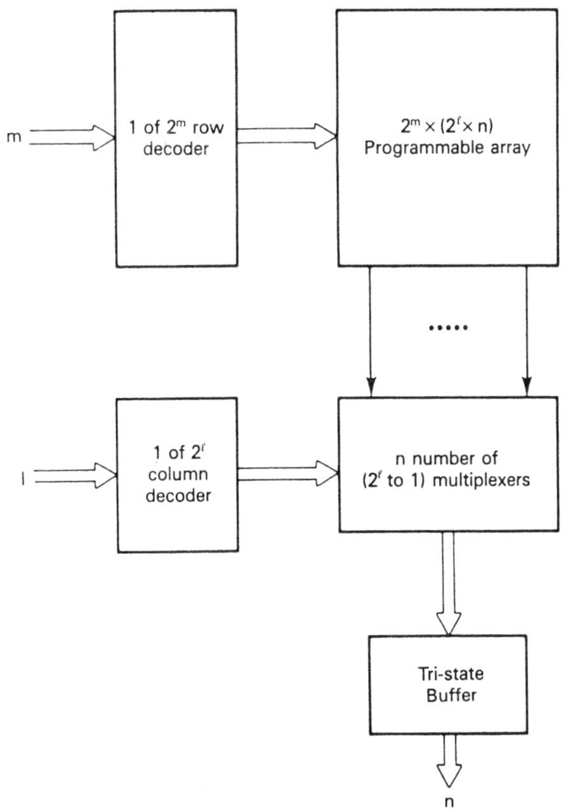

FIGURE 2.2
Block diagram of combinational PLE devices

these devices. The inputs to each device (except PLE5P8) are partitioned into two subsets, "l" and "m," which drive the column and the row decoder, respectively. The PLE5P8 does not have a column decoder.

There are four PLE devices with on-chip D flip-flops. These are:

PLE9R8
PLE10R8
PLE11RA8
PLE11RS8

The letter "R" denotes that the output of the device is registered. The "A" and "S" indicate that the tri-state buffers at the output of the corresponding device are enabled independent of the clock and in synchronization with the clock, respectively. Figure 2.3 shows the block diagram of the sequential PLE devices. If the $\overline{\text{IS}}$ (synchronous initialize) input is at logic "0," the content of one of the 16 locations addressed via inputs $I_0 = I_3$ are loaded into the 8-bit output register, irrespective of other inputs. These 16 locations contain all "0"s if they have not been programmed with other values; thus if $\overline{\text{IS}}$ is set to logic "0," an all "0" value is transferred to the register (i.e., the register is **cleared**). On the other hand, if the 16 initializing locations contain all "1"s, the register bits will be **present** when $\overline{\text{IS}}$ is set to logic "0." The PLE9R8 does not provide this initialization feature, however it has asynchronous preset ($\overline{\text{PR}}$) and clear ($\overline{\text{CLR}}$) inputs. If the tri-state buffers in the device are enabled, a logic "0" on the $\overline{\text{PR}}$ input will result in an all "1" output; a logic "0" on the $\overline{\text{CLR}}$ input will reset all the flip-flops, producing an all "0" output.

2.6 COMBINATIONAL LOGIC DESIGN USING PLEs

The implementation of combinational and sequential circuits using PLEs is a relatively trivial operation. For example, in designing combinational logic circuits there is no need to employ any of the conventional minimization techniques. The input variables in a combinational function are used as inputs to a combinational PLE with the required output values being programmed into the OR array of the PLE. Thus, when a particular input combination is presented to the PLE, the "contents" of the OR array corresponding to the input combination appear at the output of the PLE.

It will be obvious that a PLE can be used for realizing multi-output combinational circuits with each bit in the OR array output corresponding to a particular output value of the combinational circuit. To illustrate, we implement an eight output combinational function of five variables (e.g., A, B, C, D, E). A "1" programmed in the OR array represents the presence of a minterm in the function; and a "0" represents its absence. Thus, the input combination 10010 applied to the PLE5P8 would be interpreted as the minterm $A\overline{B}\overline{C}D\overline{E}$; in the output of the OR gate driven by the minterm, the

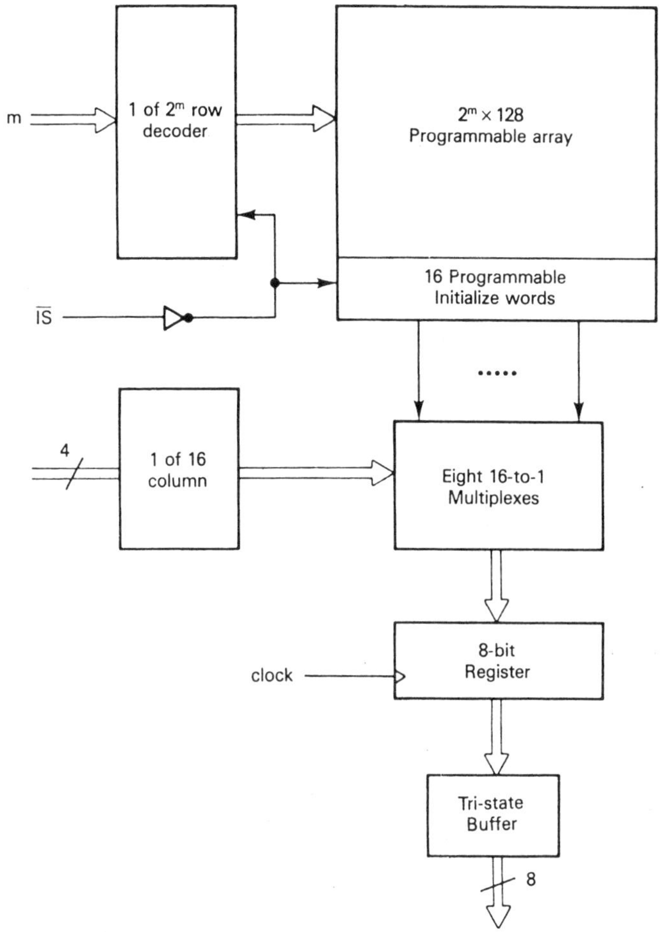

FIGURE 2.3
Block diagram of sequential PLE devices

"1"s correspond to functions containing that minterm and "0"s to functions that do not. As an example, let us consider the following function of five variables:

$$f(A,B,C,D,E) = \Sigma(2,3,4,5,8,9,10,11,18,19,22,23,24,25,26,27) + \text{don't cares } \Sigma(6,7)$$

This expression can be reduced to

$$f(A,B,C,D,E) = \overline{B}D + B\overline{C} + \overline{A}\overline{B}C$$

Seven NAND gates (three 3-input and four 2-input) are necessary to implement this function. The same function can be realized with the PLE5P8 by programming the device according to Figure 2.4. Note that the original expression rather than the reduced one has been used to specify the logic 1 outputs of O_1. In employing PLEs to implement logic functions, the minterms are programmed directly from the truth table for each of the functions; minimization process is by-passed since this does not result in any savings. In fact, if an expression is already reduced it must be expanded to its canonical

Minterm	A_0	A_1 (A)	A_2 (B)	A_3 (C)	A_4 (D)	A_5 (E)	O_1 (f)
$\bar{A}\bar{B}\bar{C}\bar{D}\bar{E}$	0	0	0	0	0	0	0
$\bar{A}\bar{B}\bar{C}\bar{D}E$	0	0	0	0	0	1	0
$\bar{A}\bar{B}\bar{C}D\bar{E}$	0	0	0	0	1	0	1
$\bar{A}\bar{B}\bar{C}DE$	0	0	0	0	1	1	1
$\bar{A}\bar{B}C\bar{D}\bar{E}$	0	0	0	1	0	0	1
$\bar{A}\bar{B}C\bar{D}E$	0	0	0	1	0	1	1
$\bar{A}\bar{B}CD\bar{E}$	0	0	0	1	1	0	0 or 1
$\bar{A}\bar{B}CDE$	0	0	0	1	1	1	0 or 1
$\bar{A}B\bar{C}\bar{D}\bar{E}$	0	0	1	0	0	0	1
$\bar{A}B\bar{C}\bar{D}E$	0	0	1	0	0	1	1
$\bar{A}B\bar{C}D\bar{E}$	0	0	1	0	1	0	1
$\bar{A}B\bar{C}DE$	0	0	1	0	1	1	1
$\bar{A}BC\bar{D}\bar{E}$	0	0	1	1	0	0	0
$\bar{A}BC\bar{D}E$	0	0	1	1	0	1	0
$\bar{A}BCD\bar{E}$	0	0	1	1	1	0	0
$\bar{A}BCDE$	0	0	1	1	1	1	0
$A\bar{B}\bar{C}\bar{D}\bar{E}$	0	1	0	0	0	0	0
$A\bar{B}\bar{C}\bar{D}E$	0	1	0	0	0	1	0
$A\bar{B}\bar{C}D\bar{E}$	0	1	0	0	1	0	1
$A\bar{B}\bar{C}DE$	0	1	0	0	1	1	1
$A\bar{B}C\bar{D}\bar{E}$	0	1	0	1	0	0	0
$A\bar{B}C\bar{D}E$	0	1	0	1	0	1	0
$A\bar{B}CD\bar{E}$	0	1	0	1	1	0	1
$A\bar{B}CDE$	0	1	0	1	1	1	1
$AB\bar{C}\bar{D}\bar{E}$	0	1	1	0	0	0	1
$AB\bar{C}\bar{D}E$	0	1	1	0	0	1	1
$AB\bar{C}D\bar{E}$	0	1	1	0	1	0	1
$AB\bar{C}DE$	0	1	1	0	1	1	1
$ABC\bar{D}\bar{E}$	0	1	1	1	0	0	0
$ABC\bar{D}E$	0	1	1	1	0	1	0
$ABCD\bar{E}$	0	1	1	1	1	0	0
$ABCDE$	0	1	1	1	1	1	0

FIGURE 2.4
Program table for the PLE5P8

form in order to properly specify the PLE program. For example, the expression $f(A,B,C) = \overline{B}\overline{C} + AC + AB$ has to be expanded as

$$f = (A + \overline{A})\overline{B}\overline{C} + A(B + \overline{B})C + AB(C + \overline{C})$$
$$= A\overline{B}\overline{C} + \overline{A}\overline{B}\overline{C} + ABC + A\overline{B}C + ABC + AB\overline{C}$$
$$= A\overline{B}\overline{C} + \overline{A}\overline{B}\overline{C} + ABC + A\overline{B}C + AB\overline{C}$$

before programming for PLE implementation.

In the following we will illustrate the application of PLE devices in the combinational logic implementation with the aid of several examples.

2.6.1 Totally Self-checking Checker for Berger Codes

A Berger code of length n has i information bits and k check bits where $k = \lceil \log_2(i + 1) \rceil$ and $n = i + k$. The k check bits are the binary number corresponding to the number of "0"s in the i information bits. For example if i = 10101000, then the k check bits are derived as follows:

Number of "0"s in information bits i = 5

Binary equivalent of 5 = 0101

Thus,

$$n = \underbrace{10101000}_{i} \quad \underbrace{0101}_{k}$$

Berger codes can detect all single and unidirectional errors in a codeword. Figure 2.5 shows the circuit for a totally self-checking checker for

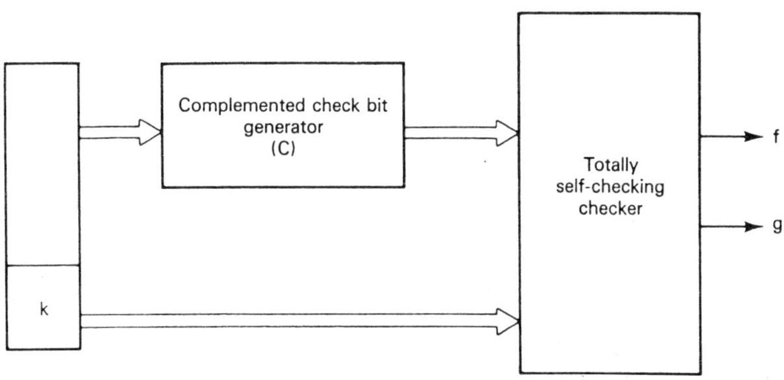

FIGURE 2.5
Totally self-checking checker for Berger codes

Berger codes. C is a combinational network which generates the complements of the check bits from the information bits. The totally self-checking checker circuit compares the k check bits with the outputs of C. It has two outputs f and g; the signals observed on the outputs f and g should always be complementary (i.e., f = 0, g = 1 or f = 1, g = 0) if and only if every pair of inputs to the checker is also complementary. Details of Berger codes and self-checking circuit design can be found in [2].

The check bit generator and the totally self-checking checker of Figure 2.5 can also be implemented by two PLE8P4 devices as shown in Figure 2.6. The program table for device 1 and device 2 are shown in Figure 2.7a and b respectively.

2.6.2 1-out-of-n Detector

A 1-out-of-n detector is a network whose output is logic "1" if, and only if, a single input out of the n inputs to the network is at logic "1," otherwise the output of the network is at logic "0" [3]. Figure 2.8 shows the design of 1-out-of-n detector using decoding gates. This network requires n inverters, n AND gates and one n-input OR gate. With decoding gates, however, the number of levels and gates becomes prohibitive for large values of n.

A 1-out-of-n detector, for large n, can be built from PLE devices. The number of inputs n, is divided into smaller groups of m inputs so that the detector can be constructed with PLEs having m inputs each. In such a detector design, the output of a PLE can be in one of the three states correspond-

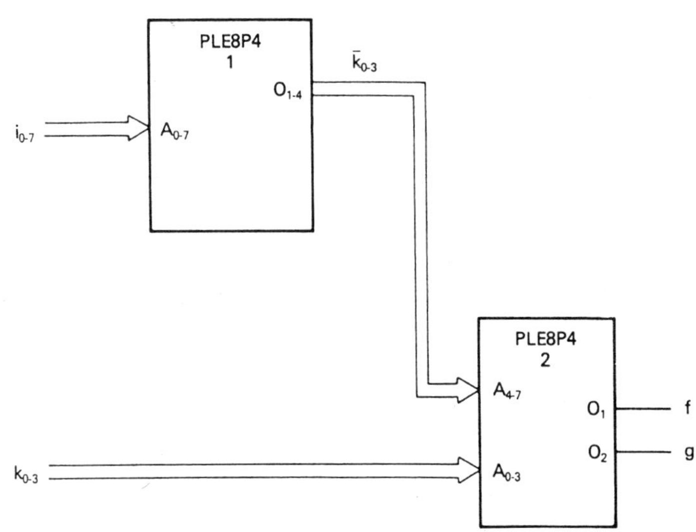

FIGURE 2.6
Implementation of totally self-checking checker using PLE8P4

A_0	A_1	A_2	A_3	A_4	A_5	A_6	A_7	O_1	O_2	O_3	O_4
0	0	0	0	0	0	0	0	0	1	1	1
0	0	0	0	0	0	0	1	1	0	0	0
0	0	0	0	0	0	1	0	1	0	0	0
0	0	0	0	0	0	1	1	1	0	0	1
0	0	0	0	0	1	0	0	1	0	0	0
				⋮					⋮		
1	1	1	1	1	1	0	0	1	1	0	1
1	1	1	1	1	1	0	1	1	1	1	0
1	1	1	1	1	1	1	0	1	1	1	0
1	1	1	1	1	1	1	1	1	1	1	1

FIGURE 2.7a

A_0	A_1	A_2	A_3	A_4	A_5	A_6	A_7	O_1	O_2	O_3	O_4
1	0	0	0	0	1	1	1	1	0	—	—
0	1	1	1	1	0	0	0	0	1	—	—
0	1	1	0	1	0	0	1	1	0	—	—
0	1	0	1	1	0	1	0	1	0	—	—
0	1	0	0	1	0	1	1	1	0	—	—
0	0	1	1	1	1	0	0	1	0	—	—
0	0	1	0	1	1	0	1	0	1	—	—
0	0	0	1	1	1	1	0	0	1	—	—
0	0	0	0	1	1	1	1	0	1	—	—
← all other combinations →								0	0	—	—
								or			
								1	1		

FIGURE 2.7b

ing to m inputs; these states are all "0"s, a single "1," and two or more "1"s. Since the state of all "0"s can be identified from the knowledge of the other two states, each PLE requires only two outputs. One output indicates logic "1" only when the number of "1"s in its inputs is two or more; the other indicates logic "1" when the number of "1"s at the input is exactly one.

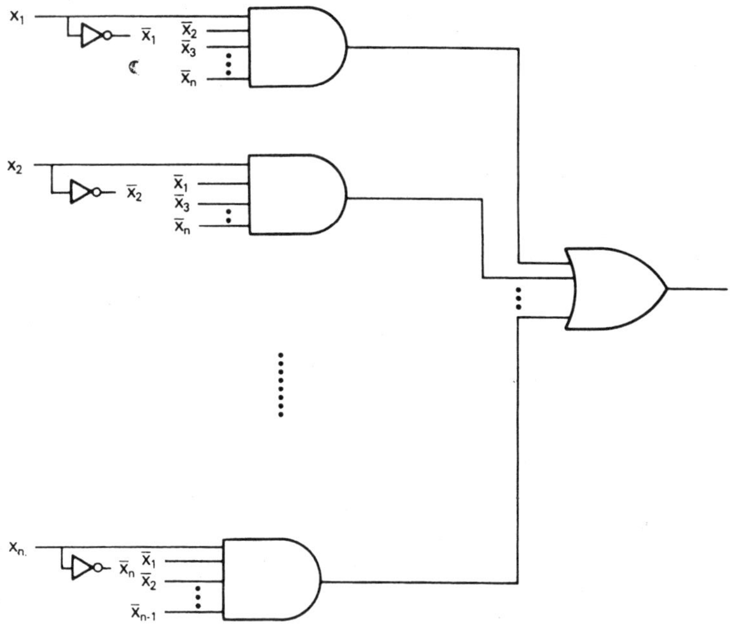

FIGURE 2.8
1-out-of-n detector using decoding gates

We shall illustrate the design procedure for 1-out-of-90 detector. The first stage of the detector consists of 9[= n/m = 90/10] PLE10P4 devices. Only two out of four outputs of each device are required. The outputs of the PLEs, which represent the state of "the number of '1's is exactly '1'" are connected to the inputs of a PLE9P4. The outputs of the PLE10P4 representing the state "the number of '1's is two or more" are connected to the A_{0-8} inputs of a PLE11P4, and the A_9 and A_{10} inputs of the device are driven by the outputs O_1 and O_2 respectively of the PLE9P4. Thus, 11 PLEs are required to implement the 1-out-of-90 detector as shown in Figure 2.9. The program tables for the PLEs used are shown in Figure 2.10.

2.6.3 Code Converter for Hamming-coded BCD to ASCII

The code converter accepts Hamming-coded 8-bit BCD characters, corrects single-bit errors, indicates the presence of multi-bit errors, and generates 7-bit ASCII data [4]. The code converter can be implemented with the PLE8P8. Figure 2.11 shows the Hamming code for BCD; the c_{1-4} and d_{1-4} correspond to the check bits and the BCD bits respectively. c_1 check bits 1, 3, 5, 7 for even

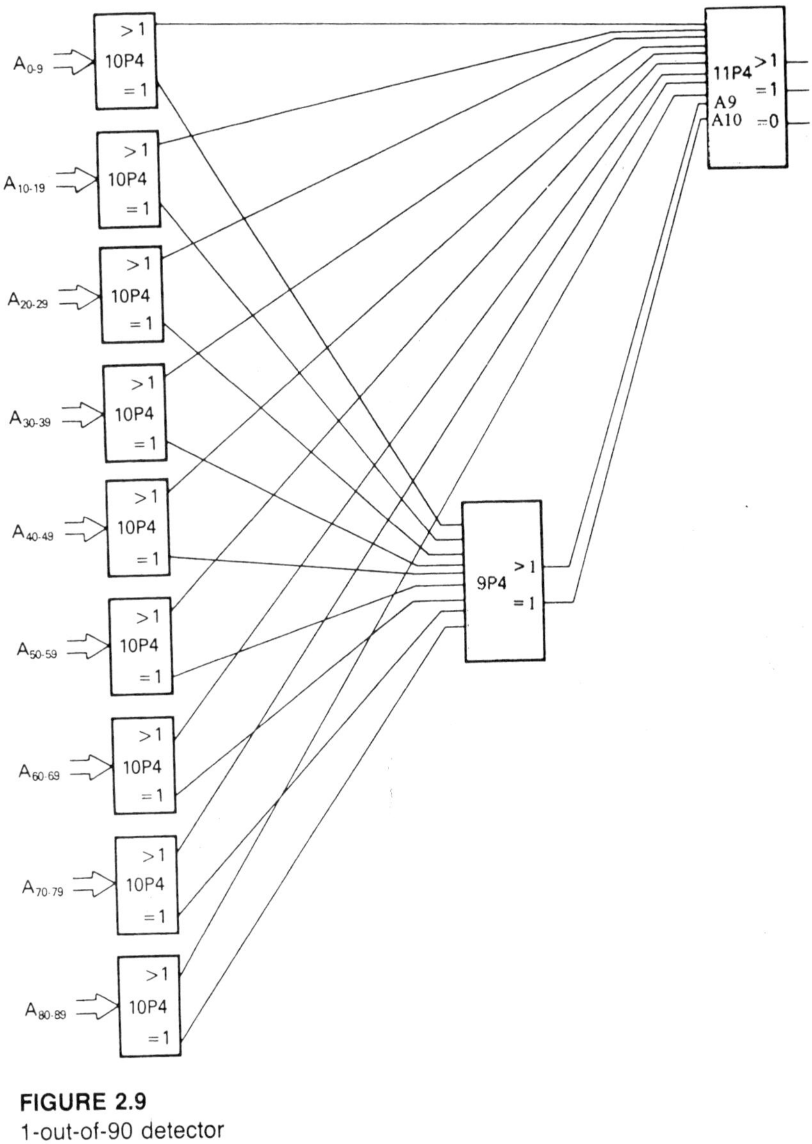

FIGURE 2.9
1-out-of-90 detector

parity, similarly, c_2 checks bits 2, 3, 6, 7 while c_3 checks bits 4, 5, 6, 7. c_4 is chosen so that all eight bits will have even parity.

A single-bit error in a codeword can result in nine erroneous codewords. For example, the correct codeword for the BCD digit 4 and its corrupted versions containing single-bit errors are as follows:

1	0	0	1	1	0	0	1	correct code for BCD 4
0	0	0	1	1	0	0	1	Codewords containing a single-bit error
1	1	0	1	1	0	0	1	
1	0	1	1	1	0	0	1	
1	0	0	0	0	0	0	1	
1	0	0	1	0	0	0	1	
1	0	0	1	1	1	0	1	
1	0	0	1	1	0	1	1	
1	0	0	1	1	0	0	0	

A_0 (x_0)	A_1 (x_1)	A_2 (x_2)	A_3 (x_3)	A_4 (x_4)	A_5 (x_5)	A_6 (x_6)	A_7 (x_7)	A_8 (x_8)	A_9 (x_9)	O_1 (>1)	O_2 $(=1)$	O_3	O_4
0	0	0	0	0	0	0	0	0	0	0	0	—	—
0	0	0	0	0	0	0	0	0	1	0	1		
0	0	0	0	0	0	0	0	1	0	0	1		
0	0	0	0	0	0	0	1	0	0	0	1		
0	0	0	0	0	0	1	0	0	0	0	1		
0	0	0	0	0	1	0	0	0	0	0	1		
0	0	0	0	1	0	0	0	0	0	0	1		
0	0	0	1	0	0	0	0	0	0	0	1		
0	0	1	0	0	0	0	0	0	0	0	1		
0	1	0	0	0	0	0	0	0	0	0	1		
1	0	0	0	0	0	0	0	0	0	0	1		
← all other combinations →										1	0		

FIGURE 2.10a
Program table for the PLE10P4s

A_0	A_1	A_2	A_3	A_4	A_5	A_6	A_7	A_8	O_1 (>1)	O_2 $(=1)$	O_3	O_4
0	0	0	0	0	0	0	0	0	0	0	-	-
0	0	0	0	0	0	0	0	1	1	1	-	-
0	0	0	0	0	0	0	1	0	0	1	-	-
0	0	0	0	0	0	1	0	0	0	1	-	-
0	0	0	0	0	1	0	0	0	0	1	-	-
0	0	0	0	1	0	0	0	0	0	1	-	-
0	0	0	1	0	0	0	0	0	0	1	-	-
0	0	1	0	0	0	0	0	0	0	1	-	-
0	1	0	0	0	0	0	0	0	0	1	-	-
1	0	0	0	0	0	0	0	0	0	1	-	-
← all other combinations →									1	0		

FIGURE 2.10b
Program table for the PLE9P4

A0	*A1*	*A2*	*A3*	*A4*	*A5*	*A6*	*A7*	*A8*	*A9*	*A10*	*O1*	*O2*	*O3*	*O4*
											(>1)	(=1)	(=0)	
0	0	0	0	0	0	0	0	0	0	0	0	0	1	-
0	0	0	0	0	0	0	0	0	1	0	1	0	0	-
0	0	0	0	0	0	0	0	0	0	1	0	1	0	-
← all other combinations →											1	0	0	-

FIGURE 2.10c
Program table for the PLE11P4

A codeword and its erroneous versions with single-bit errors are used as inputs for the PLE8P8. The OR array of the PLE8P8 is programmed so that the device will produce the output $O_1O_2O_3O_4O_5O_6O_7$ = 0 1 1 0 1 0 0, the ASCII equivalent of BCD 4, for all of these inputs. Thus, the correction of a single-bit error in a codeword is accomplished.

Similarly, nine unique addresses cover each of the other nine BCD characters, totalling 90 input combinations for the digits 0–9. For all other combinations, the PLE8P8 is programmed to produce 1 1 1 1 at its O_4 to O_7 outputs. The O_8 output of the device produces a 1 for any input combination which differs from the 90 correct and single-bit error codewords, indicating the presence of a non-correctable error. Figure 2.12 shows the program table for the PLE8P8. Note that if there are four more errors in a codeword, the converter will not be able to detect the errors.

2.6.4 Multi-function Generator

The multi-function generator is designed to perform one of the following operations on an 8-bit data: **increment, left shift, right shift, "2"s complement,**

	Bit positions in a codeword							
	1	*2*	*3*	*4*	*5*	*6*	*7*	*8*
Decimal digit	c_1	c_2	d_1	c_3	d_2	d_3	d_4	c_4
0	0	0	0	0	0	0	0	0
1	1	1	0	1	0	0	1	0
2	0	1	0	1	0	1	0	1
3	1	0	0	0	0	1	1	1
4	1	0	0	1	1	0	0	1
5	0	1	0	0	1	0	1	1
6	1	1	0	0	1	1	0	0
7	0	0	0	1	1	1	1	0
8	1	1	1	0	0	0	0	1
9	0	0	1	1	0	0	1	1

FIGURE 2.11
Hamming-coded BCD digits

A_0	A_1	A_2	A_3	A_4	A_5	A_6	A_7	O_1	O_2	O_3	O_4	O_5	O_6	O_7	O_8
0	0	0	0	0	0	0	0	0	1	1	0	0	0	0	0
0	0	0	0	0	0	0	1	0	1	1	0	0	0	0	0
0	0	0	0	0	0	1	0	0	1	1	0	0	0	0	0
0	0	0	0	0	1	0	0	0	1	1	0	0	0	0	0
0	0	0	0	1	0	0	0	0	1	1	0	0	0	0	0
0	0	0	1	0	0	0	0	0	1	1	0	0	0	0	0
0	0	1	0	0	0	0	0	0	1	1	0	0	0	0	0
0	1	0	0	0	0	0	0	0	1	1	0	0	0	0	0
1	0	0	0	0	0	0	0	0	1	1	0	0	0	0	0
			⋮								⋮				
1	1	1	1	1	1	0	1	0	1	1	1	1	1	1	1
1	1	1	1	1	1	1	0	0	1	1	1	1	1	1	1
1	1	1	1	1	1	1	1	0	1	1	1	1	1	1	1

FIGURE 2.12
Program table for the PLE8P8

left rotate, right rotate, decrement, and **transfer the data to the output.** Since there are eight operations, three bits are needed to specify each function (see Figure 2.13). These three bits together with eight bits of input data and eight bits of output data require a PLE device with 11 inputs and eight outputs for the implementation of the multi-function generator. Hence, we select the PLE11P8. The control inputs C_{0-2} are applied to the inputs A_{0-2} of the device, and the data inputs are applied to A_{3-10}. The program table for the PLE11P8 is shown in Figure 2.14.

C_0	C_1	C_2	*Function*
0	0	0	Transfer data input to the device output
0	0	1	Increment
0	1	0	Left shift
0	1	1	Right shift
1	0	0	"2"s complement
1	0	1	Decrement
1	1	0	Left rotate
1	1	1	Right rotate

FIGURE 2.13
Codes for various functions

A_0	A_1	A_2	A_3	A_4	A_5	A_6	A_7	A_8	A_9	A_{10}	O_1	O_2	O_3	O_4	O_5	O_6	O_7	O_8
0	0	0	0	0	0	0	0	0	0	0	0	0	0	0	0	0	0	0
	.		0	0	0	0	0	0	0	1	0	0	0	0	0	0	0	1
	.					.												
	.					.												
	.					.												
0	0	0	1	1	1	1	1	1	1	1	1	1	1	1	1	1	1	1
0	0	1	0	0	0	0	0	0	0	0	0	0	0	0	0	0	0	1
	.		0	0	0	0	0	0	0	1	0	0	0	0	0	0	1	0
	.					.												
	.					.												
	.					.												
0	0	1	1	1	1	1	1	1	1	1	0	0	0	0	0	0	0	0
0	1	0	0	0	0	0	0	0	0	0	0	0	0	0	0	0	0	0
	.		0	0	0	0	0	0	0	1	0	0	0	0	0	0	1	0
	.					.												
	.					.												
	.					.												
0	1	0	1	1	1	1	1	1	1	1	1	1	1	1	1	1	1	0
0	1	1	0	0	0	0	0	0	0	0	0	0	0	0	0	0	0	0
	.		0	0	0	0	0	0	0	1	0	0	0	0	0	0	0	0
	.					.												
	.					.												
	.					.												
0	1	1	1	1	1	1	1	1	1	1	0	1	1	1	1	1	1	1
0	0	0	0	0	0	0	0	0	0	0	0	0	0	0	0	0	0	0
	.		0	0	0	0	0	0	0	1	1	1	1	1	1	1	1	1
	.					.												
	.					.												
	.					.												
1	0	0	1	1	1	1	1	1	1	1	0	0	0	0	0	0	0	1
1	0	1	0	0	0	0	0	0	0	0	1	1	1	1	1	1	1	1
	.		0	0	0	0	0	0	0	1	0	0	0	0	0	0	0	0
	.					.												
	.					.												
	.					.												
1	0	1	1	1	1	1	1	1	1	1	1	1	1	1	1	1	1	0
1	1	0	0	0	0	0	0	0	0	0	0	0	0	0	0	0	0	0
	.					.												
	.					.												
	.					.												
	.		1	0	0	0	0	0	0	1	0	0	0	0	0	0	1	1
	.					.												
	.					.												
	.					.												
1	1	0	1	1	1	1	1	1	1	1	1	1	1	1	1	1	1	1
1	1	1	0	0	0	0	0	0	0	0	0	0	0	0	0	0	0	0
	.					.												
	.					.												
	.					.												
	.		1	0	0	0	0	0	0	1	1	1	0	0	0	0	0	0
1	1	1	1	1	1	1	1	1	1	1	1	1	1	1	1	1	1	1

FIGURE 2.14
Program table for the PLE11P8

2.7 SEQUENTIAL CIRCUIT REALIZATION USING PLEs

A sequential circuit is, in general, represented as shown in Figure 2.15. The output of a sequential circuit depends not only on the present inputs, but also on past input values as reflected by the state of the circuit. There are two types of sequential circuits: **synchronous** and **asynchronous.** In a synchronous sequential circuit, the secondary variables change in synchronization with a clock pulse, whereas in an asynchronous circuit, the transition between states occur when input conditions change with no synchronizing clock.

PLE devices can be used to realize both synchronous and asynchronous sequential circuits. Figure 2.16a shows a sequential circuit with direct feedback from the PLE output to the input. However, only one feedback output is allowed to change at a time, otherwise race conditions cannot be avoided. In contrast, the race conditions are irrelevant in designs based on registered PLE devices. Figure 2.16b shows a sequential circuit with feedback derived from the registered outputs. The disadvantage of both approaches is that each bit in a state of a sequential circuit uses up an input and an output pin of a PLE because of the feedback connection. In the following subsections we illustrate the implementation of both asynchronous and synchronous sequential circuits.

2.7.1 Four-bit Synchronous Counter Design Using Direct Feedback

Combinational PLEs can be used for implementing synchronous sequential circuits. To illustrate the design technique, we shall use the PLE5P8 to implement a 4-bit counter. Figure 2.17 shows the PLE5P8 interconnections required for the implementation. Input A_0 of the PLE5P8 is connected to a clock which

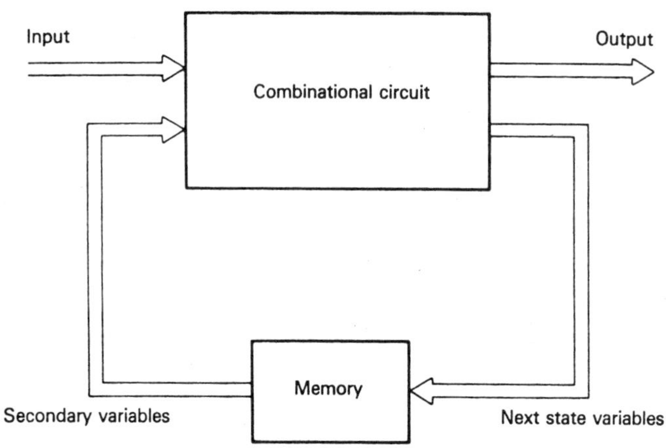

FIGURE 2.15
Model of sequential circuits

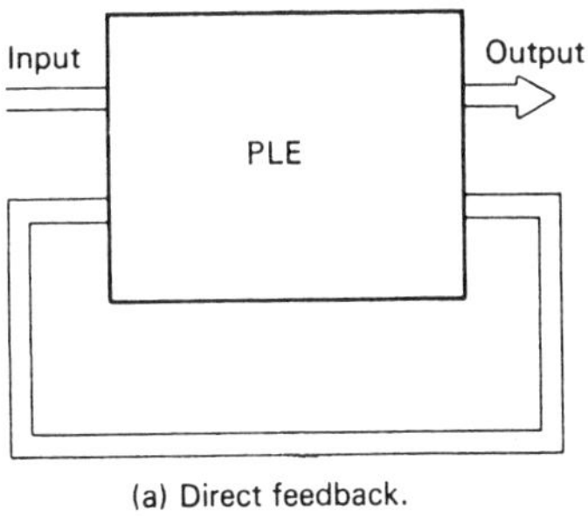

FIGURE 2.16a
Direct feedback

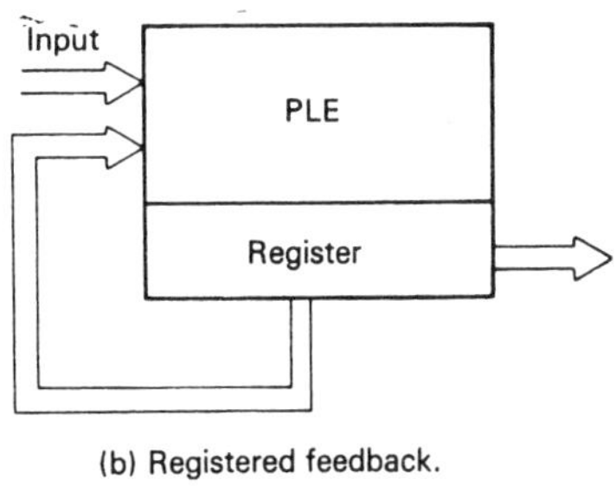

FIGURE 2.16b
Registered feedback

toggles between "0" and "1." It must remain stable for the duration equal to the propagation delay through the PLE. Figure 2.18 shows the contents of the PLE programmed to operate as the 4-bit counter. When the clock and all the input bits are "0"s, the output O_1–O_4 are also "0." When the clock goes from "0" to "1," the outputs corresponding to the inputs 10000 is 0001, and feedback inputs change the inputs to the PLE from 10000 to 10001. The OR array in the device has been programmed so that the output corresponding to this input combination is also 0001, hence the output condition remains stable.

When the A_0 bit is changed back to "0," the input becomes 00001 for which the output is 0010; this results in another stable state. The counter sequences through stable states, as A_0 is changed from "0" to "1" and vice-versa. Notice that the clocking occurs on both the rising edge and falling edge of the clock.

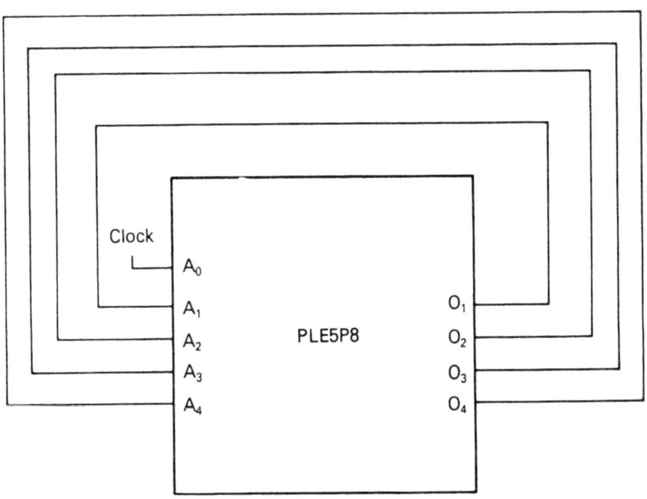

FIGURE 2.17
4-bit synchronous counter

Count state	A_0	A_1	A_2	A_3	A_4	O_1	O_2	O_3	O_4
0	0	0	0	0	0	0	0	0	0
	1	0	0	0	0	0	0	0	1
1	1	0	0	0	1	0	0	0	1
	0	0	0	0	1	0	0	1	0
2	0	0	0	1	0	0	0	1	0
	1	0	0	1	0	0	0	1	1
3	1	0	0	1	1	0	0	1	1
	0	0	0	1	1	0	1	0	0
4	0	0	1	0	0	0	1	0	0
	1	0	1	0	0	0	1	0	1
5	1	0	1	0	1	0	1	0	1
	0	0	1	0	1	0	1	1	0
6	0	0	1	1	0	0	1	1	0
	1	0	1	1	0	0	1	1	1
7	1	0	1	1	1	0	1	1	1
	0	0	1	1	1	1	0	0	0
8	0	1	0	0	0	1	0	0	0
	1	1	0	0	0	1	0	0	1
9	1	1	0	0	1	1	0	0	1
	0	1	0	0	1	1	0	1	0
10	0	1	0	1	0	1	0	1	0
	1	1	0	1	0	1	0	1	1
11	1	1	0	1	1	1	0	1	1
	0	1	0	1	1	1	1	0	0
12	0	1	1	0	0	1	1	0	0
	1	1	1	0	0	1	1	0	1
13	1	1	1	0	1	1	1	0	1
	0	1	1	0	1	1	1	1	0
14	0	1	1	1	0	1	1	1	0
	1	1	1	1	0	1	1	1	1
15	1	1	1	1	1	1	1	1	1
	0	1	1	1	1	0	0	0	0
0	0	0	0	0	0	0	0	0	0

FIGURE 2.18
Program table for the PLE5P8 for 4-bit counter implementation

2.7.2 Synchronous Sequential Circuit Design Using Registered PLEs

Registered PLE devices are ideal for implementing clocked sequential circuits. As an example we shall implement the state table of Figure 2.19 with such a device. The circuit has four outputs; **Ace, Jack, King,** and **Queen.** The outputs are coded as shown in Figure 2.20. The circuit has 15 different states hence a 4-bit register is needed. The state assignment for the circuit is given

Present state	Next states x = 0	x = 1	Outputs x = 0	x = 1
A	B	B	Ace	Ace
B	C	C	Ace	Ace
C	D	D	Ace	Ace
D	E	E	Ace	Ace
E	F	F	Ace	Ace
F	G	G	Ace	Ace
G	M	H	Ace	Ace
H	I	I	Queen	Queen
I	J	J	King	King
J	K	K	King	King
K	L	L	King	King
L	A	A	Jack	Jack
M	N	N	Ace	Ace
N	P	P	Ace	Ace
P	K	K	Queen	Queen

FIGURE 2.19
State table of the circuit to be designed

Code	Z1	Z2	Z3	Z4
Jack	0	0	0	1
King	0	0	1	0
Queen	0	1	0	0
Ace	1	0	0	0

FIGURE 2.20
Circuit output codes

in Figure 2.21. Since the circuit has four outputs and requires four state variables, a registered PLE with five inputs and eight outputs is needed. We select the PLE9R8. The implementation is as shown in Figure 2.22. The program table for the PLE9R8 is shown in Figure 2.23. Notice that the program table is identical to the state table, with "present state" and "input" specifying the input combinations to the PLE and "output" and "next state" specifying the outputs to the PLE.

2.7.3 Asynchronous Sequential Circuit Implementation

The flow table of an asynchronous sequential circuit is shown in Figure 2.24. The state assignment has to be chosen so that only one bit in a state can change

State	Assignment y_1	y_2	y_3	y_4
A	0	0	0	0
B	0	0	0	1
C	0	0	1	0
D	0	0	1	1
E	0	1	0	0
F	0	1	0	1
G	0	1	1	0
H	0	1	1	1
I	1	0	0	0
J	1	0	0	1
K	1	0	1	0
L	1	0	1	1
M	1	1	0	0
N	1	1	0	1
P	1	1	1	0

FIGURE 2.21
State assignment

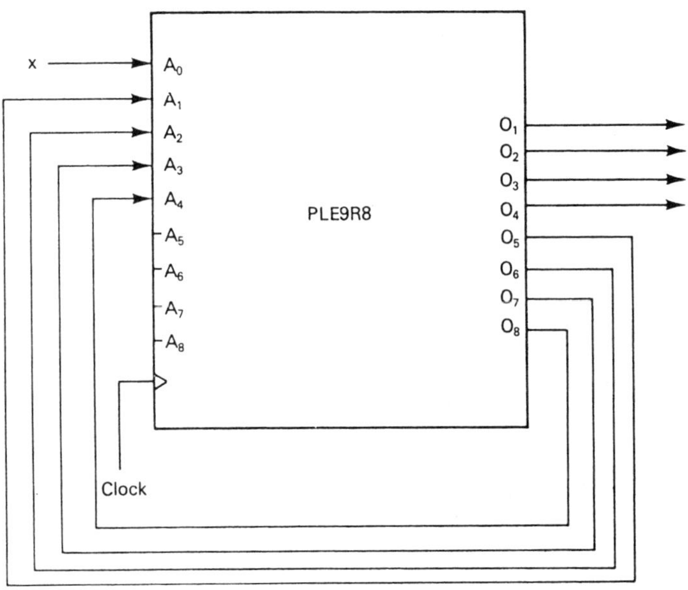

FIGURE 2.22
Implementation of the state table of Figure 2.19

Inputs						*Output*				*Next state*			
A0	*A1*	*A2*	*A3*	*A4*	*A5...A8*	*O1*	*O2*	*O3*	*O4*	*O5*	*O6*	*O7*	*O8*
0	0	0	0	0	—	1	0	0	0	0	0	0	1
0	0	0	0	1	—	1	0	0	0	0	0	1	0
0	0	0	1	0	—	1	0	0	0	0	0	1	1
0	0	0	1	1	—	1	0	0	0	0	1	0	0
0	0	1	0	0	—	1	0	0	0	0	1	0	1
0	0	1	0	1	—	1	0	0	0	0	1	1	0
0	0	1	1	0	—	1	0	0	0	1	1	0	0
0	0	1	1	1	—	0	1	0	0	1	0	0	0
0	1	0	0	0	—	0	0	1	0	1	0	0	1
0	1	0	0	1	—	0	0	1	0	1	0	1	0
0	1	0	1	0	—	0	0	1	0	1	0	1	1
0	1	0	1	1	—	0	0	0	1	0	0	0	0
0	1	1	0	0	—	1	0	0	0	1	1	0	1
0	1	1	0	1	—	1	0	0	0	1	1	1	0
0	1	1	1	0	—	0	1	0	0	1	0	1	0
1	0	0	0	0	—	1	0	0	0	0	0	0	1
1	0	0	0	1	—	1	0	0	0	0	0	1	0
1	0	0	1	0	—	1	0	0	0	0	0	1	1
1	0	0	1	1	—	1	0	0	0	0	1	0	0
1	0	1	0	0	—	1	0	0	0	0	1	0	1
1	0	1	0	1	—	1	0	0	0	0	1	1	0
1	0	1	1	0	—	1	0	0	0	0	1	1	1
1	0	1	1	1	—	0	1	0	0	1	0	0	0
1	1	0	0	0	—	0	0	1	0	1	0	0	1
1	1	0	0	1	—	0	0	1	0	1	0	1	0
1	1	0	1	0	—	0	0	1	0	1	0	1	1
1	1	0	1	1	—	0	0	0	1	0	0	0	0
1	1	1	0	0	—	1	0	0	0	1	1	0	1
1	1	1	0	1	—	1	0	0	0	1	1	1	0
1	1	1	1	0	—	0	1	0	0	1	0	1	0

FIGURE 2.23
Truth table for the PLE9R8

	Input			
State	$\bar{x}1\bar{x}2$	$\overline{x1}x2$	$x1x2$	$x1\overline{x2}$
S_0	S_0, 1	S_1	—	S_1
S_1	S_2	S_1, 0	—	S_1, 0
S_2	S_2, 1	S_3	—	S_3
S_3	S_0	S_3, 0	—	S_3, 0

FIGURE 2.24
Flow-table of an asynchronous sequential circuit

on each transition. A possible state assignment is given below:

	y_1	y_2
S_0	0	0
S_1	0	1
S_2	1	1
S_3	1	0

Since the asynchronous sequential circuit has two inputs, one output and two state variables, a PLE with at least four inputs and three outputs is required. We select the PLE5P8. Figure 2.25 shows the PLE5P8 interconnections required for the implementation of the circuit. The program table for the PLE5P8 is given in Figure 2.26. If the PLE receives an input combination which does not correspond to the input-present state of the circuit, it produces the output 00011111 indicating the presence of a fault in the device.

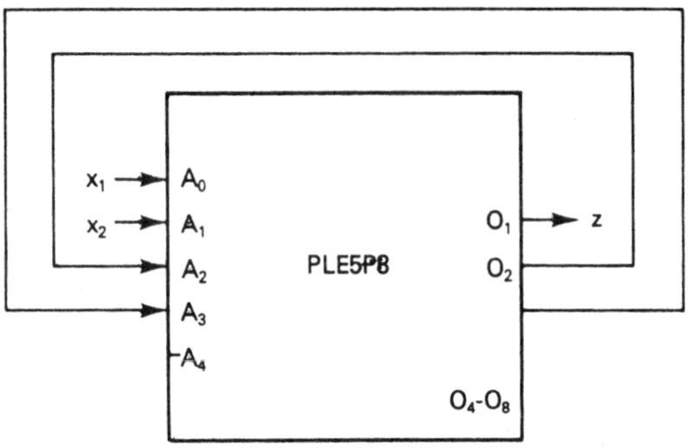

FIGURE 2.25
PLE5P8 Interconnections

A_0	A_1	A_2	A_3	A_4	O_1	O_2	O_3	O_4	O_5	O_6	O_7	O_8
0	1	0	0	—	0	0	1	—	—	—	—	—
0	1	0	1	—	0	0	1	—	—	—	—	—
1	0	0	0	—	0	0	1	—	—	—	—	—
1	0	0	1	—	0	0	1	—	—	—	—	—
0	0	0	1	—	1	1	1	—	—	—	—	—
0	0	1	1	—	1	1	1	—	—	—	—	—
0	1	1	1	—	0	1	0	—	—	—	—	—
0	1	1	0	—	0	1	0	—	—	—	—	—
1	0	1	1	—	0	1	0	—	—	—	—	—
1	0	1	0	—	0	1	0	—	—	—	—	—
0	0	1	0	—	1	0	0	—	—	—	—	—
0	0	0	0	—	1	0	0	—	—	—	—	—
← all other combinations →					0	0	0	1	1	1	1	1

FIGURE 2.26
Program table for the PLE5P8

PROBLEMS

2-1 Derive the program table for a **sinx** PROM. The PROM is to be addressed by the 6-bit binary equivalent to the angle, in 1° steps. The output is to be in 10-bit binary.

2-2 Design a BCD counter using an appropriate PLE device.

2-3 A control unit for a digital system is to be designed using a PROM and an appropriate size register. The inputs to the PROM are the values of the present state of the register and three control inputs x1, x2 and x3. The state diagram of the control unit is shown below:

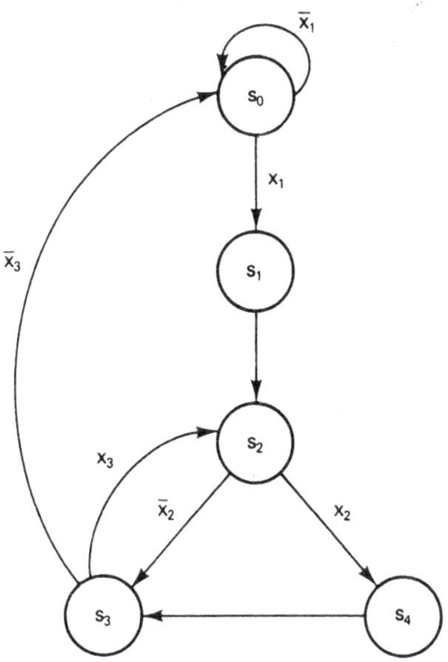

2-4 Implement the control unit of Problem 3 using an appropriate PLE.

2-5 A circuit which can detect in which direction a car is passing along a narrow path to a car park, is to be designed using a PLE. Two sensors are placed across the path of the car, spaced at less than one car length. These sensors, identified as s1 and s2, produce logic "1" when a car passes past them, and a logic "0" otherwise. Assume cars can pass only in one direction at a time. The circuit should have two outputs, z1 and z2; z1 goes to logic "1" if a car is going into the car park, and conversely, z2 indicates an outgoing car [5].

2-6 Implement a 4-bit binary to Gray code converter using PLE5P8. Write down the design equations.

2-7 Implement the 8-bit priority encoder circuit using a PLE device. Write down the design equations for the selected device.

REFERENCES

1. A. Goldberger, *E^2 PROM Endurance and Data Retention,* Exel Technology Update, June 17, 1985.
2. P. K. Lala, *Fault Tolerant and Fault Testable Hardware Design,* Prentice-Hall International, 1985.
3. A. W. Kobylar, R. L. Lindsay and S. G. Pitroda, *ROMs Cut Cost, Response Time of m-out-of-n Detector,* Electronics Int., Feb. 15, 1973, pp. 112–114.
4. K. C. Herrick, *A PROM-based Decoder Detects and Corrects Error,* EDN, June 20, 1980, pp. 169–172.
5. S. J. Cahill, *Digital and Microprocessor Engineering,* Ellis Horwood Ltd., 1982.

Chapter 3

Field-programmable Combinational Devices

As mentioned in Chapter 1, Signetics Corporation was the first to introduce **FPLA** devices. It also developed some additional devices, which may be programmed to implement specific functions. The complexity of these devices ranges from random gates to state machines. These devices include **field-programmable address decoder (FPAD), field-programmable gate-array (FPGA),** and **field-programmable logic sequencer (FPLS).** In this chapter, we will consider FPLA, FPGA, and FPAD including their applications in logic design. The FPLS will be discussed in Chapter 4.

3.1 FIELD-PROGRAMMABLE GATE-ARRAY (FPGA)

The FPGA is a programmable AND array with each product term available as an output; it does not have an OR array. Currently, the device is available in two configurations: PLS151 (16 inputs, 12 bidirectional I/O lines) and PLS103 (16 inputs, 9 outputs).

PLS151. It is a 20-pin device and has a propagation delay of 25 ns. The logic diagram of the device is shown in Figure 3.1. Each gate is programmed to the desired product term by blowing one or more of the fuses. Inputs to each

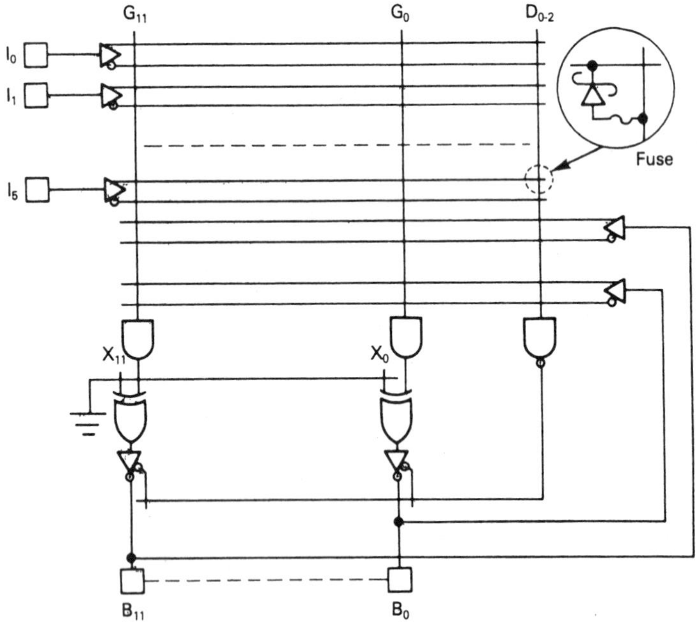

All fuses are initially intact.

FIGURE 3.1
Logic diagram of PLS151 (Courtesy of Signetics Corp.)

gate can be programmed *true, complement,* or *don't care.* In addition, the output polarity of each gate can be individually programmed to implement either AND or NAND logic functions.

As an example, let us implement the following 4-variable Boolean function using PLS151.

$$f(A,B,C,D) = \bar{A}\bar{B}D + \bar{A}B\bar{C} + ABD + A\bar{B}C$$

Since the PLS151 does not have an OR array, it cannot generate sum-of-products expressions directly. However, by representing the expression in NAND-NAND form, it is possible to utilize the built-in feedback inside the device. Thus,

$$\begin{aligned} f(A,B,C,D) &= \bar{A}\bar{B}D + \bar{A}B\bar{C} + ABD + A\bar{B}C \\ &= \overline{\overline{\bar{A}\bar{B}D + \bar{A}B\bar{C} + ABD + A\bar{B}C}} \\ &= \overline{\overline{\bar{A}\bar{B}D}\cdot\overline{\bar{A}B\bar{C}}\cdot\overline{ABD}\cdot\overline{A\bar{B}C}} \end{aligned}$$

The previous expression can be realized by blowing appropriate fuses as shown in Figure 3.2; the "X" in the diagram corresponds to the presence of a fuse. Each product term feeds an EX-OR gate. By keeping the fuse intact at the other input of the EX-OR gate, a product term is transferred to the

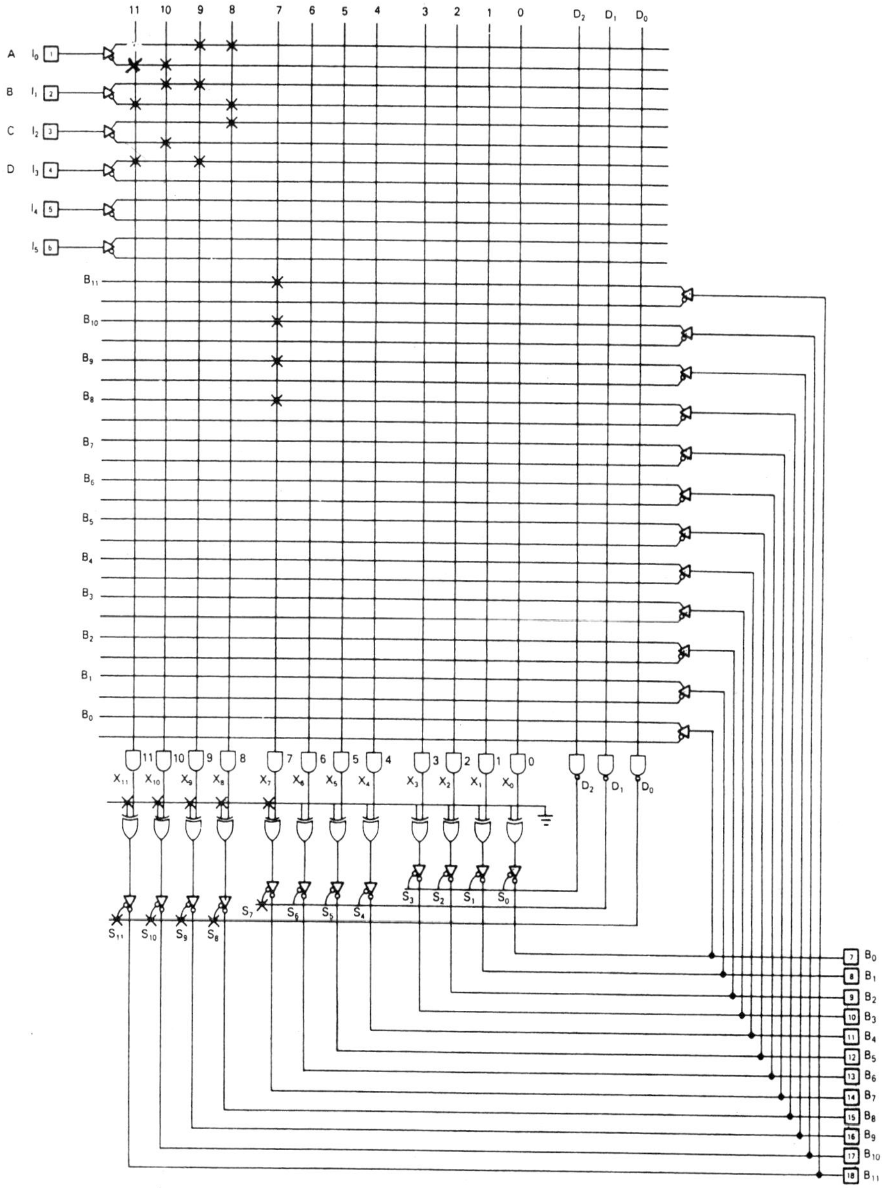

FIGURE 3.2
4-variable function implemented in NAND-NAND form (Courtesy of Signetics Corp.)

input of a tri-state inverter. All the fuses at the inputs of gates D_0 and D_1 are blown, thus their outputs will be at logic "0." Consequently the product terms generated by gates 8, 9, 10 and 11 will be inverted and fed back to the input of gate 7. The inverted output of gate 7 will be available at the I/O pin 14, thus implementing the desired function.

The PLS151 can also be programmed to implement NOR/NOR logic. For example the 4-variable expression considered above can also be expressed as,

$$f(A,B,C,D) = \overline{\overline{(A + B + D)} + \overline{(A + \bar{B} + \bar{C})} + \overline{(\bar{A} + \bar{B} + D)} + \overline{(\bar{A} + B + C)}}$$

$$= \overline{\overline{\overline{\bar{A}\bar{B}\bar{D} \cdot \bar{A}BC \cdot AB\bar{D} \cdot A\bar{B}\bar{C}}}}$$

The function is programmed into the device as shown in Figure 3.3. Notice that in this case. Besides the programmable input of the EX-OR gate following X_7, is set at logic "1" by blowing the fuse. This together with the intact fuse at S_7 realizes the double negation in the expression.

PLS103. This is a 28-pin device and has a propagation delay of 35 ns. The logic diagram of the device is shown in Figure 3.4. This device has only dedicated input and output pins, and does not have the capability of feeding back product terms to the AND array. Besides it has only nine AND gates compared to the 15 in PLS151. It, however, has a chip-enable control, which if at logic high disables the outputs (i.e., the outputs go in a high impedance state).

To illustrate the application of the device we construct a 7-to-3 cascadable priority encoder. The most significant input bit, A, of the device is assumed to come from a higher priority encoder. If A is at logic "0," then all the outputs of the encoder remain at logic "0." The truth table of the encoder is shown in Figure 3.5.

The Boolean expressions required to implement the encoder are derived from the truth table and are as follows:

$$Z_3 = A\bar{B}\bar{C}\bar{D}\bar{E}\bar{F}\bar{G}\bar{H}$$

$$Z_2 = A \cdot \overline{\bar{B}\bar{D}\bar{F}\bar{H}}$$

$$Z_1 = A\bar{B} \cdot (\overline{\bar{C}\bar{D}\bar{G}\bar{H}})$$

$$Z_0 = A\bar{B}\bar{C}\bar{D} \cdot (\overline{\bar{E}\bar{F}\bar{G}\bar{H}})$$

We program the PLS103 in such a way so that

$$F_8 = A\bar{B}\bar{C}\bar{D}\bar{E}\bar{F}\bar{G}\bar{H} = Z_3$$

$$F_7 = \overline{\bar{B}\bar{D}\bar{F}\bar{H}}$$

$$F_6 = A \cdot F_7 = Z_2$$

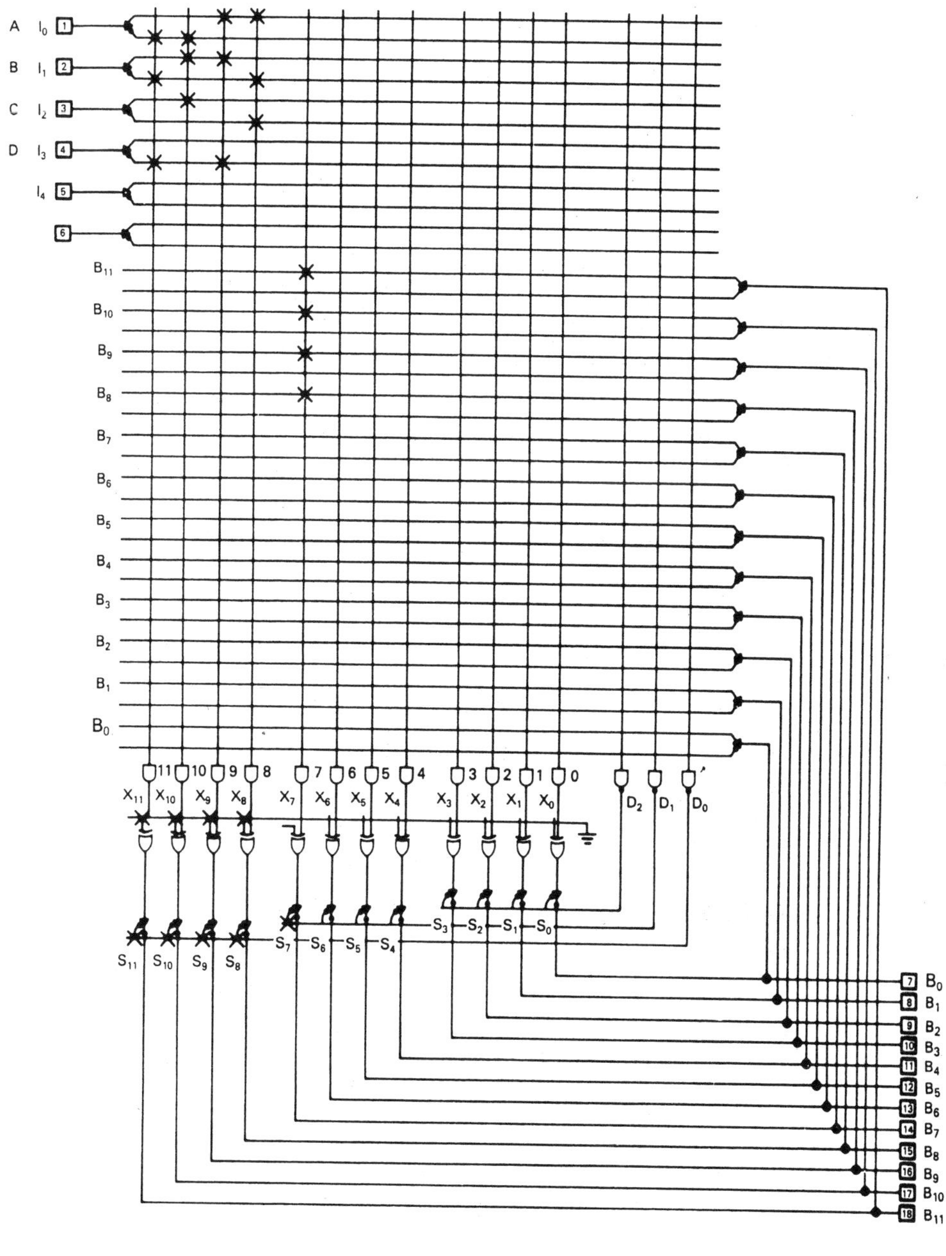

FIGURE 3.3

4-variable function implemented in NOR-NOR form (Courtesy of Signetics Corp.)

$$F_5 = \overline{\bar{C}\,\bar{D}\,\bar{G}\,\bar{H}}$$

$$F_4 = A\bar{B} \bullet F_5 = Z_1$$

$$F_3 = \overline{\bar{E}\,\bar{F}\,\bar{G}\,\bar{H}}$$

$$F_2 = A\bar{B}\,\bar{C}\,\bar{D} \bullet F_3 = Z_0$$

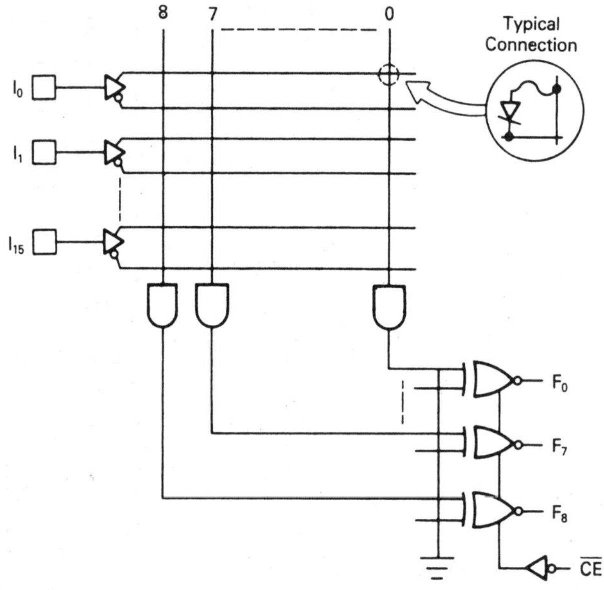

Fuses are initially intact at all array cross-points.

FIGURE 3.4
Logic diagram of PLS103 (Courtesy of Signetics Corp.)

A	B	C	D	E	F	G	H	Z_0	Z_1	Z_2	Z_3
0	X	X	X	X	X	X	X	0	0	0	0
1	0	0	0	0	0	0	0	0	0	0	1
1	1	X	X	X	X	X	X	0	0	1	0
1	0	1	X	X	X	X	X	0	1	0	0
1	0	0	1	X	X	X	X	0	1	1	0
1	0	0	0	1	X	X	X	1	0	0	0
1	0	0	0	0	1	X	X	1	0	1	0
1	0	0	0	0	0	1	X	1	1	0	0
1	0	0	0	0	0	0	1	1	1	1	0

FIGURE 3.5
Truth table for a 7-to-3 cascadable priority encoder

The device is programmed by blowing or keeping intact the appropriate fuses, as shown in Figure 3.6. Notice that the outputs F_7, F_5 and F_3 of the device are fed back to the inputs I_8, I_9 and I_{10} respectively. The fuses at X_7, X_5 and X_3 are not blown in order to achieve inversion at F_7, F_5 and F_3 respectively.

3.2 FIELD-PROGRAMMABLE ADDRESS DECODER (FPAD)

A FPAD is architecturally the same as a FPGA. It consists of only AND/NAND gates, no OR gates. Currently two configurations of FPADs are available: PLS162 (16 inputs, 5 outputs) and PLS163 (12 inputs and 9 outputs). Both devices have 24 pins and propagation delays of 30 ns. Figure 3.7 shows the logic diagram of PLS163.

As in a FPGA, all fuses in a FPAD are selectively blown to implement a certain function. To illustrate the application of a FPAD device, we shall design a 4-out-of-6 code to 1-out-of-15 code converter using two PLS163s. The truth table for the converter circuit is shown in Figure 3.8.

The Boolean equations for implementing the converter are derived from the truth table and are as follows:

$$Z_0 = ACDF \qquad Z_1 = BCDF \qquad Z_2 = ABDF$$
$$Z_3 = ABCE \qquad Z_4 = ABCF \qquad Z_5 = ABCD$$
$$Z_6 = ABDE \qquad Z_7 = ABEF \qquad Z_8 = ACDE$$
$$Z_9 = ACEF \qquad Z_{10} = ADEF \qquad Z_{11} = BCDE$$
$$Z_{12} = BCEF \qquad Z_{13} = BDEF \qquad Z_{14} = CDEF$$

Since the PLS163 contains nine AND gates, and we require 15 product terms to implement the code converter circuit, two devices have to be connected in parallel as shown in Figure 3.9. The top PLS163 generates the output Z_{0-8} and the bottom PLS163 generates the output Z_{9-14}. Figure 3.10a and b shows the logic diagrams of the programmed devices.

3.3 FIELD-PROGRAMMABLE LOGIC ARRAY (FPLA)

The FPLA structure offers a high level of flexibility because both the AND array and the OR array are programmable, as discussed in Chapter 1. Since the AND array is programmable, FPLAs do not suffer from the limitation of PROMs that the AND array must provide all possible input combinations. Since both the arrays are user-programmable it is possible for an OR gate to access any number of product terms. Moreover, all OR gates can access the same product term/s simultaneously. In other words product sharing does not require any additional resources in a FPLA architecture.

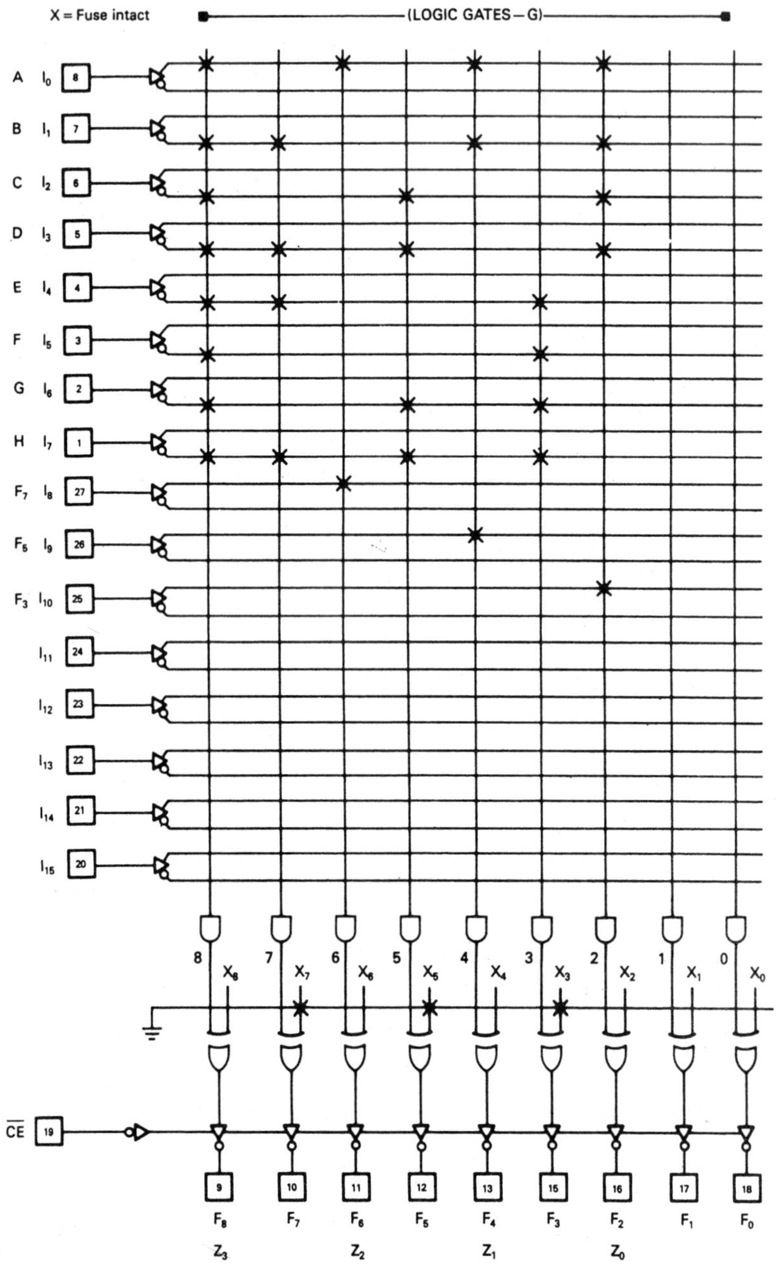

FIGURE 3.6
Implementation of a priority encoder (Courtesy of Signetics Corp.)

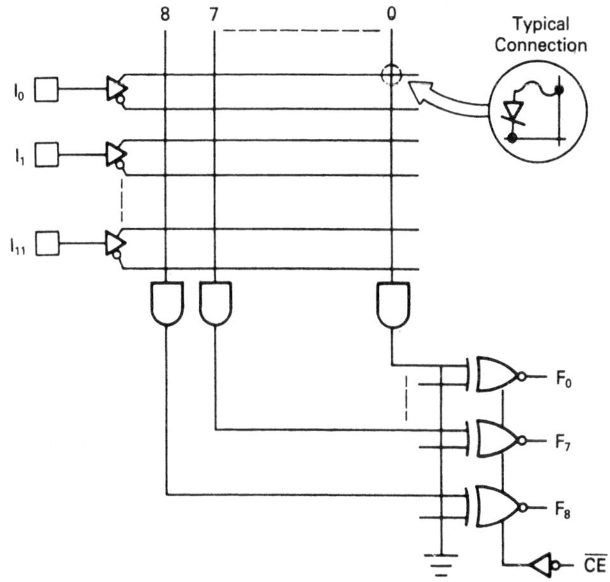

FIGURE 3.7
Logic diagram of PLS163 (Courtesy of Signetics Corp.)

4-out-of-6						*1-out-of-15*														
A	B	C	D	E	F	Z_0	Z_1	Z_2	Z_3	Z_4	Z_5	Z_6	Z_7	Z_8	Z_9	Z_{10}	Z_{11}	Z_{12}	Z_{13}	Z_{14}
0	0	1	1	1	1	0	0	0	0	0	0	0	0	0	0	0	0	0	0	1
0	1	0	1	1	1	0	0	0	0	0	0	0	0	0	0	0	0	0	1	0
0	1	1	0	1	1	0	0	0	0	0	0	0	0	0	0	0	0	1	0	0
0	1	1	1	1	0	0	0	0	0	0	0	0	0	0	0	0	1	0	0	0
1	0	0	1	1	1	0	0	0	0	0	0	0	0	0	0	1	0	0	0	0
1	0	1	0	1	1	0	0	0	0	0	0	0	0	0	1	0	0	0	0	0
1	0	1	1	1	0	0	0	0	0	0	0	0	0	1	0	0	0	0	0	0
1	1	0	0	1	1	0	0	0	0	0	0	0	1	0	0	0	0	0	0	0
1	1	0	1	1	0	0	0	0	0	0	0	1	0	0	0	0	0	0	0	0
1	1	1	1	0	0	0	0	0	0	0	1	0	0	0	0	0	0	0	0	0
1	1	1	0	0	1	0	0	0	0	1	0	0	0	0	0	0	0	0	0	0
1	1	1	0	1	0	0	0	0	1	0	0	0	0	0	0	0	0	0	0	0
1	1	0	1	0	1	0	0	1	0	0	0	0	0	0	0	0	0	0	0	0
0	1	1	1	0	1	0	1	0	0	0	0	0	0	0	0	0	0	0	0	0
1	0	1	1	0	1	1	0	0	0	0	0	0	0	0	0	0	0	0	0	0

FIGURE 3.8
4-out-of-6 to 1-out-of-15 converter

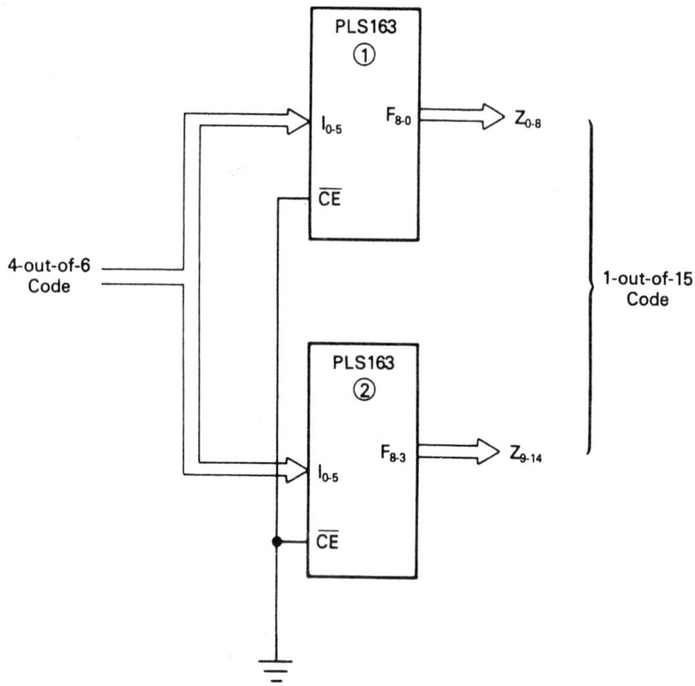

FIGURE 3.9
Two PLS163s connected in parallel

FPLAs are configured by the number of input variables (I), output functions (O) and the number of product terms (P): I × P × O. For example Signetics PLS100 is a 16 × 48 × 8 device (i.e., it has 16 input lines, 48 product terms, and 8 OR gates). Figure 3.11 shows the logic diagram of the device. The 16 input are each internally buffered and also inverted so as to provide true or complemented values; so there are 2 × I = 32 inputs to the 48 AND gates (32 × 48 input arrays). Product terms are formed by appropriate ANDing of any combination of the 16 input variables and their complements. Each of the 8 OR gates can provide a sum of any or all of the 48 product terms.

In addition, each output function can be individually programmed true or complement. This is accomplished by an EX-OR gate on each output, one input of which is connected to the ground via a fuse so that the sum-of-products function is not inverted (see Figure 3.12). If the fuse is blown, this input is forced to be at logic "1," thus providing the complement of the sum-of-products function. The programmable inversion has the added advantage in that if the complement of a sum-of-products function is simpler to realize than the original output function, then the complemented function may be programmed into the AND array and an inversion of it is obtained at the output. As an example, the function $f(x_1,x_2,x_3,x_4) = x_1 + x_2 + x_3 + x_4$ is more easily realizable as $f(x_1,x_2,x_3,x_4) = \overline{\bar{x}_1 \cdot \bar{x}_2 \cdot \bar{x}_3 \cdot \bar{x}_4}$.

The PLS100 is a 28-pin device and features tri-state outputs. For example if the chip enable input, $\overline{CE}$, is at logic "1" (see Figure 3.11), all the eight outputs of the device will be in high-impedance states. An open collector

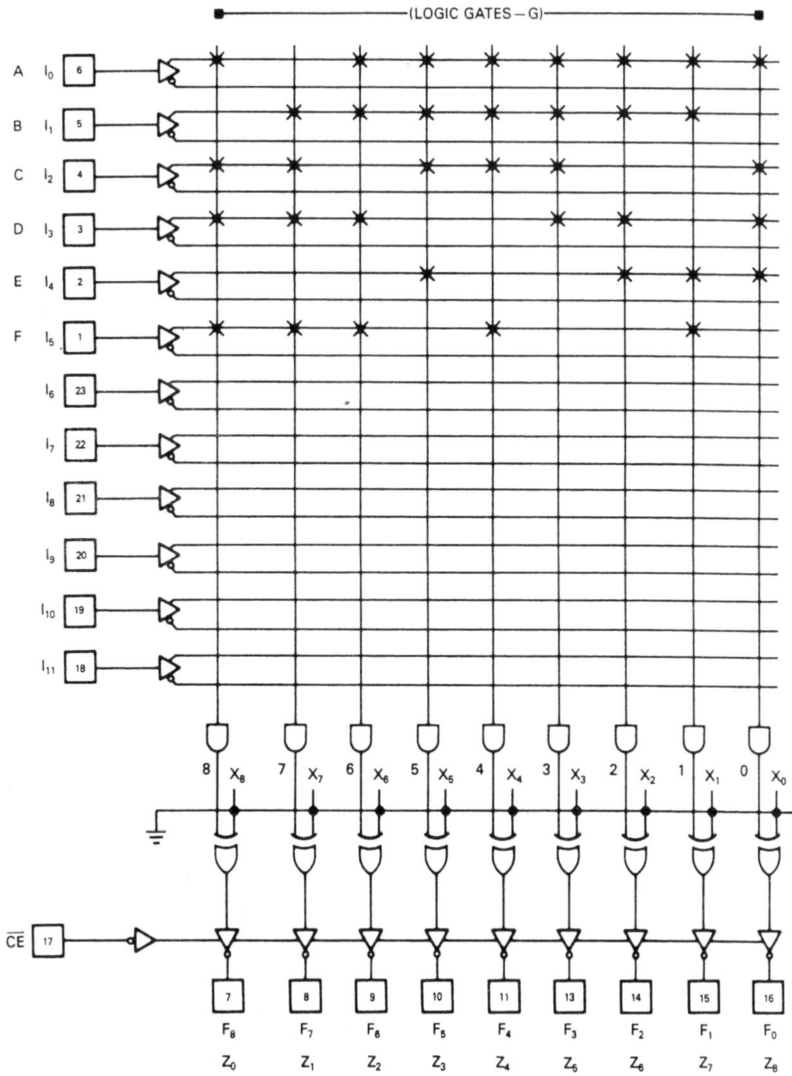

(a)

FIGURE 3.10a
Programmed devices for the 4-out-of-6 to 1-out-of-15 converter (Courtesy of Signetics Corp.)

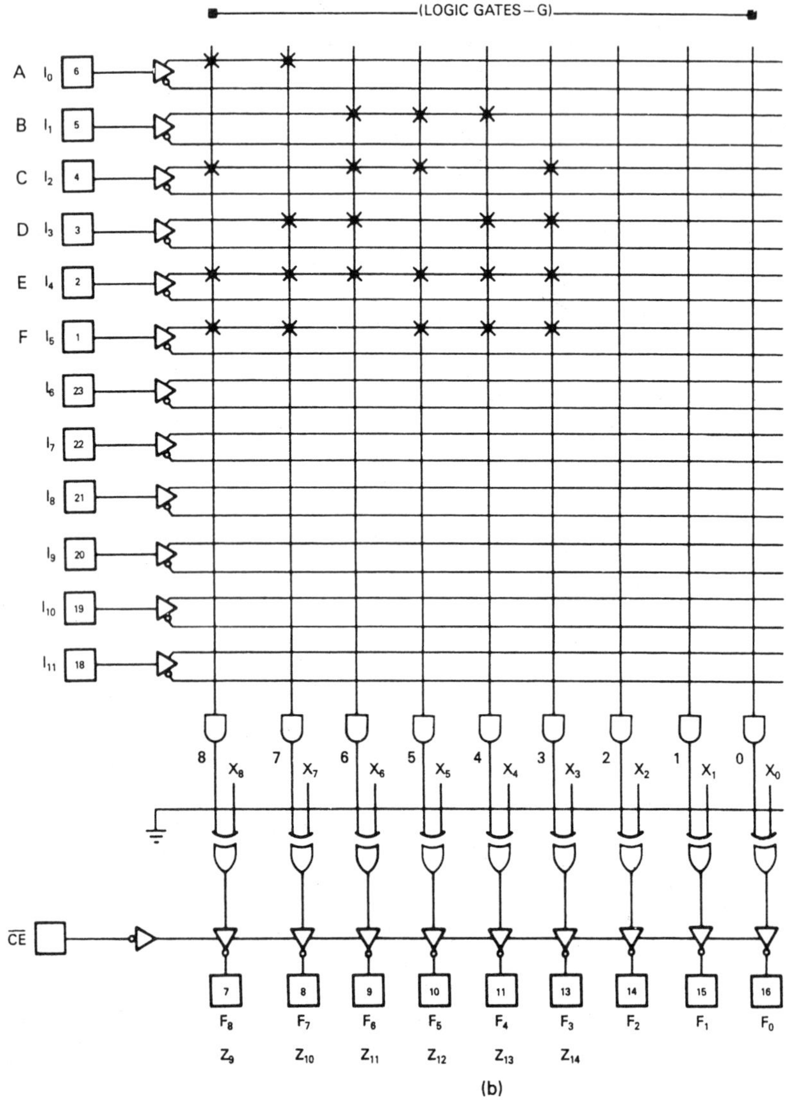

FIGURE 3.10b
Programmed devices for the 4-out-of-6 to 1-out-of-15 converter (Courtesy of Signetics Corp.)

version of the device, PLS101, is also available. Although the maximum number of inputs available is 16 in a PLS100/101, a number of these devices can be connected as shown in Figure 3.13a to increase the input variables. In this circuit four PLS100 devices are connected such that product terms corresponding to 18 input variables can be formed. Note that this scheme does not increase the number of product terms available (i.e., 48).

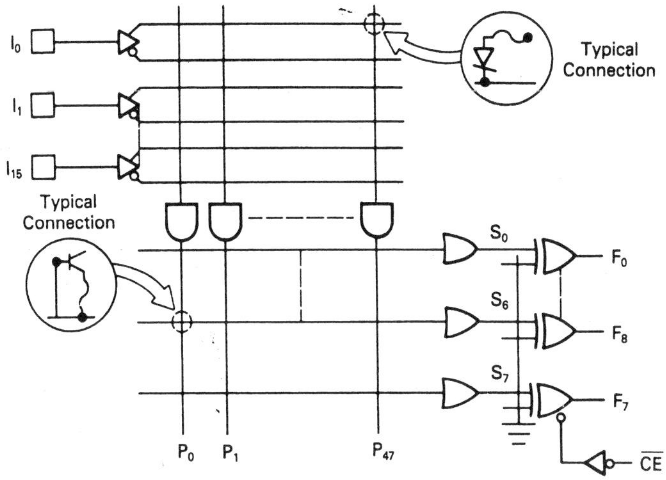

FIGURE 3.11
Logic diagram of PLS100 (Courtesy of Signetics Corp.)

It is possible to increase the number of product terms to more than 48. This involves partitioning the product terms into two groups, each containing fewer than 48 terms. Each group can then be fitted into a separate device. The partitioning process, however, often becomes complicated when a large number of product terms are involved.

In applications requiring more than eight outputs, a number of PLS100s can be connected in parallel. Figure 3.13b shows one such scheme in which the PLS100s share the same input and generate 16 outputs.

FPLAs are also available in 20-pin packages (e.g., PLS153, PLS153A, and PLHS153). All of these devices have eight dedicated input lines, 42 product terms, 10 OR gates, and 10 I/O lines which can be programmed to act as either input or output lines. Figure 3.14 shows the generic logic diagram of these devices. Eight of the 42 product terms are used to enable the buffers at the output of the EX-OR gates. Thus output lines may be selectively config-

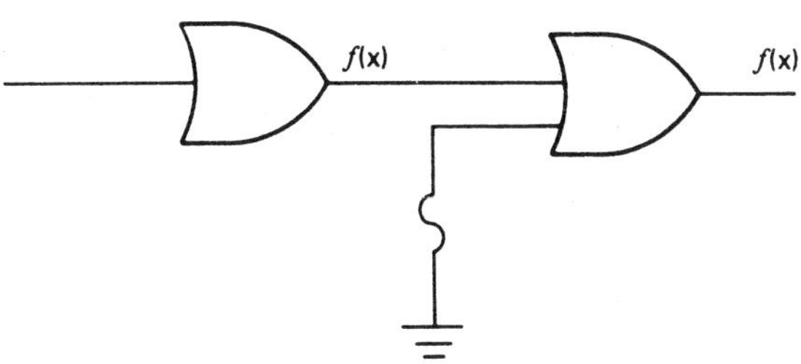

FIGURE 3.12
Programmable output inversion

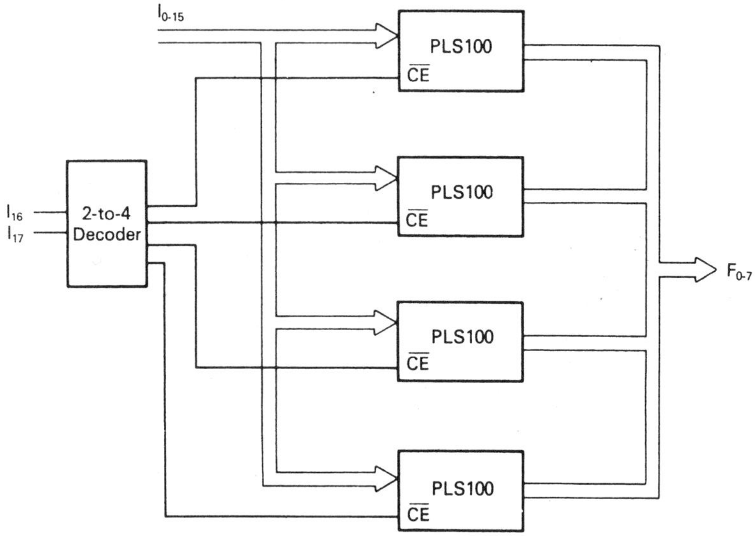

FIGURE 3.13a
Expansion of input variables

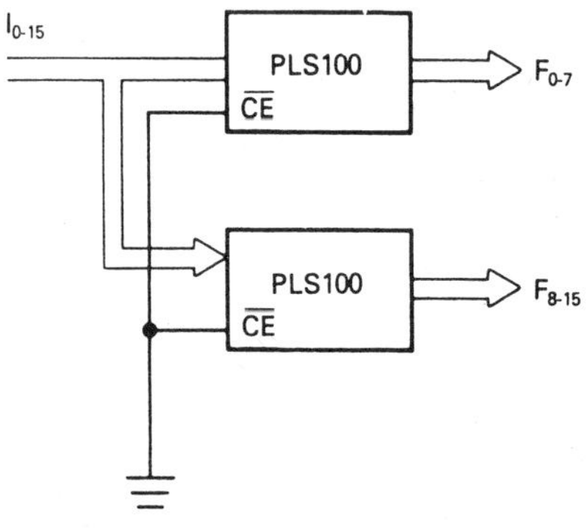

FIGURE 3.13b
Output expansion

ured as input lines by disabling the buffers driving them. Notice that this feature is not available in 28-pin PLS100/PLS101 devices. All the FPLAs in the 20-pin series can be used to implement AND-OR or AND-OR-INVERT functions. However, the devices have different propagation delays: PLS153 has 40 ns, PLS153A has 30 ns and PLHS153 has 20 ns.

The latest additions to FPLA devices are PLS161, PLS173, PLUS173, PLHS473 and PLC473; these are available in 24-pin packages. The PLS161 is basically the same as the PLS100, except that it has 12 input lines rather than 16. The PLS173 has the same features as PLS153A, except that it has more inputs (i.e., 12) and consumes 750 mw as compared to 650 mw in PLS153A.

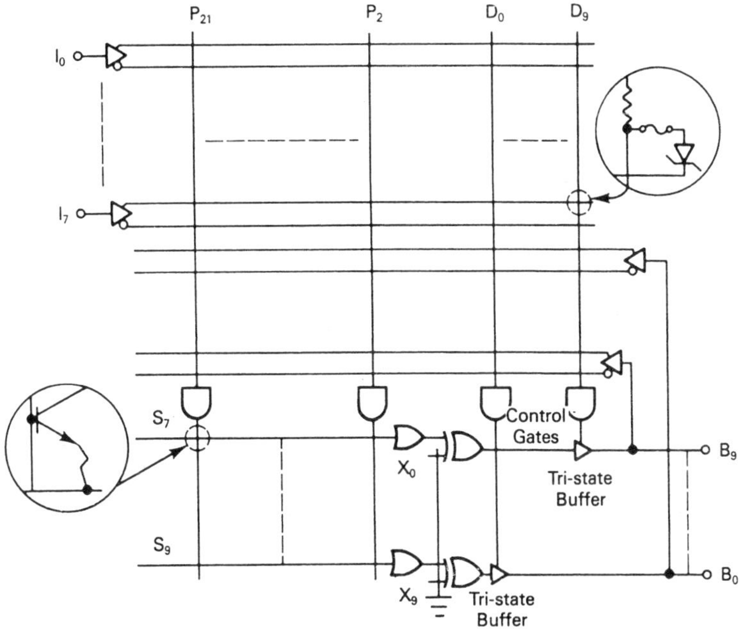

FIGURE 3.14
Logic diagram of 20-pin FPLAs (Courtesy of Signetics Corp.)

The PLUS173 is functionally identical to PLS173; however, it is three times faster than PLS173 and consumes less power.

The PLHS473 has 11 dedicated input lines, 24 product terms, 22 OR gates, two dedicated output lines and nine I/O lines which may be configured as either input or output. Figure 3.15 shows the block diagram of the device. Notice that the EX-OR gates driving the outputs, also function as tri-state output buffers. The enable input to each EX-OR gate is supplied by a dedicated OR gate. Alternatively, each output may be converted to an open-collector output by programming the output of the corresponding EX-OR gate to logic "0," and using the OR gate driving the enable input to generate the logic function, as shown in Figure 3.16 [1].

The PLHS473 has a propagation delay of about 20 ns, and consumes about 700 mw. A **security fuse** is incorporated into the device which if blown, prevents the unauthorized access to the programmed pattern corresponding to the design.

3.4 LOGIC DESIGN USING FPLAs

The FPLA's ability to set desired information in the chip after the chip has been manufactured and packaged, distinguishes it from the conventional PLA. To understand the translation of logic equations into the FPLA, let us refer to the program table shown in Figure 3.17a which defines the internal

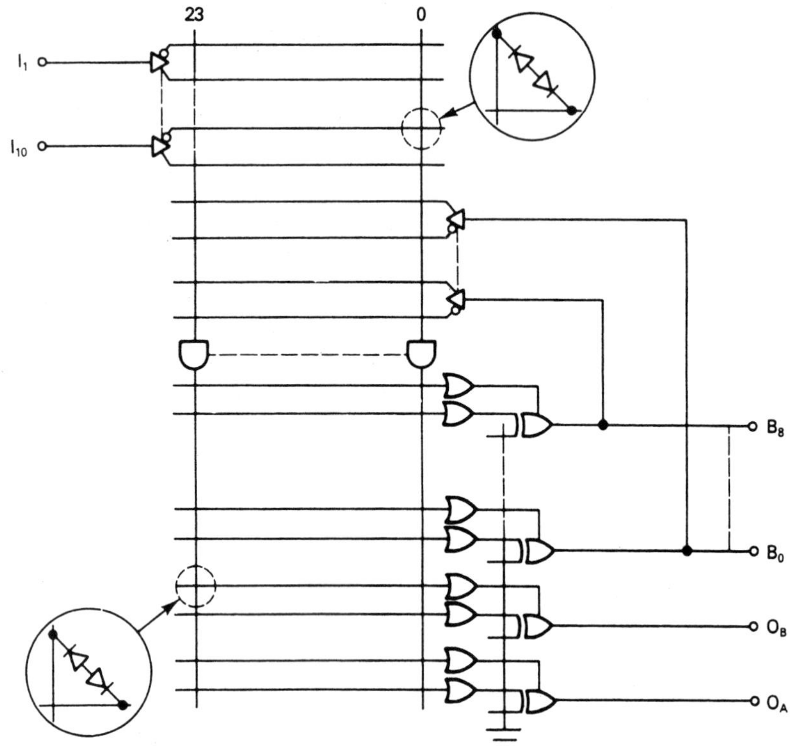

FIGURE 3.15
Logic diagram of PLHS473 (Courtesy of Signetics Corp.)

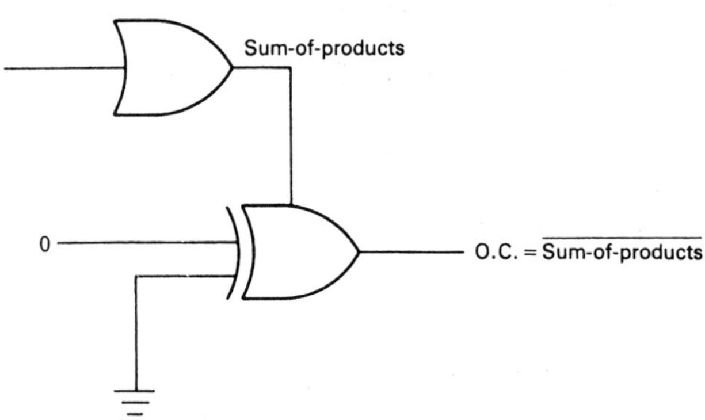

FIGURE 3.16
Conversion to open-collector output

PROGRAM TABLE ENTRIES

INPUT VARIABLE			OUTPUT FUNCTION		OUTPUT ACTIVE LEVEL	
I_m	$\bar{I}_m$	Don't Care	Prod Term Present in F_p	Prod Term Not Present in F_p	Active High	Active Low
H	L	— (dash)	A	• (period)	H	L
NOTE Enter (•) for unused inputs of used P-terms.			NOTES 1. Entries independent of output polarity. 2. Enter (A) for unused outputs of used P-terms.		NOTES 1. Polarity programmed once only. 2. Enter (H) for all unused outputs.	

CUSTOMER NAME ________
PURCHASE ORDER # ________
SIGNETICS DEVICE # ________ CF (XXXX)
CUSTOMER SYMBOLIZED PART # ________
TOTAL NUMBER OF PARTS ________
PROGRAM TABLE # ________ REV ____ DATE ____

	AND																OR							
																	POLARITY							
																						H	H	H
TERM	INPUT (I_m)																OUTPUT (F_p)							
	15	14	13	12	11	10	9	8	7	6	5	4	3	2	1	0	7	6	5	4	3	2	1	0
0	—	—	—	—	—	—	—	—	—	—	—	—	H	—	L	H	•	•	•	•	•	•	•	A
1	—	—	—	—	—	—	—	—	—	—	—	—	L	H	L	L	•	•	•	•	•	•	A	A
2	—	—	—	—	—	—	—	—	—	—	—	—	—	H	H	L	•	•	•	•	•	A	•	A
3	—	—	—	—	—	—	—	—	—	—	—	—	—	L	H	H	•	•	•	•	•	A	A	•
4	—	—	—	—	—	—	—	—	—	—	—	—	L	H	H	H	•	•	•	•	•	•	A	•
5	—	—	—	—	—	—	—	—	—	—	—	—	H	H	H	H	•	•	•	•	•	A	•	•
6																								
7																								
8																								
9																								
10																								
11																								
12																								
13																								
14																								
15																								
16																								
17																								
18																								
19																								
20																								
21																								
22																								
23																								
24																								
25																								
26																								
27																								
28																								
29																								
30																								
31																								
32																								
33																								
34																								
35																								
36																								
37																								
38																								
39																								
40																								
41																								
42																								
43																								
44																								
45																								
46																								
47																								
PIN NO.	20	21	22	23	24	25	26	27	2	3	4	5	6	7	8	9	10	11	12	13	15	16	17	18
VARIABLE NAME													A	B	C	D						F_2	F_1	F_0

FIGURE 3.17a
Implementation of the 4-input, 3-output function (Courtesy of Signetics Corp.)

connection of PLS100/PLS101. Each row represents one of the available AND gates in the matrix. In each row, opposite the appropriate product term, information is entered in the product term's input data columns.

1. An **H** is entered in an input column if that input appears in the product term as a true input.
2. An **L** is entered in an input column if that input appears in the product term as a complemented input.
3. A — (dash) is entered in an input column if that input does not appear in the product term.

If fewer than the maximum product terms are used, the spaces for the unused terms are left blank.

The OUTPUT part of the programming table specifies the product term connections to the OR gate inputs.

1. An **A** is entered in an output column if the product term is contained in the output expression.
2. A **.** (period) is entered in an output column if the product term is not contained in the output expression.
3. An **H** or **L** is entered in the polarity location corresponding to an output column, if the output is to be active-high or active-low, respectively. For example, the Boolean functions,

$$F_0(A,B,C,D) = A\overline{C}D + \overline{A}B\overline{C}\overline{D} + BC\overline{D}$$

$$F_1(A,B,C,D) = \overline{B}CD + \overline{A}B\overline{C}\overline{D} + \overline{A}BCD$$

$$F_2(A,B,C,D) = \overline{B}CD + ABCD + BC\overline{D}$$

are coded for PLS100/PLS101 implementation as shown in Figure 3.17a; input variables A, B, C, D correspond to I_3, I_2, I_1 and I_0 respectively in Figure 3.17a. The above equations can be expressed in ABEL format as shown in Figure 3.17b. The ABEL software will process the input file, and generate the programmer load file. Note that in ABEL, the device file for the PLS100 is named F100.

Single-error Detection and Correction Circuit for 8-bit Word. An 8-bit word requires four check bits; the check bits are appended to the eight data bits in order for the encoded word to be single error-correcting. The bit positions of the encoded word are labeled, with numbers 1 through 12.

Bit positions	1	2	3	4	5	6	7	8	9	10	11	12
Bit names	C_1	C_2	b_1	C_3	b_2	b_3	b_4	C_4	b_5	b_6	b_7	b_8

```
module Comb
title 'combinational logic
Parag K. Lala            23 November 1988.'
       IC1           device          'F100';
       A,B,C,D        pin      6,7,8,9;
       F2,F1,F0       pin      16,17,18,19;
equations
       F0 = A&!C&D # !A&B&!C&!D # B&C&!D;
       F1 = !B&C&D # !A&B&!C&!D # !A&B&C&D;
       F2 = !B&C&D # A&B&C&D # B&C&!D;
end Comb;
```

FIGURE 3.17b
ABEL description

The bit positions corresponding to the powers of 2 are used as check bits C_1, C_2, C_3 and C_4. The other bit positions correspond to the data bits b_1–b_8. The check bits are derived by using the following matrix:

$$\begin{array}{cccccccccccc}
C_1 & C_2 & b_1 & C_3 & b_2 & b_3 & b_4 & C_4 & b_5 & b_6 & b_7 & b_8
\end{array}$$
$$\begin{pmatrix}
0 & 0 & 0 & 0 & 0 & 0 & 0 & 1 & 1 & 1 & 1 & 1 \\
0 & 0 & 0 & 1 & 1 & 1 & 1 & 0 & 0 & 0 & 0 & 1 \\
0 & 1 & 1 & 0 & 0 & 1 & 1 & 0 & 0 & 1 & 1 & 0 \\
1 & 0 & 1 & 0 & 1 & 0 & 1 & 0 & 1 & 0 & 1 & 0
\end{pmatrix}
\begin{array}{c} e_1 \\ e_2 \\ e_3 \\ e_4 \end{array}$$

It can be seen from the matrix that:

$$C_1 = b_1 \oplus b_2 \oplus b_4 \oplus b_5 \oplus b_7$$

$$C_2 = b_1 \oplus b_3 \oplus b_4 \oplus b_6 \oplus b_7$$

$$C_3 = b_2 \oplus b_3 \oplus b_4 \oplus b_8$$

$$C_4 = b_5 \oplus b_6 \oplus b_7 \oplus b_8$$

For example, if $b_1 b_2 b_3 b_4 b_5 b_6 b_7 = 10101011$, then $C_1 = 1$, $C_2 = 1$, $C_3 = 0$ and $C_4 = 1$. Thus the corresponding encoded word is

Bit positions	1	2	3	4	5	6	7	8	9	10	11	12
	1	1	1	0	0	1	0	1	1	0	1	1

Figure 3.18 shows the block diagram of the single-error correcting system. It receives an 8-bit word of incoming data and generates the four check bits, which are stored with the eight data bits in the addressed location of the memory. When the memory location is read, the check bits are again gener-

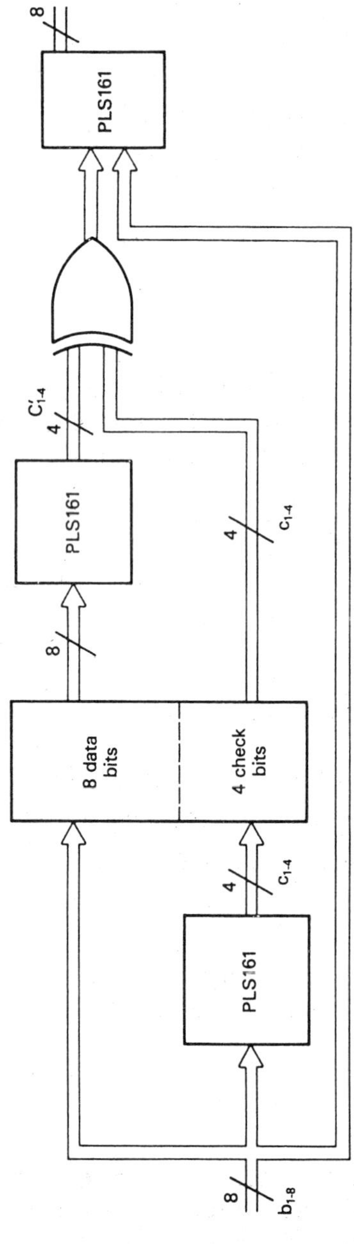

FIGURE 3.18
Block diagram of the single-error correcting system

ated from the data bits. Then these check bits are EX-ORed with the previously stored check bits to produce the syndrome bits. These syndrome bits reveal whether no error occurred, a single-bit error occurred (identifying that bit) or a multiple-bit error occurred. If a single-bit error occurred, it is corrected before the data bits are available at the output of the error-correcting system. The check bits can be generated with an FPLA. In order to use an FPLA, the check bit equations must be expressed in the sum-of-products form:

$$\begin{aligned}
C_1 &= b_1 \oplus b_2 \oplus b_4 \oplus b_5 \oplus b_7 \\
&= \bar{b}_1 b_2 b_4 b_5 \bar{b}_7 + \bar{b}_1 b_2 b_4 \bar{b}_5 b_7 + \bar{b}_1 b_2 \bar{b}_4 b_5 b_7 + \bar{b}_1 b_2 \bar{b}_4 \bar{b}_5 \bar{b}_7 \\
&\quad + b_1 \bar{b}_2 b_4 b_5 \bar{b}_7 + b_1 \bar{b}_2 b_4 \bar{b}_5 b_7 + b_1 \bar{b}_2 \bar{b}_4 b_5 b_7 + b_1 \bar{b}_2 \bar{b}_4 \bar{b}_5 \bar{b}_7 \\
&\quad + \bar{b}_1 \bar{b}_2 b_4 b_5 b_7 + \bar{b}_1 \bar{b}_2 b_4 \bar{b}_5 \bar{b}_7 + \bar{b}_1 \bar{b}_2 \bar{b}_4 b_5 \bar{b}_7 + \bar{b}_1 \bar{b}_2 \bar{b}_4 \bar{b}_5 b_7 \\
&\quad + b_1 b_2 b_4 b_5 b_7 + b_1 b_2 b_4 \bar{b}_5 \bar{b}_7 + b_1 b_2 \bar{b}_4 b_5 \bar{b}_7 + b_1 b_2 \bar{b}_4 \bar{b}_5 b_7
\end{aligned}$$

$$\begin{aligned}
C_2 &= b_1 \oplus b_3 \oplus b_4 \oplus b_6 \oplus b_7 \\
&= \bar{b}_1 b_3 b_4 b_6 \bar{b}_7 + \bar{b}_1 b_3 b_4 \bar{b}_6 b_7 + \bar{b}_1 b_3 \bar{b}_4 b_6 b_7 + \bar{b}_1 b_3 \bar{b}_4 \bar{b}_6 \bar{b}_7 \\
&\quad + b_1 \bar{b}_3 b_4 b_6 \bar{b}_7 + b_1 \bar{b}_3 b_4 \bar{b}_6 b_7 + b_1 \bar{b}_3 \bar{b}_4 b_6 b_7 + b_1 \bar{b}_3 \bar{b}_4 \bar{b}_6 \bar{b}_7 \\
&\quad + \bar{b}_1 \bar{b}_3 b_4 b_6 b_7 + \bar{b}_1 \bar{b}_3 b_4 \bar{b}_6 \bar{b}_7 + \bar{b}_1 \bar{b}_3 \bar{b}_4 b_6 \bar{b}_7 + \bar{b}_1 \bar{b}_3 \bar{b}_4 \bar{b}_6 b_7 \\
&\quad + b_1 b_3 b_4 b_6 b_7 + b_1 b_3 b_4 \bar{b}_6 \bar{b}_7 + b_1 b_3 \bar{b}_4 b_6 \bar{b}_7 + b_1 b_3 \bar{b}_4 \bar{b}_6 b_7
\end{aligned}$$

$$\begin{aligned}
C_3 &= b_2 \oplus b_3 \oplus b_4 \oplus b_8 \\
&= b_2 b_3 b_4 \bar{b}_8 + b_2 b_3 \bar{b}_4 b_8 + \bar{b}_2 \bar{b}_3 b_4 \bar{b}_8 + \bar{b}_2 \bar{b}_3 \bar{b}_4 b_8 \\
&\quad + b_2 \bar{b}_3 \bar{b}_4 \bar{b}_8 + b_2 \bar{b}_3 b_4 b_8 + \bar{b}_2 b_3 \bar{b}_4 \bar{b}_8 + \bar{b}_2 b_3 b_4 b_8
\end{aligned}$$

$$\begin{aligned}
C_4 &= b_5 \oplus b_6 \oplus b_7 \oplus b_8 \\
&= b_5 b_6 \bar{b}_7 b_8 + b_5 b_6 b_7 \bar{b}_8 + \bar{b}_5 \bar{b}_6 \bar{b}_7 b_8 + \bar{b}_5 \bar{b}_6 b_7 \bar{b}_8 \\
&\quad b_5 \bar{b}_6 \bar{b}_7 \bar{b}_8 + b_5 \bar{b}_6 b_7 b_8 + \bar{b}_5 b_6 \bar{b}_7 \bar{b}_8 + \bar{b}_5 b_6 b_7 b_8
\end{aligned}$$

There are 48 product terms in the check bit equations, hence, either PLS100 or PLS161 can be used. Since the PLS161 has fewer pins, we will use this device to generate the check bits. The coded program table for the device is shown in Figure 3.19; data bits $b_0 \ldots b_7$ correspond to $I_0 \ldots I_8$, respectively in the table, and the check bits c_1–c_4 correspond to F_0–F_3, respectively.

The equation for the syndrome bits e_1, e_2, e_3 and e_4 are as follows:

$$e_1 = C_1 \oplus C_1', \qquad e_2 = C_2 \oplus C_2', \qquad e_3 = C_3 \oplus C_3' \quad \text{and} \quad e_4 = C_4 \oplus C_4'$$

where C_1', C_2', C_3' and C_4' correspond to check bits generated using the data bits programmed into the PLS161; these check bits can be generated by using another PLS161 programmed as in Figure 3.19. The equations for the syndrome bits can be realized with an SSI chip (e.g., SN7486) containing four EX-OR gates.

The error-correcting circuit decodes the four syndrome bits, and if they match a column in the check matrix considered above the corresponding bit in the data word is inverted (assuming error correction will be performed only

TERM	AND INPUT (I_m) 11	10	9	8	7	6	5	4	3	2	1	0	OR OUTPUT (F_p) 7	6	5	4				
POLARITY																	H	H	H	H
0	—	—	—	—	L	H	—	H	H	—	—	L	•	•	•	•	A	•	•	•
1	—	—	—	—	L	H	—	H	L	—	—	H	•	•	•	•	A	•	•	•
2	—	—	—	—	L	H	—	L	L	—	—	L	•	•	•	•	A	•	•	•
3	—	—	—	—	L	H	—	L	H	—	—	H	•	•	•	•	A	•	•	•
4	—	—	—	—	H	L	—	H	L	—	—	H	•	•	•	•	A	•	•	•
5	—	—	—	—	H	L	—	L	H	—	—	H	•	•	•	•	A	•	•	•
6	—	—	—	—	H	L	—	L	L	—	—	L	•	•	•	•	A	•	•	•
7	—	—	—	—	H	L	—	H	H	—	—	L	•	•	•	•	A	•	•	•
8	—	—	—	—	L	L	—	H	H	—	—	H	•	•	•	•	A	•	•	•
9	—	—	—	—	L	L	—	H	L	—	—	L	•	•	•	•	A	•	•	•
10	—	—	—	—	L	L	—	L	H	—	—	L	•	•	•	•	A	•	•	•
11	—	—	—	—	L	L	—	L	L	—	—	H	•	•	•	•	A	•	•	•
12	—	—	—	—	H	H	—	H	H	—	—	H	•	•	•	•	A	•	•	•
13	—	—	—	—	H	H	—	H	L	—	—	L	•	•	•	•	A	•	•	•
14	—	—	—	—	H	H	—	L	H	—	—	L	•	•	•	•	A	•	•	•
15	—	—	—	—	H	H	—	L	L	—	—	H	•	•	•	•	A	•	•	•
16	—	—	—	—	L	—	H	H	—	H	—	L	•	•	•	•	•	A	•	•
17	—	—	—	—	L	—	H	H	—	L	—	H	•	•	•	•	•	A	•	•
18	—	—	—	—	L	—	H	L	—	H	—	H	•	•	•	•	•	A	•	•
19	—	—	—	—	L	—	H	L	—	L	—	L	•	•	•	•	•	A	•	•
20	—	—	—	—	H	—	L	H	L	H	—	L	•	•	•	•	•	A	•	•
21	—	—	—	—	H	—	L	H	H	L	—	H	•	•	•	•	•	A	•	•
22	—	—	—	—	H	—	L	L	H	H	—	H	•	•	•	•	•	A	•	•
23	—	—	—	—	H	—	L	L	H	L	—	L	•	•	•	•	•	A	•	•
24	—	—	—	—	L	—	L	H	H	H	—	H	•	•	•	•	•	A	•	•
25	—	—	—	—	L	—	L	H	—	L	—	L	•	•	•	•	•	A	•	•
26	—	—	—	—	L	—	L	L	—	H	—	L	•	•	•	•	•	A	•	•
27	—	—	—	—	L	—	L	L	—	L	—	H	•	•	•	•	•	A	•	•
28	—	—	—	—	H	—	H	H	—	H	—	H	•	•	•	•	•	A	•	•
29	—	—	—	—	H	—	H	H	—	L	—	L	•	•	•	•	•	A	•	•
30	—	—	—	—	H	—	H	L	—	H	L	L	•	•	•	•	•	A	•	•
31	—	—	—	—	H	—	H	L	—	L	H	H	•	•	•	•	•	A	•	•
32	—	—	—	—	—	H	H	H	—	—	H	L	•	•	•	•	•	•	A	•
33	—	—	—	—	—	H	H	L	—	—	H	H	•	•	•	•	•	•	A	•
34	—	—	—	—	—	L	L	H	—	—	H	L	•	•	•	•	•	•	A	•
35	—	—	—	—	—	L	L	L	—	—	—	H	•	•	•	•	•	•	A	•
36	—	—	—	—	—	H	L	L	—	—	—	L	•	•	•	•	•	•	A	•
37	—	—	—	—	—	H	L	H	—	—	—	H	•	•	•	•	•	•	A	•
38	—	—	—	—	—	L	H	L	—	—	—	L	•	•	•	•	•	•	A	•
39	—	—	—	—	—	L	H	H	—	—	—	H	•	•	•	•	•	•	A	•
40	—	—	—	—	—	—	—	—	H	H	L	H	•	•	•	•	•	•	•	A
41	—	—	—	—	—	—	—	—	H	H	H	L	•	•	•	•	•	•	•	A
42	—	—	—	—	—	—	—	—	L	L	L	H	•	•	•	•	•	•	•	A
43	—	—	—	—	—	—	—	—	L	L	H	L	•	•	•	•	•	•	•	A
44	—	—	—	—	—	—	—	—	H	L	L	L	•	•	•	•	•	•	•	A
45	—	—	—	—	—	—	—	—	H	L	H	H	•	•	•	•	•	•	•	A
46	—	—	—	—	—	—	—	—	L	H	L	L	•	•	•	•	•	•	•	A
47	—	—	—	—	—	—	—	—	L	H	H	H	•	•	•	•	•	•	•	A
PIN NO.	18	19	20	21	22	23	2	3	4	5	6	7	8	9	10	11	13	14	15	16
VARIABLE NAME					b_1	b_2	b_3	b_4	b_5	b_6	b_7	b_8					c_1	c_2	c_3	c_4

PROGRAM TABLE ENTRIES

INPUT VARIABLE			OUTPUT FUNCTION		OUTPUT ACTIVE LEVEL	
I_m	$\bar{I}_m$	Don't Care	Prod Term Present in F_p	Prod Term Not Present in F_p	Active High	Active Low
H	L	—(dash)	A	• (period)	H	L
NOTE Enter (•) for unused inputs of used P-terms.			NOTES 1. Entries independent of output polarity. 2. Enter (A) for unused outputs of used P-terms.		NOTES 1. Polarity programmed once only. 2. Enter (H) for all unused outputs.	

CUSTOMER NAME ______

PURCHASE ORDER # ______

SIGNETICS DEVICE # ______ CF (XXXX)

CUSTOMER SYMBOLIZED PART # ______

TOTAL NUMBER OF PARTS ______

PROGRAM TABLE # ______ REV ______ DATE ______

FIGURE 3.19
Check bit generation using PLS161 (Courtesy of Signetics Corp.)

on data bits). If the decoded bits are all "0"s, then there is no error. Alternatively, if the decoded bits have a non-zero value and do not match with any column in the check matrix, then there is a double or multi-bit error in the data word. In that case, the corrector generates an error signal (ERROR) to indicate the presence of an uncorrectable error. The equations for the corrector are:

$$\begin{aligned}
d_1 &= \bar{e}_1 \bar{e}_2 e_3 e_4 \oplus b_1 \\
&= \bar{e}_1 \bar{e}_2 e_3 e_4 \bar{b}_1 + e_1 b_1 + e_2 b_1 + \bar{e}_3 b_1 + \bar{e}_4 b_1 \\
d_2 &= \bar{e}_1 e_2 \bar{e}_3 e_4 \oplus b_2 \\
&= \bar{e}_1 e_2 \bar{e}_3 e_4 \bar{b}_2 + e_1 b_2 + \bar{e}_2 b_2 + e_3 b_2 + \bar{e}_4 b_2 \\
d_3 &= \bar{e}_1 e_2 e_3 \bar{e}_4 \oplus b_3 \\
&= \bar{e}_1 e_2 e_3 \bar{e}_4 \bar{b}_3 + e_1 b_3 + \bar{e}_2 b_3 + \bar{e}_3 b_3 + e_4 b_3 \\
d_4 &= \bar{e}_1 e_2 e_3 e_4 \oplus b_4 \\
&= \bar{e}_1 e_2 e_3 e_4 \bar{b}_4 + e_1 b_4 + \bar{e}_2 b_4 + \bar{e}_3 b_4 + \bar{e}_4 b_4 \\
d_5 &= e_1 \bar{e}_2 \bar{e}_3 e_4 \oplus b_5 \\
&= e_1 \bar{e}_2 \bar{e}_3 e_4 \bar{b}_5 + \bar{e}_1 b_5 + e_2 b_5 + e_3 b_5 + \bar{e}_4 b_5 \\
d_6 &= e_1 \bar{e}_2 e_3 \bar{e}_4 \oplus b_6 \\
&= e_1 \bar{e}_2 e_3 \bar{e}_4 \bar{b}_6 + \bar{e}_1 b_6 + e_2 b_6 + \bar{e}_3 b_6 + e_4 b_6 \\
d_7 &= e_1 \bar{e}_2 e_3 e_4 \oplus b_7 \\
&= e_1 \bar{e}_2 e_3 e_4 \bar{b}_7 + \bar{e}_1 b_7 + e_2 b_7 + \bar{e}_3 b_7 + \bar{e}_4 b_7 \\
d_8 &= e_1 e_2 \bar{e}_3 \bar{e}_4 \oplus b_8 \\
&= e_1 e_2 \bar{e}_3 \bar{e}_4 \bar{b}_8 + \bar{e}_1 b_8 + \bar{e}_2 b_8 + e_3 b_8 + e_4 b_8 \\
\text{ERROR} &= e_1 e_2 e_3 + e_1 e_2 e_4
\end{aligned}$$

The equations for d_1–d_8 are programmed into another PLS161 as shown in Figure 3.20. The ERROR signal can be generated by using a small amount of random logic.

1-out-of-90 Detector. As a further example of the application of the FPLAs in combinational logic design, we consider the implementation of a 1-out-of-90 detector using PLS153 (as discussed in Chapter 2). Figure 3.21 shows the design of 1-out-of-90 detector using these devices. It requires only six devices as compared to the PLE solution which, besides additional gate logic, need nine 4K × 4 PLE devices.

Each PLS153 utilizes 19 product terms to detect the presence of all "0"s, single "1," or multiple "1"s via outputs X and Y, as defined in the program table of Figure 3.22a. An extra PLS153 is required to examine the ten X and

CUSTOMER NAME ______
PURCHASE ORDER # ______
SIGNETICS DEVICE # ______ CF (XXXX)
CUSTOMER SYMBOLIZED PART # ______
TOTAL NUMBER OF PARTS ______
PROGRAM TABLE # ______ REV ______ DATE ______

PROGRAM TABLE ENTRIES

INPUT VARIABLE			OUTPUT FUNCTION		OUTPUT ACTIVE LEVEL	
I_m	$\bar{I}_m$	Don't Care	Prod Term Present in F_p	Prod Term Not Present in F_p	Active High	Active Low
H	L	— (dash)	A	• (period)	H	L

NOTE: Enter (•) for unused inputs of used P-terms.

NOTES: 1. Entries independent of output polarity. 2. Enter (A) for unused outputs of used P-terms.

NOTES: 1. Polarity programmed once only. 2. Enter (H) for all unused outputs.

TERM	AND INPUT (I_m) 11	10	9	8	7	6	5	4	3	2	1	0	OR OUTPUT (F_p) 7	6	5	4	3	2	1	0
POLARITY													H	H	H	H	H	H	H	H
0	L	L	H	H	L	—	—	—	—	—	—	—	A	•	•	•	•	•	•	•
1	H	—	—	—	H	—	—	—	—	—	—	—	A	•	•	•	•	•	•	•
2	—	H	—	—	H	—	—	—	—	—	—	—	A	•	•	•	•	•	•	•
3	—	—	H	—	H	—	—	—	—	—	—	—	A	•	•	•	•	•	•	•
4	—	—	—	H	H	—	—	—	—	—	—	—	A	•	•	•	•	•	•	•
5	L	H	L	H	—	L	—	—	—	—	—	—	•	A	•	•	•	•	•	•
6	H	—	—	—	—	H	—	—	—	—	—	—	•	A	•	•	•	•	•	•
7	—	L	—	—	—	H	—	—	—	—	—	—	•	A	•	•	•	•	•	•
8	—	—	H	—	—	H	—	—	—	—	—	—	•	A	•	•	•	•	•	•
9	—	—	—	L	—	H	—	—	—	—	—	—	•	A	•	•	•	•	•	•
10	L	H	H	L	—	—	L	—	—	—	—	—	•	•	A	•	•	•	•	•
11	H	—	—	—	—	—	H	—	—	—	—	—	•	•	A	•	•	•	•	•
12	—	L	—	—	—	—	H	—	—	—	—	—	•	•	A	•	•	•	•	•
13	—	—	L	—	—	—	H	—	—	—	—	—	•	•	A	•	•	•	•	•
14	—	—	—	H	—	—	H	—	—	—	—	—	•	•	A	•	•	•	•	•
15	L	H	H	H	—	—	—	L	—	—	—	—	•	•	•	A	•	•	•	•
16	H	—	—	—	—	—	—	H	—	—	—	—	•	•	•	A	•	•	•	•
17	—	L	—	—	—	—	—	H	—	—	—	—	•	•	•	A	•	•	•	•
18	—	—	L	—	—	—	—	H	—	—	—	—	•	•	•	A	•	•	•	•
19	—	—	—	L	—	—	—	H	—	—	—	—	•	•	•	A	•	•	•	•
20	H	L	L	H	—	—	—	—	L	—	—	—	•	•	•	•	A	•	•	•
21	L	—	—	—	—	—	—	—	H	—	—	—	•	•	•	•	A	•	•	•
22	—	H	—	—	—	—	—	—	H	—	—	—	•	•	•	•	A	•	•	•
23	—	—	H	—	—	—	—	—	H	—	—	—	•	•	•	•	A	•	•	•
24	—	—	—	L	—	—	—	—	H	—	—	—	•	•	•	•	A	•	•	•
25	H	L	H	L	—	—	—	—	—	L	—	—	•	•	•	•	•	A	•	•
26	L	—	—	—	—	—	—	—	—	H	—	—	•	•	•	•	•	A	•	•
27	—	H	—	—	—	—	—	—	—	H	—	—	•	•	•	•	•	A	•	•
28	—	—	L	—	—	—	—	—	—	H	—	—	•	•	•	•	•	A	•	•
29	—	—	—	H	—	—	—	—	—	H	—	—	•	•	•	•	•	A	•	•
30	H	L	H	H	—	—	—	—	—	—	L	—	•	•	•	•	•	•	A	•
31	L	—	—	—	—	—	—	—	—	—	H	—	•	•	•	•	•	•	A	•
32	—	H	—	—	—	—	—	—	—	—	H	—	•	•	•	•	•	•	A	•
33	—	—	I	—	—	—	—	—	—	—	H	—	•	•	•	•	•	•	A	•
34	—	—	—	L	—	—	—	—	—	—	H	—	•	•	•	•	•	•	A	•
35	H	H	L	L	—	—	—	—	—	—	—	L	•	•	•	•	•	•	•	A
36	L	—	—	—	—	—	—	—	—	—	—	H	•	•	•	•	•	•	•	A
37	—	L	—	—	—	—	—	—	—	—	—	H	•	•	•	•	•	•	•	A
38	—	—	H	—	—	—	—	—	—	—	—	H	•	•	•	•	•	•	•	A
39	—	—	—	H	—	—	—	—	—	—	—	H	•	•	•	•	•	•	•	A
40																				
41																				
42																				
43																				
44																				
45																				
46																				
47																				
PIN NO.	18	19	20	21	22	23	2	3	4	5	6	7	8	9	10	11	13	14	15	16
VARIABLE NAME	e_1	e_2	e_3	e_4	b_1	b_2	b_3	b_4	b_5	b_6	b_7	b_8	d_1	d_2	d_3	d_4	d_5	d_6	d_7	d_8

FIGURE 3.20
Error corrector circuit implementation (Courtesy of Signetics Corp.)

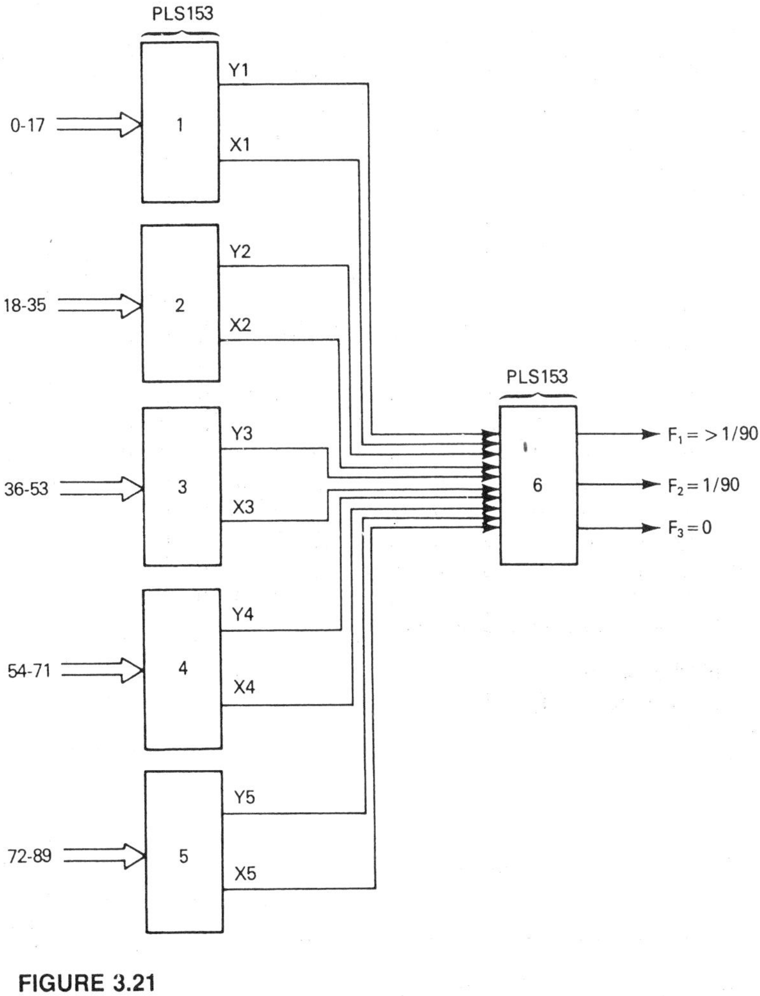

FIGURE 3.21
1-out-of-90 detector using six PLS153s

Y outputs from the first level FPLAs, and gives final indication of the number of "1"s (see Figure 3.22b).

State Machine Design. FPLAs can also be used in the realization of arbitrary state machines. All the information required to code the FPLA program table is available from the state table of the machine. To illustrate the implementation of state machines, we consider the state table/state diagram of a Moore machine shown in Figure 3.23a and b respectively.

Input																		Output	
17	*16*	*15*	*14*	*13*	*12*	*11*	*10*	*9*	*8*	*7*	*6*	*5*	*4*	*3*	*2*	*1*	*0*	*X*	*Y**
0	0	0	0	0	0	0	0	0	0	0	0	0	0	0	0	0	1	1	0
0	0	0	0	0	0	0	0	0	0	0	0	0	0	0	0	1	0	1	0
0	0	0	0	0	0	0	0	0	0	0	0	0	0	0	1	0	0	1	0
0	0	0	0	0	0	0	0	0	0	0	0	0	0	1	0	0	0	1	0
0	0	0	0	0	0	0	0	0	0	0	0	0	1	0	0	0	0	1	0
0	0	0	0	0	0	0	0	0	0	0	0	1	0	0	0	0	0	1	0
0	0	0	0	0	0	0	0	0	0	0	1	0	0	0	0	0	0	1	0
0	0	0	0	0	0	0	0	0	0	1	0	0	0	0	0	0	0	1	0
0	0	0	0	0	0	0	0	0	1	0	0	0	0	0	0	0	0	1	0
0	0	0	0	0	0	0	0	1	0	0	0	0	0	0	0	0	0	1	0
0	0	0	0	0	0	0	1	0	0	0	0	0	0	0	0	0	0	1	0
0	0	0	0	0	0	1	0	0	0	0	0	0	0	0	0	0	0	1	0
0	0	0	0	0	1	0	0	0	0	0	0	0	0	0	0	0	0	1	0
0	0	0	0	1	0	0	0	0	0	0	0	0	0	0	0	0	0	1	0
0	0	0	1	0	0	0	0	0	0	0	0	0	0	0	0	0	0	1	0
0	0	1	0	0	0	0	0	0	0	0	0	0	0	0	0	0	0	1	0
0	1	0	0	0	0	0	0	0	0	0	0	0	0	0	0	0	0	1	0
1	0	0	0	0	0	0	0	0	0	0	0	0	0	0	0	0	0	1	0
0	0	0	0	0	0	0	0	0	0	0	0	0	0	0	0	0	0	0	0

* Y output is programmed active-low.

FIGURE 3.22a
Program table for PLS153 (1–5)

Input										Output		
9	*8*	*7*	*6*	*5*	*4*	*3*	*2*	*1*	*0*			
X					*Y*					*F1**	*F2*	*F3*
0	0	0	0	0	0	0	0	0	0	0	0	1
0	0	0	0	1	0	0	0	0	0	0	1	0
0	0	0	1	0	0	0	0	0	0	0	1	0
0	0	1	0	0	0	0	0	0	0	0	1	0
0	1	0	0	0	0	0	0	0	0	0	1	0
1	0	0	0	0	0	0	0	0	0	0	1	0

* F1 output is programmed active-low.

FIGURE 3.22b
Program table for PLS153(6)

Present state	Input (l,m,n)								Output		
	000	001	010	011	100	101	110	111	Z_0	Z_1	Z_2
A	B	B	B	B	A	A	A	A	0	0	0
B	C	G	C	G	C	G	C	G	0	0	0
C	C	C	C	C	D	D	D	D	0	0	1
D	E	E	E	E	D	D	D	D	0	0	0
E	C	F	G	G	C	F	G	G	0	0	0
F	F	F	F	F	A	A	A	A	0	1	0
G	G	G	G	G	A	A	A	A	1	0	0

FIGURE 3.23a
State table of a Moore-type machine

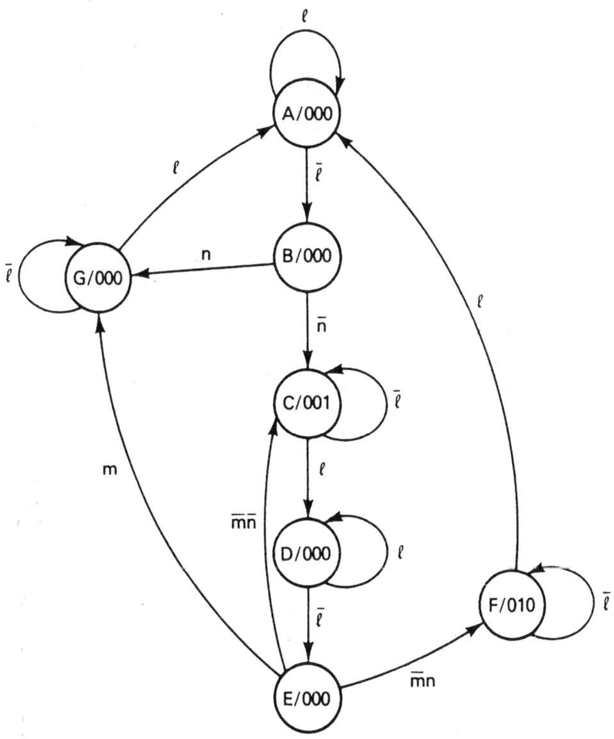

FIGURE 3.23b
State diagram of the Moore machine

A possible state assignment for the state machine is:

	Q_2	Q_1	Q_0
A =	1	0	0
B =	1	0	1
C =	0	1	0
D =	1	1	0
E =	1	1	1
F =	0	0	1
G =	0	0	0

The block diagram of the state machine implementation with a PLS153 is shown in Figure 3.24. The outputs B_2, B_1 and B_0 of the PLS153 drive the inputs of a 3-bit register; the outputs of the register $Q_2\,Q_1\,Q_6$, feed the inputs I_0, I_1, I_2, respectively. The inputs to the PLS153 are the present state of the register, and the three external inputs l, m, n. The outputs B_2, B_1, B_0 of the device generate the next state of the machine. The output of the state machine (i.e., Z_0, Z_1, and Z_2) are dependent on the present state of the register. The

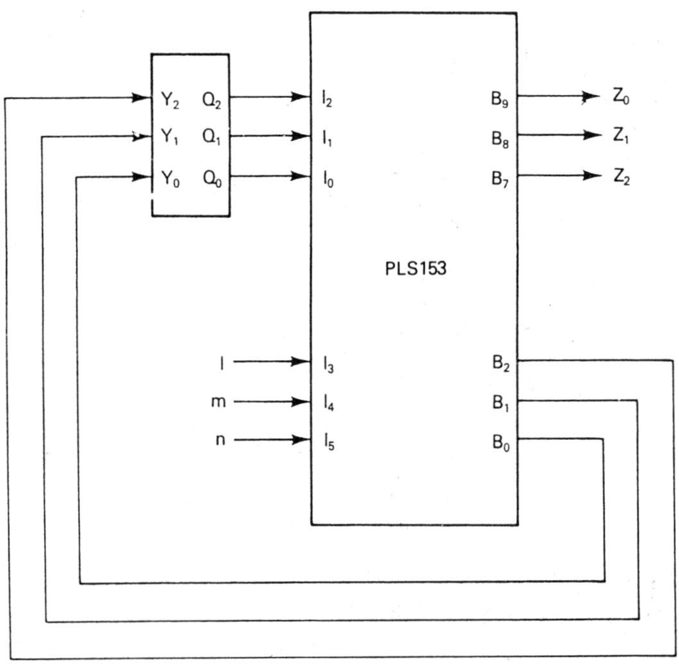

FIGURE 3.24
State machine implementation with PLS153

program table for the PLS153 is obtained directly from the state table, no simplification is required.

Figure 3.25 shows the program table for the PLS153. Note that in order to dedicate B_{0-2} and B_{7-9} as outputs, it is necessary to blow all the fuses to the inputs to the control gates D_{0-2} and D_{7-9}. This internally pulls all inputs to these control gates to logic "1," which in turn permanently enables the tri-state buffers at the selected outputs.

CUSTOMER NAME ____
PURCHASE ORDER # ____
SIGNETICS DEVICE # ____ CF (XXXX)
CUSTOMER SYMBOLIZED PART # ____
TOTAL NUMBER OF PARTS ____
PROGRAM TABLE # ____ REV ____ DATE ____

Notes
1 The FPLA is shipped with all links intact. Thus a background of entries corresponding to states of virgin links exists in the table (Shown BLANK for clarity.)
2 Unused I and B bits in the AND array must be programmed Don't Care (—).
3 Unused product terms can be left blank.

AND: INACTIVE O; I, B H; Ī, B̄ L; DON'T CARE —
OR: ACTIVE A; INACTIVE • B(O)
CONTROL: HIGH H; LOW L (POL)

TERM	AND I 7	6	5	4	3	2	1	0	B(I) 9	8	7	6	5	4	3	2	1	0	OR B(O) 9	8	7	6	5	4	3	2	1	0
POLARITY																			H	H	H	H	H	H	H	H	H	H
0	—	—	—	—	L	H	L	L											•	•	•					A	•	A
1	—	—	—	—	H	H	L	L											•	•	•					•	•	A
2	—	—	L	—	—	H	L	H											•	•	•					•	A	•
3	—	—	H	—	—	H	L	H											•	•	•					•	•	•
4	—	—	—	—	L	L	H	L											•	•	A					•	A	•
5	—	—	—	—	H	L	H	L											•	•	A					•	A	A
6	—	—	—	—	L	H	H	L											•	•	•					A	A	A
7	—	—	—	—	H	H	H	L											•	•	•					•	A	A
8	—	—	L	L	—	H	H	H											•	•	•					•	A	•
9	—	—	H	L	—	H	H	H											•	•	•					A	•	•
10	—	—	—	H	—	H	H	H											•	•	•					•	•	•
11	—	—	—	—	L	L	L	H											•	A	•					A	•	•
12	—	—	—	—	H	L	L	H											•	A	•					•	•	A
13	—	—	—	—	L	L	L	L											A	•	•					•	•	•
14	—	—	—	—	H	L	L	L											A	•	•					•	•	A
15																												
16																												
17																												
18																												
19																												
20																												
21																												
22																												
23																												
24																												
25																												
26																												
27																												
28																												
29																												
30																												
31																												
D9	—	—	—	—	—	—	—	—	—	—	—	—	—	—	—	—	—	—										
D8	—	—	—	—	—	—	—	—	—	—	—	—	—	—	—	—	—	—										
D7	—	—	—	—	—	—	—	—	—	—	—	—	—	—	—	—	—	—										
D6																												
D5																												
D4																												
D3																												
D2	—	—	—	—	—	—	—	—	—	—	—	—	—	—	—	—	—	—										
D1	—	—	—	—	—	—	—	—	—	—	—	—	—	—	—	—	—	—										
D0	—	—	—	—	—	—	—	—	—	—	—	—	—	—	—	—	—	—										
PIN	8	7	6	5	4	3	2	1	19	18	17	16	15	14	13	12	11	9	19	18	17	16	15	14	13	12	11	9
VARIABLE NAME			n	m	I	Q_2	Q_1	Q_0											Z_0	Z_1	Z_2					D_0	D_1	D_2

FIGURE 3.25
Coded program table corresponding to the state machine of Figure 3.24 (Courtesy of Signetics Corp.)

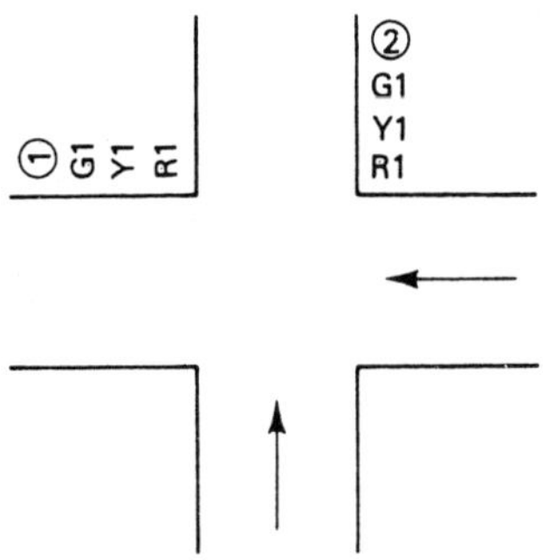

FIGURE 3.26a
Road junction

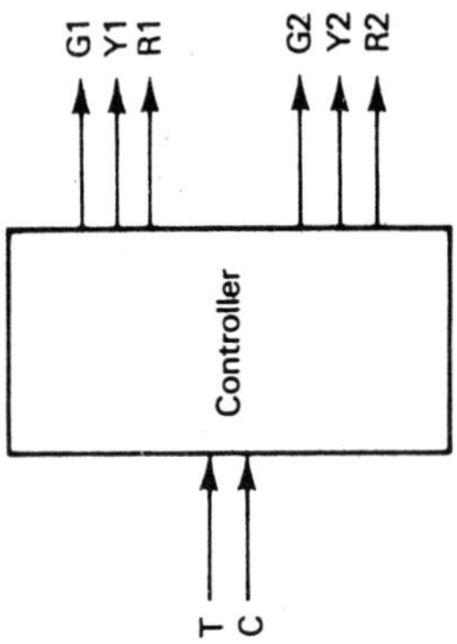

FIGURE 3.26b
Block diagram

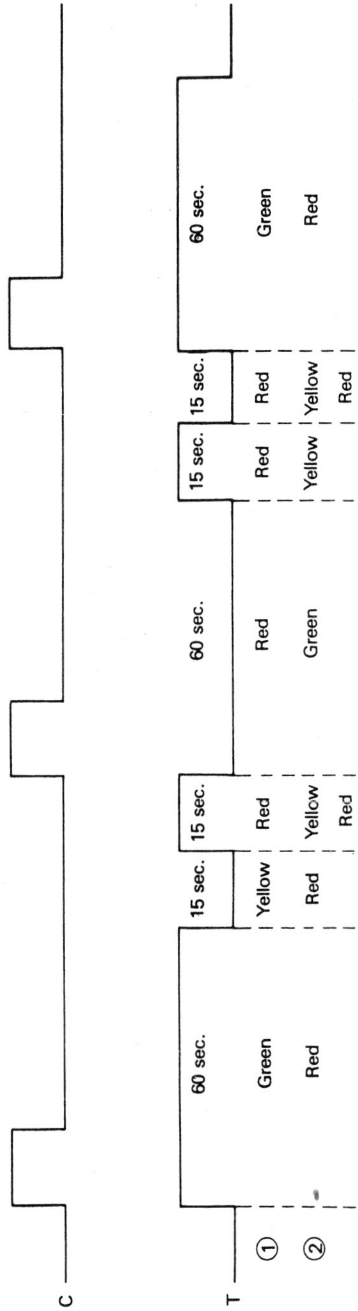

FIGURE 3.26c
Timing diagram

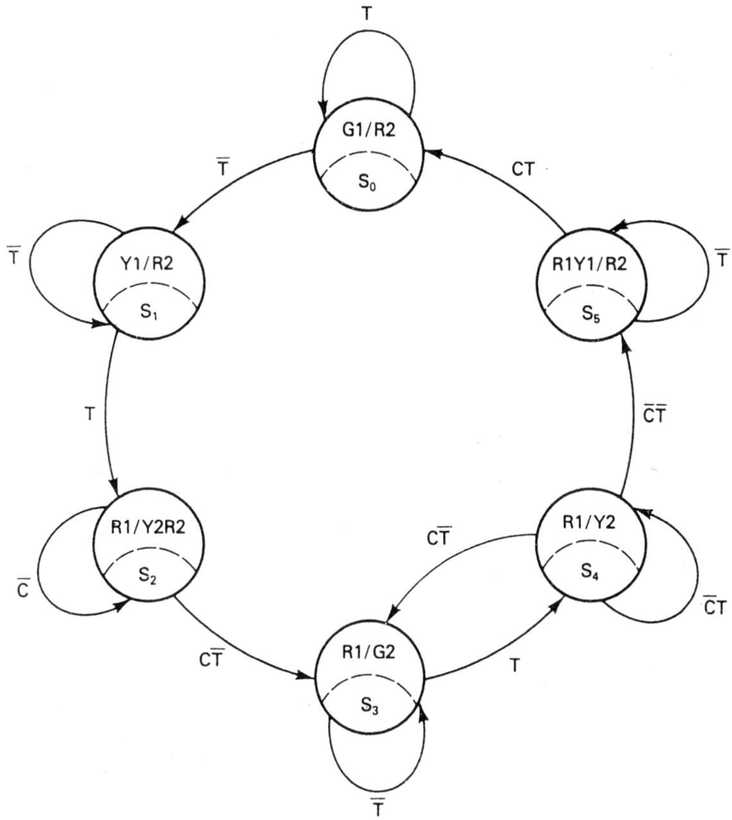

FIGURE 3.27a
State diagram

		Q_0	Q_1	Q_2
	S_0	0	0	0
	S_1	0	1	0
	S_2	1	1	0
	S_3	1	1	1
	S_4	0	1	1
	S_5	0	0	1
Invalid	S_6	1	0	0
Invalid	S_7	1	0	1

FIGURE 3.27b
State assignment

CUSTOMER NAME ____________

PURCHASE ORDER # ____________

SIGNETICS DEVICE # PLC473 CF (XXXX) ____________

CUSTOMER SYMBOLIZED PART # ____________

TOTAL NUMBER OF PARTS ____________

PROGRAM TABLE # ______ REV ______ DATE ______

AND		
INACTIVE	0	I, B (I)
I, B	H	
Ī, B̄	L	
DON'T CARE	—	

OR		
ACTIVE	A	B (O)
INACTIVE	•	
CONTROL		
HIGH	H	(POL)
LOW	L	

TERM	I 10	I 9	I 8	I 7	I 6	I 5	I 4	I 3	I 2	I 1	I 0	B(I) 8	B(I) 7	B(I) 6	B(I) 5	B(I) 4	B(I) 3	B(I) 2	B(I) 1	B(I) 0
0										H	—							L	L	L
1										L	—							L	L	L
2										L	—							L	H	L
3										H	L							L	H	L
4										—	L							H	H	L
5										L	H							H	H	L
6										L	—							H	H	H
7										H	—							H	H	H
8										H	L							L	H	H
9										L	H							L	H	H
10										L	L							L	H	H
11										L	—							L	L	H
12										H	H							L	L	H
13										—	—							H	L	L
14										—	L							H	L	H
15										L	H							H	L	H
16																				
17																				
18																				
19																				
20																				
21																				
22																				
23																				
PIN	11	10	9	8	7	6	5	4	3	2	1	23	22	21	20	17	16	15	14	13
										T	C							Q_1	Q_2	Q_3

TERM	E B	E A	D 8	D 7	D 6	D 5	D 4	D 3	D 2	D 1	D 0	O B	O A	B(O) 8	B(O) 7	B(O) 6	B(O) 5	B(O) 4	B(O) 3	B(O) 2	B(O) 1	B(O) 0
POLARITY														H	H	H	H	H	H	H	H	H
0			H	H	H	H	H	H	H	H	H			A	•	•	•	•	A	•	•	•
1			H	H	H	H	H	H	H	H	H			A	•	•	•	•	A	•	A	•
2			H	H	H	H	H	H	H	H	H			•	A	•	•	•	A	•	A	•
3			H	H	H	H	H	H	H	H	H			•	A	•	•	•	A	A	A	•
4			H	H	H	H	H	H	H	H	H			•	•	A	•	A	A	A	A	•
5			H	H	H	H	H	H	H	H	H			•	•	A	•	A	A	A	A	A
6			H	H	H	H	H	H	H	H	H			•	•	A	A	•	•	A	A	A
7			H	H	H	H	H	H	H	H	H			•	•	A	A	•	•	•	A	A
8			H	H	H	H	H	H	H	H	H			•	•	A	•	A	•	•	A	A
9			H	H	H	H	H	H	H	H	H			•	•	A	•	A	•	A	A	A
10			H	H	H	H	H	H	H	H	H			•	•	A	•	A	•	•	•	A
11			H	H	H	H	H	H	H	H	H			•	A	A	•	•	A	•	•	A
12			H	H	H	H	H	H	H	H	H			•	A	A	•	•	A	•	•	•
13			H	H	H	H	H	H	H	H	H			•	•	A	•	•	A	A	•	A
14			H	H	H	H	H	H	H	H	H			•	•	A	•	•	A	A	•	A
15			H	H	H	H	H	H	H	H	H			•	•	A	•	•	A	A	A	A
16																						
17																						
18																						
19																						
20																						
21																						
22																						
23																						
PIN												19	18	23	22	21	20	17	16	15	14	13
														G_1	Y_1	R_1	G_2	Y_2	R_2	Q_1	Q_2	Q_3

Notes
1. The FPLA is shipped with all links open.
2. Unused I and B bits in the AND array exist as Don't Care (—) in the virgin state.
3. All P-terms are inactive on all outputs (B, O) in the virgin array.
4. Unused product terms can be left blank.

FIGURE 3.28a
Coded program table

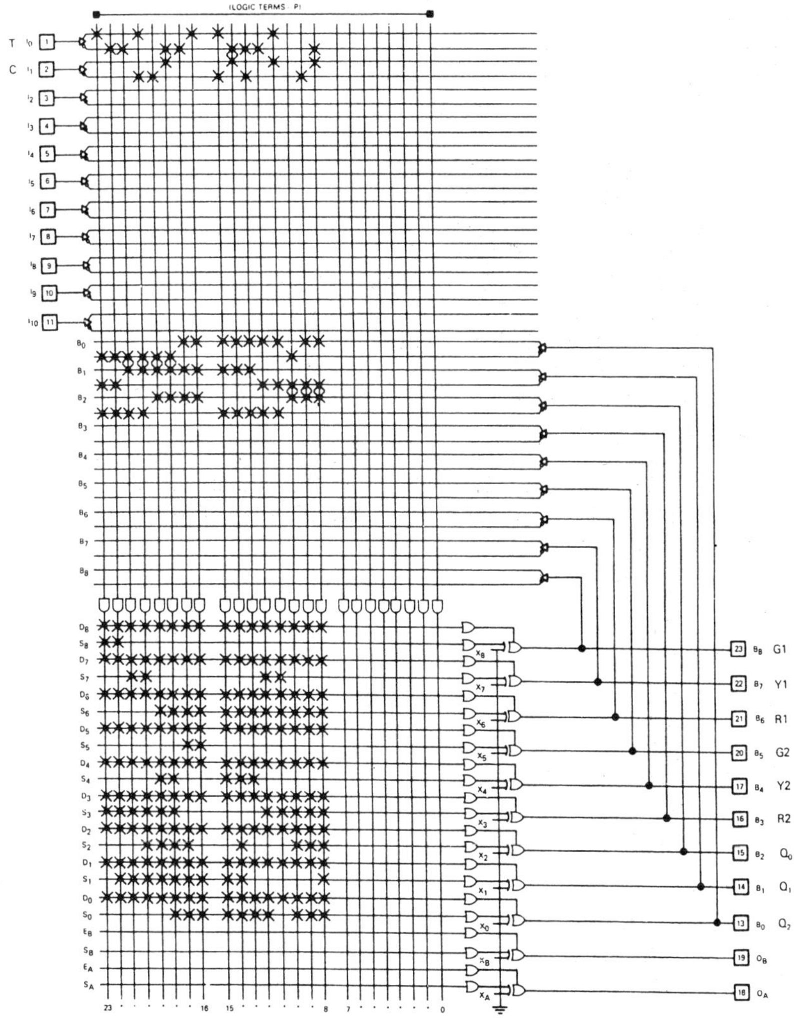

(b)

FIGURE 3.28b
Programmed logic diagram (Courtesy of Signetics Corp.)

As a further example of the state machine design using FPLAs, we consider a sequential circuit for controlling the traffic lights at a road junction (see Figure 3.26a) [2]. The controller generates the appropriate signals for turning on or off the red, yellow, and green lamps. Each traffic light is assigned a time frame of certain length; the start of a time frame is initiated by a logic "1" signal at the C input (see Figure 3.26b). A time frame is divided into three slots. The input signal at the T input remains at logic "1" or logic "0" in a slot as indicated in Figure 3.26c.

```
module traffic_light
title '3-bit state machine
Parag K. Lala          May 10, 1989.'
     traffic_light          device          'F473';
     T,C            pin 1,2;
     R2,Y2,G2       pin 16,17,20;
     R1,Y1,G1       pin 21,22,23;
     Q2,Q1,Q0       pin 13,14,15;
     Qstate         =[Q2,Q1,Q0];
     R2.OE,Y2.OE,G2.OE      istype     'eqn';
     R1.OE,Y1.OE,G1.OE      istype     'eqn';
     Q2.OE,Q1.OE,Q0.OE      istype     'eqn';
     S0 = 0;     S1 = 2;     S2 = 3;     S3 = 7;
     S4 = 6;     S5 = 4;     S6 = 1;     S7 = 5;
equations;
     R2.OE = 1;     Y2.OE = 1;     G2.OE = 1;all outputs are
     R1.OE = 1;     Y1.OE = 1;     G1.OE = 1;permanently
     Q2.OE = 1;     Q1.OE = 1;     Q0.OE = 1;enabled
state_diagram Qstate;
     State S0;
       G1 = 1;
       Y1 = 0;
       R1 = 0;
       G2 = 0;
       Y2 = 0;
       R2 = 1;
       IF(!T) THEN S1
       ELSE S0;
     State S1:
       G1 = 0;
       Y1 = 1;
       R1 = 0;
       G2 = 0;
       Y2 = 0;
       R2 = 1;
       IF(T) THEN S2
       ELSE S1;
     State S2:
       G1 = 0;
       Y1 = 0;
       R1 = 1;
       G2 = 0;
       Y2 = 1;
       R2 = 1;
       CASE C & !T : S3;
               !C    : S2;
       ENDCASE;
     State S3:
       G1 = 0;
```

```
      Y1 = 0;
      R1 = 1;
      G2 = 1;
      Y2 = 0;
      R2 = 0;
      IF(T) THEN S4
      ELSE S3;
    State S4:
      G1 = 0;
      Y1 = 0;
      R1 = 1;
      G2 = 0;
      Y2 = 1;
      R2 = 0;
      CASE C & !T  : S3;
           !C & !T : S5;
           !C & T  : S4;
      ENDCASE;
    State S5:
      G1 = 0;
      Y1 = 1;
      R1 = 1;
      G2 = 0;
      Y2 = 0;
      R2 = 1;
      CASE C & T   : S0;
           !T      : S5;
      ENDCASE;
    State S6:
      G1 = 0;
      Y1 = 0;
      R1 = 1;
      G2 = 0;
      Y2 = 0;
      R2 = 1;
      GOTO S7;
    STATE S7:
      G1 = 0;
      Y1 = 0;
      R1 = 1;
      G2 = 0;
      Y2 = 0;
      R2 = 1;
      CASE !T & C  : S3;
           !C      : S7;
      ENDCASE;
end
```

FIGURE 3.29
ABEL source file

The state diagram of the controller is shown in Figure 3.27a. The next step in the design process is the state assignment which is done as shown in Figure 3.27b, using a 3-bit Gray code. There are two unused states S6 ($Q_0 Q_1 Q_2$ = 100) and S7 ($Q_0 Q_1 Q_2$ = 101). If the controller enters one of these states due to some malfunction, both the red lights will go on simultaneously. The controller is initialized to state S0 by setting input T at logic "1." Figure 3.28 shows the programmed logic diagram of PLC473 to implement the traffic controller. The ABEL source file for the design is given in Figure 3.29.

PROBLEMS

3-1. A 8-to-1 multiplexer circuit is to be implemented using PLS103. Show the program table for the device.

3-2. A combinational circuit whose input is a 4-bit number and whose output is the 2's complement of the input number, is to be implemented using a FPAD. Show the appropriately coded logic diagram of the selected device.

3-3. Implement the following Boolean expressions using PLS100. Use minimum number of product terms to implement the expressions.

$$f_1(x,y,z) = \Sigma(3,5,6,7)$$

$$f_2(x,y,z) = \Sigma(0,2,4.7)$$

3-4. The following functions are to be implemented using PLS153. Encode the program table of the device.

$$f_1(w,x,y,z) = \bar{x}y \oplus x\bar{y}z \oplus w\bar{x}\,\bar{y}\,\bar{z}$$

$$f_2(w,x,y,z) = (wy \oplus \bar{x}y \oplus w\bar{z}) + wy\bar{z}$$

3-5. A BCD-to-Excess 3-code converter is shown below.

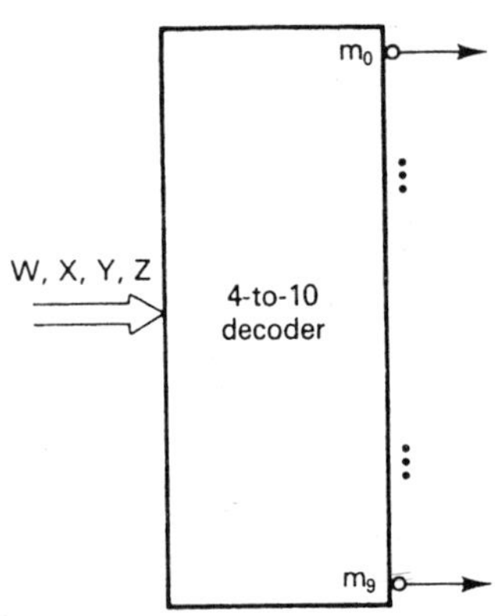

$$W = \overline{m_5 m_6 m_7 m_8 m_9}$$

$$X = \overline{\bar{m}_1 \bar{m}_2 \bar{m}_3 \bar{m}_4 \bar{m}_9}$$

$$Y = \overline{\bar{m}_0 \bar{m}_3 \bar{m}_4 \bar{m}_7 \bar{m}_8}$$

$$Z = \overline{\bar{m}_0 \bar{m}_2 \bar{m}_4 \bar{m}_6 \bar{m}_8}$$

Code the logic diagram of PLHS473 to implement the above circuit.

3-6. A sequential circuit, whose state diagram is shown below, is to be implemented using a PLC473 and a register. Show the circuit implementation, and the coded program table for PLC473.

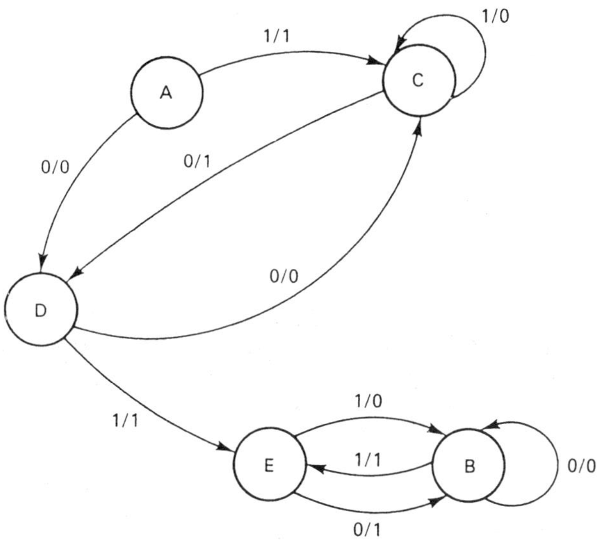

3-7. Design a 4-bit programmable counter using a FPLA and an appropriate register, which will count in binary when input x = 0, and in Gray code when x = 1. Show the program table for the selected FPLA.

REFERENCES

1. "Signetics Application Note AN27," *PLHS473 Primer.*
2. B. Holdsworth, *Digital Logic Design,* Butterworth, 1987.
3. *Programmable Logic Data Manual,* Signetics Corp., 1986.

Chapter 4

Field-programmable Logic Sequencer (FPLS)

The PLDs we have considered in Chapter 3 are combinational devices, their outputs at any instant of time are functions of their inputs at that instant. Although it is possible to implement state machines using these devices with memory elements, this results in an increase in the number of packages. Therefore, the incorporation of memory elements within AND-OR programmable devices has significant advantages in that a state machine may be implemented using a single package, limited only by the storage and the combinational logic available per package.

The FPLS devices are self-contained state machines of the Mealy type. Currently, the FPLS family consists of the following devices:

Series 28	PLS105 (16 inputs, 8 outputs, 48 product terms).
	PLUS405A (16 inputs, 8 outputs, 64 product terms).
Series 20	PLS155/157/159 (16 inputs, 12 outputs, 45 product terms).
Series 24	PLS167 (14 inputs, 6 outputs, 48 product terms).
	PLS168 (12 inputs, 8 outputs, 48 product terms).
	PLS179 (20 inputs, 12 outputs, 45 product terms).

4.1 ORGANIZATION OF SERIES 28 SEQUENCERS

The first member of this series, PLS105 (originally 82S105), was in fact the first FPLS device to appear in the market. Figure 4.1 shows the basic organization of the PLS105. It is an extension of the static logic structure of the PLS100 FPLA. It consists of a programmable AND array and a programmable OR array. The OR array controls the set and the reset (S and R) inputs of six SR flip-flops which constitute a 6-bit state register. The OR array also controls an independent 8-bit output register which stores the output generated after the inputs have been applied. If the change in inputs produces state transitions but the output does not change, the contents of the output register remain constant.

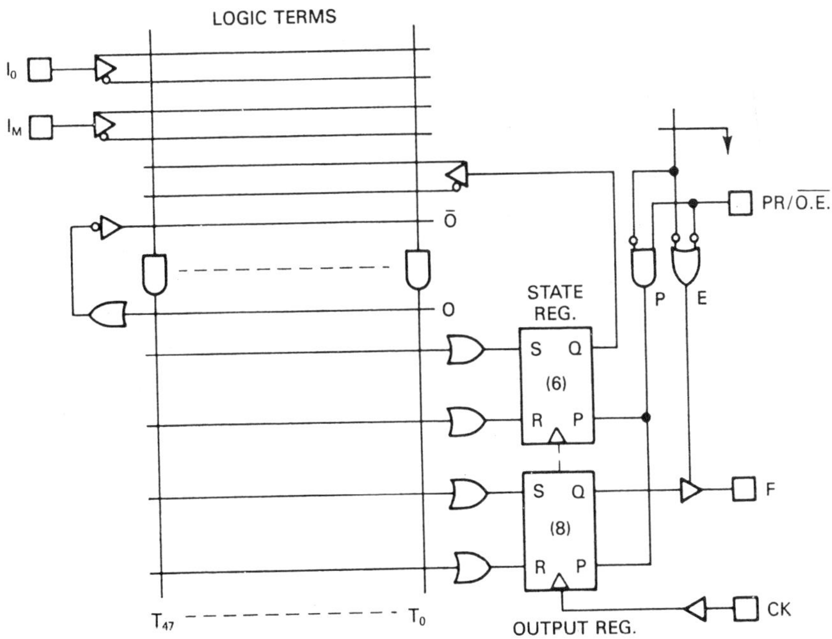

FIGURE 4.1
Basic organization of PLS105 (Courtesy of Signetics Corp.)

Figure 4.2 shows a more detailed diagram of the PLS105. It has 16 external inputs and 6 internal inputs, fed back from the 6-bit state register. The inputs are applied to the AND array through a set of true/complement buffers. The AND array consists of 48 AND gates each with 45 input connections. The AND gates form products of sixteen external input variables (I_0–I_{15}) with six state variables (P_0–P_5) fed back from the state register. These products are propagated through the OR array, and change the contents of the state regis-

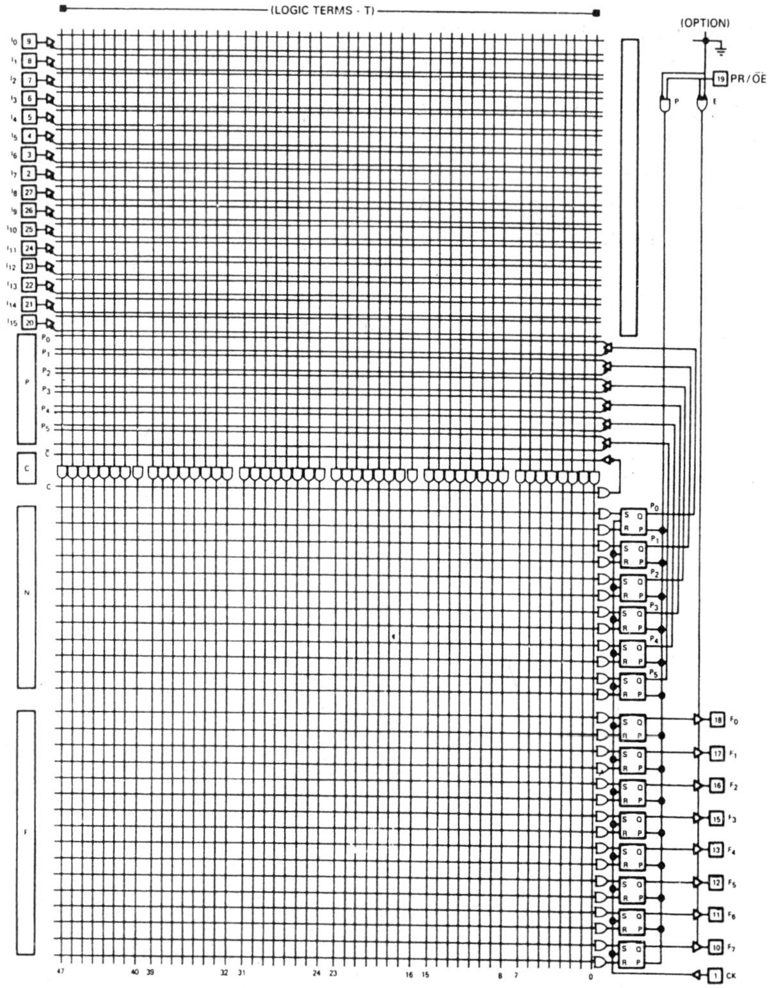

FIGURE 4.2
Logic diagram of PLS105 (Courtesy of Signetics Corp.)

ter from the present state (P) to the next state (N). Since the product terms determine the next states like the transition terms in state diagrams, they are called **transition terms.**

Figure 4.3 shows transition terms generated using arbitrary inputs and state variables. A transition term does not necessarily require a state variable (e.g., T_3 in Figure 4.3). The outputs of the AND gates are also used to drive the output register, thus making the output of the PLS105 a function of the inputs and the present state.

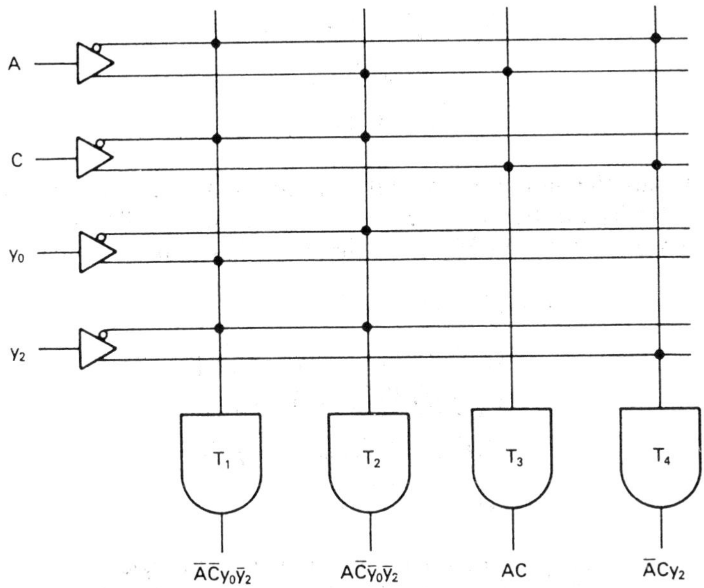

FIGURE 4.3
Transition terms generated using inputs A and C, and state variables y_0 and y_2

The SR flip-flops in the state register of the PLS105 are set or reset using the transition terms. This is accomplished by selectively ORing all the AND gate outputs necessary to drive a particular flip-flop control input. The PLS105 has 28 OR gates, each with 48 input connections to all 48 AND gates. The outputs of OR gates drive the set and the reset inputs of the 14 SR flip-flops. Figure 4.4 shows how the OR array gates the transition terms of Figure 4.3 to control the arbitrary state and output register stages.

The PLS105 also has a **complement array** which consists of a single 48-input OR gate that drives an inverter. The output of the inverter is fed back as inputs to the AND array as shown in Figure 4.5.

Thus, each AND gate in the FPLS has an extra input in addition to the 44 input connections derived from the 22 true/complement input buffers.

The complement array can be utilized to implement transition terms which are true only when certain direct transition terms are false in a state diagram. For example Figure 4.6 shows the part of the state diagram of a sequential machine. It can be seen from the figure that the transition from state C to state B occurs only if the transition from state C to state D or from state C to state E cannot occur.

The transition terms T_1, T_2 and T_3 corresponding to the transitions from state C to state B, D and E, respectively, are given by

$$T_1 = \overline{\bar{x}\,\bar{y}\cdot\bar{z}}\bullet\overline{yz}\bullet\bar{Q}_1\bar{Q}_0$$

$$T_2 = \bar{x}\,\bar{y}\,\bar{z}\bullet\bar{Q}_1\bar{Q}_0$$

$$T_3 = y\,z\bullet\bar{Q}_1\bar{Q}_0$$

where Q_1, Q_0 are the outputs of the state register, and x and y are inputs. The transition term T_1 can be implemented by using three AND gates (Figure 4.7a). However, by using DeMorgan's theorem, T_1 can be represented as

$$\begin{aligned} T_1 &= \bar{Q}_1\,\bar{Q}_0(\overline{\bar{x}\,\bar{y}\,\bar{z} + yz}) \\ &= \bar{Q}_1\,\bar{Q}_0[\overline{\overline{\bar{Q}_1\,\bar{Q}_0} + (\bar{x}\,\bar{y}\,\bar{z} + yz)}] \\ &= \bar{Q}_1\,\bar{Q}_0[\overline{\bar{Q}_1\,\bar{Q}_0(\bar{x}\,\bar{y}\,\bar{z} + yz)}] \\ &= \bar{Q}_1\,\bar{Q}_0[\overline{\bar{x}\,\bar{y}\,\bar{z}\,\bar{Q}_1\,\bar{Q}_0 + yz\bar{Q}_1\,\bar{Q}_0}] \\ &= \bar{Q}_1\,\bar{Q}_0[\overline{T_2 + T_3}] \end{aligned}$$

Thus, the logic expression for T_1 corresponds to the logic structure of the complement array. T_1 requires a single AND gate if implemented using the complement array as shown in Figure 4.7b.

The clocked SR flip-flops that make up the state and output registers, can be asynchronously preset via an input to all 1's. Besides during power-on all the flip-flops are unconditionally preset to 1's. The state register has six flip-flops, therefore, the maximum number of states the register can represent

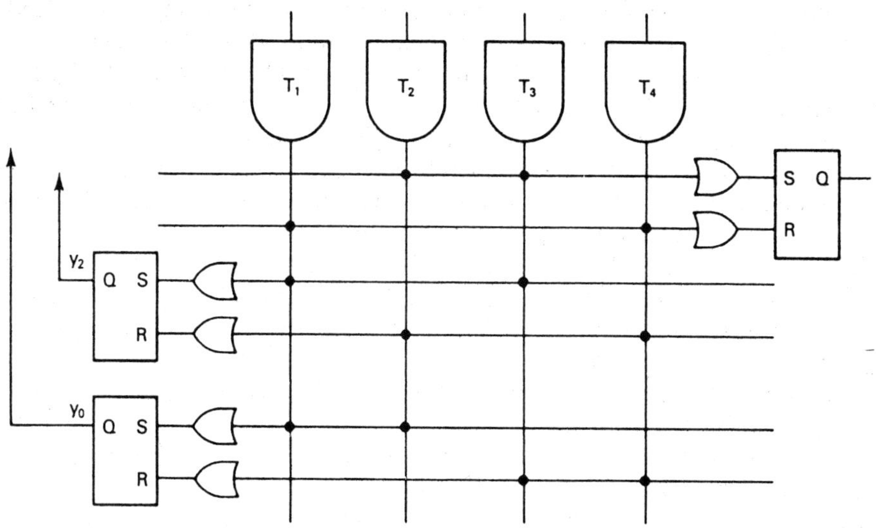

FIGURE 4.4
Control of the state and the output registers

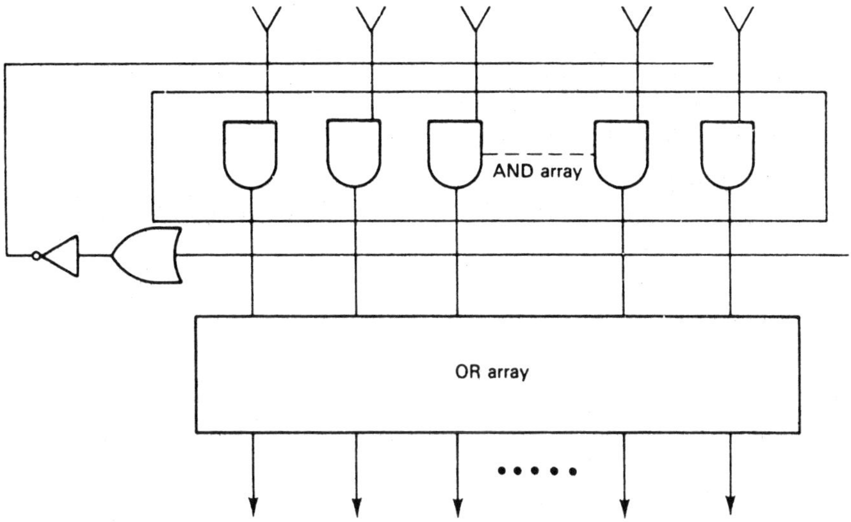

FIGURE 4.5
Complementary array

is 64. However, since there are only 48 transition terms available, this limit cannot in general be reached. The output register is similar to the state register except that it has eight states. It accepts the next state terms from the OR array and then transfers them to the Q outputs of each of the flip-flops. The present input pin of the PLS105 can also function as an active low ouptut enable. Figure 4.8 illustrates the function of the present/enable input. If the fuse is

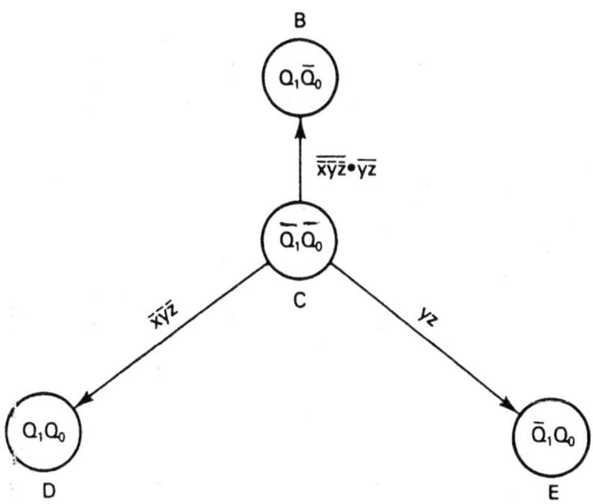

FIGURE 4.6
Example of a state sequence

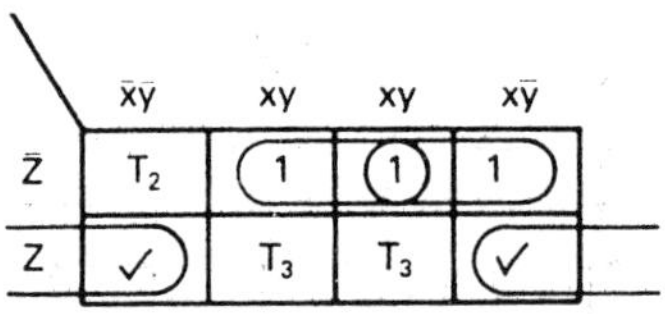

FIGURE 4.7a
Transition term $T_1 = y\bar{z} + x\bar{z} + \bar{y}z$ needs three AND gates in the FPLS

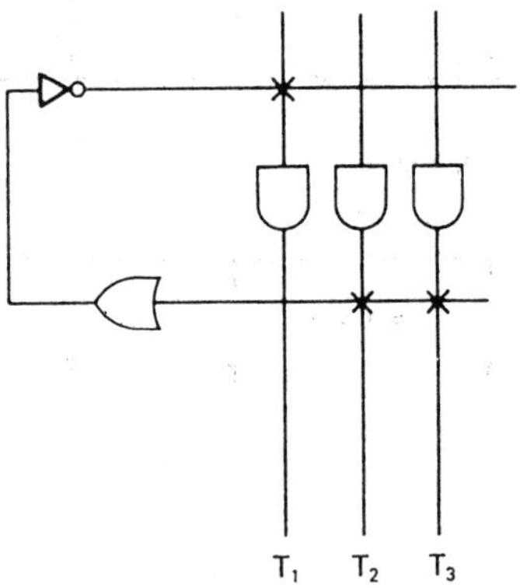

FIGURE 4.7b
Implementation of $T_1 = \overline{T_2 + T_3}$ using the complementary array

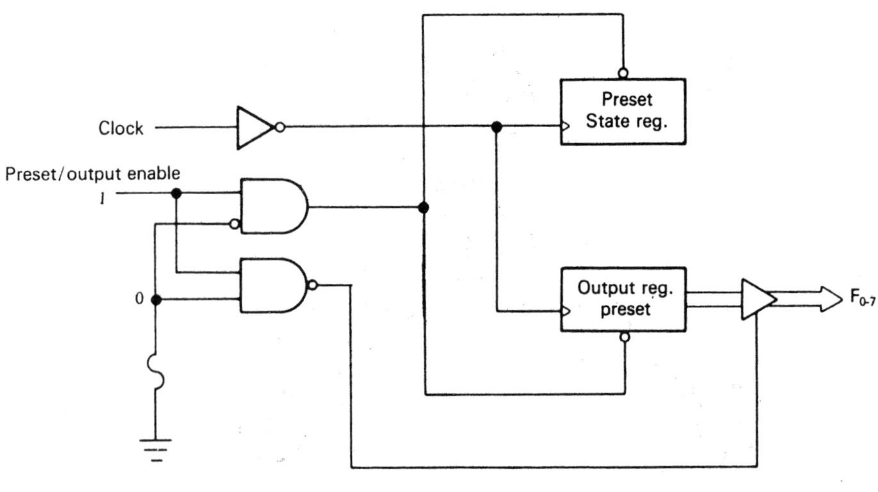

FIGURE 4.8
Circuit for preset/output enable in PLS105

blown, then a logic "0" on this input will inhibit the clock, and all the flip-flops in the state and the clock pulse affects state transition on its positive edge only if the preset/output enable input is at logic "1" and the fuse is intact.

The maximum frequency at which the PLS105 can be clocked is 13.9 MHz; a faster version PLS105A, which can be clocked at 20 MHz, is also available. In practice, the clock frequency of PLS105 is dependent on the number of transition terms connected to the OR gates. This is because the clock frequency is inversely proportional to the length of the time the inputs must remain valid before the positive transition of the clock pulse. The set up time in turn increases with the number of transition terms connected to the OR gates as shown in the graph of Figure 4.9. Once the number of transition terms connected to an OR gate is the set-up time can be determined from the graph. For example, if the number of transition terms connected to the OR gates driving the state registers are 8, 10, 32, 20, 24, and 16, then the set-up time for the inputs is 50 ns (from Figure 4.9), because the maximum number of transition terms connected to an OR gate is 32 in this case. Therefore, by eliminating all unused transition terms from the OR array the set-up time can be reduced to the minimum, thereby maximizing the speed of operation of the device.

In an unprogrammed FPLS device all the fuses remain intact. As a result all the transition terms remain inactive and all the SR flip-flops are disabled. In addition, the preset/output enable is set to logic "1." A transition term in

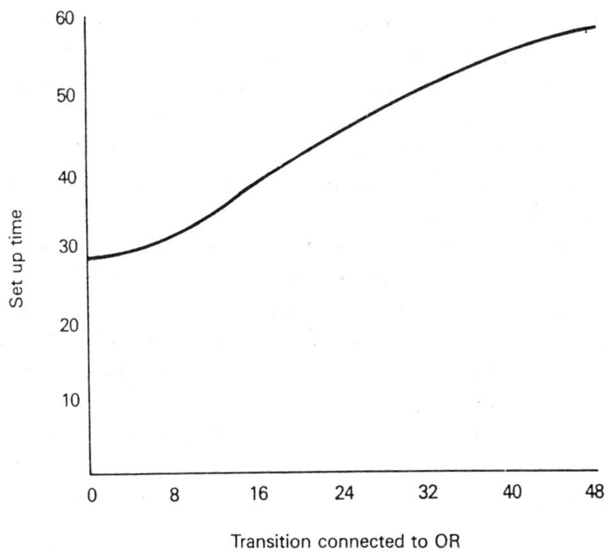

FIGURE 4.9
Set up time vs. terms connected to the OR gates (Courtesy of Signetics Corp.)

an FPLS can be formed by programming the logic state of the input and the state variables associated with the transition term. Figure 4.10 illustrates how each of the input or the state variable in a transition term is programmed in the PLS105. If an AND gate is connected to the true/complement pair of an input buffer (i.e., if both the fuses from the input buffer are left intact, then the resulting transition term is inactive (Fig. 4.10c)). On the other hand, if both the fuses from the input buffer are blown then a don't care situation results, and the transition term is independent of the input A (see Figure 4.10d).

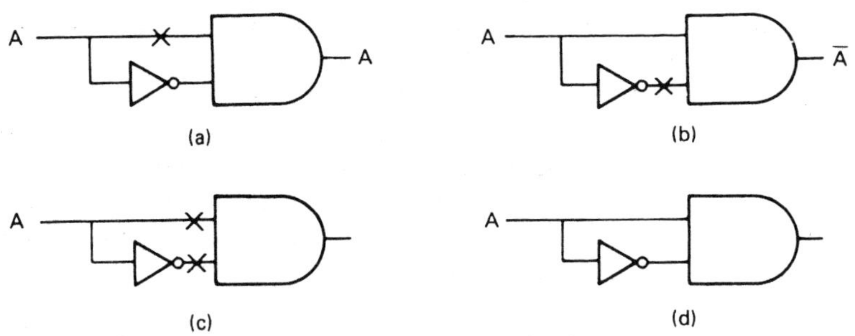

FIGURE 4.10
Input/state variable a) Active-high; b) Active-low; c) Inactive; d) Don't care (Courtesy of Signetics Corp.)

The set and the reset inputs of the state and the output registers are driven by the transition terms, as shown in Figure 4.11a. Since in an SR flip-flop the set and the reset inputs are not allowed to be at 1's simultaneously (in order to avoid a race condition), the same transition term cannot drive both the S and R inputs of a flip-flop in the FPLS (see Figure 4.11b). If the S and R inputs are not connected to a transition term, then the flip-flop retains its previous state (see Figure 4.11c).

The complement array may be used to generate and propagate the complements of transition terms. The generation of the complement of a transition term is illustrated in Figure 4.12a; the complemented term may be propagated (i.e., fed back) to the input of another AND gate. The complement of a transition term corresponding to an AND gate cannot be fed back to the input of the same AND gate; this is necessary in order to avoid oscillation (see Figure 4.12b). If the complement of a transition term is not generated, and the AND gate corresponding to the transition term does not propagate a complemented term either, then the transition term is known to be transparent (see Figure 4.12c).

The second member of the Series 28 sequencer family, PLUS405A, is the fastest FPLS chip currently available. It can operate at 40 MHz. Figure 4.13 shows the logic diagram of the device. It has 16 dedicated input lines, eight output lines and 64 product terms. The device incorporates 16 JK flip-

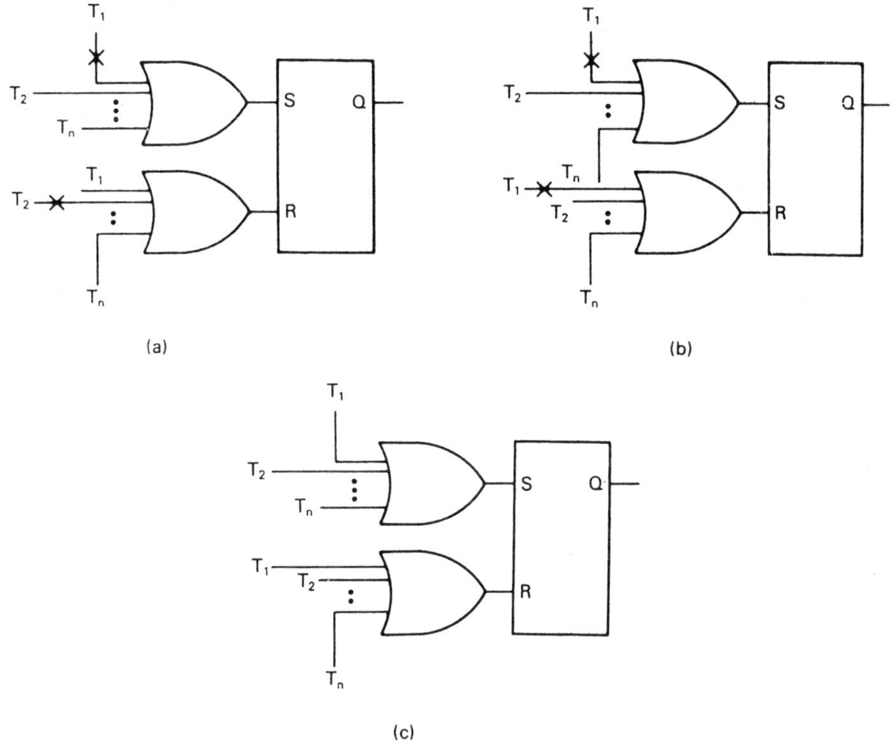

FIGURE 4.11
a) Flip-flop is set by transition term T_1 and is reset by T_2;
b) Invalid condition; c) No change (Courtesy of Signetics Corp.)

flops, and has two complement arrays. It has two clock lines, one is dedicated while the other may be used as an input line. Figure 4.14 shows the circuit used for routing the two clock signals. If the fuse is intact, the state flip-flops and the output flip-flops are triggered by the positive edge of the Clk1. On the other hand, if the fuse is blown, the state flip-flops are triggered by Clk2 and the output flip-flops are triggered by Clk1. Note that if Clk2 is employed, the corresponding input lines cannot contribute to the formation of product terms in the AND array. Each flip-flop may also be individually programmed to be set or reset when initialization input (INIT) is set at logic "1." The clocking of the flip-flops are inhibited when INIT is held at logic "1."

4.2 ORGANIZATION OF SERIES 20 SEQUENCERS

This family of sequencers are all similar in organization; however each device has different number of outputs that are registered. The PLS155, PLS157 and

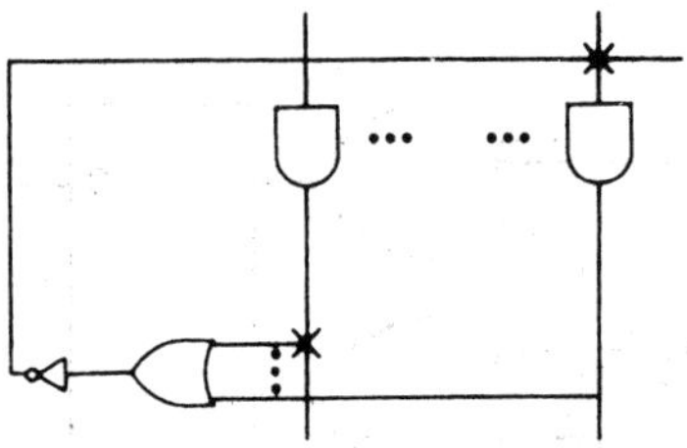

FIGURE 4.12a
Generation and propagation of a complemented transition term

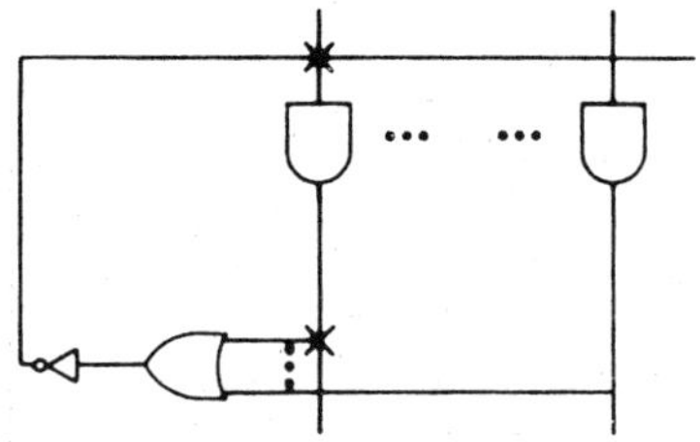

FIGURE 4.12b
Invalid state

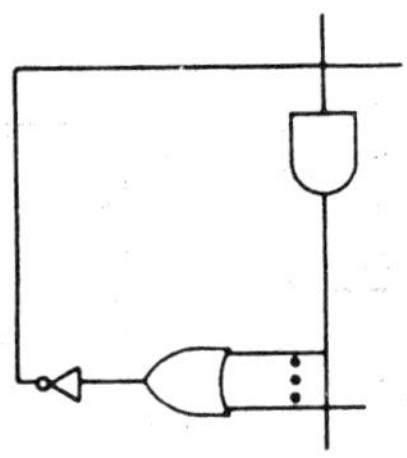

FIGURE 4.12c
Transparent term (Courtesy of Signetics Corp.)

PLS159 have respectively 4-bit, 6-bit, and 8-bit tri-state registered outputs; open collector versions of these devices are PLS154, PLS156 and PLS158, respectively.

Figure 4.15 shows the basic organization of the Series 20 sequencers. The output register of these sequencers are made up of JK flip-flops. A JK flip-flop may be converted into a D flip-flop using the product term F_c. A tri-state inverter is placed between the J and K inputs with a wired-OR connection at the K input. The control term F_c is programmed in the same way as the other 32 transition terms. If F_c is at logic "1" (i.e., node $M = 1$), then the tri-state inverter is disabled and the flip-flop is configured as a JK type as shown in Figure 4.16a. When F_c is at logic "0" (i.e., $M = 0$), the tri-state inverter is enabled and the flip-flop functions as a D type, as shown in Figure 4.16b. The output of the OR gate driving the K input of a JK flip-flop must not be at logic "1," when the flip-flop functions as a D type.

All the flip-flops are used in the output register are positive edge triggered. The output data is fed back to the AND array, thus forming the present state of the sequencer. The AND array consists of 32 transition terms and 13 control terms. One group of control terms **D** is used to drive the bidirectional I/O lines **B**, whereas the other group **L** allows parallel loading of the output register from the **F** lines on the rising edge of the clock pulse. While parallel

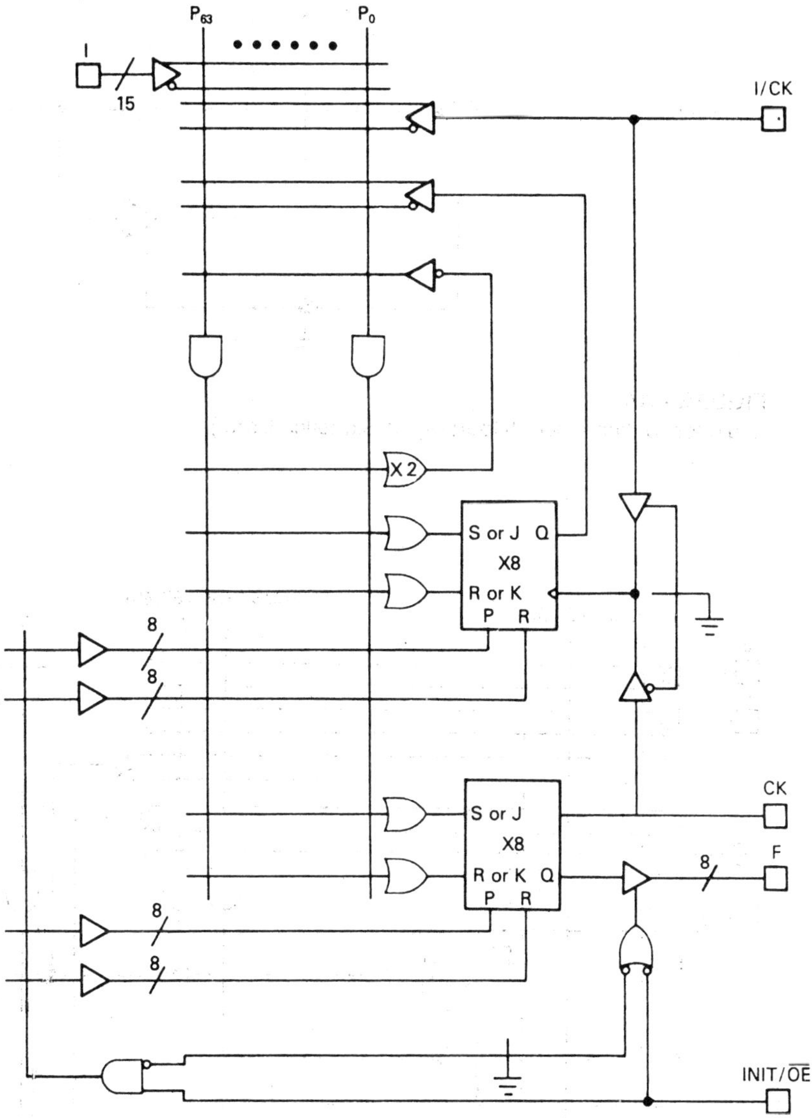

FIGURE 4.13
Logic diagram of PLUS405A (Courtesy of Signetics Corp.)

loading the output register from the **F** lines, the other active transition terms must be disabled via the input lines **I**, bidirectional I/O lines **B** or by asynchronous preset/reset of the flip-flops. Asynchronous preset and reset capability of the flip-flops is controlled via the AND array on PLS159 and via the OR array on PLS155. The asynchronous preset/reset lines for two of the flip-flops

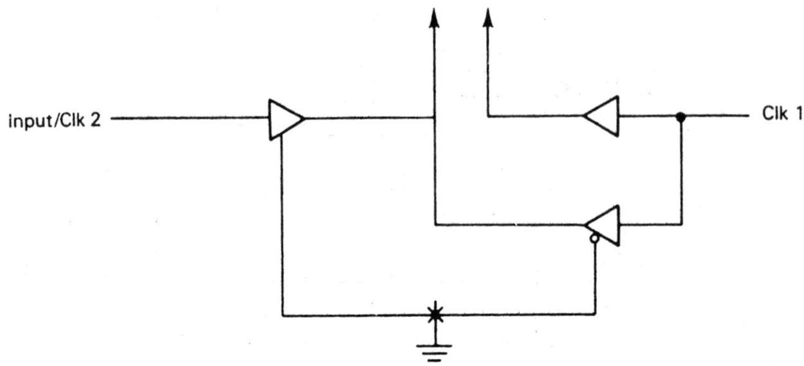

FIGURE 4.14
Logic for routing clock (Courtesy of Signetics Corp.)

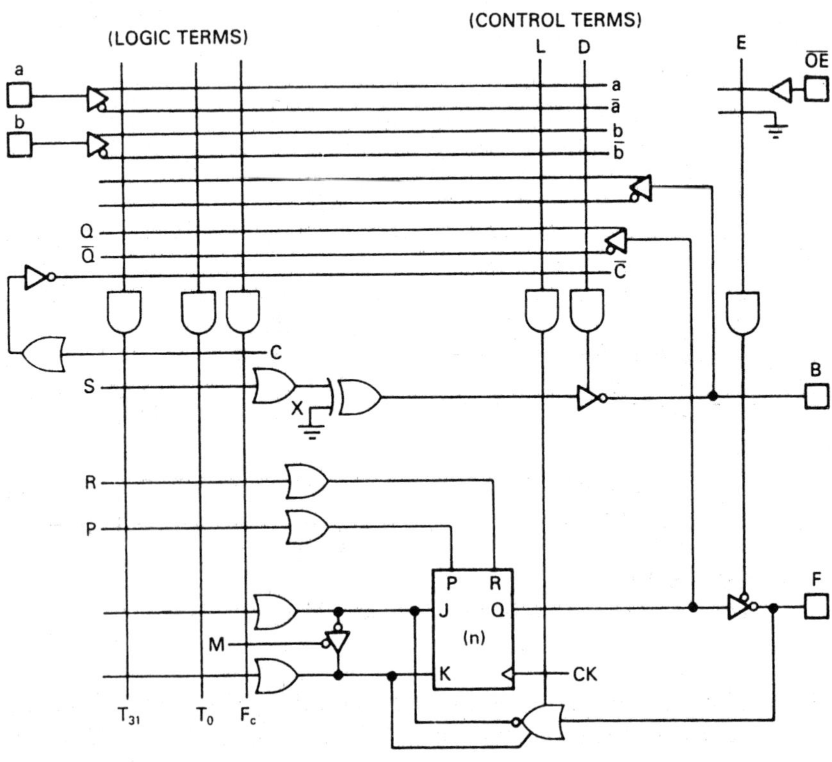

FIGURE 4.15
Organization of Series 20 Sequencers (Courtesy of Signetics Corp.)

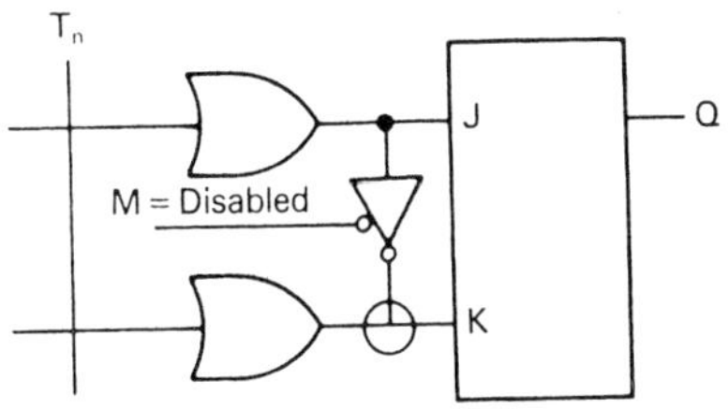

FIGURE 4.16a
JK flip-flop (Courtesy of Signetics Corp.)

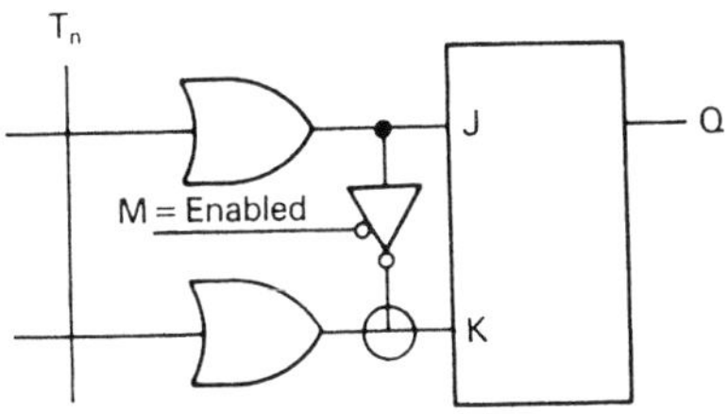

FIGURE 4.16b
D flip-flop (Courtesy of Signetics Corp.)

in PLS157 are driven from the AND array, whereas those for the other four flip-flops are driven from the OR array.

The output polarity of each of the AND gates driving the bidirectional I/O is individually programmable through a set of EX-OR gates. The programmable select lines E_A and E_B are used to enable or disable the outputs of the flip-flops as shown in Figure 4.17. The idle and enable states shown in Figure 4.17a and Figure 4.17b, respectively, are logically equivalent because both enable the flip-flop outputs. If the fuse connecting the input of either of the AND gates to the ground is blown, the input floats to logic "1," and the corresponding **E** line is controlled by the signal on the $\overline{OE}$ input (see Figure 4.17c).

The complementary array functions the same way as in PLS105. It consists of a NOR gate which may be linked to all AND gates to generate and to propagate complementary transition terms.

4.3 SERIES 24 SEQUENCER FAMILY

The Series 24 family consists of three sequencers: PLS167, PLS168, and PLS179. Like the PLS105, both PLS167 and PLS168 are Mealy-type state machines. The PLS167 has a 8-bit state register and a 4-bit output register, whereas the PLS168 has a 10-bit state register and a 4-bit output register. The registers are made up of positive edge-triggered SR flip-flops. The two least

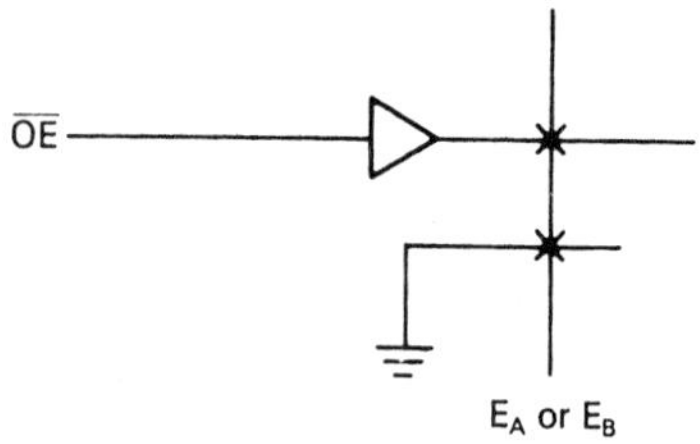

FIGURE 4.17a
E_A or E_B is in idle state

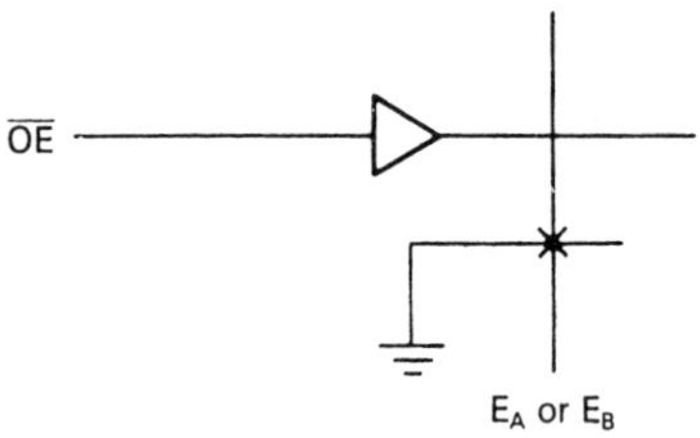

FIGURE 4.17b
E_A or E_B is enabled

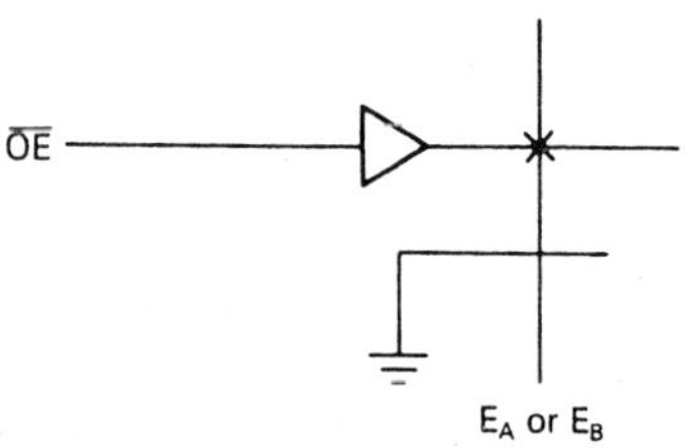

FIGURE 4.17c
E_A or E_B is controlled by $\overline{OE}$ (Courtesy of Signetics Corp.)

significant bits of the state register in PLS167 can be used as output bits, thus extending the output register to 6 bits; these two bits are then considered as the most significant output register bits. In PLS168, four least significant bits of the state register can be used as output bits. As in PLS105, both PLS167 and PLS168 have complementary array which consists of a single 48-input OR gate. The OR gate feeds an inverter, the output of which is fed back to the AND gates in order to generate and propagate complement transition terms. All the flip-flops are automatically preset to logic "1" when power is applied. As a final programming option (similar to PLS105), a pin can function as either an active-high asynchronous preset (PR) or an active-low output enable ($\overline{OE}$). The output enable forces the outputs to high impedance states when it is at logic "1." The preset input signal, when at logic "1," forces the state and output register bits to logic "1," irrespective of the clock pulse; only when the preset input is at logic "0" do the registers change state in response to a clock pulse.

Both PLS167 and PLS168 have tri-state outputs and can operate at the maximum clock frequency of 13.9 MHz; the faster versions of these devices, PLS167A/PLS168A, can operate at 20 MHz. The actual clocking frequency is inversely proportional to the set-up time of the flip-flop control inputs. With the increase of the number of transition terms connected to the OR gates, the set up time increases as shown in Figure 4.18. This results in a decrease of the clock frequency of the devices.

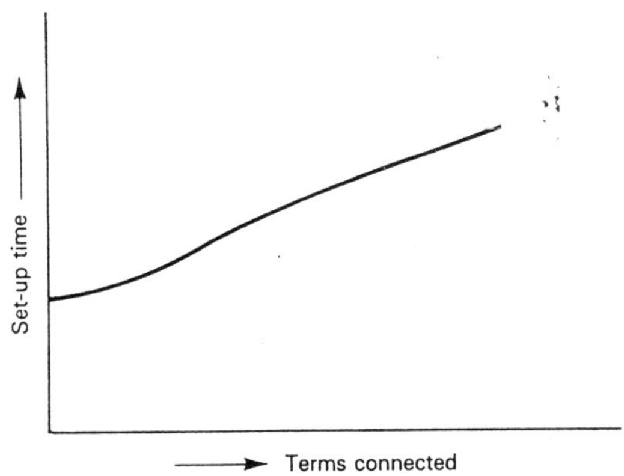

FIGURE 4.18
Set-up time vs. loading of OR gates (Courtesy of Signetics Corp.)

The PLS179 provides 8 dedicated inputs, 4 I/O lines (which can function as either input or output lines), and 45 product terms. There are 8 positive edge-triggered JK flip-flops incorporated into the device. Figure 4.19 shows the input and the output connections of the flip-flops. If the fuse is intact, then the JK flip-flop is converted into D flip-flop provided the NOR gate is disabled and the output of the OR gate B is at logic "0." If the fuse is blown and the outputs of both the OR gates A and B are at logic "1," the JK flip-flop functions as a T flip-flop. Alternatively, if the output of either OR gate A or OR gate B is at logic "1," then the flip-flop functions as a SR flip-flop. If the outputs of both gate A and gate B are at logic "0," then the flip-flop retains its previous value. It is assumed that the output inverter and the NOR gate are disabled in all cases. It is also possible to drive the J and K inputs of the ith flip-flop from the I/O pin F_i; in this mode the flip-flop functions as a D flip-flop. In order to achieve this, the output inverter must be disabled; besides the outputs of the OR gates A and B must also be at logic "0," and the fuse has to be blown.

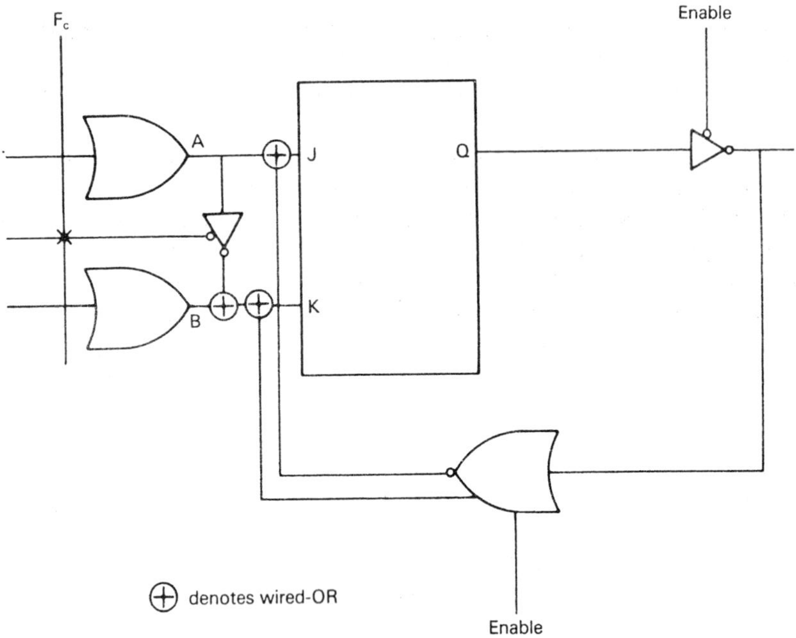

FIGURE 4.19
Programmable flip-flop (Courtesy of Signetics Corp.)

4.4 APPLICATION OF FPLS DEVICES

In designing with logic sequencers, the user need concern himself only with generating truth tables associated with the state diagrams. This section deals with a few design examples; the objective of these examples is to familiarize the readers with the application of FPLS devices in sequential circuit design.

Example 1: This example illustrates the implementation of the state diagram shown in Figure 4.20 using PLS105. The five states of the machine are assigned with the straight binary codes as shown below:

	y_2	y_1	y_0
A	0	0	0
B	0	0	1
C	0	1	0
D	0	1	1
E	1	0	0

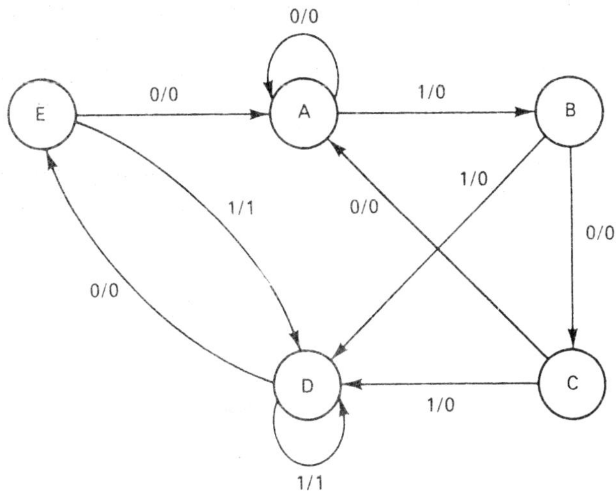

FIGURE 4.20
State diagram

Since there are only five states, three out of six flip-flops in the state register of PLS105 will be used. The sequential machine has only 1 output, hence only one bit of the output register in the PLS105 is needed. Figure 4.21 shows the truth table for the sequential machine derived from its state table.

The information obtained in the truth table is then mapped onto the programming table for PLS105, as shown in Figure 4.22a. The first row in the programming table indicates that if the present state $y_2\,y_1\,y_0$ = LLL (i.e., 000), then for input x = L (i.e., 0) the next state of the sequencer is the same as the

Present state			*Input*	*Next state*			*Output*
y_2	y_1	y_0	x	Y_2	Y_1	Y_0	Z
0	0	0	0	0	0	0	0
0	0	0	1	0	0	1	0
0	0	1	0	0	1	0	0
0	0	1	1	0	1	1	0
0	1	0	0	0	0	0	0
0	1	0	1	0	1	1	0
0	1	1	0	1	0	0	0
0	1	1	1	0	1	1	1
1	0	0	0	0	0	0	0
1	0	0	1	0	1	1	1

FIGURE 4.21
Truth table for the sequential machine of Figure 4.20

present state (i.e., there are no changes in the state variables). The corresponding next state entries are, therefore, "—" (dash). The output associated with state 000 is 0; hence the corresponding SR flip-flop in the output register has to be programmed for a reset input condition. Therefore, the entry in the output column is L.

The second row generates the next state 001 corresponding to the present state 000 and input 1. The only change is in the flip-flop y_0 of the state

CUSTOMER NAME
PURCHASE ORDER #
SIGNETICS DEVICE # CF (XXXX)
CUSTOMER SYMBOLIZED PART #
TOTAL NUMBER OF PARTS
PROGRAM TABLE
REV
DATE

AND			OR		
INACTIVE	0	Cn	INACTIVE	0	Ns, Fr
GENERATE	A		SET	H	
PROPAGATE	•		RESET	L	
TRANSPARENT	—		NO CHANGE	—	
INACTIVE	0	Im, Ps	OPTION		
I, P	H		PRESENT	H	P/E
I, P	L		OE	L	
DON'T CARE	—				

OPTION (P/E): L

AND

TERM	C_n	INPUT (Im)																PRESENT STATE (Ps)						REMARKS
		15	14	13	12	11	10	9	8	7	6	5	4	3	2	1	0	5	4	3	2 (y_2)	1 (y_1)	0 (y_0)	
0	—	—	—	—	—	—	—	—	—	—	—	—	—	—	—	—	L	—	—	—	L	L	L	
1	—	—	—	—	—	—	—	—	—	—	—	—	—	—	—	—	H	—	—	—	L	L	L	
2	—	—	—	—	—	—	—	—	—	—	—	—	—	—	—	—	L	—	—	—	L	L	H	
3	—	—	—	—	—	—	—	—	—	—	—	—	—	—	—	—	H	—	—	—	L	L	H	
4	—	—	—	—	—	—	—	—	—	—	—	—	—	—	—	—	L	—	—	—	L	H	L	
5	—	—	—	—	—	—	—	—	—	—	—	—	—	—	—	—	H	—	—	—	L	H	L	
6	—	—	—	—	—	—	—	—	—	—	—	—	—	—	—	—	L	—	—	—	L	H	H	
7	—	—	—	—	—	—	—	—	—	—	—	—	—	—	—	—	H	—	—	—	L	H	H	
8	—	—	—	—	—	—	—	—	—	—	—	—	—	—	—	—	L	—	—	—	H	L	L	
9	—	—	—	—	—	—	—	—	—	—	—	—	—	—	—	—	H	—	—	—	H	L	L	
10	—	—	—	—	—	—	—	—	—	—	—	—	—	—	—	—	—	—	—	—	H	H	H	
11																								
12																								
13																								
14																								
15																								
16																								
17																								
18																								
19																								
20																								
21																								
22																								
23																								
24																								
25																								
26																								
27																								
28																								
29																								
30																								
31																								
32																								
33																								
34																								
35																								
36																								
37																								
38																								
39																								
40																								
41																								
42																								
43																								
44																								
45																								
46																								
47																								
PIN NO.		20	21	22	23	24	25	26	27	2	3	4	5	6	7	8	9							
VARIABLE NAME																	x							

OR

TERM	NEXT STATE (Ns)						OUTPUT (Fr)							
	5	4	3	2 (Y_2)	1 (Y_1)	0 (Y_0)	7	6	5	4	3	2	1	0
0	0	0	0	—	—	—	0	0	0	0	0	0	0	L
1	0	0	0	—	—	H	0	0	0	0	0	0	0	L
2	0	0	0	—	H	L	0	0	0	0	0	0	0	—
3	0	0	0	—	H	—	0	0	0	0	0	0	0	—
4	0	0	0	—	L	—	0	0	0	0	0	0	0	—
5	0	0	0	—	—	H	0	0	0	0	0	0	0	—
6	0	0	0	H	L	L	0	0	0	0	0	0	0	—
7	0	0	0	—	—	—	0	0	0	0	0	0	0	H
8	0	0	0	L	—	—	0	0	0	0	0	0	0	L
9	0	0	0	L	H	H	0	0	0	0	0	0	0	H
10	0	0	0	L	L	L	0	0	0	0	0	0	0	—
11														
12														
13														
14														
15														
16														
17														
18														
19														
20														
21														
22														
23														
24														
25														
26														
27														
28														
29														
30														
31														
32														
33														
34														
35														
36														
37														
38														
39														
40														
41														
42														
43														
44														
45														
46														
47														
PIN NO.							10	11	12	13	15	16	17	18
VARIABLE NAME														z

FIGURE 4.22a
Coded program table for PLS105

register, which has to be set to 1 (H). The entry in the output column is "—" because the output associated with state 001 is also 0. The rest of the entries are derived in a similar fashion. Since the PLS105 powers up in a state with all the bits in the state and output register being foced to logic "1," the next state corresponding to the present state, 111, is made to be 000 as shown in Figure 4.22a.

The ABEL source file for the above state machine is shown in Figure 4.22b. Note that **state** is a keyword in ABEL design language. A double quotation mark (") indicates the beginning of a comment, which ends with another double quotation mark or the end of the line.

Example 2: This example describes how the PLS155 can be used to implement the controller of the dice game "craps." The rules of the game are quite straightforward and may be summarized as follows [1]:

1. A player throws two dice obtaining a number between 2 and 12.
2. He wins if the number is 7 or 11.

```
module mealy
title 'state machine description

Parag K. Lala          25 November 1988'
      IC3                device 'F105';

      Clk,Clr,x,Z      pin 1,8,9,19;

      State               =[S2,S1,S0];        "State flip-flops
equations

      [S2.AR,S1.AR,S0.AR] = Clr;         "Asynchronous reset
      "Output          Next State     Present State         Input
      [Z.R                        := !S2&!S1&!S0&!x;
      [Z.R                    S0] := !S2&!S1&!S0&x;
      [                 S1,S0.R] := !S2&!S1&S0&!x;
      [                 S1      ] := !S2&!S1&S0&x;

      [                 S1.R    ] := !S2&S1&!S0&!x;

      [                       S0] := !S2&S1&!S0&x;
      [Z.R         S2,S1.R,S0.R] := !S2&S1&S0&!x;
      [Z                        ] := !S2&S1&S0&x;
      [               S2.R      ] :=  S2&!S1&!S0&!x;
      [Z              S2.R,S1,S0] := S2&!S1&!S0&x;

end
```

FIGURE 4.22b
ABEL input file

3. Any number other than 7 or 11 is the player's point and is recorded.
4. The player throws the two dice again.
5. If the number is 7 or 11 he loses.
6. If the number is equal to the recorded value of the first of the first two throw he wins.
7. If the conditions of steps 5 and 6 are not satisfied, the game is continued to step 4.

In designing a digital system to meet the above specification, the functional subsystem tasks must be identified first, followed by that of the controller required to co-ordinate these tasks. The craps game requires four subsystems, the roles of which are as follows:

1. A dice simulator that generates numbers in the range of 2 to 12 with the correct probability distribution (there are 36 combinations of two randomly thrown dice).
2. Combinational logic that detects the value 7 or 11.
3. A register enabling the value of the first throw to be stored.
4. Combinational logic that compares current value of the dice with that stored in the register.

A Moore machine having seven states can be used as a controller. The tasks of the controller at each state are as follows:

S_0: Simulate the first throw of the dice.
S_1: Compare number with 7 or 11. Prepare to store value in register.
S_2: Throw again (a wait state).
S_3: Simulate further throw of dice.
S_4: Compare number with 7 or 11 and with the number stored in the register
S_5: LOSE (a wait state).
S_6: WIN (a halt state).

The state diagram of the controller is shown in Figure 4.23a (and in the tabular form in Figure 4.23b) where

P is a primary input from a user operated button.
C is an input from the combinational logic that compares the number with that stored in the register.
F is an input from the combinational logic that compares the number with 7 or 11.

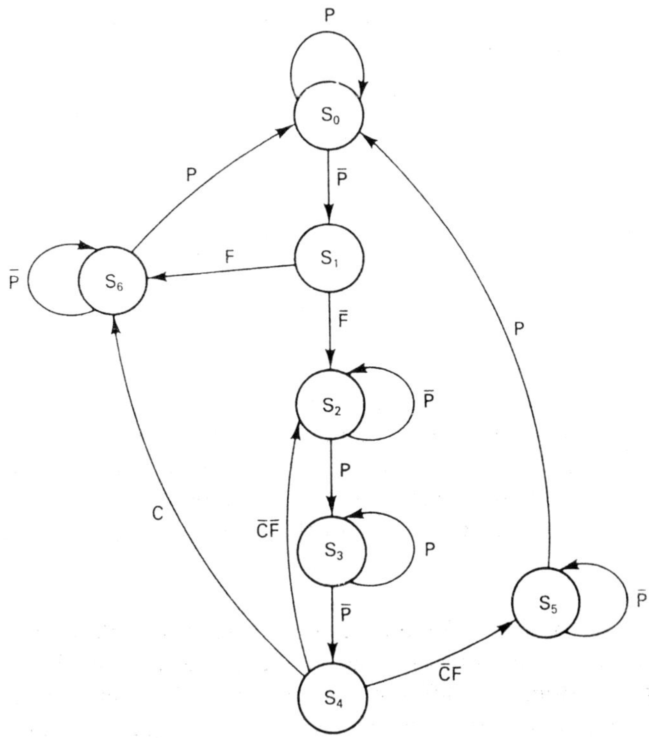

FIGURE 4.23a
State diagram of the controller

The controller remains in one of the waiting states (S_2, S_5 or S_6) when P is at logic "0"; only when P is at logic "1" does the controller move to one of the states in which the dice simulator operates (i.e., state S_0 or S_3).

	Input PCF							
State	*000*	*001*	*010*	*011*	*100*	*101*	*110*	*111*
S_0	S_1	S_1	S_1	S_1	S_0	S_0	S_0	S_0
S_1	S_2	S_6	S_2	S_6	S_2	S_6	S_2	S_6
S_2	S_2	S_2	S_2	S_2	S_3	S_3	S_3	S_3
S_3	S_4	S_4	S_4	S_4	S_3	S_3	S_3	S_3
S_4	S_2	S_5	S_6	S_6	S_2	S_5	S_6	S_6
S_5	S_5	S_5	S_5	S_5	S_0	S_0	S_0	S_0
S_6	S_6	S_6	S_6	S_6	S_0	S_0	S_0	S_0

FIGURE 4.23b
State table for the controller

Since the controller has seven states, it requires three flip-flops. A possible state assignment for the controller is:

State	y_2	y_1	y_0
S_0	1	0	0
S_1	1	0	1
S_2	0	1	0
S_3	1	1	0
S_4	1	1	1
S_5	0	0	1
S_6	0	0	0

The control information in the state diagram/state table can be represented by the truth table of Figure 4.24. The truth table can be directly mapped onto the program table for FPLS PLS155 as shown in Figure 4.25a. The appropriate fuses in the device can then be blown to implement the controller circuit. The ABEL source file for the controller circuit is shown in Figure 4.25b.

Example 3: A controller for an elevator serving four floors is to be designed using PLS167. The controller has ten inputs I_0–I_9. Inputs I_0 through I_5 are "request" buttons on different floors; input I_6–I_9 are inside the elevator—each one is used to request a particular floor. Figure 4.26 shows the functions of each input.

	Present state			*Input*			*Next state*			*Output*		
	y_2	y_1	y_0	*P*	*C*	*F*	y_2	y_1	y_0	*Again*	*Win*	*Lose*
S_0	1	0	0	0	X	X	1	0	1	0	0	0
	1	0	0	1	X	X	1	0	1	0	0	0
S_1	1	0	1	X	X	0	0	1	0	0	0	0
	1	0	1	X	X	1	0	0	0	0	0	0
S_2	0	1	0	0	X	X	0	1	0	1	0	0
	0	1	0	1	X	X	1	1	0	1	0	0
S_3	1	1	0	0	X	X	1	1	1	0	0	0
	1	1	0	1	X	X	1	1	0	0	0	0
S_4	1	1	1	X	0	0	0	1	0	0	0	0
	1	1	1	X	0	1	0	0	1	0	0	0
	1	1	1	X	1	X	0	0	0	0	0	0
S_5	0	0	1	0	X	X	0	0	1	0	0	1
	0	0	1	1	X	X	1	0	0	0	0	1
S_6	0	0	0	0	X	X	0	0	0	0	1	0
	0	0	0	1	X	X	1	0	0	0	1	0

FIGURE 4.24

The elevator controller is designed as a Moore machine with twelve states. The state diagram of the controller is shown in Figure 4.27; the operations performed at each state are as follows:

S_0: the elevator is on the first floor.
Keep the floor and the elevator doors open.

S_1: the elevator is on the first floor and is ready to go up.
Shut the floor and the elevator doors.

S_2: the elevator is going up and is on the second floor.
Keep the floor and the elevator doors open.

S_3: the elevator is on the second floor and is ready to go up.
Shut the floor and the elevator doors.

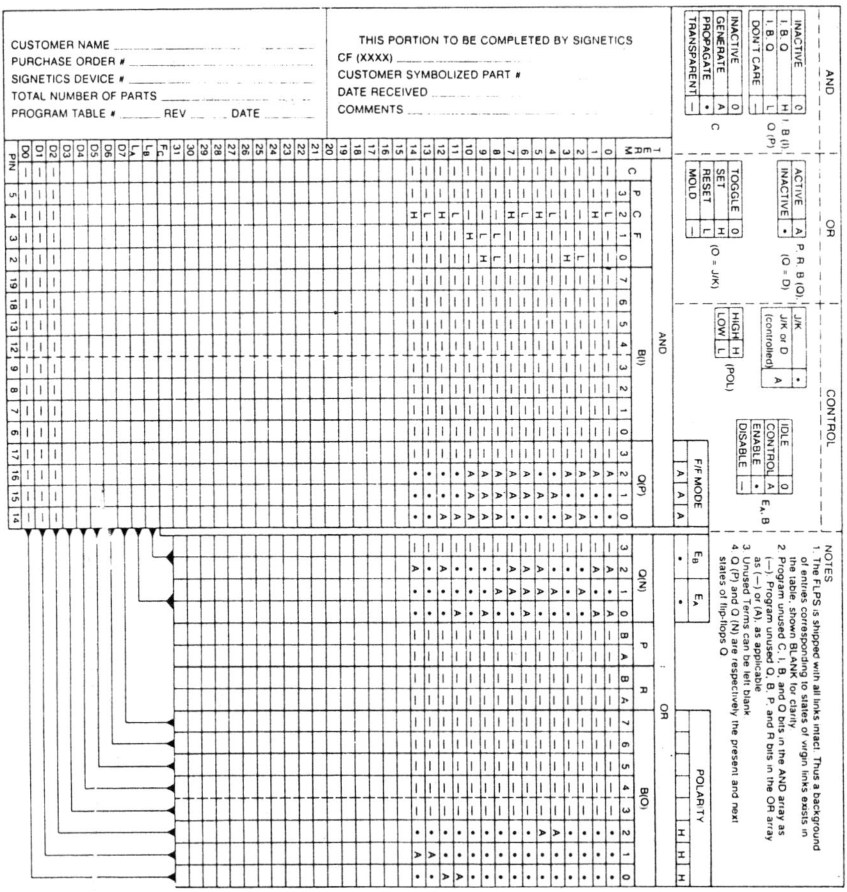

FIGURE 4.25a
Coded program table PLS155

```
module moore
title 'CRAPS sample design
Parag K. Lala            20 November 1988';

        m1          device 'F155';

        q2,q1,q0                pin 14,15,16;
        clock,p,c,f             pin 1,2,3,4;
        again,win,lose          pin 6,7,8;
        sreg                    =  [q2,q1,q0];

        "State Values...
        S0 = 4; S1 = 5; S2 = 2; S3 = 6; S4 = 7; S5 = 1; S6 = 0;

state_diagram sreg;
        State S0:
          again = 0;
            win = 0;
           lose = 0;
          IF (!p) THEN S1;
        ELSE S0;

        State S1:
          again = 0;
            win = 0;
           lose = 0;
          IF (!f) THEN S2;
          ELSE S6;

        State S2:
          again = 1;
            win = 0;
           lose = 0;
          IF (p) THEN S3;
          ELSE S2;

        State S3:
          again = 0;
            win = 0;
           lose = 0;
          IF (!p) THEN S4;
          ELSE S3;

        State S4:
          again = 0;
            win = 0;
           lose = 0;
          IF (c) THEN S6;
          IF (f) THEN S5;
          ELSE S2;

        State S5:
          again = 0;
            win = 0;
           lose = 1;
          IF (p) THEN S0;
          ELSE S5;

        State S6:
          again = 0;
            win = 1;
           lose = 0;
          IF (p) THEN S0;
          ELSE S6;

end
```

FIGURE 4.25b
Source file for CRAPS state machine

S_4: the elevator is going down and is on the second floor.
Keep the floor door and the elevator door open.

S_5: the elevator is on the second floor and is ready to go down.
Shut the floor and the elevator doors.

S_6: the elevator is going up and is on the third floor.
Keep the floor and the elevator doors open.

S_7: the elevator is on the third floor and is ready to go up.
Shut the floor and the elevator doors.

S_8: the elevator is going down and is on the third floor.
Keep the floor and the elevator doors open.

S_9: the elevator is on the third floor and is ready to go down.
Shut the floor and the elevator doors.

S_{10}: the elevator is on the fourth floor.
Keep the floor and the elevator doors open.

S_{11}: the elevator is on the fourth floor and is ready to go down.
Shut the floor and the elevator doors.

The elevator remains on the first floor whenever it is idle. If the elevator is moving up, any request to go up has a higher priority over a request to go down. For example, if somebody gets in on the first floor and has requested to go to the fourth floor then if there are simultaneous requests from the third floor to go up and to go down, the request to go up is served first. Similarly, when the elevator is moving down, a request to go down has higher priority over a request to go up.

The outputs F_0–F_3 of PLS167 control the doors on floors one to four, respectively. The doors are opened when the corresponding output is at logic "1" and shut when the output is at logic "0." The state assignments and the

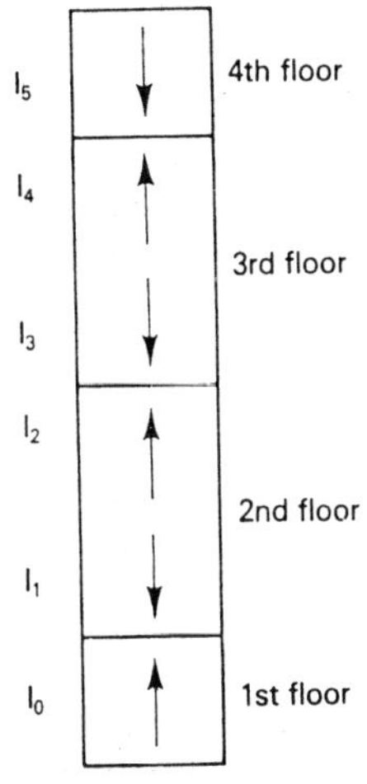

FIGURE 4.26a
Input buttons on different floors

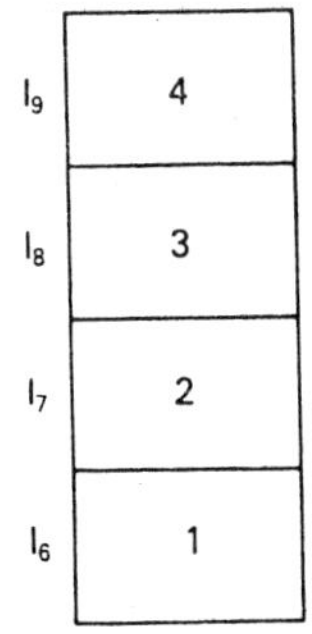

FIGURE 4.26b
Input buttons inside the elevator

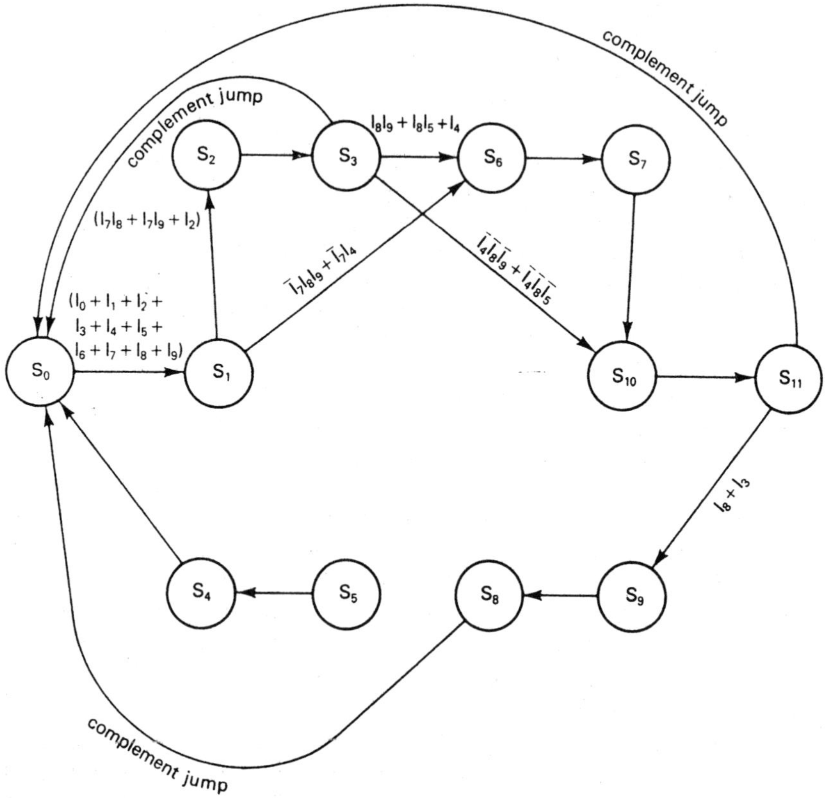

FIGURE 4.27
State diagram of the elevator controller

State	y_3	y_2	y_1	y_0	F_3	F_2	F_1	F_0
S_0	0	0	0	0	0	0	0	1
S_1	0	0	0	1	0	0	0	0
S_2	0	0	1	0	0	0	1	0
S_3	0	0	1	1	0	0	0	0
S_4	0	1	0	0	0	0	1	0
S_5	0	1	0	1	0	0	0	0
S_6	0	1	1	0	0	1	0	0
S_7	0	1	1	1	0	0	0	0
S_8	1	0	0	0	0	1	0	0
S_9	1	0	0	1	0	0	0	0
S_{10}	1	0	1	0	1	0	0	0
S_{11}	1	0	1	1	0	0	0	0

FIGURE 4.28a
State assignments and outputs

CUSTOMER NAME
PURCHASE ORDER #
SIGNETICS DEVICE # CF (XXXX)
CUSTOMER SYMBOLIZED PART #
TOTAL NUMBER OF PARTS
PROGRAM TABLE
REV
DATE

AND			OR		
INACTIVE	0	Cn	INACTIVE	0	Ns, Fr
GENERATE	A		SET	H	
PROPAGATE	•		RESET	L	
TRANSPARENT	—		NO CHANGE	—	
INACTIVE	0	Im, Ps	OPTION		
I, P	H		PRESET	H	P/E
Ī, P̄	L		OE	L	
DON'T CARE	—				

TERM	Cn	AND: INPUT (Im)														PRESENT STATE (Ps)								REMARKS	OR: NEXT STATE (Ns)								OUTPUT (Fr)			
		13	12	11	10	9	8	7	6	5	4	3	2	1	0	7	6	5	4	3	2	1	0		7	6	5	4	3	2	1	0	F_3 3	F_2 2	F_1 1	F_0 0
0	—	—	—	—	—	—	—	—	—	—	—	—	—	—	H	—	—	—	—	L	L	L	L		0	0	0	0	—	—	—	H	L	L	L	H
1	—	—	—	—	—	—	—	—	—	—	—	—	—	H	—	—	—	—	—	L	L	L	L		0	0	0	0	—	—	—	H	L	L	L	H
2	—	—	—	—	—	—	—	—	—	—	—	—	H	—	—	—	—	—	—	L	L	L	L		0	0	0	0	—	—	—	H	L	L	L	H
3	—	—	—	—	—	—	—	—	—	—	—	H	—	—	—	—	—	—	—	L	L	L	L		0	0	0	0	—	—	—	H	L	L	L	H
4	—	—	—	—	—	—	—	—	—	—	H	—	—	—	—	—	—	—	—	L	L	L	L		0	0	0	0	—	—	—	H	L	L	L	H
5	—	—	—	—	—	—	—	—	—	H	—	—	—	—	—	—	—	—	—	L	L	L	L		0	0	0	0	—	—	—	H	L	L	L	H
6	—	—	—	—	—	—	—	—	H	—	—	—	—	—	—	—	—	—	—	L	L	L	L		0	0	0	0	—	—	—	H	L	L	L	H
7	—	—	—	—	—	—	—	H	—	—	—	—	—	—	—	—	—	—	—	L	L	L	L		0	0	0	0	—	—	—	H	L	L	L	H
8	—	—	—	—	—	—	H	—	—	—	—	—	—	—	—	—	—	—	—	L	L	L	L		0	0	0	0	—	—	—	H	L	L	L	H
9	—	—	—	—	—	H	—	—	—	—	—	—	—	—	—	—	—	—	—	L	L	L	L		0	0	0	0	—	—	—	H	L	L	L	H
10	—	—	—	—	—		H	H	—	—	—	—	—	—	—	—	—	—	—	L	L	L	H		0	0	0	0	—	—	H	L	L	L	L	L
11	—	—	—	—	—	H	—	H	—	—	—	—	—	—	—	—	—	—	—	L	L	L	H		0	0	0	0	—	—	H	L	L	L	L	L
12	—	—	—	—	—	—	—	—	—	—	—	—	H	—	—	—	—	—	—	L	L	L	H		0	0	0	0	—	—	H	L	L	L	L	L
13	—	—	—	—	—	H	H	L	—	—	—	—	—	—	—	—	—	—	—	L	L	L	H		0	0	0	0	—	H	H	L	L	L	L	L
14	—	—	—	—	—	—	—	L	—	—	H	—	—	—	—	—	—	—	—	L	L	L	H		0	0	0	0	—	H	H	L	L	L	L	L
15	—	—	—	—	—	H	L	L	—	—	L	—	L	—	—	—	—	—	—	L	L	L	H		0	0	0	0	H	—	H	L	L	L	L	L
16	—	—	—	—	—	—	L	L	—	H	L	—	L	—	—	—	—	—	—	L	L	L	H		0	0	0	0	H	—	H	L	L	L	L	L
17	—	—	—	—	—	—	—	—	—	—	—	—	—	—	—	—	—	—	—	L	L	H	L		0	0	0	0	—	—	—	H	L	L	H	L
18	A	—	—	—	—	H	H	—	—	—	—	—	—	—	—	—	—	—	—	L	L	H	H		0	0	0	0	—	H	—	L	L	L	L	L
19	A	—	—	—	—	—	H	—	—	H	—	—	—	—	—	—	—	—	—	L	L	H	H		0	0	0	0	—	H	—	L	L	L	L	L
20	A	—	—	—	—	—	—	—	—	—	H	—	—	—	—	—	—	—	—	L	L	H	H		0	0	0	0	—	H	—	L	L	L	L	L
21	A	—	—	—	—	H	L	—	—	—	L	—	—	—	—	—	—	—	—	L	L	H	H		0	0	0	0	H	—	—	L	L	L	L	L
22	A	—	—	—	—	—	L	—	—	H	L	—	—	—	—	—	—	—	—	L	L	H	H		0	0	0	0	H	—	—	L	L	L	L	L
23	•	—	—	—	—	—	—	—	—	—	—	—	—	—	—	—	—	—	—	L	L	H	H		0	0	0	0	—	—	L	L	L	L	L	L
24	—	—	—	—	—	—	—	—	—	—	—	—	—	—	—	—	—	—	—	L	H	H	L		0	0	0	0	—	—	—	H	L	H	L	L
25	—	—	—	—	—	—	—	—	—	—	—	—	—	—	—	—	—	—	—	L	H	H	H		0	0	0	0	H	L	—	L	L	L	L	L
26	—	—	—	—	—	—	—	—	—	—	—	—	—	—	—	—	—	—	—	H	L	H	L		0	0	0	0	—	—	—	H	H	L	L	L
27	A	—	—	—	—	L	L	L	H	—	—	L	—	—	—	—	—	—	—	H	L	H	H		0	0	0	0	L	—	L	L	L	L	L	L
28	A	—	—	—	—	L	L	L	—	—	—	L	—	—	H	—	—	—	—	H	L	H	H		0	0	0	0	L	—	L	L	L	L	L	L
29	A	—	—	—	—	—	H	—	—	—	—	—	—	—	—	—	—	—	—	H	L	H	H		0	0	0	0	—	—	L	L	L	L	L	L
30	A	—	—	—	—	—	—	—	—	—	—	H	—	—	—	—	—	—	—	H	L	H	H		0	0	0	0	—	—	L	L	L	L	L	L
31	A	—	—	—	—	—	L	—	—	—	—	L	—	H	—	—	—	—	—	H	L	H	H		0	0	0	0	L	H	L	L	L	L	L	L
32	A	—	—	—	—	—	L	H	—	—	—	L	—	—	—	—	—	—	—	H	L	H	H		0	0	0	0	L	H	L	L	L	L	L	L
33	—	—	—	—	—	—	—	—	—	—	—	—	—	—	—	—	—	—	—	H	L	L	L		0	0	0	0	—	—	—	H	L	H	L	L
34	A	—	—	—	—	—	—	H	—	—	—	—	—	—	—	—	—	—	—	H	L	L	H		0	0	0	0	L	H	—	L	L	L	L	L
35	A	—	—	—	—	—	—	—	—	—	—	—	—	H	—	—	—	—	—	H	L	L	H		0	0	0	0	L	H	—	L	L	L	L	L
36	•	—	—	—	—	—	—	—	—	—	—	—	—	—	—	—	—	—	—	H	L	L	H		0	0	0	0	L	—	—	L	L	L	L	L
37	—	—	—	—	—	—	—	—	—	—	—	—	—	—	—	—	—	—	—	L	H	L	L		0	0	0	0	—	—	—	H	L	L	H	L
38	—	—	—	—	—	—	—	—	—	—	—	—	—	—	—	—	—	—	—	L	H	L	H		0	0	0	0	—	L	—	L	L	L	L	L
39	•	—	—	—	—	—	—	—	—	—	—	—	—	—	—	—	—	—	—	H	L	H	H		0	0	0	0	L	—	L	L	L	L	L	L
40	—	—	—	—	—	—	—	—	—	—	—	—	—	—	—	—	—	—	—	H	H	H	H		0	0	0	0	L	L	L	L	L	L	L	L
41																																				
42																																				
43																																				
44																																				
45																																				
46																																				
47																																				
PIN NO.		17	18	19	20	21	22	23	2	3	4	5	6	7	8																15	14	13	11	10	9
VARIABLE NAME						I_9	I_8	I_7	I_6	I_5	I_4	I_3	I_2	I_1	I_0																					

FIGURE 4.28b
Coded program table (Courtesy of Signetics Corp.)

outputs associated with each state are shown in Figure 4.28a. The transition terms are indicated in Figure 4.27. Complement jumps are used from certain states (S_2, S_8, S_{11}). This restricts the number of transition terms to 41, while ensuring that all requests are served. The program table for PLS167 is shown in Figure 4.28b.

PROBLEMS

4-1. A parity bit generator circuit for a 4-bit input sequence is to be designed. The circuit receives the four bits of the input sequence and generates an even parity bit which is to be added to the original sequence. After generating the parity bit for the last sequence, the circuit is ready to receive the next input sequence. Implement the circuit using PLS105.

4-2. The following state diagram is to be implemented using PLS155. Show the program table for the device.

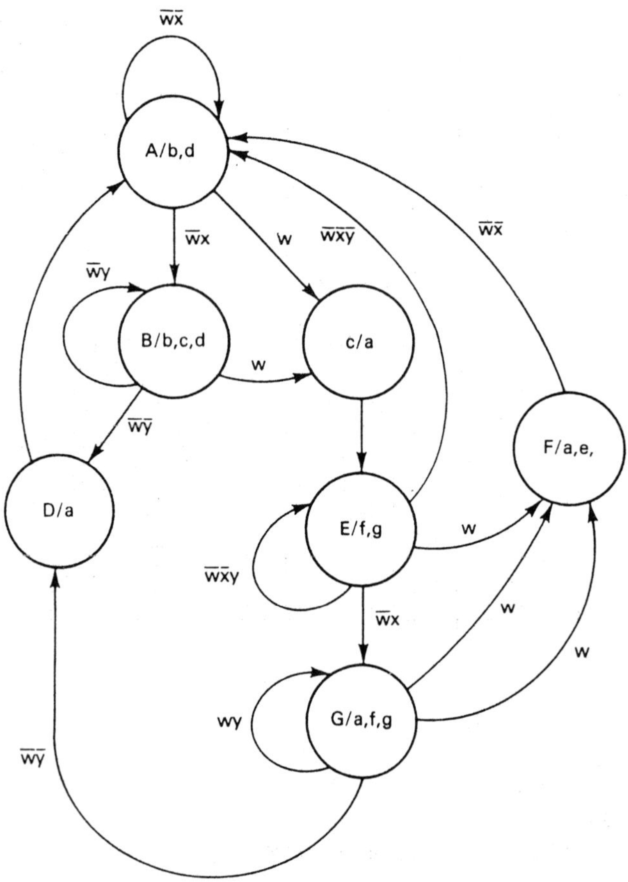

4-3. A sequential circuit has one input (x) and two outputs (l and m). If the circuit receives the input sequence 010, it produces l = 1, provided input sequence 110 has never occurred. The output m is set to 1, if the input sequence 110 is received. In other words, if m is ever set to 1, l can never be set to 1 again; however, the converse is not true. Implement the circuit using PLS105; show its program table.

4-4. A digital system that multiplies two unsigned binary numbers is to be designed. It evaluates a product by adding the multiplicand n times, where n is the value of the multiplier. Assume that the multiplicand is in register A, the multiplier in register B and the product is stored in register C. An adder circuit adds the contents of A to C. A zero-detect circuit D, checks to see if the content of B is 0 after it has been decremented. Design the control circuit for the digital system using PLS167; show the program table for the device.

REFERENCES

1. V. T. Rhyne, *Fundamentals of Digital System Design,* Prentice-Hall, Inc., 1973
2. *Programmable Logic Data Manual,* Signetics Corp., 1986.

Chapter 5

Programmable Array Logic (PAL)

The basic PAL architecture is exactly the opposite to that of a PROM. It comprises of a programmable AND array and a fixed OR array. The programmability in the AND array removes one of the main deficiencies in PROMs that the AND plane must be large enough to produce product terms corresponding to all possible input combinations. Thus, as in FPLAs only the desired input combinations have to be programmed. Moreover, logic minimization techniques can be employed to further reduce the required number of product terms. However, since the OR array is not programmable, only a fixed number of product terms, typically eight, can drive a specific OR gate.

5.1 PAL SERIES 20

The first family of PAL devices, Series 20, was introduced by Monolithic Memories (now AMD, Inc.) in the late 1970s. These devices were aimed at relatively simple substitutions of SSI/MSI chips, rather than replacing complex blocks of logic on a circuit board. All 15 PALs in the Series 20 have 20 pins, with input-to-output gate delay of 25 ns. They have varying number of inputs and outputs. Some of these devices have feedback paths from the outputs back to the AND array. Some devices have programmable I/O pins (i.e., the pins can be configured to function either as inputs or outputs). All the members of Series 20 PAL family can have active-high or active-low outputs. Some devices have built-in D flip-flops and can be utilized in realizing finite state machines. The PAL Series 20 devices include both combinational and sequential units. The combinational group consists of nine devices:

PAL10H8	PAL10L8
PAL12H6	PAL10L6
PAL14H4	PAL14L4
PAL16H2	PAL16L2
PAL16C1	

The first two digits in a device number specify the number of inputs, the last digit the number of outputs. Letter **H** or **L** indicates that the corresponding device has an active-high or active-low output respectively. The letter **C** denotes that both the true output and its complement are available.

Four other PAL devices in the series have been designed to be used in implementing state machines. These are:

PAL16L8
PAL16R8
PAL16R6
PAL16R4

The **L** has the same meaning as in combinational logic devices; the **R** indicates that the device has built-in flip-flops, varying from zero (16L8), eight (16R8), six (16R6) and four (16R4).

The smallest group of devices in the Series 20 consists of two units. They are:

PAL16A4
PAL16X4

The **A** stands for arithmetic registered and the **X** denotes exclusive-OR registered.

During the last few years, eight more devices have been added to the original 15 in the Series 20. They are:

PAL16P8
PAL16RP8
PAL16RP6
PAL16RP4
PAL16H8
PAL16HD8
PAL18LD8
PAL18P8

The **P** indicates that each output in the device can be programmed as active-high or active-low. The **R** has the same meaning as in sequential PAL devices. The PAL16H8 is an active-high output version of PAL16L8. The PAL16HD8 has 10 dedicated and 6 feedback inputs. Each of the eight dedicated outputs can generate the sum of eight product terms. The PAL16LD8 is an active-low output version of the PALHD8. The PAL18P8 is an enhanced version of PAL16P8. In addition, to two extra inputs, the PAL18P8 generates the sum of eight product terms at each output, compared to seven in the PAL16P8. Figure 5.1 shows the functional diagrams of all the devices in Series 20.

5.1.1. Combinational PAL Devices

The devices in this group are used to implement combinational logic functions. The units with active-high outputs can implement AND-OR logic, and the units with active-low outputs can implement AND-NOR logic. Figure 5.2a and b show the logic for a cell from an active-high and an active-low PAL, respectively. Any combinational function represented by NAND-NAND, OR-NAND, or NOR-OR, logic can be replaced by a PAL with active-high output. Similarly, a function in NAND-AND, OR-AND or NOR-NOR form can be realized by a PAL with active-low outputs.

To illustrate the application of combinational PAL devices in logic design, let us implement a circuit with four inputs (A, B, C, D) and two outputs (X, Y). One output (X) is high when the majority of the inputs are high, and low at other times. The remaining output (Y) is high only during a **tie** (i.e., when two inputs are high and two are low) [1]. Figure 5.3 shows the block diagram and the truth table for the circuit.

The output expressons for X and Y can be minimized by using Karnaugh maps as shown in Figure 5.4.

From the Karnaugh map for X we get

$$X = ABD + ABC + BCD + ACD \quad \ldots \quad \ldots \text{①}$$

The expression for X can also be represented as

$$X = \overline{\bar{C}\bar{D} + \bar{A}\bar{B} + \bar{B}\bar{C}D + \bar{A}C\bar{D} + \bar{B}C\bar{D} + \bar{A}\bar{C}D} \quad \ldots \quad \ldots \text{②}$$

Similarly,

$$Y = \bar{A}\bar{B}CD + \bar{A}B\bar{C}D + \bar{A}BC\bar{D} + AB\bar{C}\bar{D} + A\bar{B}\bar{C}D + A\bar{B}C\bar{D} \ldots \quad \ldots \text{③}$$

and also

$$Y = \overline{\bar{A}\bar{B}\bar{C} + \bar{A}\bar{B}C\bar{D} + \bar{A}B\bar{C}\bar{D} + \bar{A}BCD + AB\bar{C}D + ACD + ABC\bar{D} + A\bar{B}\bar{C}\bar{D}} \quad \ldots \quad \ldots \quad \ldots \quad \ldots \text{④}$$

It is also possible to use either an active-high or an active-low output PAL to implement the expressions for X and Y. If we wish to use an active-high PAL then the expressions (1) and (3) will have to be employed, whereas the expressions (2) and (4) will be required for implementation using an active-low PAL. Figure 5.5a and b show the implementation of the expressions in a PAL16H2 and PAL16L2 device, respectively.

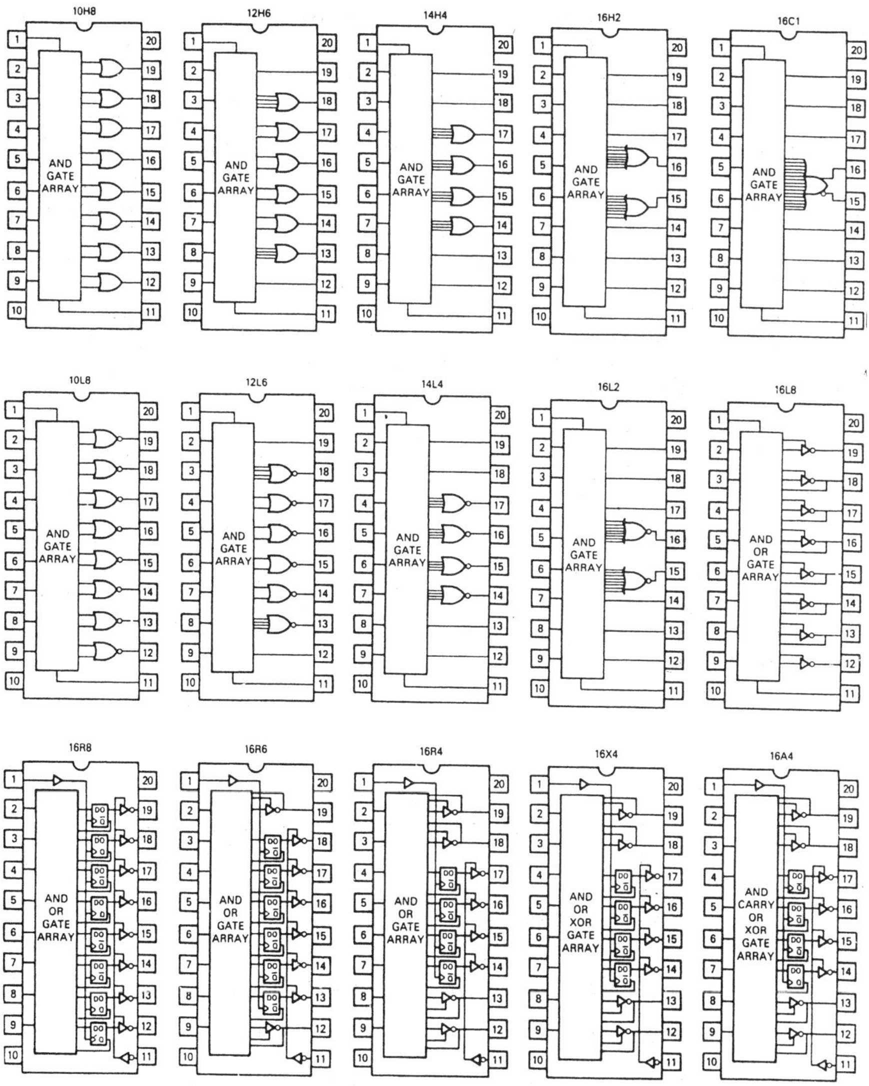

FIGURE 5.1
PAL Series 20 (Courtesy of AMD, Inc.)

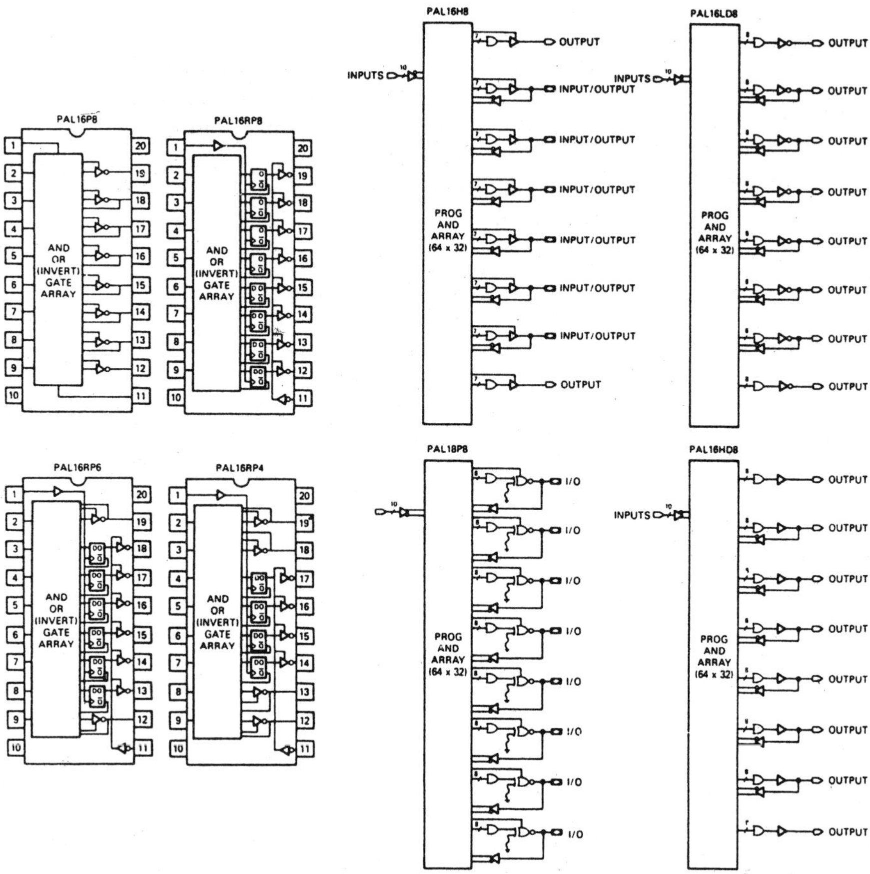

FIGURE 5.1
Part II

Thus, in order to realize a Boolean function with a combinational PAL device, the function must be expressed in the sum-of-products form. The reduction of terms to the minimum is not essential. As a further example of the combinational function implementation using a PAL, let us consider the following six variable functions; these functions are not necessarily minimal.

$$W(A,B,C,D,E,F) = A\overline{B}C + \overline{B}\,\overline{D} + BC\overline{D}E\overline{F} + \overline{E}\,\overline{F}$$

$$X(A,B,C,D,E,F) = A\overline{B}CF + \overline{B}\,\overline{D} + \overline{B}EF$$

$$Y(A,B,C,D,E,F) = C\overline{D}F + \overline{A}B\overline{C}D\overline{E}F + \overline{B}C\overline{F}$$

$$Z(A,B,C,D,E,F) = A\overline{C}F + \overline{B}EF + \overline{B}\,\overline{D} + AC\overline{F}$$

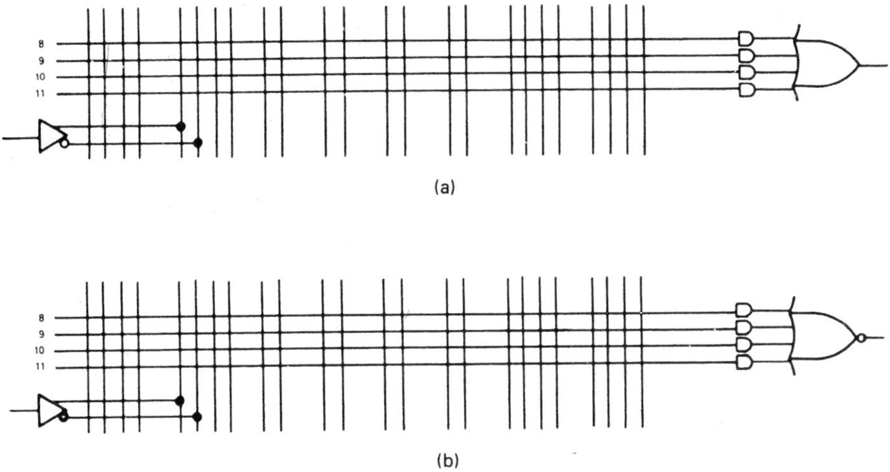

FIGURE 5.2
Structure of active-high/active-low output PALs (Courtesy of AMD, Inc.)

It is clear that the above functions can be implemented with a PAL having active-high outputs. However, two of the functions produce the summation of four product terms, and the remaining two produce the summation of three product terms. As can be seen from Figure 5.1, only the PAL14H4 has the capability to realize the functions. Figure 5.5c shows the programmed logic diagram of the device.

In certain cases the unused inputs in the PAL device can be utilized to modify a logic function. For example in Figure 5.5c, when input T (= Pin 7) is at logic "1," the product term 32 remains unaffected and the product term 35 generates a logic "0"; the output Y still implements the same function. However, if it becomes necessary to change the product term 32, then the product term 35 can be programmed appropriately and $\overline{T}$ is included as a literal in that product term. Thus, when T is set at logic "0," the product term 32 is replaced with the product term 35 in the expression for Y.

8-bit Comparator Design Using PAL16C1. The PAL16C1 is different from the other devices in the combinational group. In this device, the summation of the 16 product terms are gated to the two output pins via an OR-NOR gate; thus the outputs are complements of each other. The device can be used to implement a single output combinational circuit of sixteen input variables. As an example of the application of the device, let us design an 8-bit comparator circuit.

Let the two 8-bit numbers to be compared be $(x_0 x_1 x_2 x_3 x_4 x_5 x_6 x_7)$ and $(y_0 y_1 y_2 y_3 y_4 y_5 y_6 y_7)$. If any input pair does not match, then the output of the

A	B	C	D	X	Y
0	0	0	0	0	0
0	0	0	1	0	0
0	0	1	0	0	0
0	0	1	1	0	1
0	1	0	0	0	0
0	1	0	1	0	1
0	1	1	0	0	1
0	1	1	1	1	0
1	0	0	0	0	0
1	0	0	1	0	1
1	0	1	0	0	1
1	0	1	1	1	0
1	1	0	0	0	1
1	1	0	1	1	0
1	1	1	0	1	0
1	1	1	1	1	0

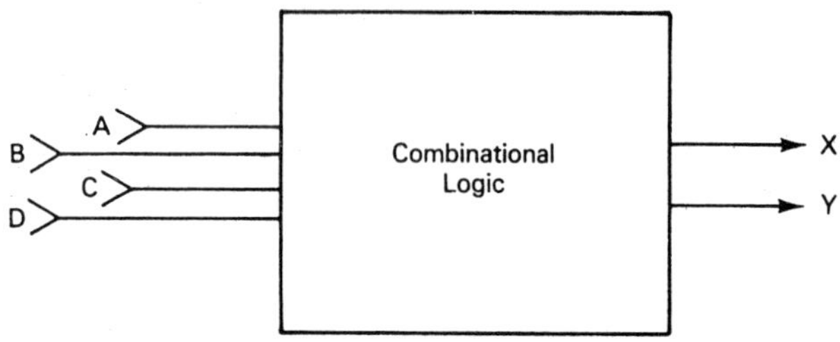

FIGURE 5.3
Truth table for a 4-input and 2-output combinational logic circuit

	$\bar{C}\bar{D}$	$\bar{C}D$	CD	$C\bar{D}$
$\bar{A}\bar{B}$				
$\bar{A}B$			1	
AB		1	1	1
$A\bar{B}$			1	

X

	$\bar{C}\bar{D}$	$\bar{C}D$	CD	$C\bar{D}$
$\bar{A}\bar{B}$			1	
$\bar{A}B$		1		1
AB	1			
$A\bar{B}$		1		1

Y

FIGURE 5.4
Karnaugh maps for output expressions X and Y.

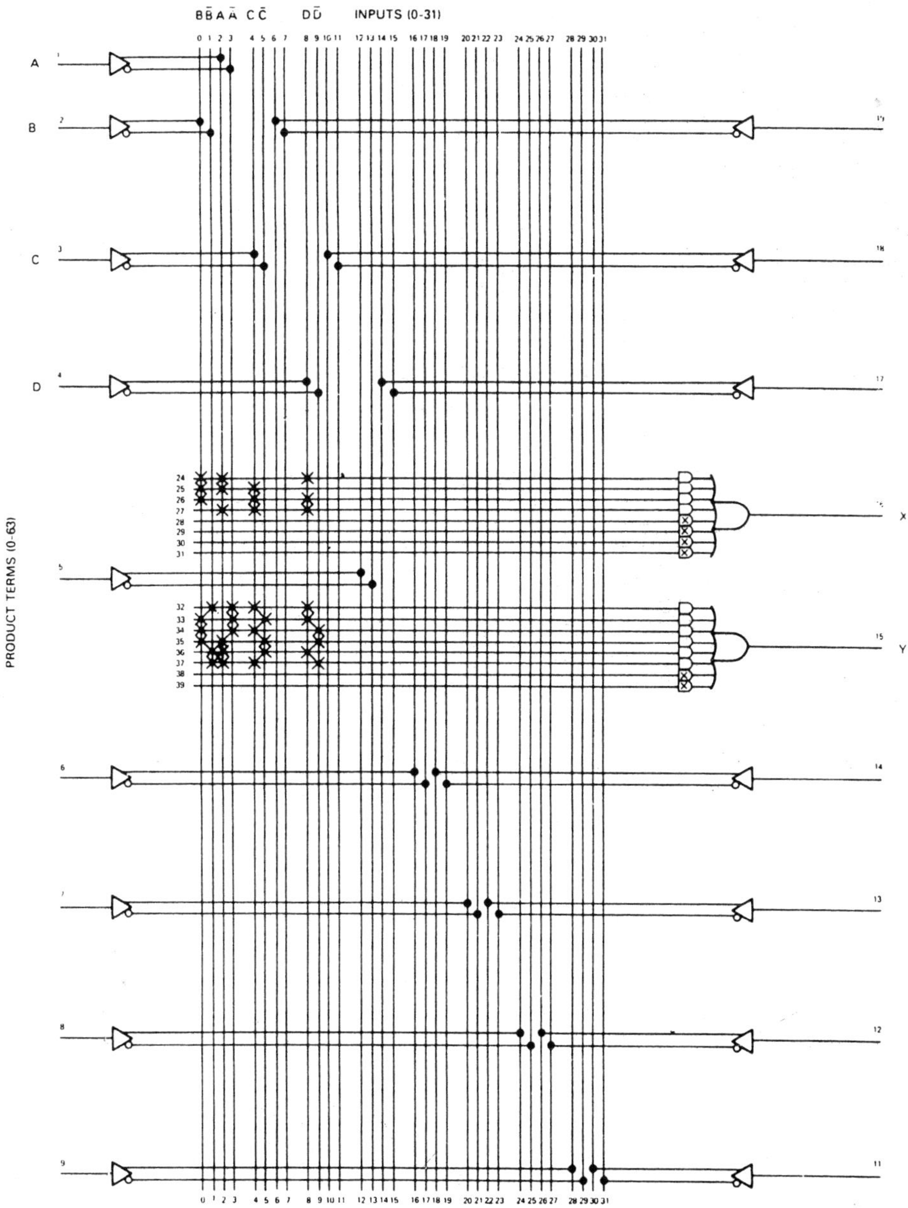

(a)

FIGURE 5.5a
Implementation of Boolean expressions using 16H2 (Courtesy of AMD, Inc.)

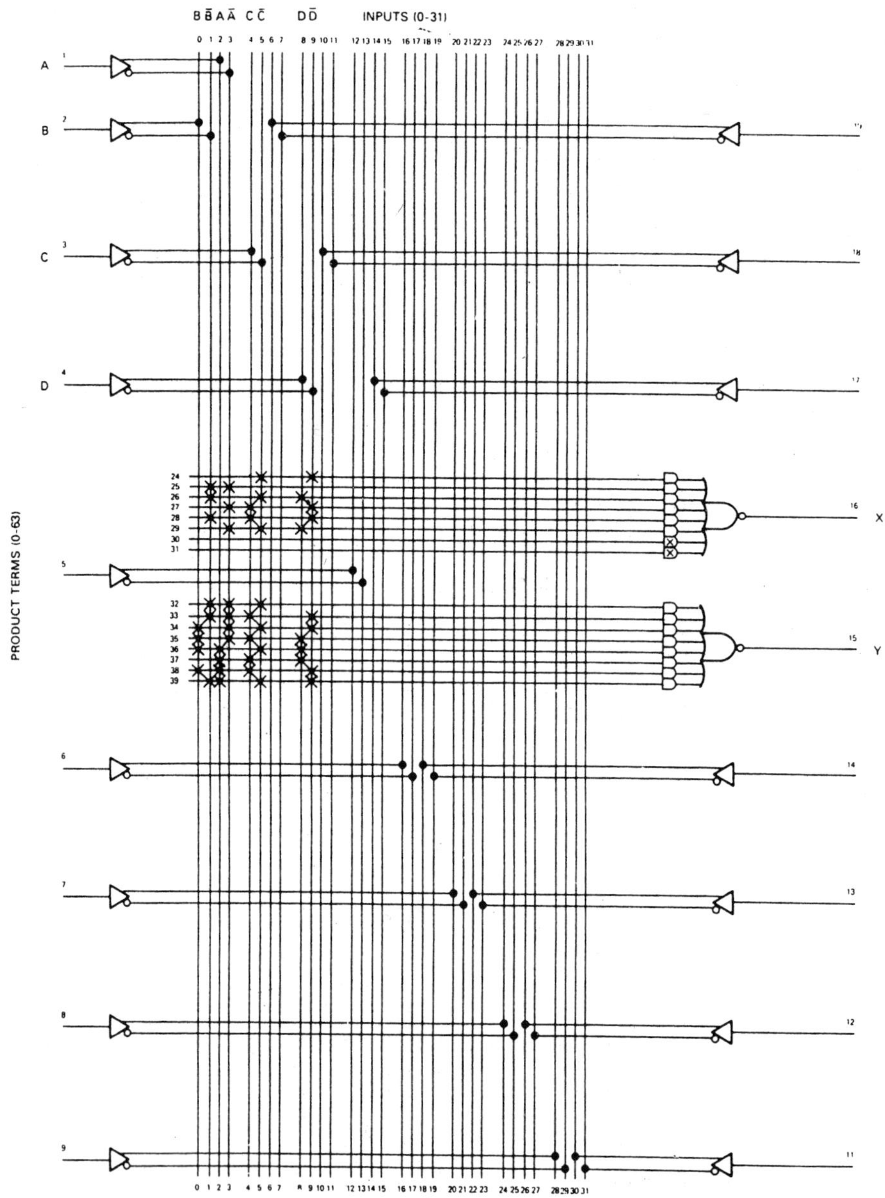

(b)

FIGURE 5.5b
Implementation of Boolean expressions using 16L2 (Courtesy of AMD, Inc.)

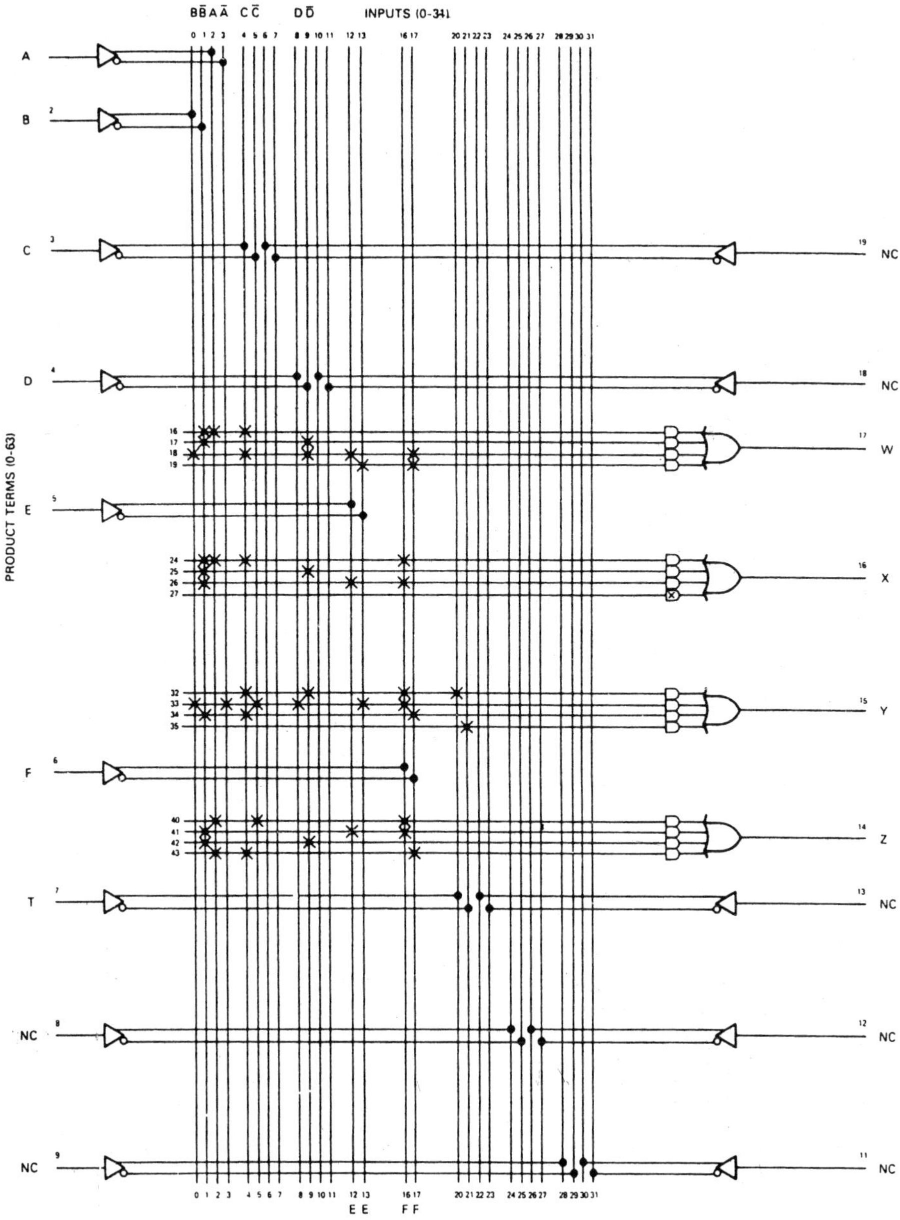

(c)

FIGURE 5.5c
Implementation of the 6 input, 4-output function (Courtesy of AMD, Inc.)

comparator is assumed to be at logic "1." Thus, the Boolean expression for the comparator output, f, is

$$f = (x_0 \oplus y_0) + (x_1 \oplus y_1) + (x_2 \oplus y_2) + (x_3 \oplus y_3)$$
$$+ (x_4 \oplus y_4) + (x_5 \oplus y_5) + (x_6 \oplus y_6) + (x_7 \oplus y_7)$$
$$= x_0\overline{y}_0 + \overline{x}_0 y_0 + x_1\overline{y}_1 + \overline{x}_1 y_1 + x_2\overline{y}_2 + \overline{x}_2 y_2 + x_3\overline{y}_3 + \overline{x}_3 y_3$$
$$+ x_4\overline{y}_4 + \overline{x}_4 y_4 + x_5\overline{y}_5 + \overline{x}_5 y_5 + x_6\overline{y}_6 + \overline{x}_6 y_6 + x_7\overline{y}_7 + \overline{x}_7 y_7$$

Each one of the above 16 product terms can be implemented with a product term in PAL16C1. The active-high output of the device generates a logic "1" signal if the two 8-bit numbers are not equal, while the active-low output produces a logic "1" if they are equal. Figure 5.6 shows the programmed logic diagram of the PAL16C1.

5.1.2 Sequential PAL Devices

This group of PAL devices are designed to be used as state machines—Mealy and Moore. However, they can also be used to realize combinational functions. Each output pin in these devices has eight product terms associated with it. The lower seven product terms in a group drive an OR gate, while the upper product term controls the enable input of an inverting tri-state buffer. When this product term is activated, the output is enabled and the sum of the product terms is gated to the output.

On the other hand, if the product term is not activated, the tri-state buffer remains in the high-impedance state and the output pin can be used as an input. Figure 5.7 illustrates this bidirectional capability of the sequential PAL devices.

The output structure of the registered PALs is shown in Figure 5.8. The sum of eight product terms produced by an OR gate is fed to the D-input of the flip-flop. The clock signal is shared by all the flip-flops, and on its rising edge the output of the OR gate is loaded into the flip-flop. The output of the flip-flop can be fed back into the AND array or can be gated to the output by enabling the tri-state inverter. An output enable signal, which controls the enable inputs of all the tri-state buffers, is supplied via a dedicated input pin.

4-bit Binary Counter. As an example of the state machine design using a PAL chip, let us implement a 4-bit binary counter. The state table of the counter is shown in Figure 5.9. The counter has one input terminal which receives pulse signals, and one output (overflow) terminal. It counts up in binary number system up to fifteen. After the count value of fifteen is reached, the next pulse will reset the counter to its initial state (i.e., to a count of zero). Since the registered PALs contain D flip-flops only, we will derive the excita-

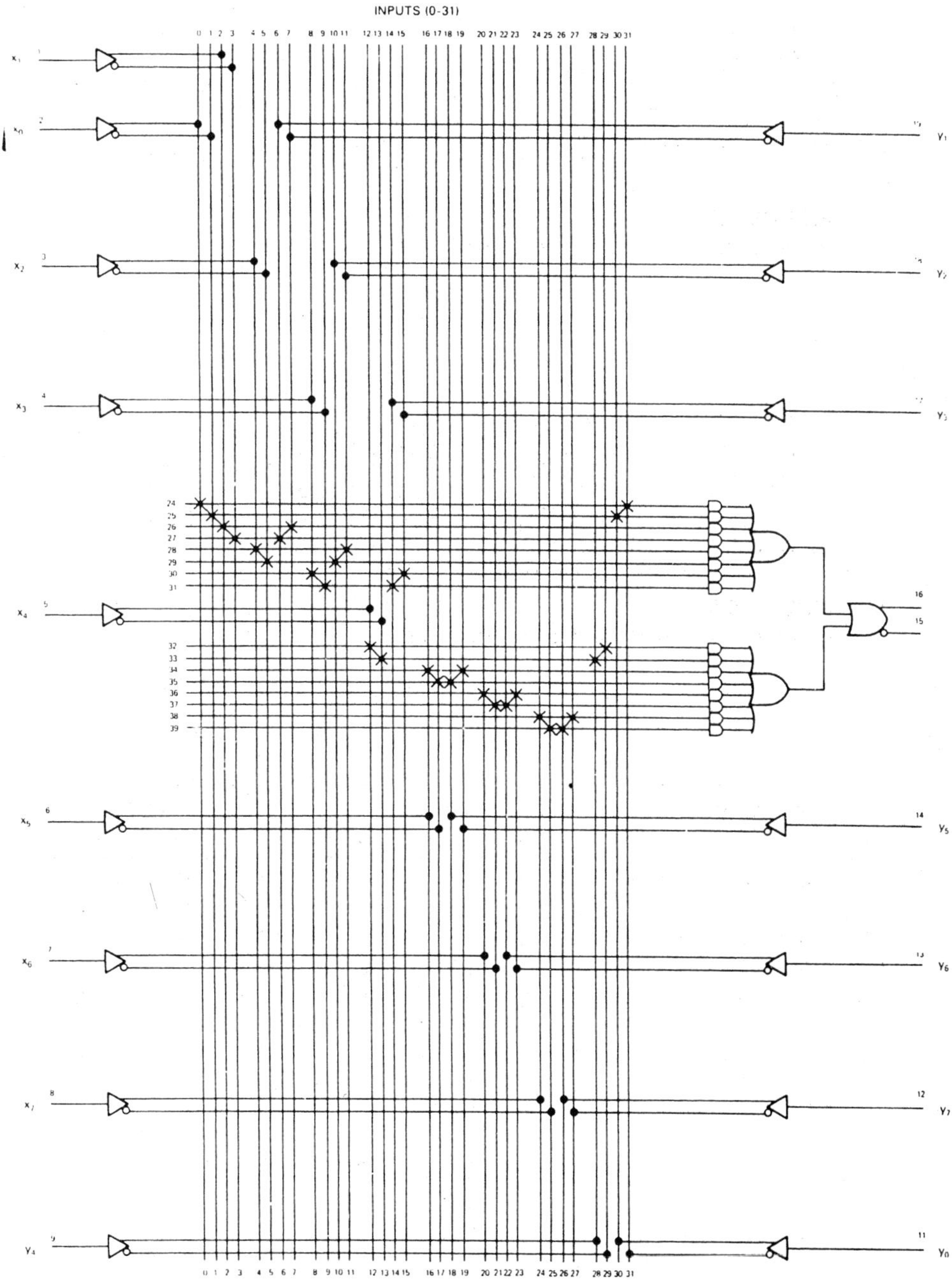

FIGURE 5.6
A 8-bit comparator (Courtesy of AMD, Inc.)

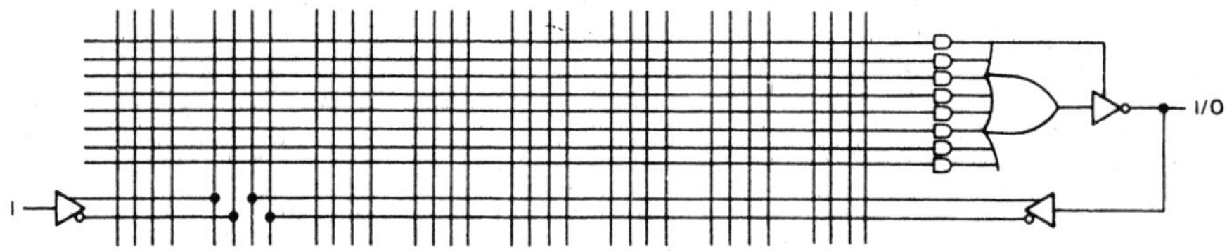

FIGURE 5.7
Programmable I/O (Courtesy of AMD, Inc.)

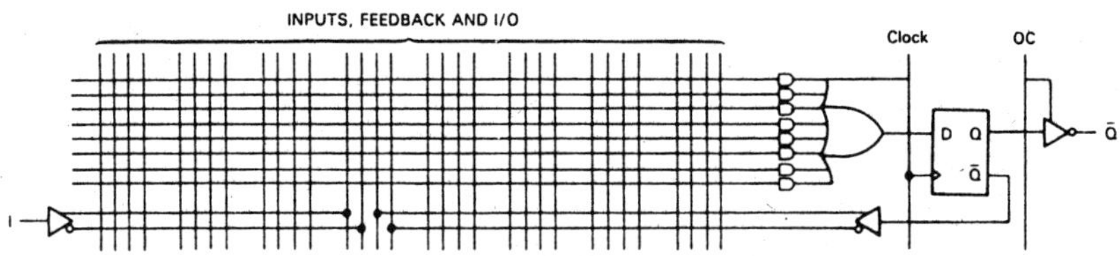

FIGURE 5.8
Registered output (Courtesy of AMD, Inc.)

Present state						*Input*						*Output*	
x_1	x_2	x_3	x_4	$A = 0$				$A = 1$				$A = 0$	$A = 1$
0	0	0	0	0	0	0	0	0	0	0	1	0	0
0	0	0	1	0	0	0	1	0	0	1	0	0	0
0	0	1	0	0	0	1	0	0	0	1	1	0	0
0	0	1	1	0	0	1	1	0	1	0	0	0	0
0	1	0	0	0	1	0	0	0	1	0	1	0	0
0	1	0	1	0	1	0	1	0	1	1	0	0	0
0	1	1	0	0	1	1	0	0	1	1	1	0	0
0	1	1	1	0	1	1	1	1	0	0	0	0	0
1	0	0	0	1	0	0	0	1	0	0	1	0	0
1	0	0	1	1	0	0	1	1	0	1	0	0	0
1	0	1	0	1	0	1	0	1	0	1	1	0	0
1	0	1	1	1	0	1	1	1	1	0	0	0	0
1	1	0	0	1	1	0	0	1	1	0	1	0	0
1	1	0	1	1	1	0	1	1	1	1	0	0	0
1	1	1	0	1	1	1	0	1	1	1	1	0	0
1	1	1	1	1	1	1	1	0	0	0	0	0	1

FIGURE 5.9
State table of the 4-bit counter

tion equations for the 4-bit counter circuit using D flip-flops as memory elements. The minimized excitation equation for each of the D flip-flop can be derived directly from the corresponding Karnaugh map as shown in Figure 5.10a, b, c, and d. The output expression is derived as shown in Figure 5.10e.

Since there are four flip-flops in the circuit, the PAL16R4 is the best choice for implementing the counter. The PAL16R4 has active-low outputs, hence the excitation equations and the output expression have to be complemented. The complemented equations can be derived from the Karnaugh maps and are as follows:

$$\bar{x}_1 = x_1 x_2 x_3 x_4 A + \bar{x}_1 \bar{A} + \bar{x}_1 \bar{x}_3 + \bar{x}_1 \bar{x}_4$$

$$\bar{x}_2 = x_2 x_3 x_4 A + \bar{x}_2 \bar{A} + \bar{x}_2 \bar{x}_3 + \bar{x}_2 \bar{x}_4$$

$$\bar{x}_3 = \bar{x}_3 \bar{A} + x_3 x_4 A + \bar{x}_3 \bar{x}_4$$

$$\bar{x}_4 = \bar{x}_4 \bar{A} + x_4 A$$

$$\bar{Z} = \bar{x}_1 + \bar{x}_2 + \bar{x}_3 + \bar{x}_4 + \bar{A}$$

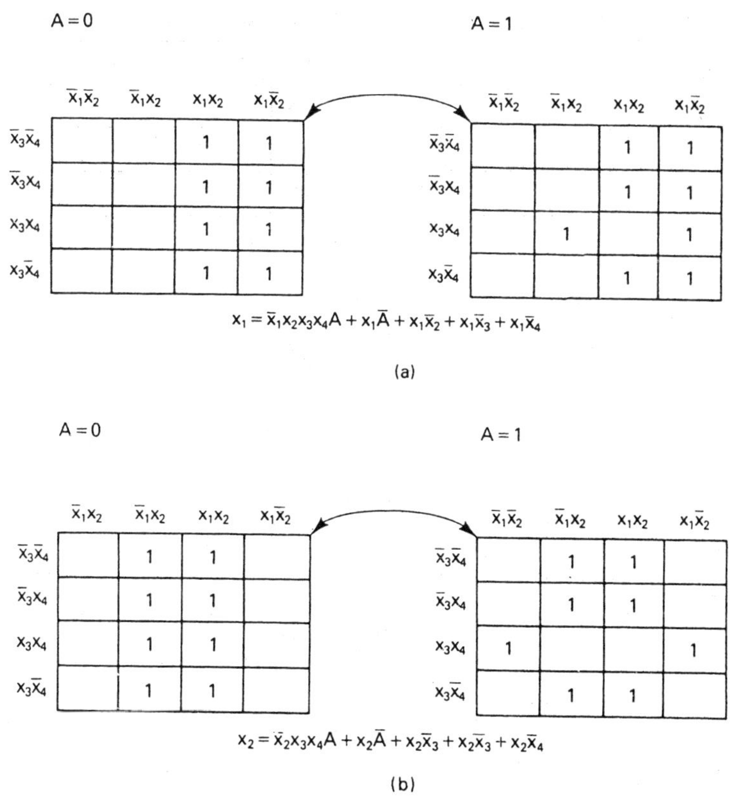

FIGURE 5.10
Karnaugh maps

A = 0

	$\bar{x}_1\bar{x}_2$	$\bar{x}_1x_2$	x_1x_2	$x_1\bar{x}_2$
$\bar{x}_3\bar{x}_4$				
$\bar{x}_3x_4$				
x_3x_4	1	1	1	1
$x_3\bar{x}_4$	1	1	1	1

A = 1

	$\bar{x}_1\bar{x}_2$	$\bar{x}_1x_2$	x_1x_2	$x_1\bar{x}_2$
$\bar{x}_3\bar{x}_4$				
$\bar{x}_3x_4$	1	1	1	1
x_3x_4				
$x_3\bar{x}_4$	1	1	1	1

$$x_3 = x_3\bar{A} + \bar{x}_3x_4A + x_3\bar{x}_4$$

(c)

A = 0

	$\bar{x}_1\bar{x}_2$	$\bar{x}_1x_2$	x_1x_2	$x_1\bar{x}_2$
$\bar{x}_3\bar{x}_4$				
$\bar{x}_3x_4$	1	1	1	1
x_3x_4	1	1	1	1
$x_3\bar{x}_4$				

A = 1

	$\bar{x}_1\bar{x}_2$	x_1x_2	x_1x_2	$x_1\bar{x}_2$
$\bar{x}_3\bar{x}_4$	1	1	1	1
$\bar{x}_3x_4$				
x_3x_4				
$x_3\bar{x}_4$	1	1	1	1

$$x_4 = x_4\bar{A} + \bar{x}_4A$$

(d)

A = 0

	$\bar{x}_1\bar{x}_2$	$\bar{x}_1x_2$	x_1x_2	$x_1\bar{x}_2$
$\bar{x}_3\bar{x}_4$				
$\bar{x}_3x_4$				
x_3x_4				
$x_3\bar{x}_4$				

A = 1

	$\bar{x}_1\bar{x}_2$	$\bar{x}_1x_2$	x_1x_2	$x_1\bar{x}_2$
$\bar{x}_3\bar{x}_4$				
$\bar{x}_3x_4$				
x_3x_4			1	
$x_3\bar{x}_4$				

$$Z = x_1x_2x_3x_4A$$

(e)

FIGURE 5.10
Karnaugh maps (cont'd)

The programmed logic diagram of the PAL16R4 is shown in Figure 5.11. Notice that the logic value corresponding to the complemented sum-of-products expressions are loaded into the D flip-flops; the outputs of the D flip-flops are inverted by the tri-state inverters, resulting in true outputs.

8-bit Parallel CRC Generator. **Cyclic redundancy check** (CRC) codes are primarily used for checking data stored in sequential access memory devices such as magnetic tapes and floppy disks. With serial input data, CRC codes are generated using linear feedback shift registers. In a parallel bus-oriented system however, it is more appropriate to have a CRC generator in which a word of data can be loaded into the code generator circuit. In other words, if the word length is 8 bits, then all 8 bits should be clocked into the CRC register for each bus cycle. In addition, there should be combinational logic to generate the next state of the CRC register corresponding to the 8-bit word.

Figure 5.12 shows the implementation of an 8-bit CRC code generator circuit for serial data [2]. Initially, the shift register is reset so that it contains all 0's. Let us define Y_n to be the state of the shift register after n shifts. Thus, after the shift register has been reset, $Y_0 = 0$. Let d_0 through d_{n-1} be the n serial data bits. After the first data bit d_0 has been clocked into the shift register, $Y_1 = d_0 x$, where x is an elementary vector. After the second data bit d_1 has been clocked into the shift register, $Y_2 = d_0 Tx \oplus d_1 x$, where T is a 8×8 matrix as shown below:

$$T = \begin{vmatrix} 0 & 0 & 0 & 0 & 0 & 1 & 0 & 1 \\ 1 & 0 & 0 & 0 & 0 & 0 & 0 & 0 \\ 0 & 1 & 0 & 0 & 0 & 0 & 0 & 0 \\ 0 & 0 & 1 & 0 & 0 & 0 & 0 & 0 \\ 0 & 0 & 0 & 1 & 0 & 0 & 0 & 0 \\ 0 & 0 & 0 & 0 & 1 & 0 & 0 & 0 \\ 0 & 0 & 0 & 0 & 0 & 1 & 0 & 0 \\ 0 & 0 & 0 & 0 & 0 & 0 & 1 & 0 \end{vmatrix}$$

The first row in the matrix indicates the feedback connections (e.g., column 6 and column 8 being 1 indicate feedback from y_5 and y_7, respectively). The remaining rows in T form an identity matrix. After the third bit d_2 has been clocked into the CRC register $Y_3 = d_0 T^2 x \oplus d_1 Tx \oplus d_2 x$. The state of the CRC register after n data bits have been shifted into it is:

$$Y_n = d_0 T^{n-1} x \oplus \cdots \oplus d_{n-2} Tx \oplus d_{n-1} x$$

This equation can be used to develop the logic equations for implementing the 8-bit parallel CRC generator. The input data is first relabeled as:

$$d_0 d_1 \cdots d_6 d_7 d_0 d_1 \cdots d_6 d_7 d_0 d_1 \cdots d_6 d_7$$

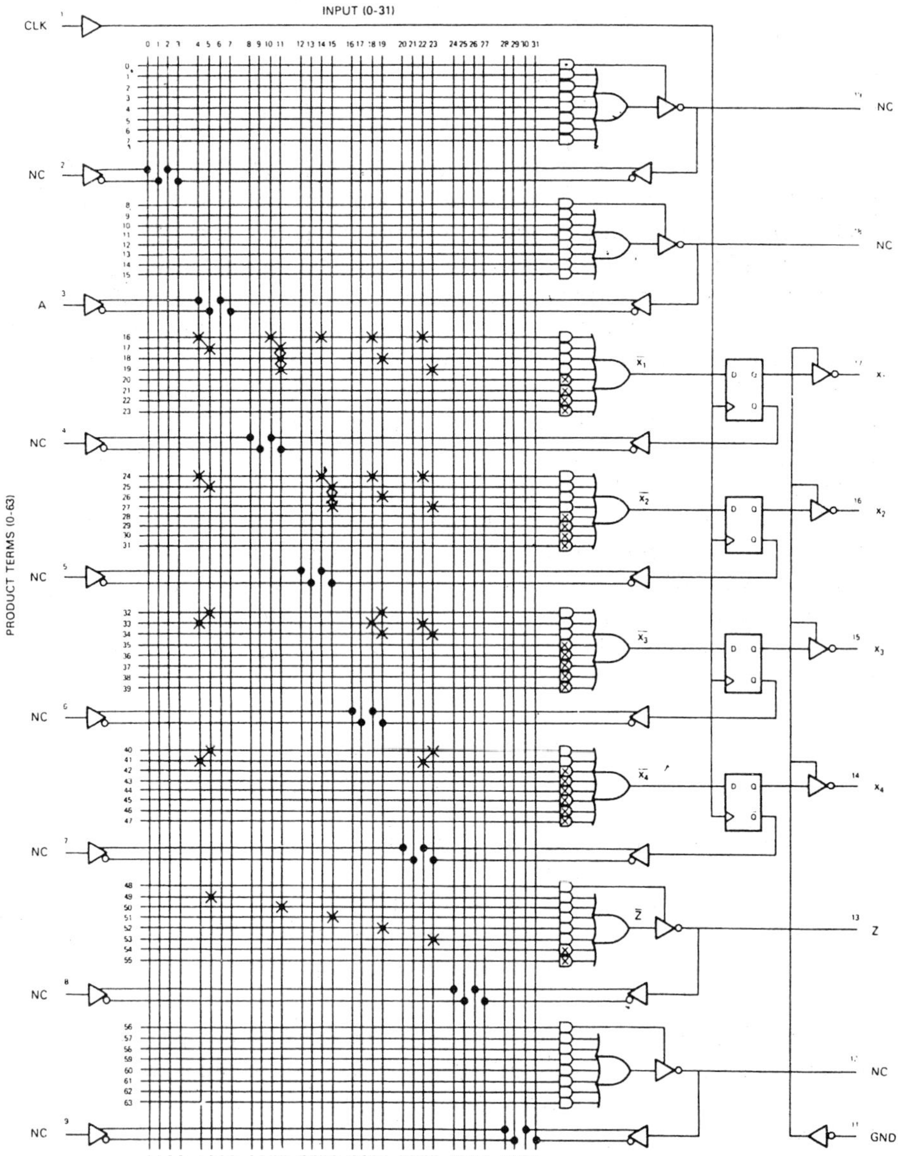

FIGURE 5.11a
4-bit binary counter (Courtesy of AMD, Inc.)

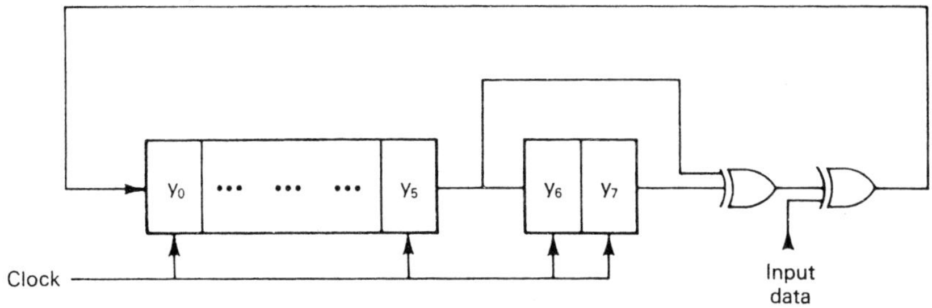

FIGURE 5.12
Serial CRC code generator

Thus, the input data can be considered to be a serial bit stream with a length equal to 8 times the number of words in the data stream. The next state of the shift register, Y_{n+8}, corresponding to the present input data, d_0 to d_7 and the present state Y_n is given by:

$$\begin{aligned} Y_{n+8} &= [d_0 T^7 x \oplus \cdots \oplus d_6 Tx \oplus d_7 x] \oplus [T^8 Y_n] \\ &= d_0 T^7 x \oplus d_1 T^6 x \oplus d_2 T^5 x \oplus d_3 T^4 x \oplus d_4 T^3 x \\ &\quad \oplus d_5 T^2 x \oplus d_6 Tx \oplus d_7 x \oplus T^8 Y_n \end{aligned}$$

The next state equation, Y_i, for each bit of the parallel CRC generator can be derived from the above expression:

$$\begin{aligned} Y_7 &= d_0 \oplus y_5 \oplus y_7 = d_0 y_5 y_7 + \bar{d}_0 \bar{y}_5 y_7 + d_0 \bar{y}_5 \bar{y}_7 + \bar{d}_0 y_5 \bar{y}_7 \\ Y_6 &= d_1 \oplus y_4 \oplus y_6 = d_1 y_4 y_6 + \bar{d}_1 \bar{y}_4 y_6 + d_1 \bar{y}_4 \bar{y}_6 + \bar{d}_1 y_4 \bar{y}_6 \\ Y_5 &= d_2 \oplus y_3 \oplus y_5 = d_2 y_3 y_5 + \bar{d}_2 \bar{y}_3 y_5 + d_2 \bar{y}_3 \bar{y}_5 + \bar{d}_2 y_3 \bar{y}_5 \\ Y_4 &= d_3 \oplus y_2 \oplus y_4 = d_3 y_2 y_4 + \bar{d}_3 \bar{y}_2 y_4 + d_3 \bar{y}_2 \bar{y}_4 + \bar{d}_3 y_2 \bar{y}_4 \\ Y_3 &= d_4 \oplus y_1 \oplus y_3 = d_4 y_1 y_3 + \bar{d}_4 \bar{y}_1 y_3 + d_4 \bar{y}_1 \bar{y}_3 + \bar{d}_4 y_1 \bar{y}_3 \\ Y_2 &= d_5 \oplus y_0 \oplus y_2 = d_5 y_0 y_2 + \bar{d}_5 \bar{y}_0 y_2 + d_5 \bar{y}_0 \bar{y}_2 + \bar{d}_5 y_0 \bar{y}_2 \\ Y_1 &= d_0 \oplus d_6 \oplus y_1 \oplus y_5 \oplus y_7 \\ &= d_0 d_6 \\ Y_0 &= d_1 \oplus d_7 \oplus y_0 \oplus y_4 \oplus y_6 \end{aligned}$$

The above expressions can be directly implemented using two PAL16R4s, interconnected as shown in Figure 5.13. Each device implements part of the next state equations. Note that the value on the data bus is the inversion of the CRC register contents. The coded logic diagram of the PAL16R4s are shown in Figure 5.14a (chip 1) and Figure 5.14b (chip 2).

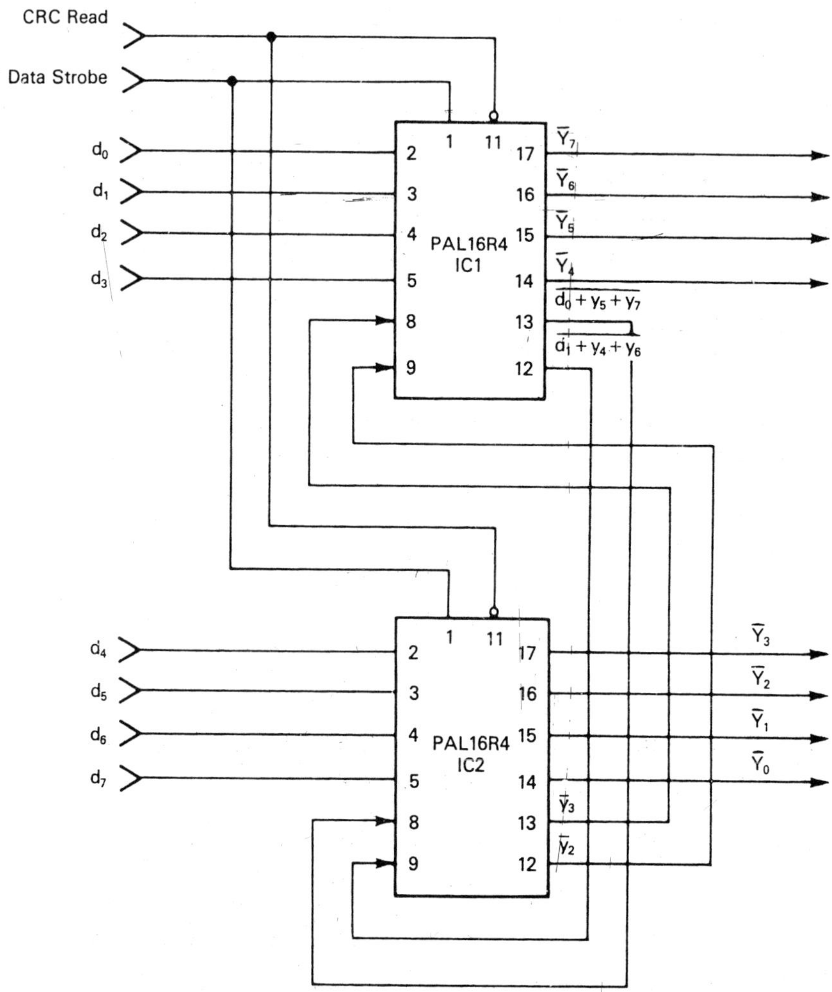

FIGURE 5.13
8-bit parallel CRC generator

BCD Adder. The adder receives a pair of BCD digits and produces their sum in BCD format; any carry bit generated is stored and is added to the next pair of BCD digits. The block diagram of the adder is shown in Figure 5.15.

The Boolean expressions required to implement the adder are as follows:

$$b_0 = cs \oplus x_0 \oplus y_0 = \overline{cs}\,\overline{x}_0\,y_0 + \overline{cs}x_0\,\overline{y}_0 + cs\overline{x}_0\,\overline{y}_0 + csx_0\,y_0$$

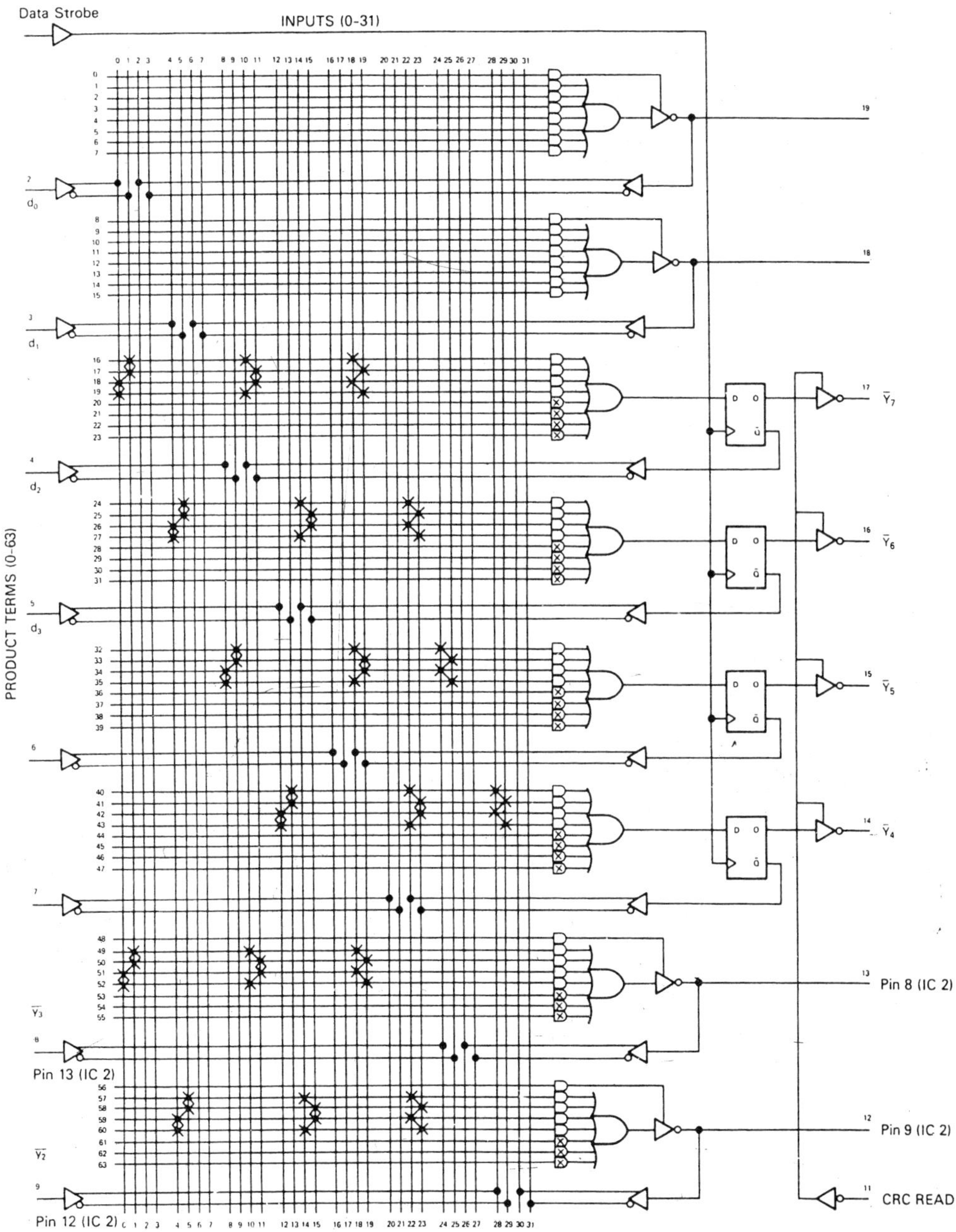

(a)

FIGURE 5.14a
CRC generator IC1 (Courtesy of AMD, Inc.)

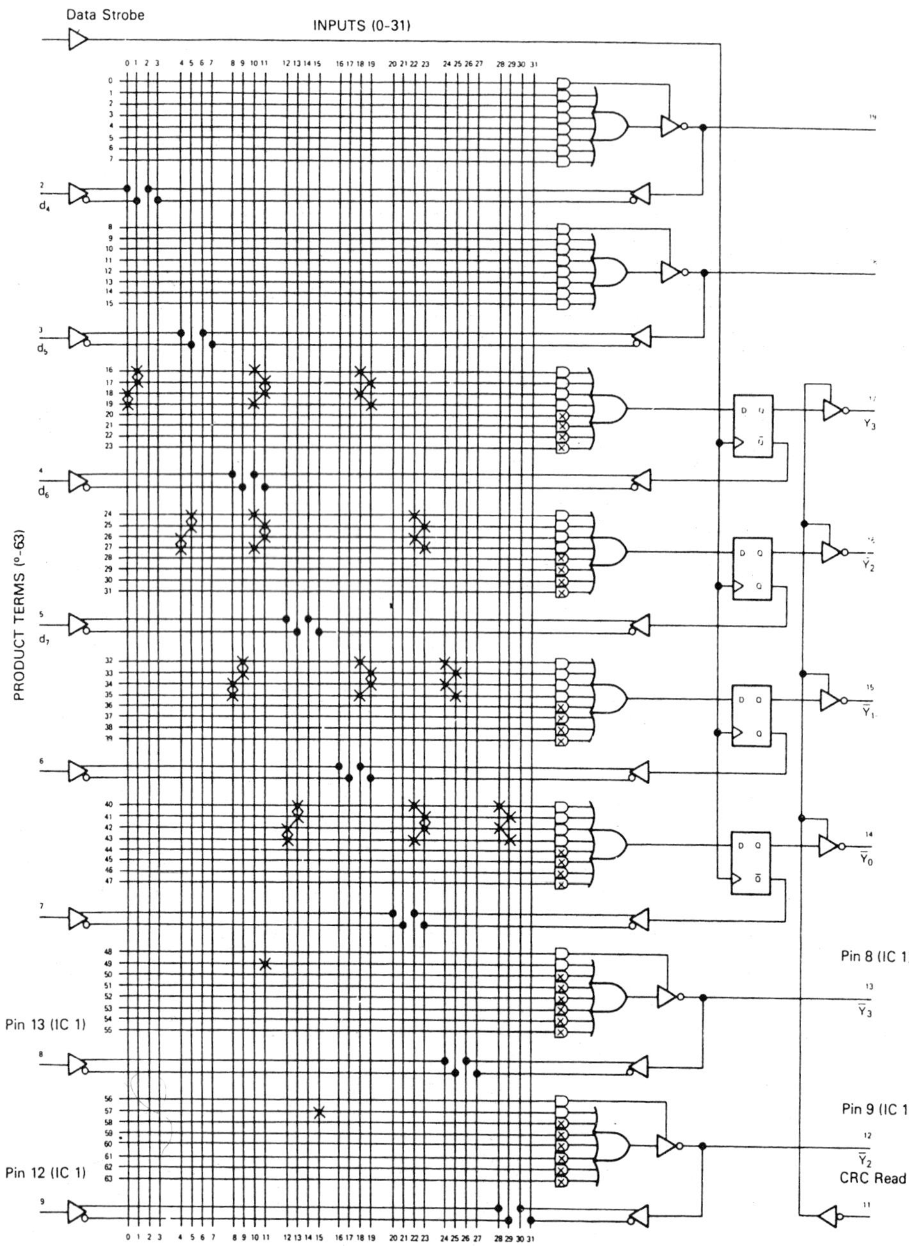

(b)

FIGURE 5.14b
CRC generator IC2 (Courtesy of AMD, Inc.)

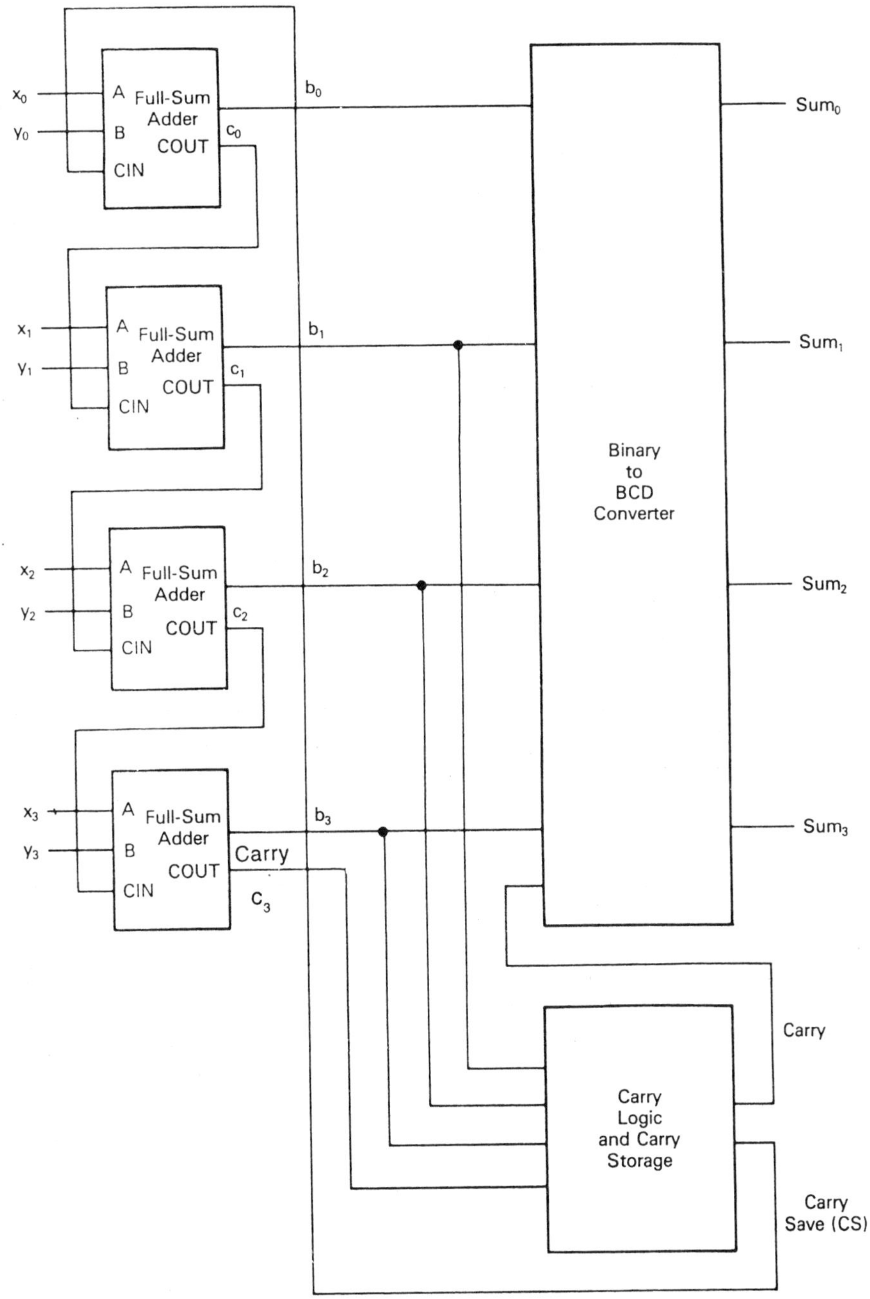

FIGURE 5.15
Bit-parallel, digit serial BCD adder (© Reprinted with the permission of tl GE Microelectronics Center.)

Similarly,

$$b_1 = \bar{c}_0 \bar{x}_1 y_1 + \bar{c}_0 x_1 \bar{y}_1 + c_0 \bar{x}_1 \bar{y}_1 + c_0 x_1 y_1$$

$$b_2 = \bar{c}_1 \bar{x}_2 y_2 + \bar{c}_1 x_2 \bar{y}_2 + c_1 \bar{x}_2 \bar{y}_2 + c_1 x_2 y_2$$

$$b_3 = \bar{c}_2 \bar{x}_3 y_3 + \bar{c}_2 x_3 \bar{y}_3 + c_2 \bar{x}_3 \bar{y}_3 + c_2 x_3 y_3$$

$$c_0 = csx_0 + csy_0 + x_0 y_0$$

$$c_1 = c_0 x_1 + c_0 y_1 + x_1 y_1$$

$$c_2 = c_1 x_2 + c_1 y_2 + x_2 y_2$$

$$\text{Carry} = c_3 + (b_1 + b_2)b_3$$

$$= c_2 x_3 + c_2 y_3 + x_3 y_3 + b_1 b_3 + b_2 b_3$$

The output expressions for the binary to BCD converter are as follows:

$$\text{Sum}_0 = b_0$$

$$\text{Sum}_1 = \text{carry} \oplus b_1$$

$$\text{Sum}_2 = b_1 b_2 + \overline{\text{carry}} \bullet b_2 + \text{carry} \bullet \bar{b}_1 \bar{b}_2$$

$$\text{Sum}_3 = \text{carry} \bullet b_1 \bullet \bar{b}_3 + \text{carry} \bullet b_2 \bullet \bar{b}_3 + \overline{\text{carry}} \bullet b_3 + \bar{b}_1 \bar{b}_2 b_3$$

The carry bit generated during the addition of two BCD digits is "saved" in a D flip-flop. The output of the flip-flop is connected to the carry-in input of the least significant adder. The excitation equation for the D flip-flop is:

$$cs = \text{carry} \bullet \overline{\text{Reset}}$$

The BCD adder can be implemented by using a PAL16L8 and PAL16R4 as shown in Figure 5.16. The PAL16L8 generates the sum and the intermediate carry bits, whereas the PAL16R4 converts the binary to BCD and generates the carry-save output bit. The coded logic diagram of the PAL16L8 and the PAL16R4 are shown in Figure 5.17. The PAL16L8 actually generates the complements of all the sum and carry bits. The PAL16R4 generates the complements of the BCD code corresponding to the sum bits, as well as the inverted carry-save bit. Hence, the complements of Sum_{0-3} and cs are programmed into the PAL16R4. The complemented expressions are given by:

$$\overline{\text{Sum}_0} = \bar{b}_0$$

$$\overline{\text{Sum}_1} = \text{carry} \bullet b_1 + \overline{\text{carry}} \bullet \bar{b}_1$$

$$\overline{\text{Sum}_2} = b_1 \bullet \bar{b}_2 + \overline{\text{carry}} \bullet \bar{b}_2 + \text{carry} \bullet \bar{b}_1 \bullet b_2$$

$$\overline{\text{Sum}_3} = \text{carry} \bullet b_1 \bullet b_2 + \text{carry} \bullet b_2 \bullet b_3 + \overline{\text{carry}} \bullet \bar{b}_3 + \bar{b}_1 \bar{b}_2 \bar{b}_3$$

$$\overline{cs} = \overline{\text{carry}} + \text{Reset}$$

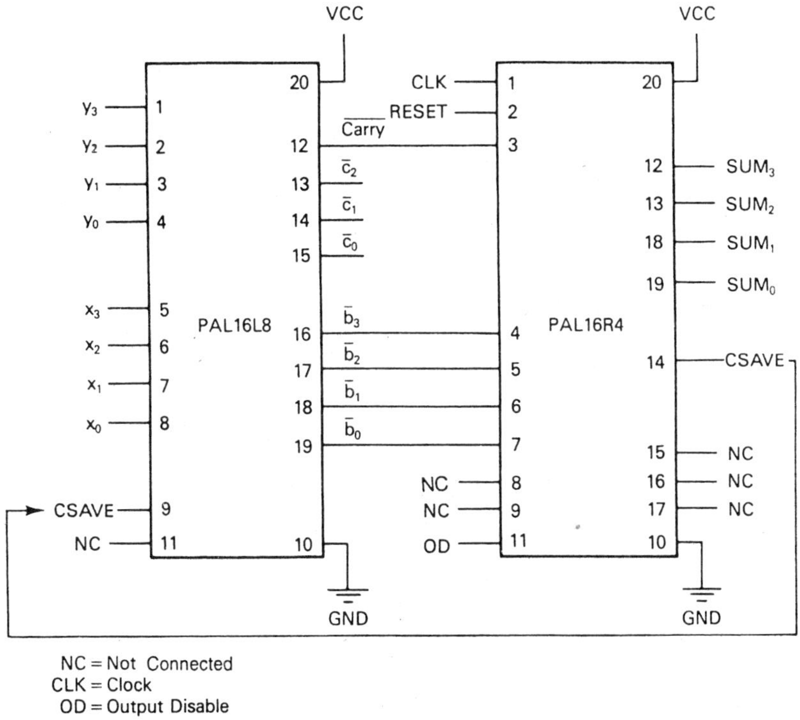

FIGURE 5.16
Implementation of the BCD adder using PAL chips

Asynchronous State Machine Design. The registered PALs are used to implement synchronous state machines. The PALs with programmable I/O capability can be employed to implement asynchronous state machines. We shall illustrate the application of the PAL16L8 in the design of the asynchronous state machine as specified in Figure 5.18. The minimum-row flow table corresponding to Figure 5.18 is shown in Figure 5.19. If we use the state assignment at the left below, the following Boolean equations result:

	$y_1\,y_2$	
A $\longrightarrow$	0 0	$y_1 = x_1y_1 + x_2y_1 + \bar{x}_1\bar{x}_2y_2$
(B,F) $\longrightarrow$	0 1	
C $\longrightarrow$	1 1	$y_2 = x_1\bar{y}_1 + x_2\bar{y}_1 + \bar{x}_1\bar{x}_2y_2$
(D,E) $\longrightarrow$	1 0	$Z = y_1 + y_2$

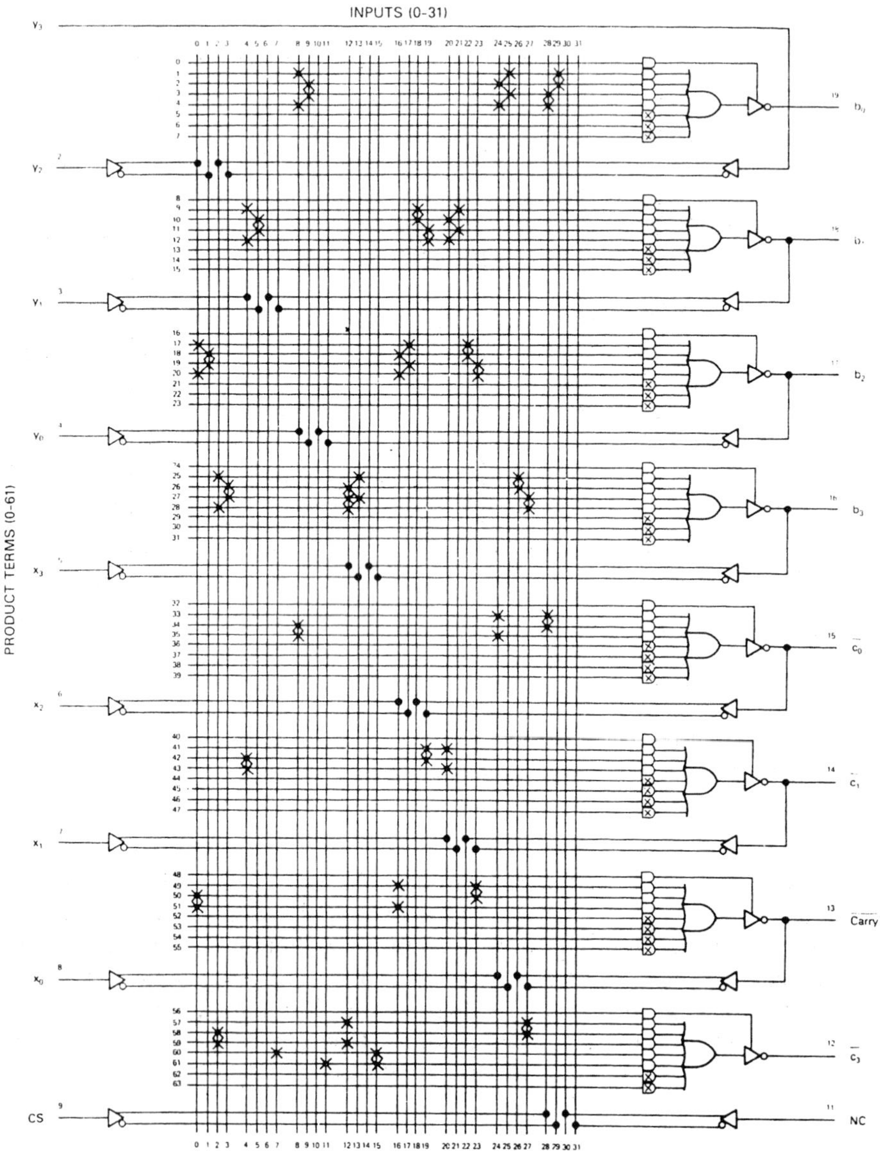

(a)

FIGURE 5.17a
4-bit adder (Courtesy of AMD, Inc.)

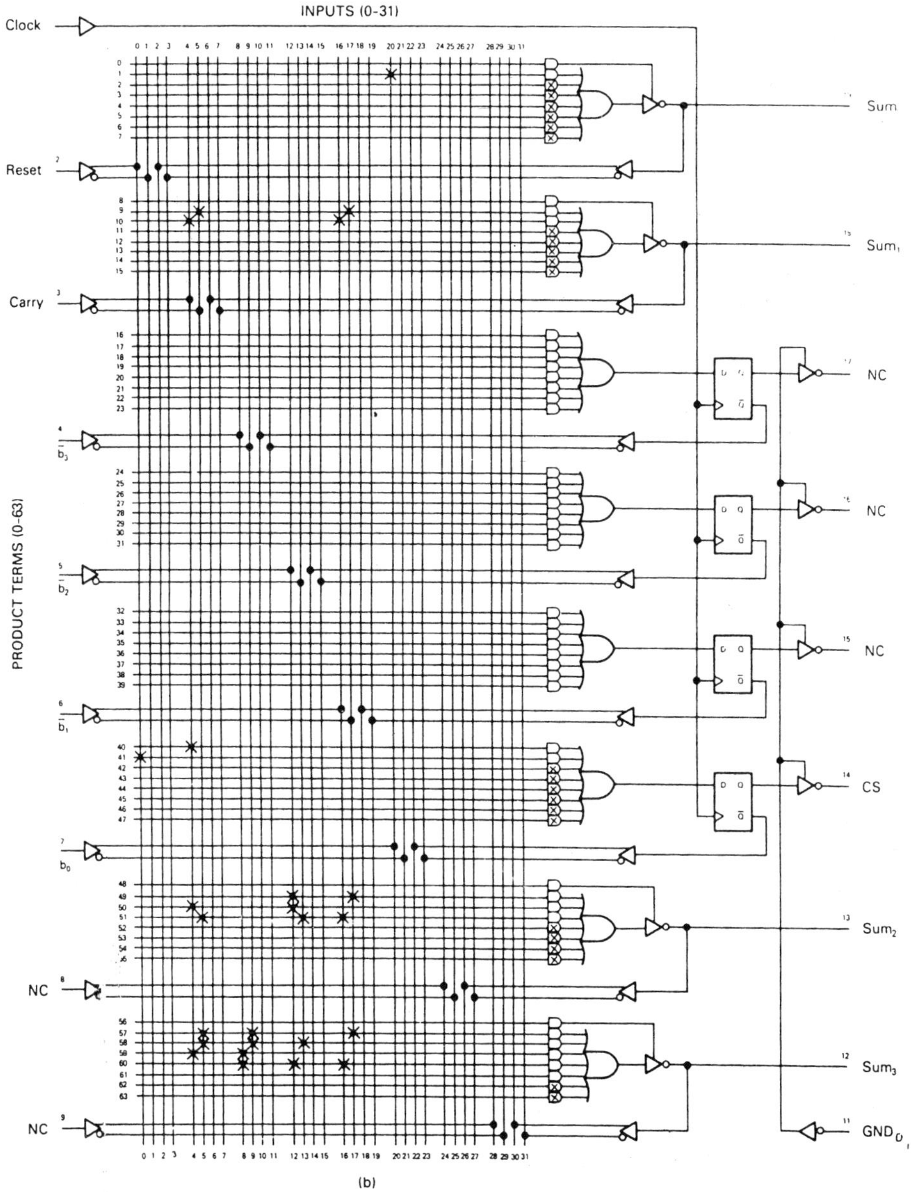

FIGURE 5.17b
Binary-to-BCD converter and carry-save generator (Courtesy of AMD, Inc.)

Present state \ Input	$\bar{x}_1\bar{x}_2$	$\bar{x}_1 x_2$	$x_1 x_2$	$x_1\bar{x}_2$
A	Ⓐ,0	B	—	F
B	C	Ⓑ,1	—	—
C	Ⓒ,1	E	—	D
D	A	—	—	Ⓓ,1
E	A	Ⓔ,1	—	—
F	C	—	—	Ⓕ,1

FIGURE 5.18
An asynchronous state machine

Present state	$\bar{x}_1\bar{x}_2$	$\bar{x}_1 x_2$	$x_1 x_2$	$x_1\bar{x}_2$
A	Ⓐ,0	B	—	F
(B,F)	C	Ⓑ,1	—	Ⓕ,1
C	Ⓒ,1	E	—	D
(D,E)	A	Ⓔ,1	—	Ⓓ,1

FIGURE 5.19
Minimized flow table

Since the PAL16L8 has active-low output, the complement of the above expressions have to be programmed into the device. The complement of the expressions are:

$$\bar{y}_1 = \bar{x}_1\bar{x}_2\bar{y}_2 + x_1\bar{y}_1 + x_2\bar{y}_1$$

$$\bar{y}_2 = \bar{x}_1\bar{x}_2\bar{y}_2 + x_1 y_1 + x_2 y_1$$

$$\overline{Z} = \bar{y}_1\bar{y}_2$$

Figure 5.20 shows the coded logic diagram of PAL16L8.

5.1.3 Arithmetic PAL Devices

This is the smallest group of PAL devices, consisting of two units: PAL16A4 and PAL16X4. In these devices, the sum-of-products is partitioned into two blocks which are combined by EX-OR gates at the input of a D flip-flop, as shown in Figure 5.21. This feature allows carrys from previous operations to be EX-ORed with the sum of two variables generated within the device.

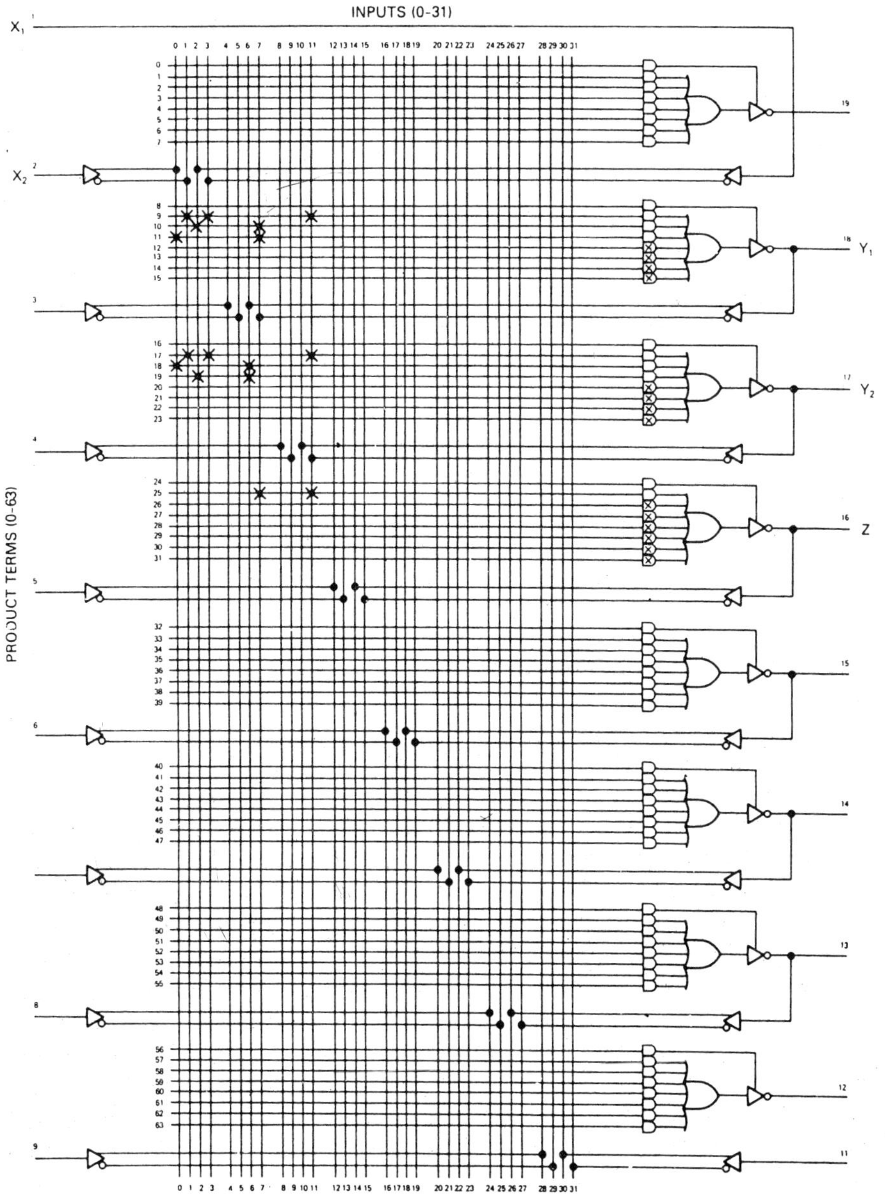

FIGURE 5.20
Implementation of the asynchronous state machine of Figure 5.19 (Courtesy of AMD, Inc.)

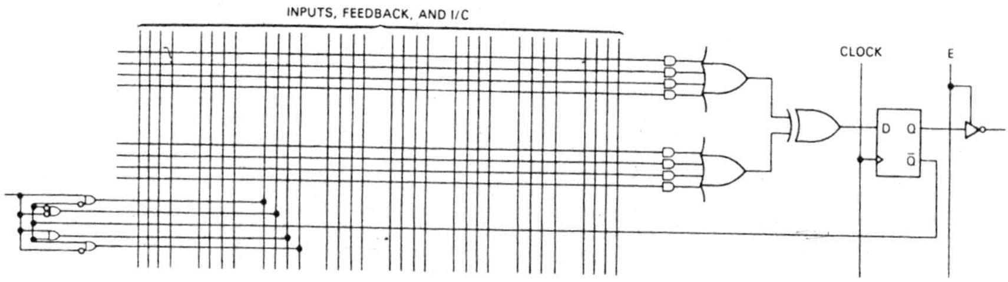

FIGURE 5.21
Arithmetic-gated feedback (Courtesy of AMD, Inc.)

Furthermore, in these two devices, the inverted output of a D flip-flop, B, is combined with input A to form:

$$A + B, \quad \overline{A} + B, \quad A + \overline{B} \text{ and } \overline{A} + \overline{B}$$

These are then used as inputs to the PAL. This capability allows the formation of sixteen Boolean functions corresponding to variables A and B (Figure 5.22).

As an example of the application of these devices we shall design a 4-bit ALU using PAL16A4. The ALU can perform nine operations, an operation is selected by a 4-bit opcode. Figure 5.23 lists the opcodes and the corresponding operations of the ALU. We assume that the 4 flip-flops inside the PAL16A4 constitute a 4-bit accumulator which we identify as A. Thus A + B in Figure 5.23 indicates that the first operand is already in A and operand $B(= b_3 b_2 b_1 b_0)$ supplied via the input pins 4, 5, 6, and 7 of the PAL16A4, is added to the contents of $A(= a_3 a_2 a_1 a_0)$ and the sum is stored back in A. In the case of subtraction it is assumed that the 1's complement of B is available on the input pins of the PAL16A4.

The PAL16A4 has active-low outputs, hence, the logic expressions required to implement the ALU must be complemented first before programming into the device in order to get true outputs. The logic expressions are as follows:

$$\bar{a}_0 = [\bar{I}_2 \bar{I}_1 (\overline{a_0 \oplus b_0}) + \bar{I}_2 I_1 I_0 (\bar{a}_0 + \bar{b}_0) + \bar{I}_2 I_1 \bar{I}_0 \bullet \bar{b}_0 + I_2 \bar{I}_1 \bar{I}_0 \bullet b_0]$$

$$\oplus [I_2 \bar{I}_1 I \cdot \bar{a}_0 \bar{b}_0 + \bar{I}_2 \bar{I}_1 I_0]$$

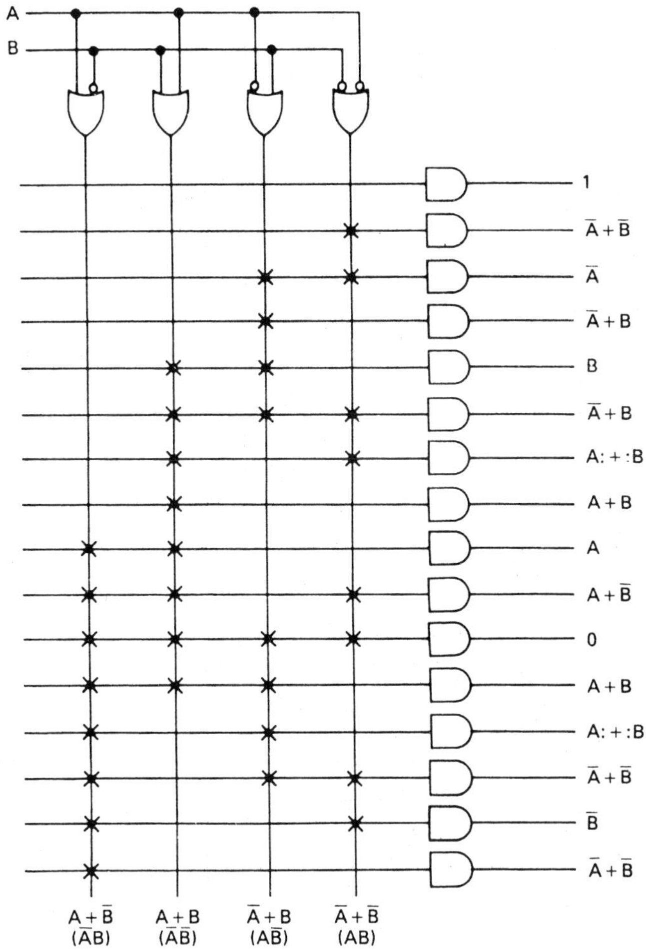

FIGURE 5.22
Formation of Boolean functions (Courtesy of AMD, Inc.)

Opcode I_2	I_1	I_0	*Mnemonic*	*Operation*
0	0	0	ADD B	A := A + B
0	0	1	SUB B	A := A − B (2"s complement)
1	0	0	COMPLEMENT	A := $\overline{B}$
1	0	1	OR	A := A .OR. B
0	1	0	LOAD B	A := B
0	1	1	A AND B	A := A AND B

FIGURE 5.23
ALU operations

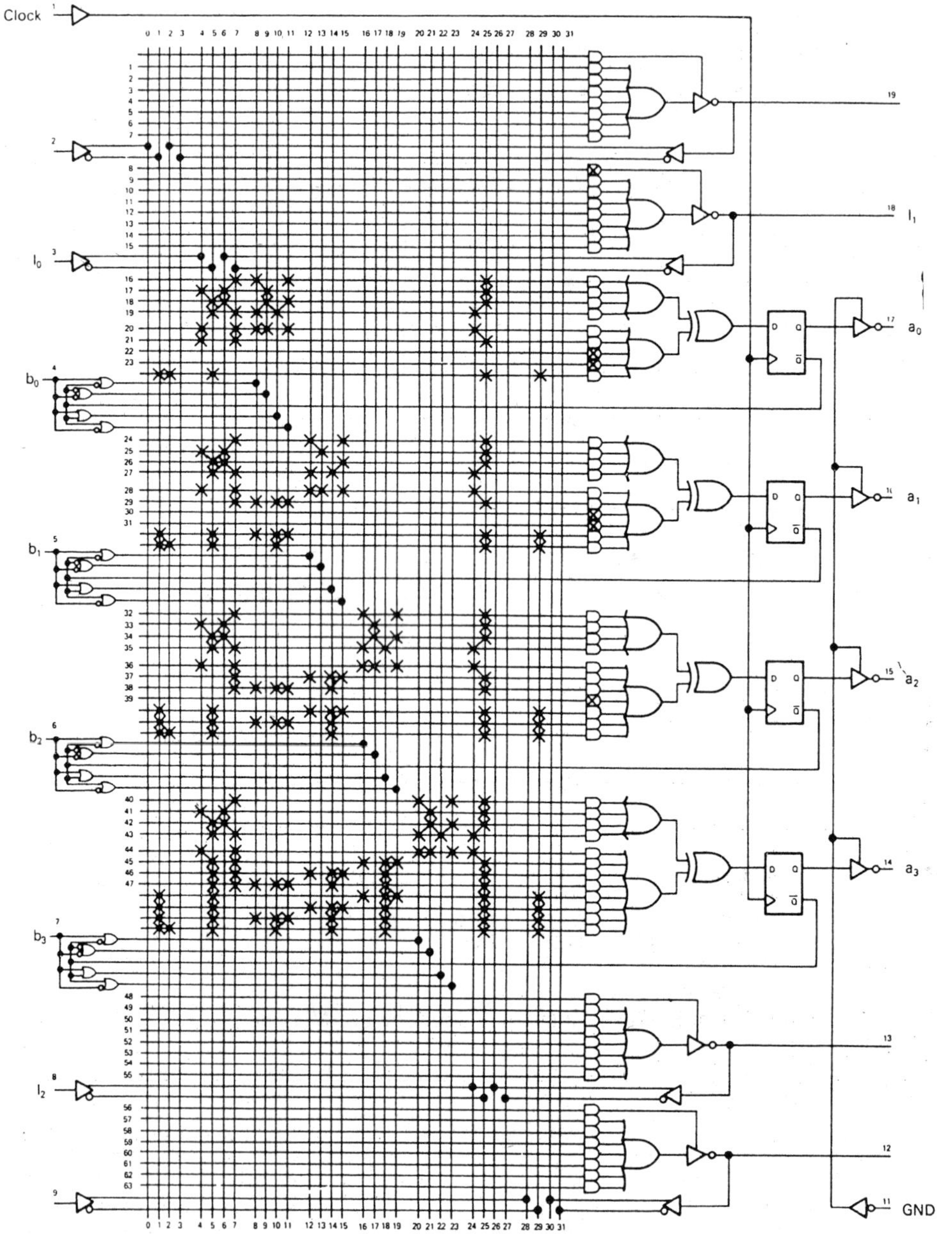

FIGURE 5.24
4-bit ALU. (Courtesy of AMD, Inc.)

Add 1 for 2's complement subtraction,

$$\begin{aligned}
\bar{a}_1 = {} & [\bar{I}_2 \bar{I}_1(\overline{a_1 \oplus b_1}) + \bar{I}_2 I_1 I_0(\bar{a}_1 + \bar{b}_1) + \bar{I}_2 I_1 \bar{I}_0 \bullet \bar{b}_1 + I_2 \bar{I}_1 \bar{I}_0 \bullet b_1] \\
& \oplus [I_2 \bar{I}_1 I_0 \bullet \bar{a}_1 \bar{b}_1 + \bar{I}_2 \bar{I}_1 \bullet a_0 b_0] \\
\bar{a}_2 = {} & [\bar{I}_2 \bar{I}_1(\overline{a_2 \oplus b_2}) + \bar{I}_2 I_1 I_0(\bar{a}_2 + \bar{b}_2) + \bar{I}_2 I_1 \bar{I}_0 \bullet \bar{b}_2 + I_2 \bar{I}_1 \bar{I}_0 \bullet b_2] \\
& \oplus [I_2 \bar{I}_1 I_0 \bullet \bar{a}_2 \bar{b}_2 + \bar{I}_2 \bar{I}_1 \bullet a_1 b_1 + \bar{I}_2 \bar{I}_1(a_1 + b_1) a_0 b_0] \\
\bar{a}_3 = {} & [\bar{I}_2 \bar{I}_1(\overline{a_3 \oplus b_3}) + \bar{I}_2 I_1 I_0(\bar{a}_3 + \bar{b}_3) + \bar{I}_2 I_1 \bar{I}_0 \bullet \bar{b}_3 + I_2 \bar{I}_1 \bar{I}_0 \bullet b_3] \\
& \oplus [I_2 \bar{I}_1 I_0 \bullet \bar{a}_3 \bar{b}_3 + \bar{I}_2 \bar{I}_1 \bar{I}_0 \bullet a_2 b_2 + \bar{I}_2 \bar{I}_1 \bar{I}_0(a_2 + b_2) a_1 b_1 \\
& + \bar{I}_2 \bar{I}_1 \bar{I}_0(a_2 + b_2)(a_1 + b_1) a_0 b_0]
\end{aligned}$$

These expressions have been coded into the logic diagram of the PAL16A4 as shown in Figure 5.24.

5.2 PAL SERIES 24

The 24-pin versions of PALs were introduced to extend the range and size of designs that could be accommodated by using PALs. Initially, this group included ten devices:

- PAL12L10
- PAL14L8
- PAL16L6
- PAL18L4
- PAL20L2
- PAL20C1
- PAL20L10
- PAL20X10
- PAL20X8
- PAL20X4

These devices are simple extensions of the original Series 20 PAL family. For example 12L10, 14L8, and 16L6 have the same features as 10L8, 12L6, and 14L4, respectively, except the 24-pins versions have two additional inputs and outputs. The 18L4, 20L2, 20C1, 20X4 are similar to 14L4, 16L2, 16C1 and 16X4, respectively, except that they have four extra inputs. Both 20L10 and

20X10 have 10 dedicated inputs as well as 10 outputs. However, in the 20L10, the output pins if not used can be used as inputs whereas this is not possible in 20X10. The 20X8 has 8 registered outputs (compared to 10 in 20X10), and two non-registered outputs which can also be used as inputs.

More recently, several other devices have been included in the Series 24 PAL family by AMD, Texas Instruments, and others.

PAL20L8
PAL20R8
PAL20R6
PAL20R4
PAL20S10
PAL20RS4
PAL20RS8
PAL20RS10
PAL20RA10
PAL32VX10
PAL22V10

The 20L8, 20R8, 20R6, and 20R4 have the same characteristics as their 20-pin counterparts. In addition, they have four extra inputs. The PAL20S10 has 12 dedicated inputs, 2 dedicated outputs, and eight programmable I/O lines. This device allows "sharing" of 16 product terms between two output cells (the "S" denotes shared), as shown in Figure 5.25. Either output can use any of the 16 product terms, however if a product term is used by one output, the same product term cannot be used by the other output. Thus, the term **product sharing** is probably misused in this case; it is basically partitioning the product terms into two disjoint blocks, each block being used by one output. The output polarity of the device is programmable.

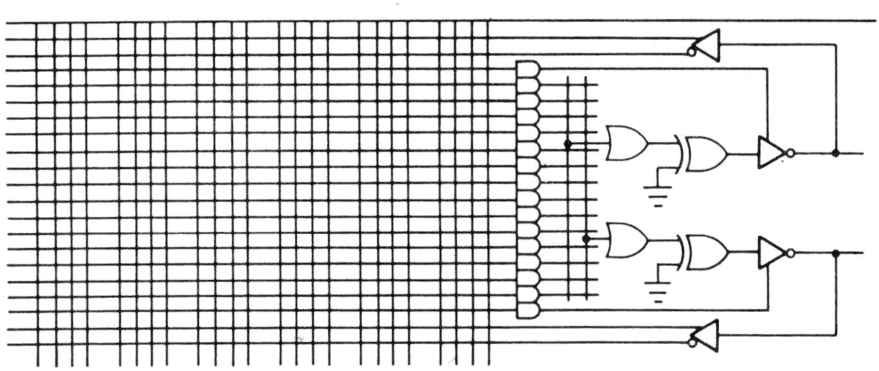

FIGURE 5.25
Registered output with product sharing (Courtesy of AMD, Inc.)

The 20RS4, 20RS8 and 20RS10 have 10 dedicated inputs, and 4, 8 and 10 registered outputs, respectively. In addition, the 20RS4 has 6 programmable I/O lines, and the 20RS8 has 2 programmable I/O lines. All three devices, like the 20S10, have the product term sharing capability, as well as the programmable output polarity feature.

PAL20RA10. The PAL20RA10 has certain features which make it unique among the PAL devices considered so far. It has 10 dedicated inputs, and 10 programmable I/O lines. The outputs can be registered or non-registered; the "RA" in the device identification number denotes "registered asynchronous." A 20-pin version of this device, PAL16RA8, is already in production.

The PAL20RA10 basically consists of 10 identical cells. Figure 5.26 shows the logic diagram of a cell. As can be seen in the diagram the clock, the set, and the reset inputs of the D flip-flop are controlled by individual product terms. When the set product term is high, the output of the D flip-flop becomes logic "1." Alternatively, if the reset product term is high, the output of the D flip-flop is forced to logic "0." The set and reset functions override the clock. If both the set and reset product terms are activated simultaneously, the flip-flop becomes transparent, and the output of the cell corresponds to the sum of four product terms or its complement. This feature enables each output to be either registered or combinational. In addition, since the clock input of the flip-flop is driven by a product term, the flip-flop can be triggered only by activating

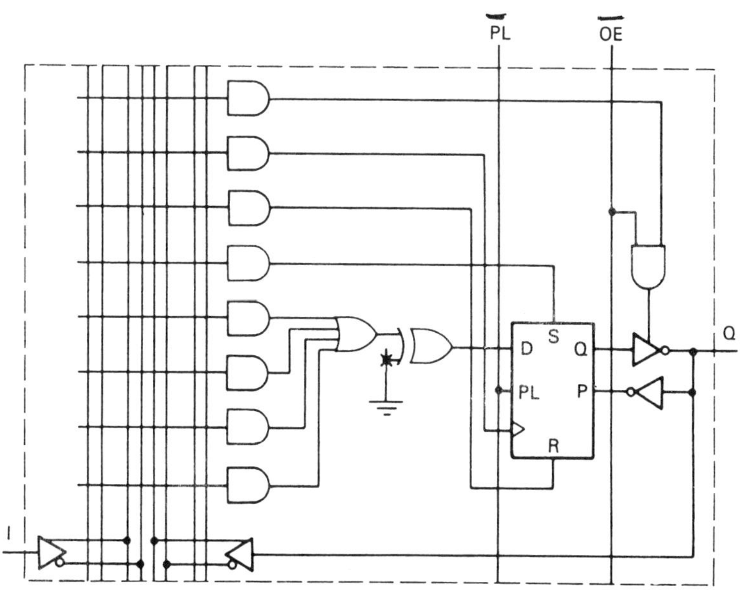

FIGURE 5.26
A cell of PAL20RA10 (Courtesy of AMD, Inc.)

the product term. Thus, each flip-flop in the PAL20RA10 can be clocked independently of the others by activating the appropriate product terms in the corresponding cell.

The device has two dedicated inputs, one is used to provide an output enable signal, the other is used for preloading the flip-flops with a known state. The enable signal for the tri-state inverter at the output of each cell is generated by ANDing the externally applied enable signal with the dedicated product term inside the cell. When the signal on the enable input line is at logic "0," the tri-state inverters are enabled or disabled depending on whether the corresponding product term is activated or not activated, respectively. On the other hand if the externally applied enable signal is at logic "1," the device is disabled. This facility, together with preloading, significantly improves the testability of the PAL20RA10. The preloading value to the flip-flops are supplied via the PL-inputs, shown in Figure 5.26.

To illustrate the application of the PAL20RA10, we will implement the state machine specified in Figure 5.27 using this device. This is a Moore-type machine. Let us choose the following state assignment for the machine:

State	y_1	y_2	y_3
A	0	0	0
B	0	0	1
C	0	1	1
D	0	1	0
E	1	0	0
F	1	1	0

The resulting equations for the machine are:

$$y_1 = x_2 x_3 \bullet \bar{y}_2 y_3 + y_1 \bar{y}_2 + x_1 y_2 y_3 + \bar{x}_2 y_2 y_3$$

$$y_2 = x_2 \bullet \bar{y}_2 y_3 + y_1 \bar{y}_2 + \bar{x}_1 x_2 y_2 y_3$$

$$y_3 = x_2 \bar{x}_3 \bar{y}_1 \bar{y}_2 + x_1 \bar{x}_2 \bar{y}_2 y_3$$

The output expressions are given by:

$$Z_1 = y_1 \bar{y}_3 + y_2 \bar{y}_3$$

$$Z_2 = \bar{y}_1 y_3 + y_1 y_2$$

$$Z_3 = \bar{y}_2 \bar{y}_3 + \bar{y}_1 y_3$$

These expressions are coded in the logic diagram of the PAL20RA10 as shown in Figure 5.28a. Notice that the programmable input of the EX-OR gates feeding the D flip-flops are at logic "1" (i.e., the fuses are blown). Thus,

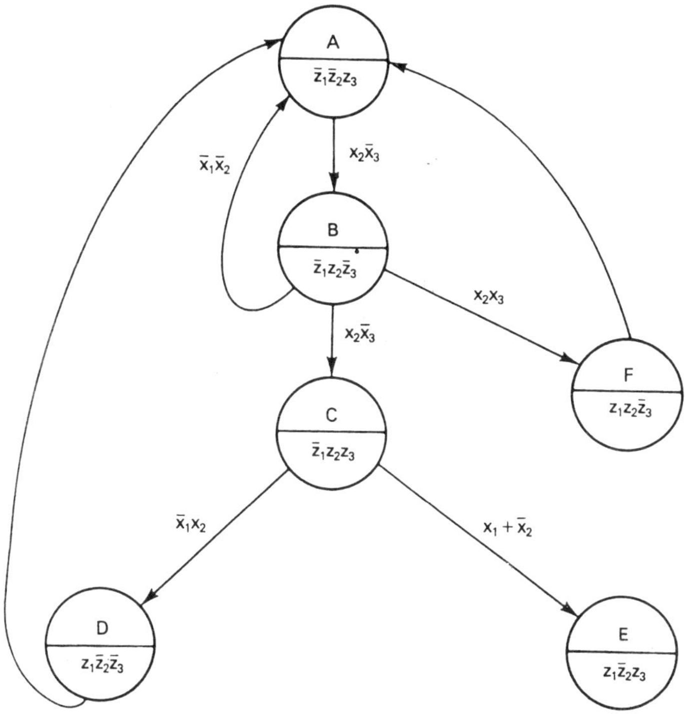

FIGURE 5.27
A state diagram

the logic values corresponding to the complements of the above expressions are stored in the D flip-flops. The inverters at the outputs of the D flip-flops are used to regenerate the true values. The R and S inputs of the D flip-flops are also programmed to be at logic "0." The PALASM2 source file for the state machine is shown in Figure 5.28b. Note that PALASM2 does not support direct state diagram coding for 20RA10 implementation.

PAL22V10. The PAL22V10 is one of the most versatile PAL devices available in the market. The chip features propagation delays of 15 ns compared to 30 ns of PAL20RA10. Figure 5.29a shows the block diagram of PAL22V10. It has 12 dedicated inputs including a clock line, and 10 I/O pins which can be configured either as inputs or outputs. It employs a variable product-term distribution which allocates from 8 to 16 terms to each output. Each output is user programmable for registered or combinational operation. This is accomplished by incorporating a **macrocell** between the fuse array and each output pin. The macrocells can be programmed to emulate the output

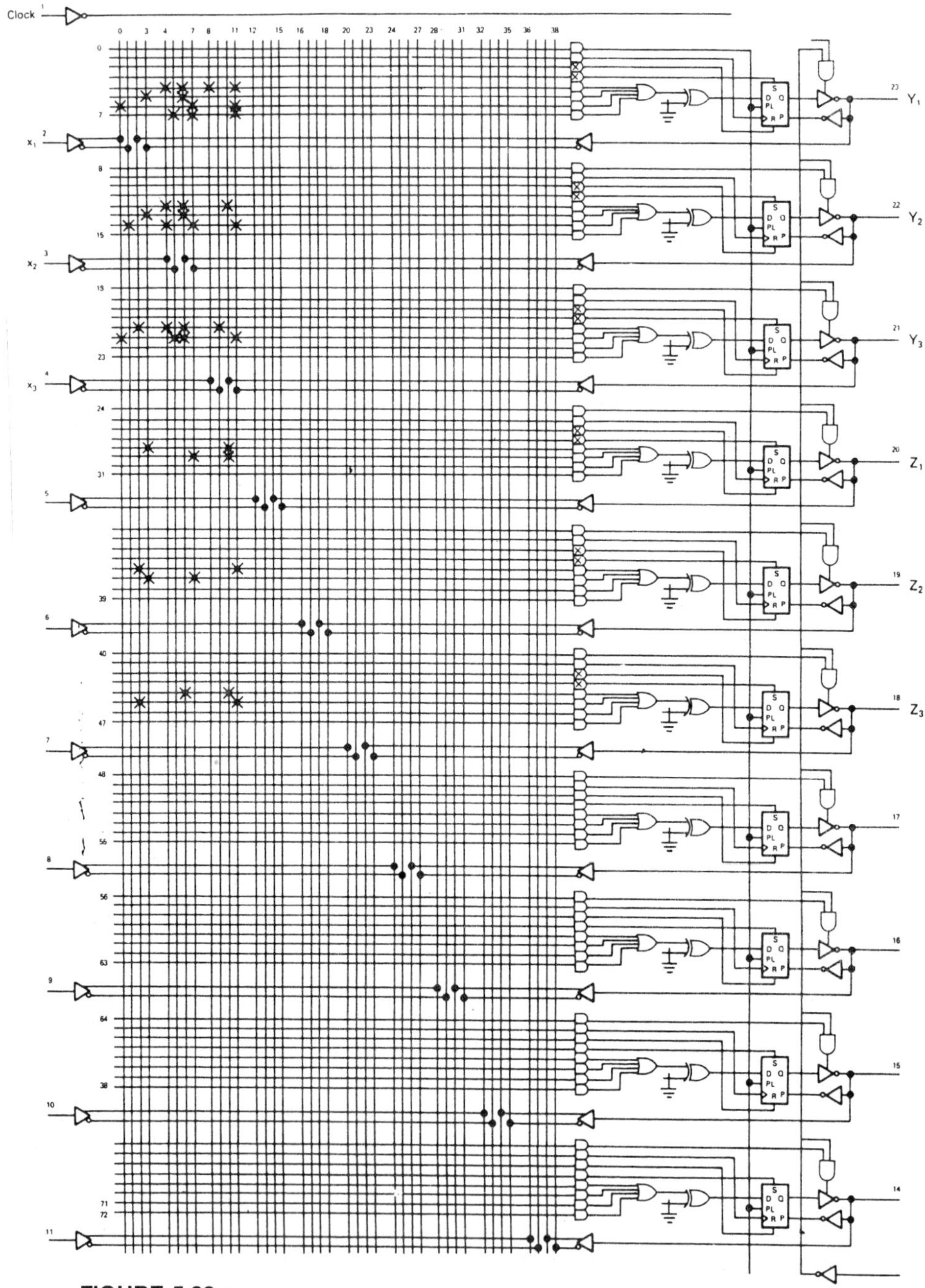

FIGURE 5.28a
Coded logic diagram corresponding to the state diagram of Figure 5.27 (Courtesy of AMD, Inc.)

```
TITLE       MY_EXAMPLE
PATTERN     STATE_MACHINE
AUTHOR      PARAG K LALA
DATE        MAY 9, 1989

CHIP    STATE_MACHINE          PAL20RA10

;PINS   1    2    3    4    5    6    7    8    9    10   11   12
        PL   CLK  X1   X2   X3   NC   NC   NC   NC   NC   INIT GND

;PINS   13   14   15   16   17   18   19   20   21   22   23   24
        OE   NC   NC   NC   Z1   Z2   Z3   Y1   Y2   Y3   NC   VCC

EQUATIONS

Y1          := X2 * X3 * /Y2 * Y3;
             + Y1 * /Y2;
             + X1 * Y2 * Y3;
             + /X2 * Y2 * Y3;
            ;clock flip-flop
Y1.CLKF      = CLK
Y1.RSTF = INIT       ;reset when INIT = 1
Y1.TRST = VCC        ;output pin 20 permanently enabled

Y2          := X2 * /Y2 * Y3;
             + Y1 * /Y2;
             + /X1 * X2 * Y2 * Y3;
Y2.CLKF      = CLK;
Y2.RSTF = INIT;
Y2.TRST = VCC;

Y3          := X2 * /X3 * /Y1 * /Y2;
             + X1 * /X2 * /Y2 * Y3;
Y3.CLKF      = CLK;
Y3.RSTF = INIT;
Y3.TRST = VCC;

Z1           = Y1 * /Y3 + Y2 * /Y3;
Z2           = /Y1 * Y3 + Y1 * Y2;
Z3           = /Y2 * /Y3 + /Y1 * Y3;
Z1.TRST      = VCC;
Z2.TRST      = VCC;
Z3.TRST      = VCC;

;{SIMULATION not included}
```

FIGURE 5.28b
Input file for PALASM2

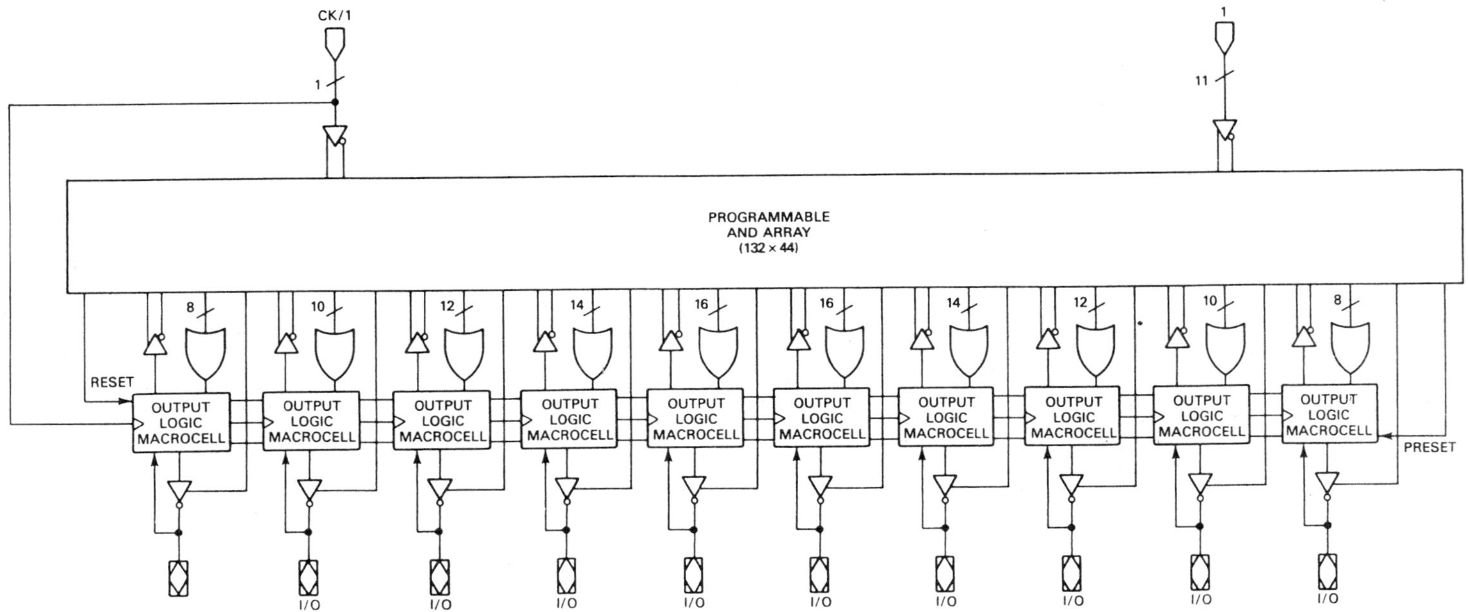

FIGURE 5.29a
Block diagram of PAL22V10 (Courtesy of AMD, Inc.)

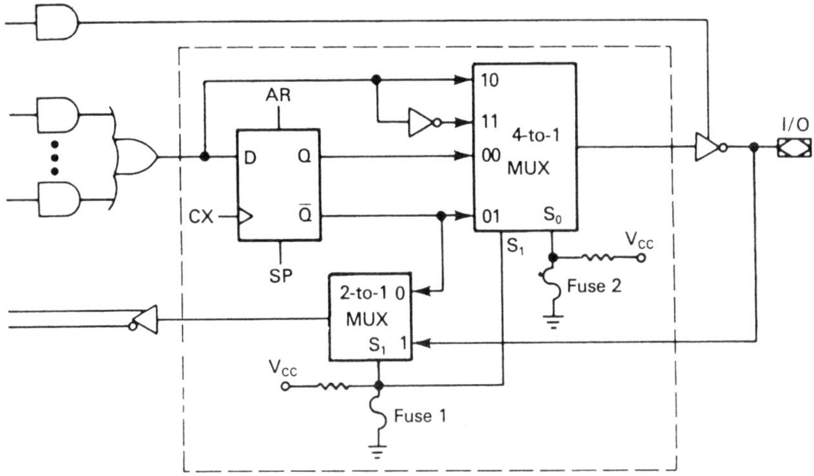

FIGURE 5.29b
A macrocell of PAL22V10 (Courtesy of AMD, Inc.)

structure of any existing 20-pin PAL device. The logic diagram of a macrocell is shown in Figure 5.29b. When fuse 1 is blown, the control input S_1 of both multiplexers will be at logic "1." Similarly, S_0 input of the 4-to-1 MUX becomes logic "1" when fuse 2 is blown. If both fuses remain intact, the select inputs of both the multiplexers will remain at logic "0." A macrocell operates in four different modes depending on the status of the fuses 1 and 2.

Mode 1: Fuse 1 blown, Fuse 2 blown

This results in both S_1 and S_0 being at logic "1." Consequently, the output of the OR gate is directly transferred to the output pin provided the tri-state inverter at the output is enabled.

Mode 2: Fuse 1 blown, Fuse 2 intact

This results in S_1 being at logic "1" and S_0 at logic "0." Thus, the inverted value of the output of the OR gate is available on the output pin.

Mode 3: Fuse 1 intact, Fuse 2

This makes S_1 to get logic "0" and S_0 to get logic "0." Therefore, the output of the D flip-flop is transferred to the output pin, and is also fed back to the AND array. However, because of the presence of the inverter at the output of the 4-to-1 MUX, the complement of the registered output is available on the output pin.

Mode 4: Fuse 1 intact, Fuse 2

This makes S_1 and S_0 to get logic "0." and logic "1" respectively. The complemented output of the D flip-flop is transferred to the output pin via the inverter—thus giving the true registered output.

The PAL22V10 has a **preset** and a **reset** product term. When the preset product term is activated, all the D flip-flops in the device are loaded with logic "1" values on the positive edge of the clock pulse. If the reset product term is enabled, the flip-flops are loaded with logic "0" independent of the clock. It is not possible however to individually set and reset a flip-flop as in PAL22RA10.

It is clear from the Mode 3 and Mode 4 operating modes of PAL22V10 that it can be programmed to implement arbitrary state machines. As in PAL20RA10, any desired state values can be preloaded into the flip-flops of the PAL22V10. As an example of the state machine design using this device we will implement the state machine specified in Figure 4.23 (see Chapter 4). The excitation equations for the state machine are:

$$y_0 = \overline{P} y_0 \overline{y}_2 + \overline{P}\overline{y}_0 y_2 + \overline{C} F y_0 y_1$$

$$y_1 = \overline{y}_0 y_1 + \overline{C}\,\overline{F} y_1 + \overline{F} y_2 \overline{y}_1 y_0$$

$$y_2 = P\overline{y}_0 + P\overline{y}_2 + \overline{y}_0 y_2$$

These equations are coded in the logic diagram of the PAL22V10 as shown in Figure 5.30a. Figure 5.30b shows the PALASM2 input file created directly from the excitation equations.

PAL32VX10. The PAL32VX10, like the PAL22V10, has 12 dedicated input lines and 10 I/O macrocells. In fact, it is pin compatible with PAL22V10, however the two devices have different macrocell structure. As shown in Figure 5.31 the macrocell of the PAL32VX10 provides two independent feedback paths from the flip-flop output and the output pin to the AND array. Unlike the PAL22V10 in which the output pin of a macrocell cannot be used if the macrocell sends its output back to the AND array (registered feedback), the PAL32VX10 allows the use of the output pin of a macrocell even if the flip-flop's output is fed back to the AND array. Furthermore, if the I/O pin of a macrocell is configured as a dedicated input, the dual feedback paths permit the flip-flop in the macrocell to function as an input register or as a buried state flip-flop, thus avoiding the loss of the flip-flop. The output of a macrocell can be configured as combinational, through simple bypassing of the flip-flop. This is accomplished by the appropriate selection of the control input of the output multiplexer. The control input of the output multiplexer is driven by a dedicated product term which can be made active-high by blowing all the fuses or made active-low by keeping all the fuses intact. Depending on whether the product term is active-high or active-low, the output multiplexer routes combinational output or registered output respectively to the output pin.

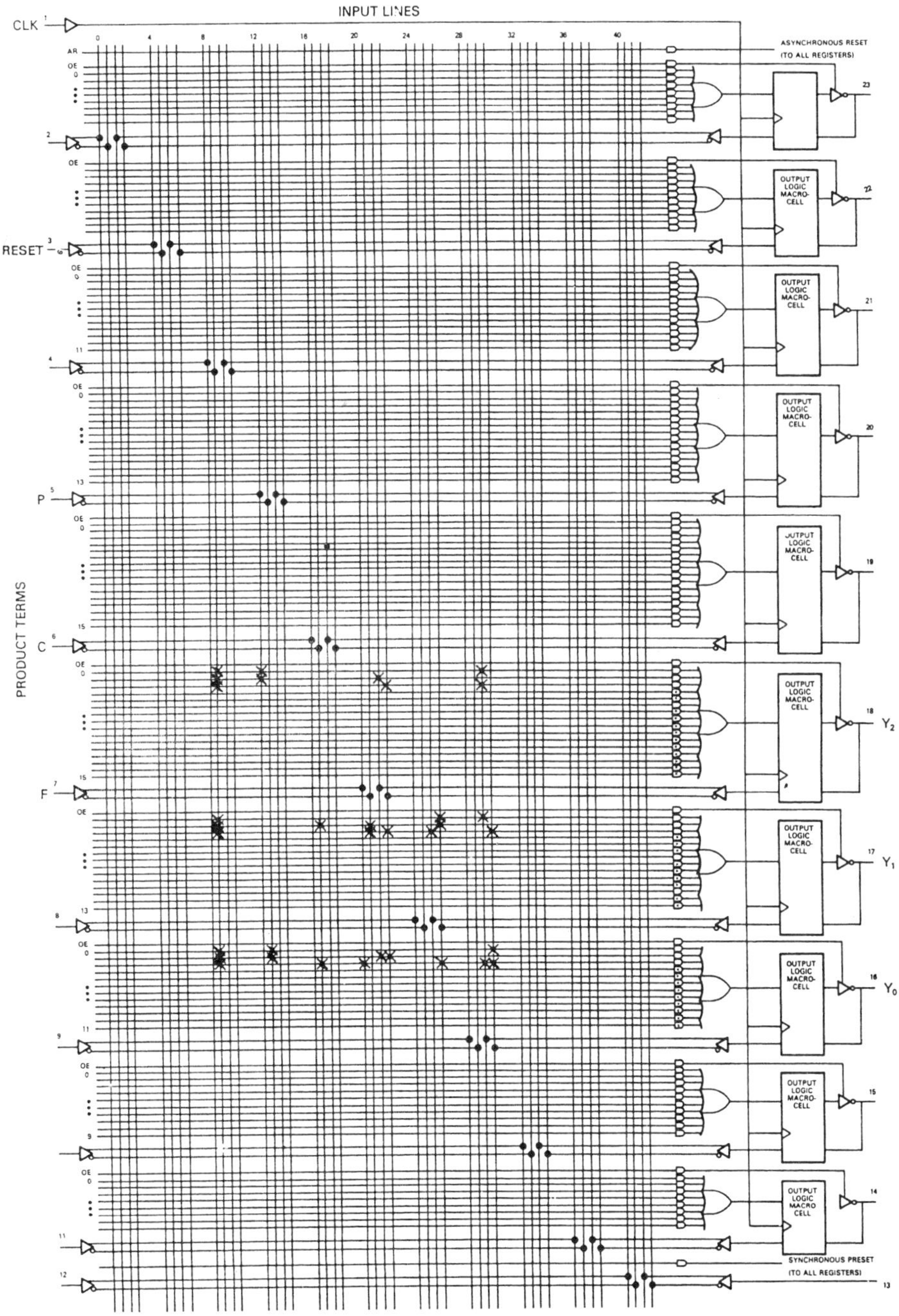

FIGURE 5.30a
Coded logic diagram corresponding to the state machine of Figure 4.23 (Courtesy of AMD, Inc.)

```
TITLE      AN_EXAMPLE
PATTERN    STATE_MACHINE
AUTHOR     PARAG K LALA
DATE       MAY 11, 1989

CHIP     STATE_MACHINE          PAL22V10

;PINS    1    2    3    4    5    6    7    8    9    10   11   12
         CLK  NC   MR   P    C    F    NC   NC   NC   NC   NC   GND

;PINS    13   14   15   16   17   18   19   20   21   22   23   24
         NC   NC   NC   Y0   Y1   Y2   NC   NC   NC   NC   NC   VCC

GLOBAL; a fictional pin used to globally set or reset the registers

EQUATIONS

GLOBAL.RSTF = MR;

Y0 := /P * Y0 * /Y2;
      + /P * /Y0 * Y2;
      + /C * F * Y0 * Y1;
Y0.TRST = VCC                         ; output pin 13 permanently enabled
Y1 := /Y0 * Y1;
      + /C * /F * Y1;
      + /F * Y2 * /Y1 * Y0;
Y1.TRST = VCC;

Y2 := P * /Y0;
      + P * /Y2;
      + /Y0 * Y2;
Y2.TRST = VCC;

;{SIMULATION not included}
```

FIGURE 5.30b
Input file for PALASM2

The flip-flop in the macrocell is fed by an EX-OR gate, one input of which is derived from a dedicated product term and the other input is driven by the output of the OR gate. As in the PAL22V10, each OR gate produces a sum of varied number of product terms, with pairs of macrocells having 8, 10, 12, 14 and 16 product terms.

The D flip-flop in a macrocell can be converted to a JK flip-flop if the next state equation for the D flip-flop is represented as follows:

$$D = \overline{K} \cdot Q + J \cdot \overline{Q}$$

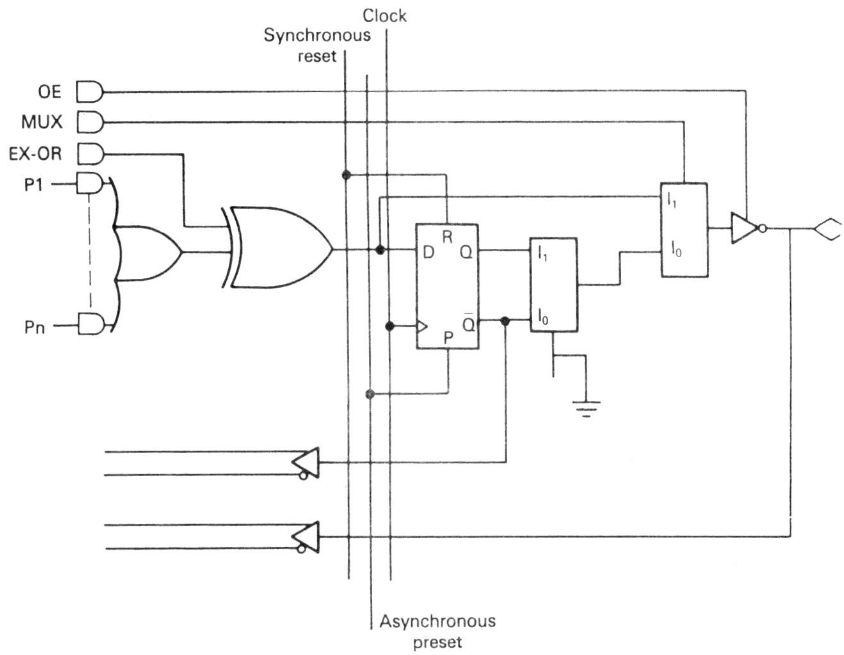

FIGURE 5.31
Macrocell of PAL32VX10 (Courtesy of AMD, Inc.)

This equation can be rewritten as:

$$\begin{aligned} D &= Q \oplus (J \cdot \overline{Q} + K \cdot Q) \\ &= Q \oplus [(J_1 + J_2 + \ldots)\overline{Q} + (K_1 + K_2 + \ldots)Q] \end{aligned}$$

Since J and K are in general sum-of-products, the expressions for J and K cannot contain more than the maximum number of product terms associated with a macrocell.

The D flip-flop can be programmed as a T flip-flop by rewriting its next state equation as:

$$D = Q \oplus T$$

All the flip-flops in the PAL32VX10 share common programmable reset and preset inputs. On power-up, the outputs of all flip-flops are set to logic high. The device also features the preload capability, as in PAL22V10, to set the flip-flops in a particular state. A security fuse is incorporated in the device, which if blown prevents the logic pattern verification.

To illustrate the application of PAL32VX10, let us implement the

Mealy-type state machine shown in Figure 5.32. The PALASM2 input file for the Mealy machine is shown in Figure 5.33a. The ABEL input file is shown in Figure 5.33b. This file uses ISTYPE and WITH-ENDWITH statements. The ISTYPE statement can be used to explicitly define a macrocell configuration. In Figure 5.33b, the ISTYPE statements define output pins q1 and q2 as feedback points; furthermore, q1 and q2 are defined to be registered outputs having positive polarity. The WITH-ENDWITH statement, when used in conjunction with the IF-THEN statement, permits the specification of output equations in terms of transitions.

State \ Input	$\bar{x}_1\bar{x}_2$	$\bar{x}_1x_2$	x_1x_2	$x_1\bar{x}_2$
A	B,0−	A,01	D,11	A,01
B	A,1−	C,1−	D,00	C,10
C	A,1−	C,1−	A,10	A,10
D	C,00	B,10	B,1−	D,01

Next state, output

FIGURE 5.32
A state table

5.3 PAL23S8

The PAL23S8 is a 20-pin device and used specifically for state machine design. It provides 9 dedicated input lines and 8 output lines (see Figure 5.34). Four of the outputs are derived from the 4 macrocells the device contains. Figure 5.35 shows the logic diagram of an output macrocell. It is very similar to a macrocell used in PAL22V10. By blowing the appropriate fuses, a macrocell can be configured to provide a direct sum-of-products output (active-high or low) or the output can be propagated via the D flip-flop. In addition, the true and complement of the output signal can be fed back to the AND array. By disabling the tri-state buffer at the macrocell output, the I/O pin is configured as an additional input pin to the device.

The device also has 4 output registers, the output of which may be fed back to the AND array by disabling the tri-state buffers at their outputs.

The 23S8 has 6 buried state registers, the output of which are directly fed back to the AND array. These registers are used for implementing state machines. The D-input of such a register is driven by an OR gate, which generates the sum of a number of product terms. Two registers have 6 product terms feeding the OR gate, 2 have 8 and the remaining two have 10 product terms. One of the 135 product terms in the device is dedicated for improving the observability of an implemented state machine. When the product term, known as the **observability product term** is enabled, the outputs of 2 specific macrocells and 4 output registers are disabled and the outputs of the six buried registers are made available on the associated I/O pins. As in PAL22V10, this

```
TITLE       STATE_MACHINE
AUTHOR      PARAG K LALA
DATE        MAY 11, 1989.

CHIP          STATE_MACHINE          PAL32VX10

;PINS          1    2    3    4    5    6    7    8    9    10   11   12
               CLK  X1   X2   MR   NC   NC   NC   NC   NC   NC   NC   GND

;PINS          13   14   15   16   17   18   19   20   21   22   23   24
               NC   Y1   Y2   NC   NC   NC   NC   NC   NC   Z1   Z2   VCC

GLOBAL         Q1   Q2   NC   NC   NC   NC   NC   NC   NC   NC

STATE

  MEALY_MACHINE;

  ;state assignment
  A = /Q1 • /Q2; 0 – 0
  B = /Q1 • Q2; 0 – 1
  C =  Q1 • /Q2; 1 – 0
  D =  Q1 • Q2; 1 – 1

A  := C1 → B;
    + C4 → D;
    +  → A;
B  := C1 → A;
    + C4 → D;
    +  → C;
C  := C2 → C;
    +  → A;
D  := C1 → C;
    + C3 → D;
    +  → B;

CONDITIONS

  C1 = /X1 • /X2;
  C2 = /X1 •  X2;
  C3 =  X1 • /X2;
  C4 =  X1 •  X2;

EQUATIONS :

  GLOBAL.RSTF = MR               ;asynchronous reset
  Y1 = Q1;
  Y1.CMBF = GND;
  Y2 = Q2;
  Y2.CMBF = GND;

  Z1 = /X1 • Q2                  ; enable pin Z1 as a
     + /X2 • Q2                  ;combinational output
     + X1 • X2 • /Q2;
     + X2 • Q1;
  Z1.CMBF = VCC;

  Z2 = /X1 • /Q1;
     + X1 • /Q2;
  Z2.CMBF = VCC;

;{SIMULATION not included}
```

FIGURE 5.33a
PALASM2 input file

```
module          state_machine
title           'state machine design
Parag K Lala          May 7, 1989.'


        state_machine           device    'P32VX10';
        clk,x1,x2               pin 1,2,3;
        q1,q2                   pin 14,15;
        sreg                    = [q2,q1];
        z1,z2                   pin 22,23;

        q1          istype          'pos,reg,feed_pin';
        q2          istype          'pos,reg,feed_pin';

state_diagram sreg;
        state A:
        q1 = 0;
        q2 = 0;
        IF(!x1 & !x2) THEN B WITH z1 := 0;
        ELSE IF(x1 & x2) THEN D WITH z1 := 1;
        ELSE A WITH z1 := 0;
                        z2 := 1;
        ENDWITH;

        state B:
        q1 = 0;
        q2 = 1;
        IF(!x1 & !x2) THEN A WITH z1 := 1;
        ELSE IF(x1 & x2) THEN D WITH z1 := 0;
        ELSE C WITH z1 := 1;

        state C:
        q1 = 1;
        q2 = 0;
        IF(!x1 & x2) THEN C WITH z1 := 0;
        ELSE A WITH z1 := 1;

        state D:
        q1 = 1;
        q2 = 1;
        IF(!x1 & !x2) THEN C
                    WITH z1 := 0;
                    WITH z2 := 1;
        ENDWITH
        ELSE IF(x1 & !x2) THEN D WITH z1 := 1;
        ELSE B WITH z1 := 1;
end
```

FIGURE 5.33b
ABEL input file

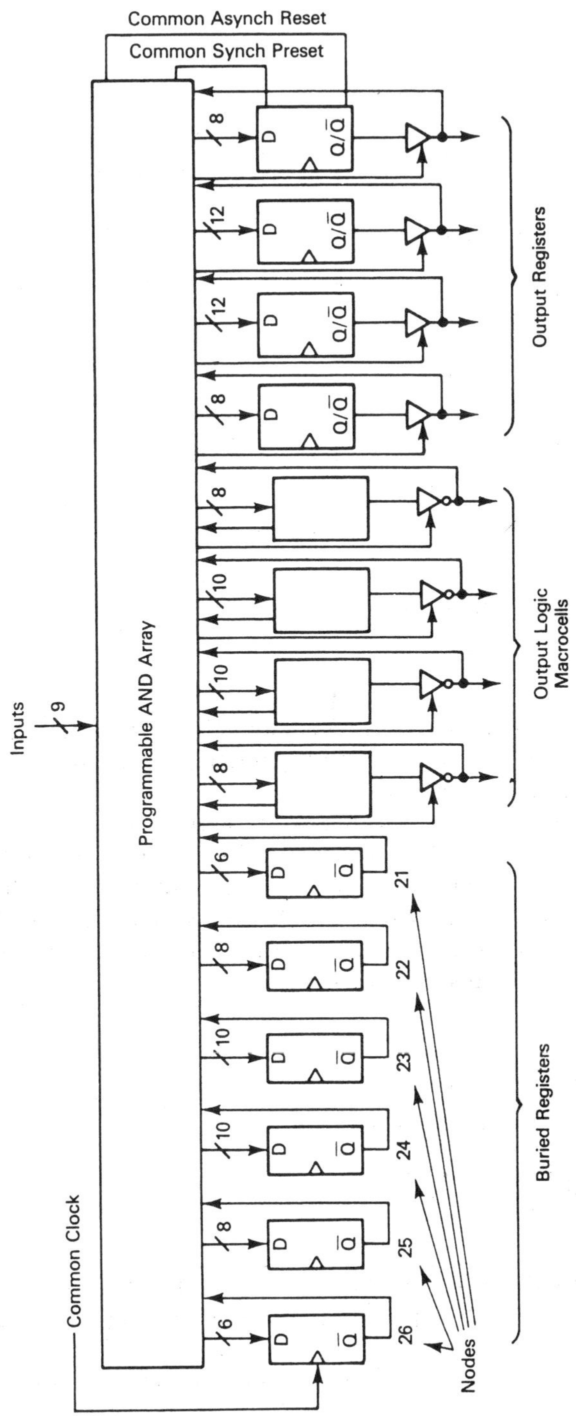

FIGURE 5.34
Block diagram of PAL2358 (Courtesy of AMD, Inc.)

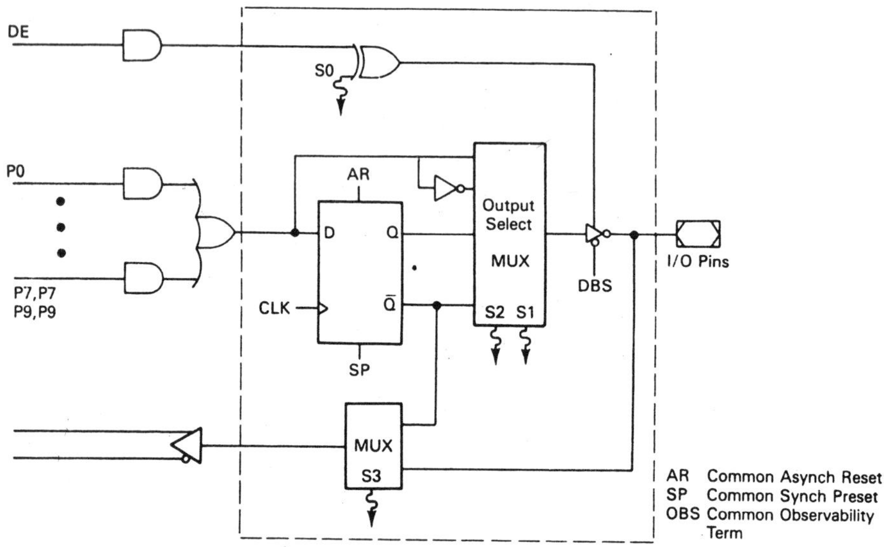

FIGURE 5.35
Output macrocell (Courtesy of AMD, Inc.)

device has the preload capability. The combination of preload facility and the buried state registers being observable simplifies the verification of a state machine designed using the 23S8.

As an example of the application of the PAL23S8, let us implement the Mealy-type state machine shown in Figure 5.36. Three buried flip-flops of the 23S8 are used to represent the states. The outputs of the buried flip-flops are specified as nodes in ABEL source file; these nodes are identified in Figure 5.34. The ABEL source file for the state machine is shown in Figure 5.37. PALASM2 does not support PAL23S8.

5.4 MegaPALs

There are two devices in this group:

PAL32R16
PAL64R32

These devices are the results of efforts to develop more complex PALs. They incorporate features such as product sharing, buried flip-flops and programmable clock for internal asynchronous operations. Both devices also offer preload capability in order to simplify testing. On power-up the flip-flops in

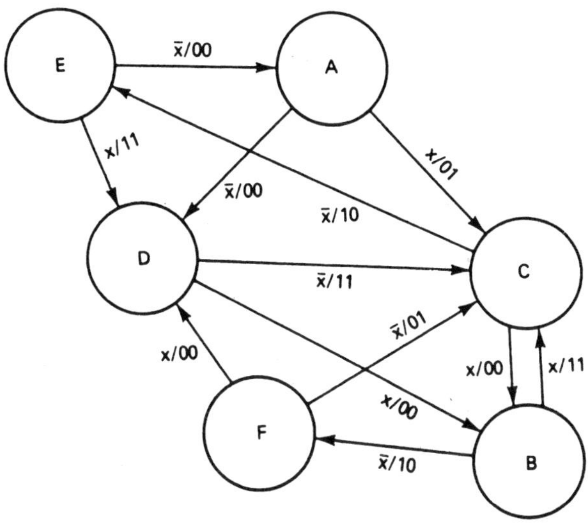

FIGURE 5.36
A state diagram

these devices assume logic "0" values, resulting in logic "1" values at the outputs of the devices. The flip-flops in each device can be bypassed in groups of 8, thus allowing combinational outputs in sets of 8. In addition, the PAL64R32 incorporates a dedicated reset product term for each group of 8 flip-flops. When a reset product term is activated, the outputs of the corresponding set of 8 flip-flops are reset to logic "0." The MegaPALS are considerably slower than conventional PALs; the PAL32R16 has a propagation delay of 40 ns and the PAL64R32 has a propagation delay of 50 ns.

5.5 HARD ARRAY LOGIC (HAL)

HAL devices are **mask-programmable** versions of PALs. They are recommended for use when a PAL design specification has been finalized and the devices are required in volume. The HAL devices are produced using standard low-power Schottky TTL technology. A mask replaces the fuses of the programmable prototype and permanently metallizes the interconnection pattern. Typical turnaround time for HAL chips is said to be 6 to 8 weeks.

The HAL devices have a worst-case propagation delay of 35 ns. For high-speed operation, the ZHAL (Zero Hard Array Logic) devices may be more appropriate. They use CMOS technology and feature zero standby power and a maximum of 25 ns propagation delay. A CMOS mask-programmable version of the MegaPAL64R32 is also available.

```
module          state_machine
title           'state machine design example
Parag K Lala          May 9, 1989'

      state_machine          device          'PAL23S8';

      clock,x,y,mr        pin 1,2,3,4;
      z1,z2               pin 16,17;
      aa,bb,cc            nodes 21,22,23;
      sreg                = [cc,bb,aa];

      z1.OE,z2.OE         istype      'pos,eqn';

      A = 0;     B = 4;     C = 2;
      D = 6;     E = 1;     F = 5;          "state values

State_diagram sreg;
      State A:
        IF (!x)   THEN D
                  WITH z1 := 0;
                       z2 := 0;
                  ENDWITH
        ELSE C WITH
                       z1 := 0;
                       z2 := 1;
                  ENDWITH;
      State B:
        IF (!x)   THEN F
                  WITH z1 := 1;
                       z2 := 0;
                  ENDWITH
        ELSE C WITH
                       z1 := 1;
                       z2 := 1;
                  ENDWITH;
      State C:
        IF (!x)   THEN E
                  WITH z1 := 1;
                       z2 := 0;
                  ENDWITH
        ELSE B WITH
                       z1 := 0;
                       z2 := 0;
                  ENDWITH;
      State D:
        IF (!x)   THEN B
                  WITH z1 := 1;
                       z2 := 1;
                  ENDWITH
        ELSE E WITH
                       z1 := 0;
                       z2 := 0;
                  ENDWITH;
      State E:
        If (!x)   THEN A
                  WITH z1 := 0;
                       z2 := 0;
                  ENDWITH
        ELSE D WITH
                       z1 := 1;
                       z2 := 1;
                  ENDWITH;
      State F:
        IF (!x)   THEN C
                  WITH z1 := 0;
                       z2 := 1;
                  ENDWITH
        ELSE D WITH
                       z1 := 0;
                       z2 := 0;
                  ENDWITH;

      equations
        [aa.AR,bb.AR,cc.AR] = mr;      "asynchronous reset
          z1.OE = 1;
          z2.OE = 1;      "output enable

      end
```

FIGURE 5.37
ABEL Input file for Figure 5.36

VLSI Technology, Inc. offers two CMOS mask-programmable logic array, VP16RP8M and VP20RP8M. Using their company's in-house design automation system, custom masks for these devices can be created directly from the logic equations or from programmed PALs or GALs (see Chapter 6). These devices, like the ZHAL chips, offer 25 ns propagation delay.

PROBLEMS

5-1. A sequential circuit represented by the following state diagram, is to be implemented using an appropriate PAL chip. Write down the design equations for the circuit in the PALASM2 format.

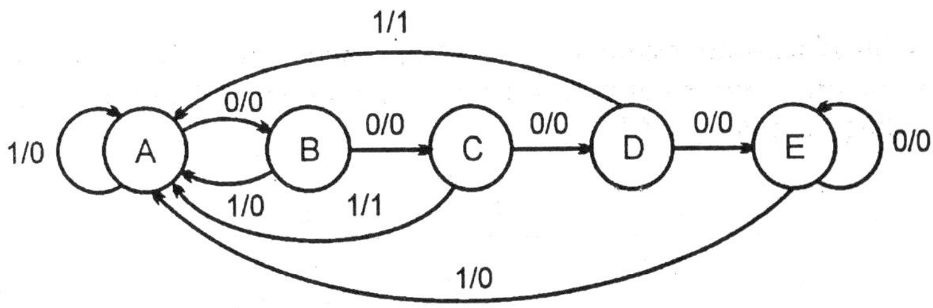

5-2. The function table for a 6-bit bidirectional shift register with parallel load capability is shown below

Mode *s1*	*Control* *s2*	*Register operation*
0	0	No change
0	1	Shift right
1	0	Shift left
1	1	Parallel Load

The shift register is to be implemented using one of the following PAL chips: 16L8, 16R6, 16R8 or 16R4. Select an appropriate PAL chip and write its design equations in PALASM2 format.

5-3. Implement the following Boolean equations using both 14H2 and 14L2 chips. Show the coded logic diagrams of the devices.

$$f_1(x,y,z) = \bar{x}\bar{y}z + x\bar{y}\bar{z} + \bar{x}y\bar{z} + xyz$$

$$f_2(x,y,z) = \bar{x}yz + x\bar{y}z + xy\bar{z} + xyz$$

5-4. Show how to implement dual 8-to-1 multiplexer using a 20L2. Give the design equations.

5-5. A circuit for converting a serial stream of binary data into a parallel BCD representation is to be designed. The block diagram of the circuit is shown below. The input data is entered into the BCD register I starting with the most significant bit. After each clock pulse, the outputs of the BCD registers indicate the correct BCD representation of the binary data shifted into the BCD register so far. Show the implementation of the circuit using PAL chips only, and also the design equations.

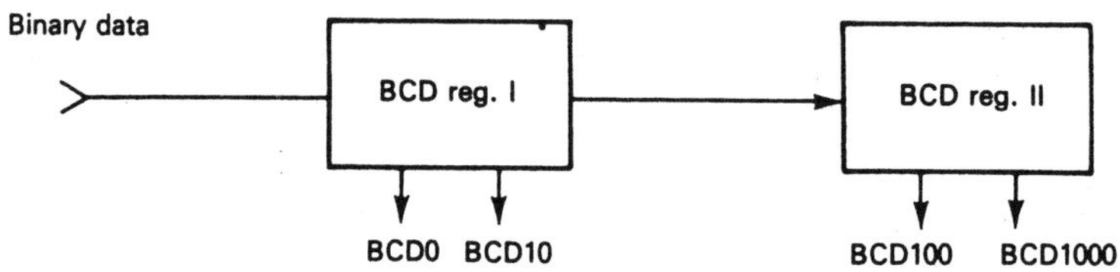

5-6. A 4-bit synchronous counter is to be designed using 16X4. The counter may be programmed to perform any of the following four functions, depending on bits I_1 and I_2

I_1	I_2	*Function*
0	0	Clear
1	0	Parallel load
1	1	Count
0	1	Hold

Write down the design equations for the counter.

5-7. An 8-bit Johnson counter is to be implemented with a single PAL22V10. The design should be such that the counter be able to get out of invalid states. Code the logic diagram of the device to show the implementation of the counter.

REFERENCES

1. F. Cave and D. Terrell, *Digital Technology with Microprocessors,* Reston Publishing Company, Inc., 1981.
2. J. F. Nebus, "Parallel Data Compression for Fault Tolerant Computer Design," *Computer Design,* April 15, 1983, pp. 127–134.
3. *PAL/PLE Device Programmable Logic Array Handbook,* Monolithic Memories, 1986.
4. *PAL Device Handbook,* Advanced Micro Devices, Inc., 1988.
5. *PAL Device Data Book,* Advanced Micro Devices, Inc., 1988.

Chapter 6

New Generation of Programmable Logic Devices

A major drawback of programmable logic based on bipolar fuse technology is that they cannot be reprogrammed. Thus, they are not suitable in applications requiring alteration of logic functions or in situations when a new logic design has to be modified several times before a satisfactory design is obtained. In addition, the power consumption in bipolar programmable logic devices is high. Consequently there has been a gradual shift from bipolar to CMOS technology, resulting in programmable logic devices which consume significantly less power than the equivalent bipolar devices; however it has been argued that this is not always true [1].

One additional advantage of CMOS devices is that they use EPROM cells or EEPROM cells instead of fuses as programmable connections. A fuse takes up a large amount of silicon area whereas the EPROM and EEPROM cells are significantly smaller than fuses, thus more functions can be packed into a smaller device. The devices based on EPROM cells are known as **erasable programmable logic devices** (EPLD), and those based on EEPROM cells are referred to as **electrically erasable programmable logic devices** (EEPLD).

The most important advantage of erasable devices is that they can be fully tested before being delivered to the customer. The only way to reliably test PLDs, is to program them to perform a particular function, and then exercising them to that function. The erasable technology allows the manufacturer to program functions into each device and exercise them in automated test systems. If a device is found to be satisfactory, its contents can be erased, and it can be supplied to the user with the same quality level as fixed-function devices. However, this test strategy is not applicable to fuse-programmable PLDs, because they can be programmed only once. Thus, it is up to the user to develop a test pattern for exercising such a device in order to avoid the risk of building a system from defective components; this obviously adds to the system cost.

Altera Corporation introduced the first EPLD in 1984. Since then, many other companies have marketed EPLDs (e.g., VLSI Technology, Intel, and Cypress Semiconductors). The first company to introduce EEPLDs was the Lattice Semiconductor Corporation. Lattice's electrically erasable CMOS **generic array logic** (GAL™) is pin-for-pin and fuse-map compatible with 21 devices of Advanced Micro Devices Series 20 PALs. International CMOS Technology is another firm which offers EEPLDs, known as **programmable electrically erasable logic** (PEEL™), that can emulate the 20-pin and 24-pin PAL devices.

One of the major problems of the traditional AND-OR architecture of programmable logic devices is that even if one needs to implement an AND or an OR function, both the AND and the OR array must be used. This introduces 2 levels of gate delay for implementing a function which requires only a single level of gates (e.g., a decoder). Moreover, in most of the AND-OR based devices, if a feedback is required the signal available on an output pin has to be routed back to the AND array, which again results in two-levels of gate delay. Two approaches for internal feedback have been developed by Exel Microelectronics and Signetics, to eliminate the additional gate delay. Exel's approach relies on folded-NOR architecture, while Signetics' approach uses folded-NAND architecture. In this chapter, we will discuss the architectural features and applications of the following devices:

- EPLDs (Altera, Cypress Semiconductors, Signetics).
- EEPLDs (Lattice Semiconductors, International CMOS Technology, Advanced Micro Devices).
- Folded-NOR/NAND devices (Exel, Signetics).
- Programmable state machines (Texas Instruments, Advanced Micro Devices, Cypress Semiconductors).
- Programmable gate-array (Actel Corporation).

6.1 ERASABLE PROGRAMMABLE LOGIC DEVICES

EP300. The EP300 was the first member of the EPROM-based programmable logic devices introduced by Altera Corporation. It can have up to 18 inputs and 3 outputs. The device consists of 8 macrocells, each of which has

9 product terms. Eight product terms feed an 8-input OR gate and the remaining term is used to enable the output. Figure 6.1 shows the block diagram of the EP300. The composition of a macrocell is shown in Figure 6.2. The output multiplexer in a cell allows the selection of the direct output of the OR gate or

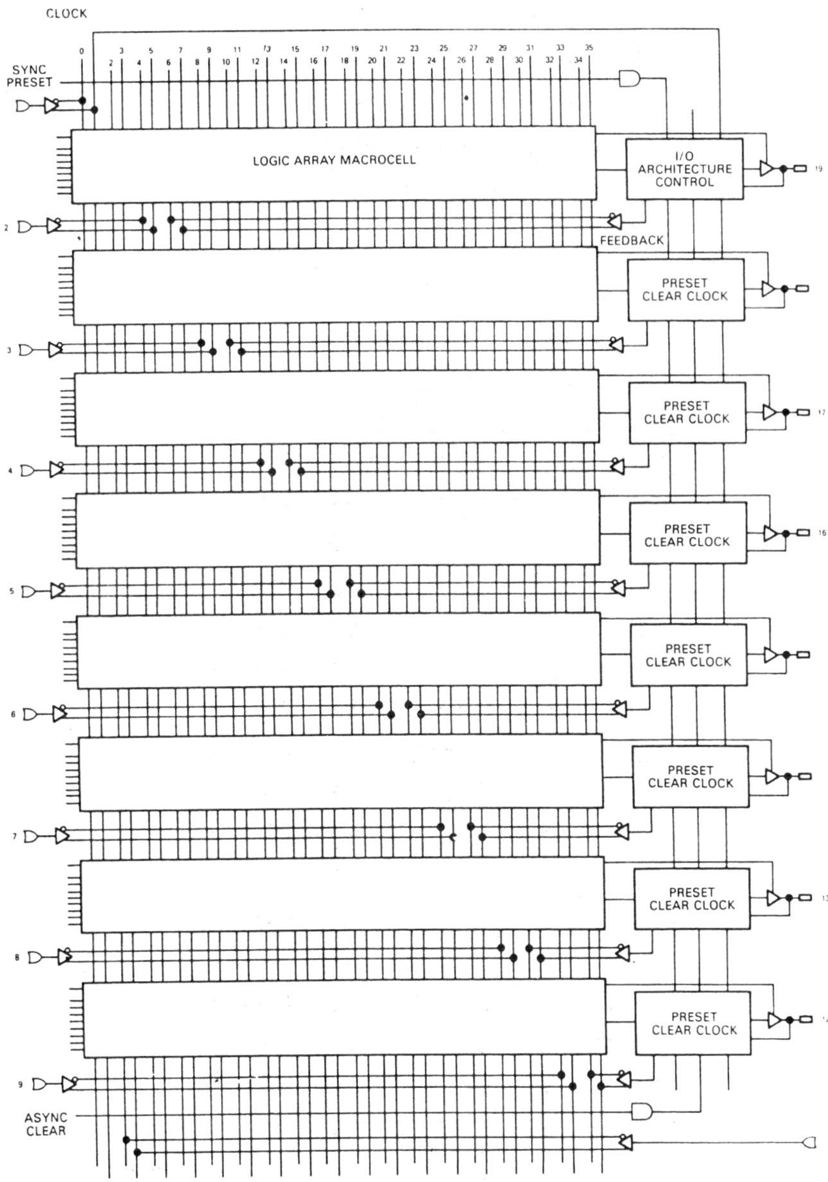

FIGURE 6.1
Block diagram of EP300 (Copyright Altera Corp.)

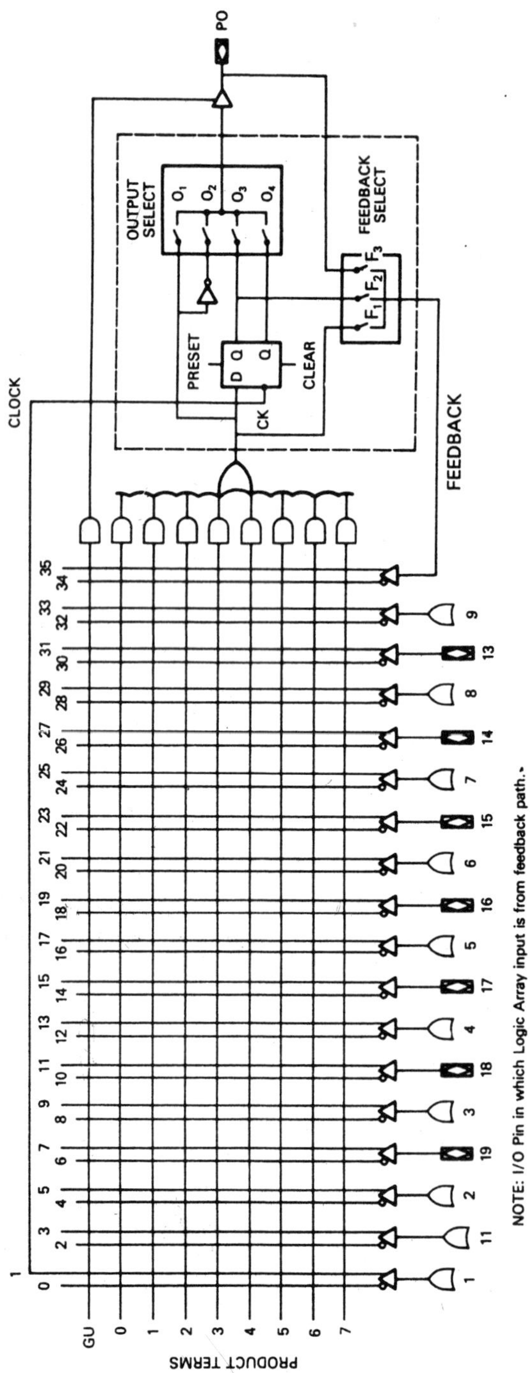

FIGURE 6.2
EP300 Macrocell (Copyright Altera Corp.)

the registered output, or their complements. The feedback multiplexer allows feedback from the output of the OR gate, the output of the register or from the bidirectional I/O pin.

The EP300 has two additional product terms which are used for output register set and clear functions (shown in Figure 6.1). When the preset input of a register is asserted high, the register is loaded with a logic "1" on the next positive edge of the clock pulse. On the other hand, if the clear input of a register is asserted high, it is loaded with a logic "0" independent of the clock pulse. When both preset and clear inputs are asserted high simultaneously, the clear input dominates (i.e., the register is loaded with a logic "0"). On power-up, all registers in an EP300 are cleared automatically.

The EP300 is a 20-pin device and operates with a maximum clock frequency of about 18 MHz. A faster version of the device, EP310, operates with a maximum clock frequency of 40 MHz. Besides EP310 requires less power than EP300. Both devices include a security bit that prevents unauthorized reading of the data programmed into the device.

EP320. Like EP300/EP310, the EP320 is also a 20-pin device. It has 10 dedicated inputs, one of which may be used as a clock input. The device also has 8 I/O pins which may be used as inputs or outputs depending on whether the OE (output enable) product term is asserted low or high, respectively. The EP320 has eight separate OE product terms, thus it is possible to individually enable or disable each output as in EP300/EP310. However unlike these two devices the EP320 does not have dedicated product terms for preset and clear operations. Moreover, the output of each OR gate in the device is fed to the input of the corresponding register via an EX-OR gate, whereas in EP300/EP310 the output of an OR gate is fed directly to the register input. The I/O configuration of the device can be done in exactly the same manner as in EP300/EP310; each I/O pin can provide either combinational or registered output (see Figure 6.3). In each mode, the output polarity is selected by setting the unused input of the EX-OR gate appropriately (logic "1" for active-low, logic "0" for active-high).

In both combinational and registered modes, there is an option for feedback or no feedback of output. The major advantage of EP320 is that it can be configured as one of the 20-pin PAL devices. This is done by appropriate selection of I/O configuration mode, output polarity, and feedback path. Figure 6.4 shows the coded logic diagram of EP320 used to implement the state machine of Figure 3.24.

EP600. This is a 24-pin device, and has 4 inputs, 2 dedicated clock inputs, and 16 I/O pins which may be configured as either input or output. It has two important architectural features which EP300 and EP320 do not possess:

1. It contains **programmable flip-flops,** each of which can be configured to a particular type (e.g., D, T, JK, or SR).

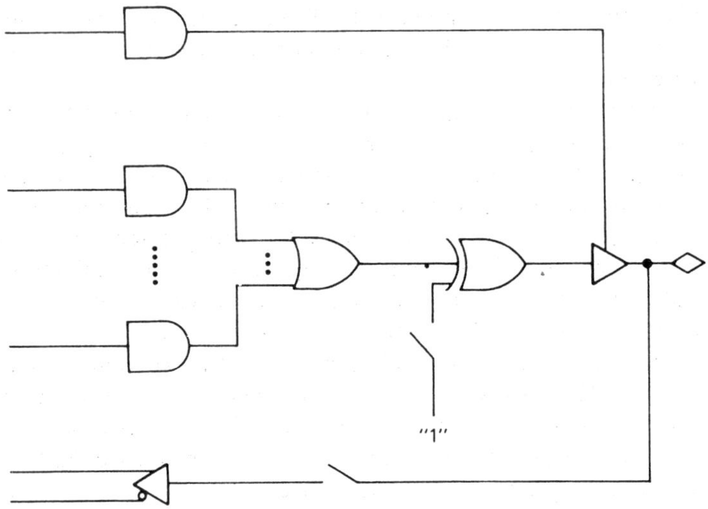

(a)

FIGURE 6.3a
Combinational output

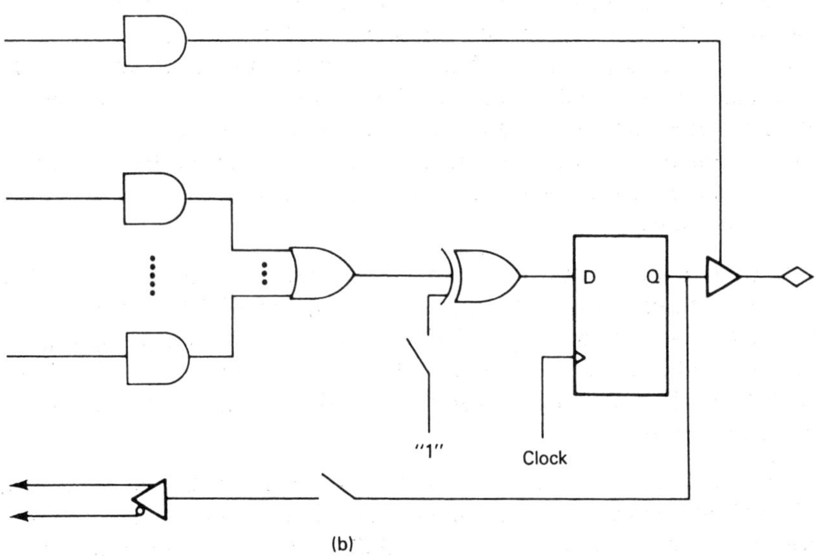

(b)

FIGURE 6.3b
Registered output

2. Each flip-flop can be triggered by an asynchronous clock signal generated by a dedicated product term, or by the clock signal applied via the dedicated input.

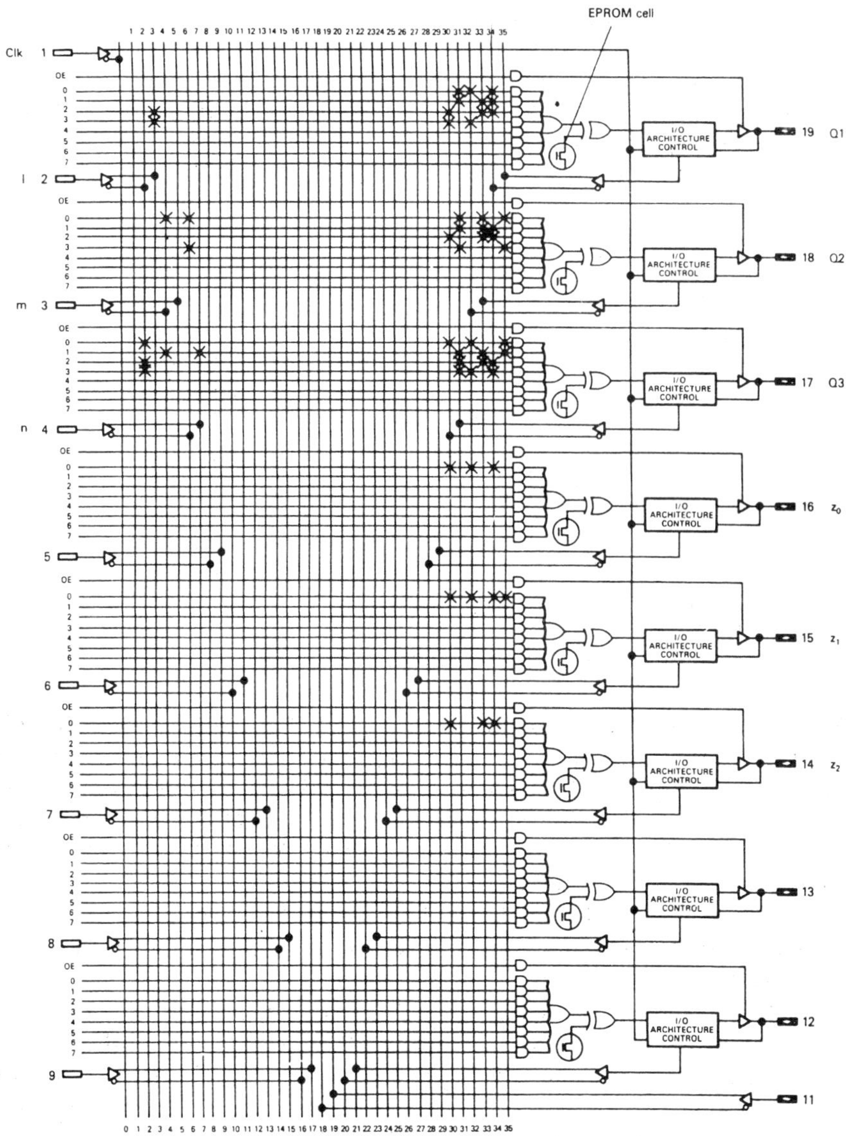

FIGURE 6.4
Implementation of the state machine of Figure 3.24 using EP320 (Copyright Altera Corp.)

The EP600 has 16 macrocells; each macrocell has 40-input/10-output programmable AND array. Eight of the AND array's product terms are used to implement the excitation equation(s) for the flip-flop in the macrocell's architectural control block. Out of the remaining 2 product terms, 1 is dedicated to control the clear input of the flip-flop, and the other is used for output enable/gated clock implementation.

As mentioned previously, the flip-flop within the architectural control block of a macrocell is programmable; it can be programmed by a single EPROM cell to operate as a D or a T flip-flop. The T flip-flop is used to perform the JK function by adding 2 AND gates, an OR gate and an inverter as shown in Figure 6.5.

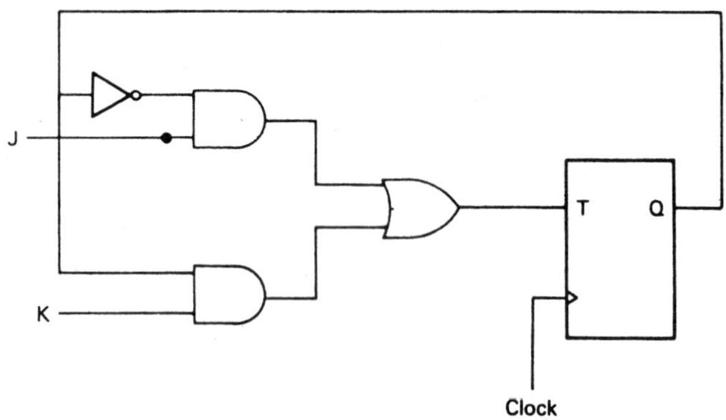

FIGURE 6.5
JK flip-flop constructed from T flip-flop

When the choice is D or T, the 8 non-dedicated product terms of the AND array are ORed together to form the input to the flip-flop (see Figure 6.6a and b). Alternatively, if the choice is JK or SR, a subset of these 8 product terms are fed via an OR gate to one control input of the flip-flop, and the remaining product terms are fed via another OR gate to the other control input (see Figure 6.6c and d).

As in EP300 and EP320, an I/O pin in an EP600 can be configured to provide a combinational output or a registered output with or without feedback, and also as an input.

The EP600 has two separate clock inputs, one provides clock signals to the flip-flops associated with macrocells 1 through 8, and the other does the same for flip-flops associated with macrocells 9 through 16. By programming an appropriate EPROM bit in the device, the designer can select either the dedicated product term in a macrocell for individual clocking of its flip-flop, or the clock signal synchronous with other macrocells. Figure 6.7 illustrates these two possible clocking schemes. In Figure 6.7a the EPROM bit is programmed such that the multiplexer within the I/O control block of the macro-

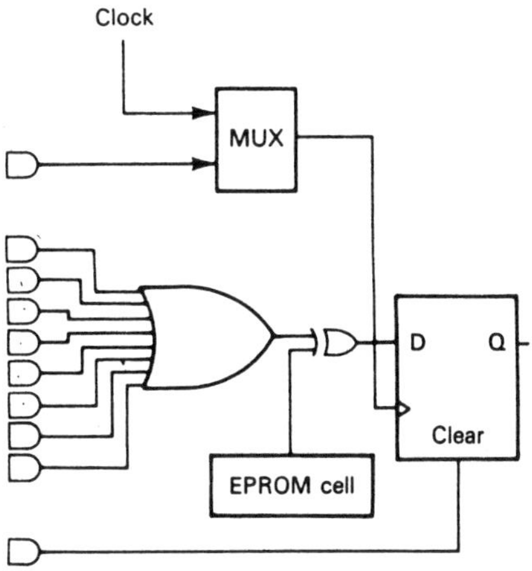

FIGURE 6.6a
D flip-flop

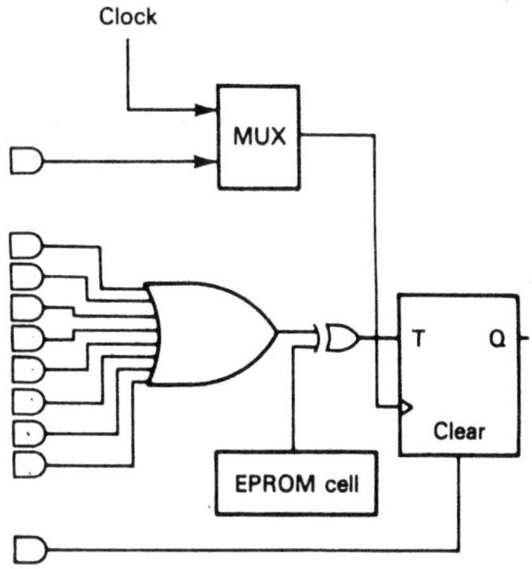

FIGURE 6.6b
T flip-flop

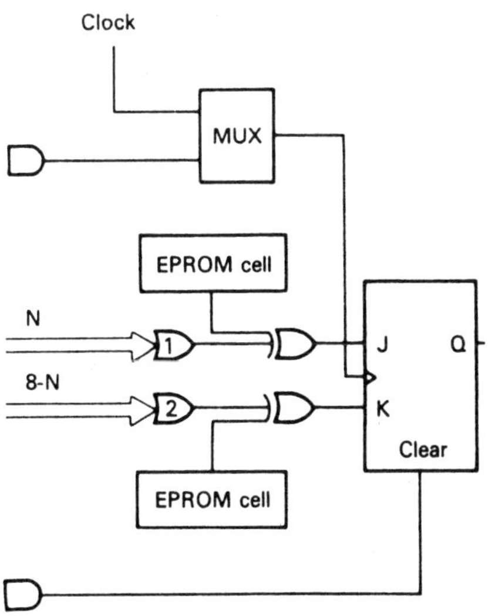

N. Subset of product terms feeding the OR gate 1.

FIGURE 6.6c
JK flip-flop

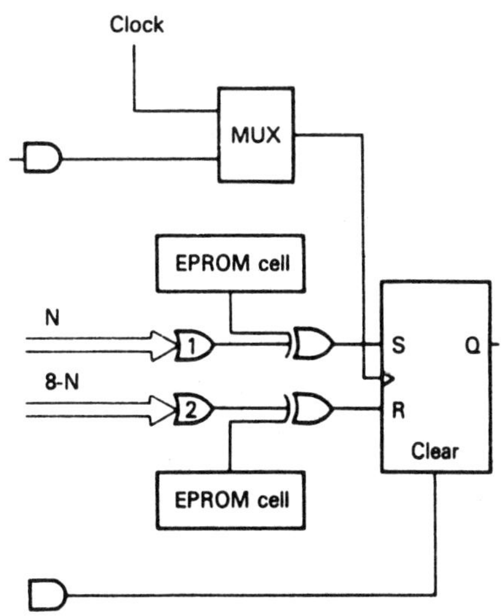

N. Subset of product terms feeding the OR gate 1.

FIGURE 6.6d
SR flip-flop (Copyright Altera Corp.)

cell, transfers the output of the AND gate (i.e., the dedicated product term to the enable input of the tri-state buffer at the output pin of the macrocell). The output buffer is enabled only if the output of the AND gate is at logic "1." The multiplexer also connects the dedicated clock input line to the corresponding input of the flip-flop, thus the flip-flop changes state in synchronization with flip-flops in other macrocells when a clock signal is applied.

The EPROM bit controlling the multiplexer associated with a macrocell, can also be programmed such that the enable input of the tri-state buffer at the output of the macrocell is connected to the supply voltage V_{CC}, and the clock input of the flip-flop is driven by the output of the AND gate corresponding to the dedicated product term (see Figure 6.7b). Thus, the output buffer is permanently enabled and the flip-flop is triggered by a product term (i.e., asynchronous clocking).

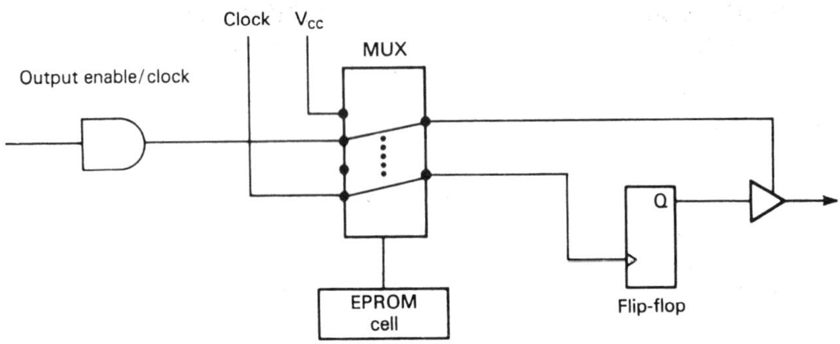

FIGURE 6.7a
Synchronous clock

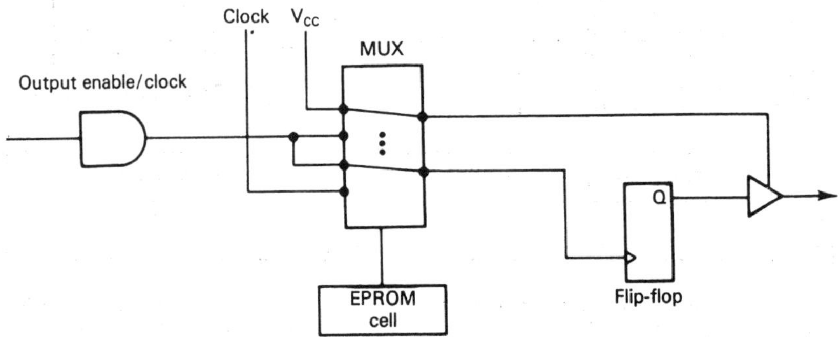

FIGURE 6.7b
Asynchronous clock (Copyright Altera Corp.)

In the erased state of the EP600, the EPROM bits controlling the multiplexer operation in the macrocells are set such that synchronous clocking is automatically selected and the output buffers are disabled.

EP900. The EP900 is architecturally similar to EP600. It offers up to 38 inputs and 24 outputs in a 24-pin package. It has 24 macrocells which have similar features as those in EP600. The EP900 provides equivalent of 1,104 2-input NAND gates compared to 716 in EP600. However, the power dissipation of EP900 is twice to that of EP600, and it is significantly slower with the maximum clock speed of 33.3 MHz.

EP1800. The EP1800 is currently the most complex device among the general purpose erasable PLDs offered by the Altera Corp. It has 12 dedicated inputs, 4 clock inputs, and 48 I/O pins each of which can be configured as an input or an output.

Figure 6.8 shows the block diagram of EP1800. It is partitioned into 4 quadrants, each containing 12 macrocells. A separate clock line is provided for each group of macrocells. Each quadrant of macrocells has its own local bus; these bus lines are driven by the true and complemented outputs of the macrocells within the quadrant. Thus, a local bus has 24 lines. The global bus runs through all 4 quadrants and has 64 lines. These bus lines are driven by the true and complement signals of the 12 dedicated inputs, 4 clock inputs, and the I/O pins of 4 **global** macrocells in each quadrant.

The macrocells within each quadrant are categorized into 2 different types:

1. Local macrocell; and
2. Global macrocells.

The combinational or registered output of local macrocell, or the signal on its I/O pin are fed back to the local bus of the quadrant to which the macrocell belongs (see Figure 6.9a). On the other hand, the combinational or registered output of a global macrocell is fed back to the local bus of the quadrant, and the signal on its I/O pin is fed back to the global bus (see Figure 6.9b); this requires that the output buffer of the macrocell be disabled. Thus, local and global macrocells provide feedback within and between the quadrants, respectively. Out of 12 macrocells in a quadrant, 8 are local and 4 are global.

As in EP600, a flip-flop associated with a macrocell in EP1800 is programmable (i.e., it can be configured for D, T, JK, or SR operation) and can be clocked by the quadrant clock of the macrocell for synchronous operation, or by the dedicated output enable/clock product term of the macrocell when asynchronous clocking is desired. When a flip-flop is triggered by the quadrant clock, the enable input of the macrocell output buffer is controlled by the dedicated product term. Alternatively, if a flip-flop is clocked via the product

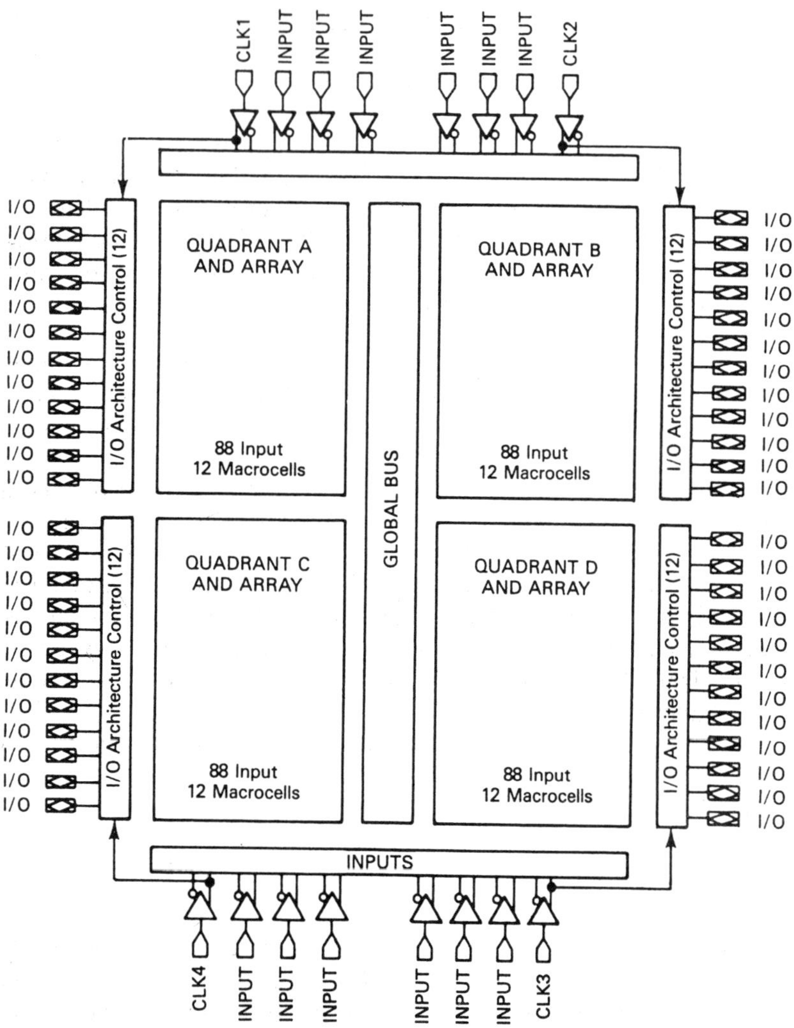

FIGURE 6.8
Block diagram of EP1800 (Copyright Altera Corp.)

term, the output buffer is permanently enabled. Both local and global macrocells can be configured to operate in either mode. The selection of a particular mode for a local macrocell is done by a single EPROM, as in EP600 (see Figure 6.7). Whereas, for global macrocells, 2 EPROM cells are needed (see Figure 6.10a and b).

One additional mode of operation is allowed for global macrocells. In this mode, the EPROM cells are programmed such that the flip-flop in a

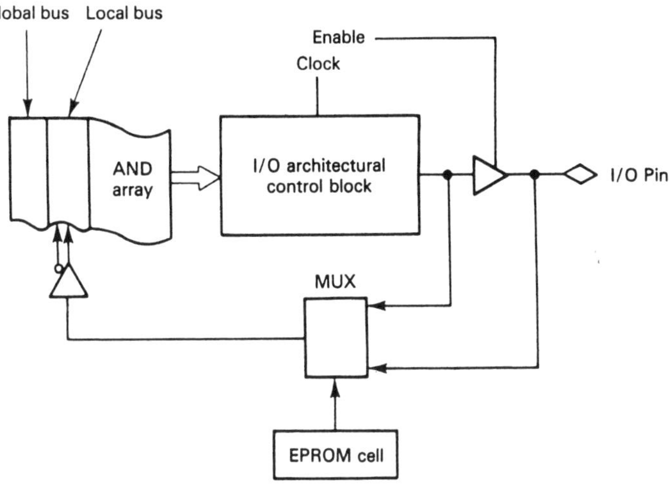

FIGURE 6.9a
Local macrocell

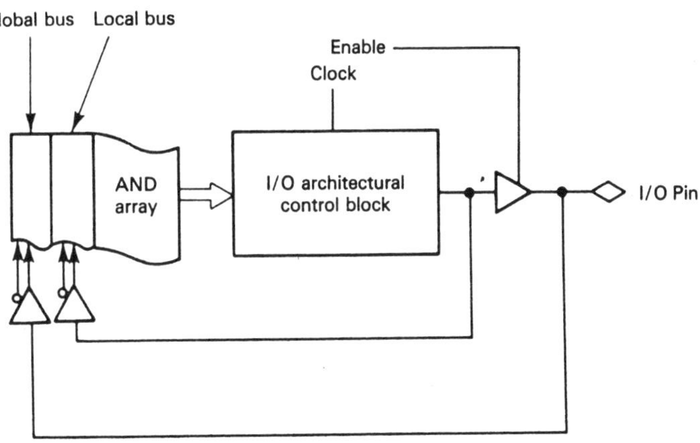

FIGURE 6.9b
Global macrocell (Copyright Altera Corp.)

macrocell is triggered by the dedicated product term and the output buffer is permanently disabled (see Figure 6.10c). Thus, the I/O pin associated with the macrocell can be used as an additional input. All the flip-flops in EP1800 have an individual clear input which is controlled by a dedicated product term. If the product term results in a logic "1" signal, the flip-flop is reset to 0 irrespective of the clock signal. In the combinational configuration, a macrocell in the EP1800 like that in the EP600, generates an output signal by taking

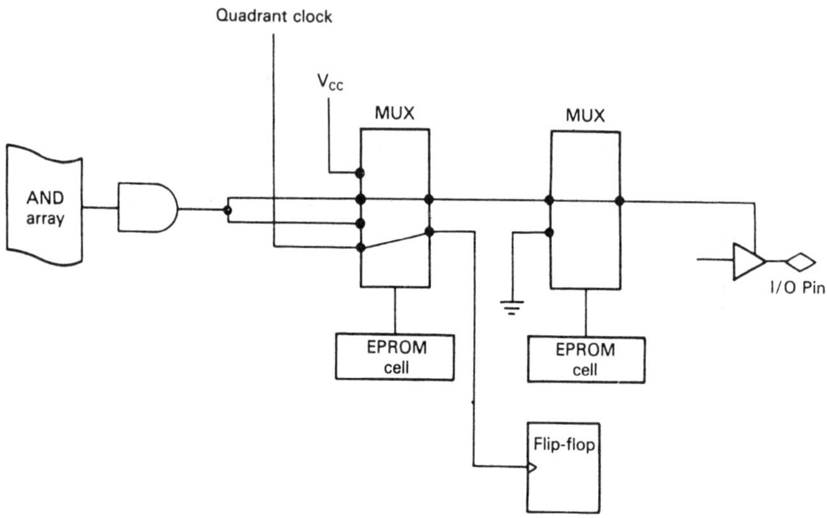

FIGURE 6.10a
Synchronous clock, output enabled by a product term

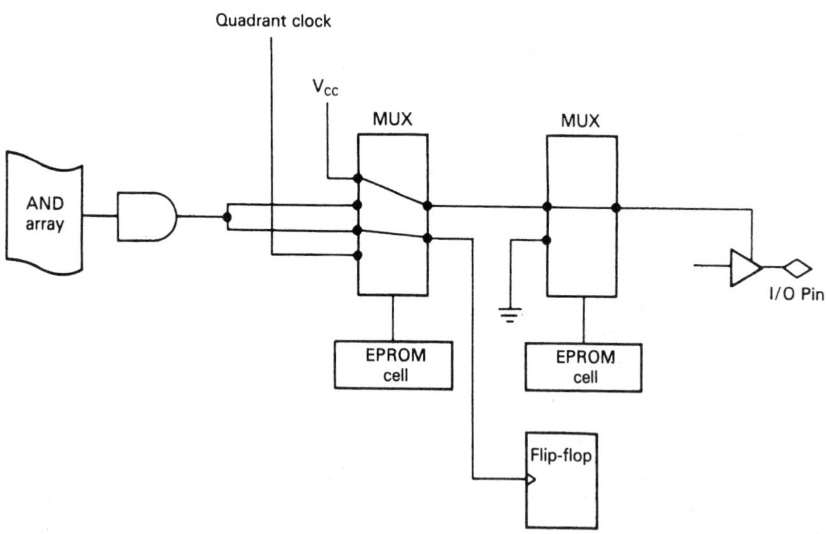

FIGURE 6.10b
Asynchronous clock, output permanently enabled

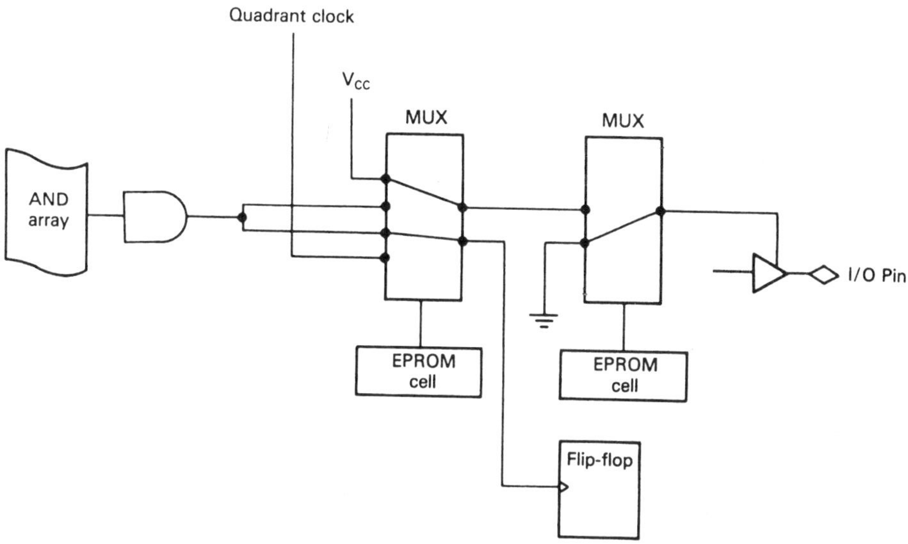

FIGURE 6.10c
Asynchronous clock, output permanently disabled (Copyright Altera Corp.)

the OR of the 8 product terms. The polarity of the output can be controlled by programming the appropriate EPROM cell. In the registered mode, 8 product terms are ORed together and the resulting output is applied to the input of the flip-flop when the flip-flop is configured as D or T type. If JK or SR flip-flop configuration is selected, the 8 product terms are shared between the 2 inputs of the flip-flop.

EP1210. This is a 40-pin device and has 12 latchable inputs and a dedicated clock input. It also has 24 I/O pins each of which can be programmed as inputs or outputs; besides one I/O pin can also be used as a second clock input line. Figure 6.11 shows the block diagram of the device. As can be seen from the diagram, the EP1210 is partitioned into 2 symmetrical segments, each segment containing 14 macrocells. Each segment is further divided into 4 blocks. Both block 1 and block 2 contain 4 macrocells, which generate sums of 4, 10, 8, and 6 product terms. Block 3 also has 4 macrocells, which produce sums of 12, 4, 8 and 8 products; besides 2 of the macrocells share 4 product terms and the other 2 share another set of 4 product terms. Block 4 contains 2 macrocells each of which forms the sum of 8 product terms.

The two segments in EP1210 communicate over a series of buses. Within each segment of the device, 8 out of the 14 macrocells transmit their true and complemented outputs on a 16-bit bus local to that segment; these 8 macrocells can also transfer their output to their respective I/O pins. Global communica-

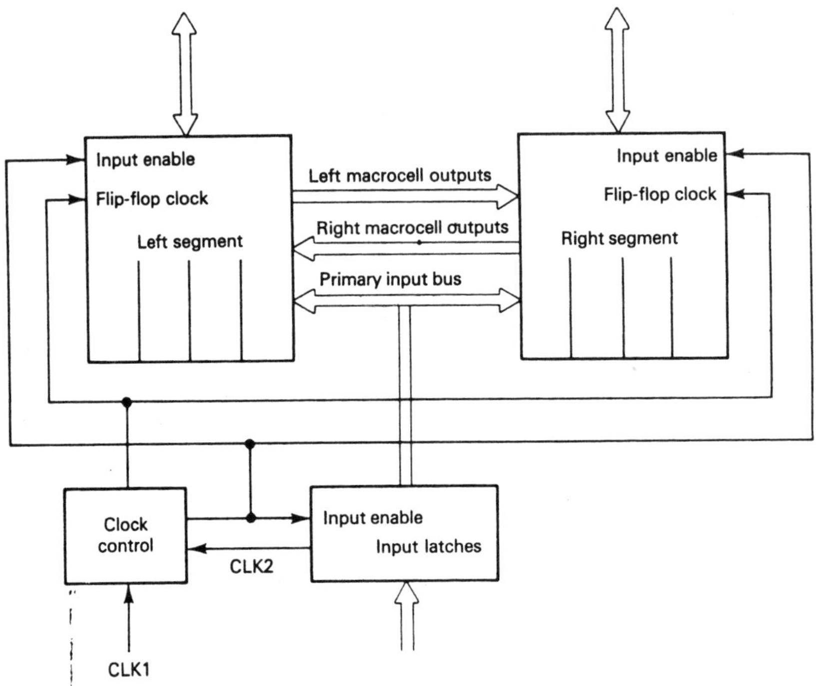

FIGURE 6.11
Block diagram of EP1210 (Copyright Altera Corp.)

tion throughout the device is done via a 48-bit bus, which carries the true and complement of signals applied at the 12 dedicated inputs, outputs of the 4 **buried flip-flops** (i.e., flip-flops whose outputs feed back into rather than out of the AND-OR array) and the outputs of the 4 macrocells in block 3 of each segment. Each EP1210 macrocell contains an AND-OR structure and a programmable I/O block. The AND array can be programmed to generate 4 to 16 product terms. These product terms of the macrocells are ORed together and may be fed back to other macrocells, or directly to itself (see Figure 6.12a) or via a D flip-flop (see Figure 6.12b). Alternatively, the output of the OR gate may be transferred to the I/O pin of the macrocell by enabling the tri-state buffer with the dedicated product term. The resulting output may also be directly fed back to the AND array or via the D flip-flop; in both cases the output latch must be enabled (see Figure 6.12c and d). The polarity of the OR gate, in all cases, is determined by the EPROM cell.

The EP1210 contains 2 internal signal paths which are used to distribute clock and latch enable sequals. One path drives the enable inputs of the latches associated with the I/O pins, as well as the enable inputs of the dedicated input latches. The other path provides clock signals to the D flip-flops within the out-

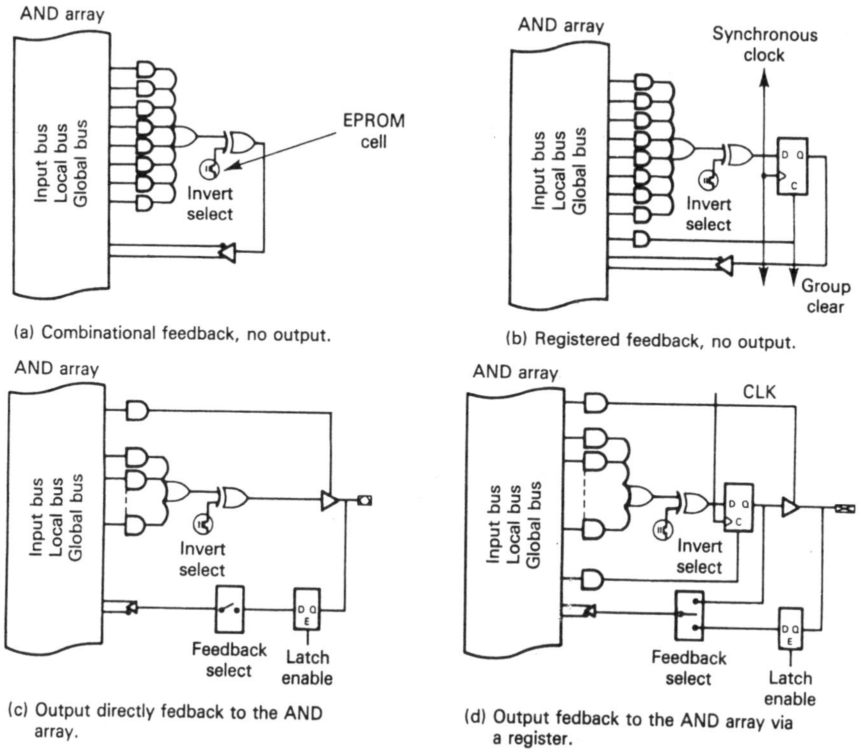

(a) Combinational feedback, no output.

(b) Registered feedback, no output.

(c) Output directly fedback to the AND array.

(d) Output fedback to the AND array via a register.

FIGURE 6.12
EP1210 Macrocell configurations (Copyright Altera Corp.)

put blocks of the macrocells. By programming 3 EPROM cells appropriately it is possible to select one of 8 operating modes of the clocking signals (see Table 6.1). For example, in the erased or 0 mode, the inputs on the dedicated lines are latched when Clk 1 (the clock signal applied via the dedicated clock input line) reaches a high level. On the high-to-low transition of Clk 1 the latches become disabled, and the D flip-flop is triggered. In mode 2 thc input data is not latched and the flip-flops change state on the negative edge of Clk 1. In modes 4 to 7, an additional clock sequel Clk 2 is applied by a dedicated I/O line (pin 38). In these modes, Clk 1 enables the latches; and Clk 2 triggers the D flip-flops.

MAX EPLDs. The **multiple array matrix** (MAX) family of EPLDS was introduced by Altera Corp. in 1988. This family consists of 6 chips with gate capacities ranging from 600 to 1200. The architecture of the chips is based on **logic array block** (LAB) concept. A LAB consists of a macrocell array, an expander product-term array and an I/O block (see Figure 6.13a). A central programmable array, known as **programmable interconnection array** (PIA), is

Programming mode	Operation
0	Input data is latched when Clk 1 goes from low to high; flip-flops change state on the negative edge of Clk 1.
1	Input data is latched when Clk 1 goes from high to low; flip-flops change state on the positive edge of Clk 1.
2	Input data is not latched; flip-flops change state on the negative edge of Clk 1.
3	Input data is not latched; flip-flops change state on the positive edge of Clk 1.
4	Input data is latched when Clk 1 goes from low to high; flip-flops change state on the negative edge of Clk 2.
5	Input data is latched when Clk 1 goes from high to low; flip-flops change state on the negative edge of Clk 2.
6	Input data is latched when Clk 1 goes from low to high; flip-flops change state on the positive edge of the Clk 2.
7	Input data is latched when Clk 1 goes from high to low; flip-flops change state on the positive edge of Clk 2.

TABLE 6.1
Operation modes of clock control block

used to interconnect the LABs. Devices containing a single LAB, use a global bus.

A macrocell consists of an array of product terms, and a flip-flop which can be programmed as a D, T, JK, or SR type (see Figure 6.13b). The flip-flop may also be used as a latch for flow-through operation, or bypassed entirely while implementing purely combinational logic functions. Individual asynchronous preset and clear capabilities are also part of the flip-flop. A flip-flop can be independently clocked of flip-flops in other macrocells (i.e., asynchronous clocking), or can be triggered synchronously with other flip-flops. The typical clock frequency for the MAX family of chips is 50 MHz.

The expander product term array in a LAB, is a group of uncommitted product terms. Each of these product terms may feed a single product term or multiple product terms in a macrocell (see Figure 6.13c). Furthermore, an expander product term may feed all the macrocells in a LAB. Such a product term is also allowed to feed or to be shared by other expander product terms.

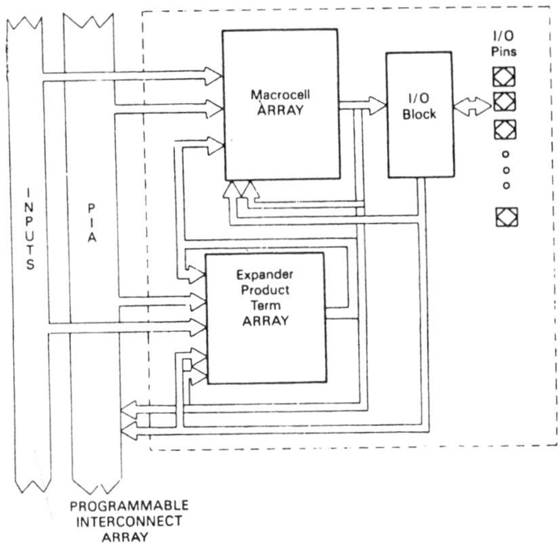

FIGURE 6.13a
LAB architecture (Copyright Altera Corp.)

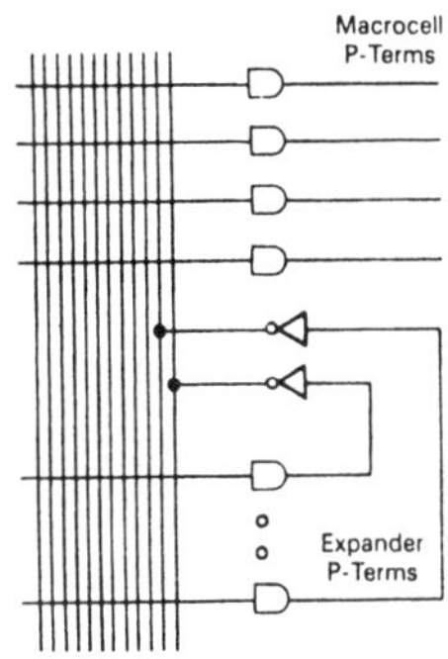

FIGURE 6.13c
Expander product terms.
(Copyright Altera Corp.)

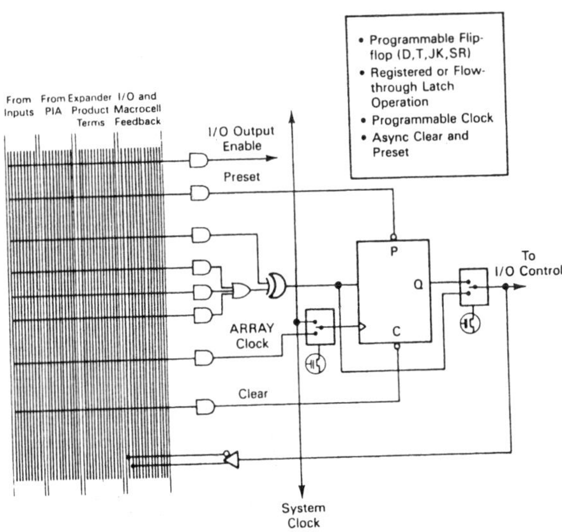

FIGURE 6.13b
Macrocell structure (Copyright Altera Corp.)

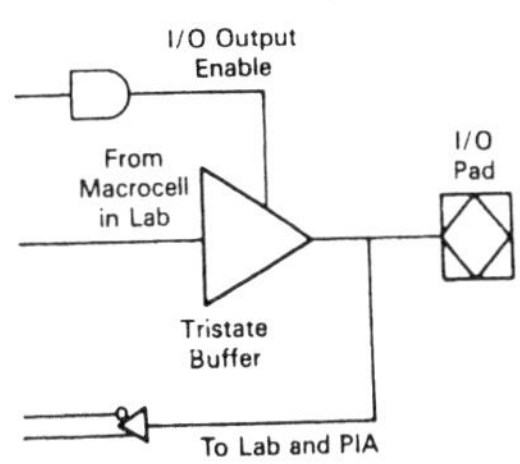

FIGURE 6.13d
I/O block
(Copyright Altera Corp.)

Device	No. of LABs	Macrocells/ LAB	Expander	PIA	Dedicated inputs	I/O pins
5016	1	16	32	No	8	8
5024	1	24	48	No	8	12
5032	1	32	64	No	8	16
5064	4	16	128	Yes	8	28
5127	8	16	256	Yes	8	28
5128	8	16	256	Yes	8	52

TABLE 6.1
MAX family members

The I/O block of a LAB is shown in Figure 6.13d. The tri-state buffer in the block drives the I/O pad, and is controlled by a product term of the macrocell array. By disabling the buffer, the macrocell flip-flop and the I/O pin can be used independently. Therefore, the flip-flops in the LAB can be **buried**, without sacrificing the input function of an I/O pin. Table 6.1 lists the features of the MAX family.

Altera offers a software package, known as **Programmable Logic Development System** (PLDS-MAX), for implementing designs using MAX EPLDs. PLDS-MAX includes design entry, processing, timing simulation, and device programming. It can be run on IBM PS/2, PC-AT or compatible machines. MAX-PLDS also accepts existing EPLD designs implemented with Altera's general purpose A+PLUS development software.

6.2 REPROGRAMMABLE GENERIC LOGIC DEVICE

Cypress Semiconductors offers a 24-pin ultraviolet-erasable CMOS device, PLDC20G10, which can emulate the functions of most of the 24-pin PAL devices. It can have up to 22 inputs, 10 programmable output cells, and features propagation delay of 25 ns. Figure 6.14 shows the block diagram of the device.

Each output cell receives the sum of 8 product terms as an input, which drives the built-in D flip-flop (see Figure 6.15). It also contains 2 multiplexers. The output enable multiplexer selects either the dedicated product term or the signal on the common output enable line to drive the enable input of the tri-state inverter at the output of the cell.

Each output cell contains 3 EPROM cells (C_0–C_2) which can be programmed to obtain a desired output configuration. Figure 6.16 shows the output configurations corresponding to each of the 8 combinations of $C_0\,C_1\,C_2$.

The PLDC20G10 provides the preload feature for simplifying the testing of a programmed device. Cypress Semiconductors also offers the reprogram-

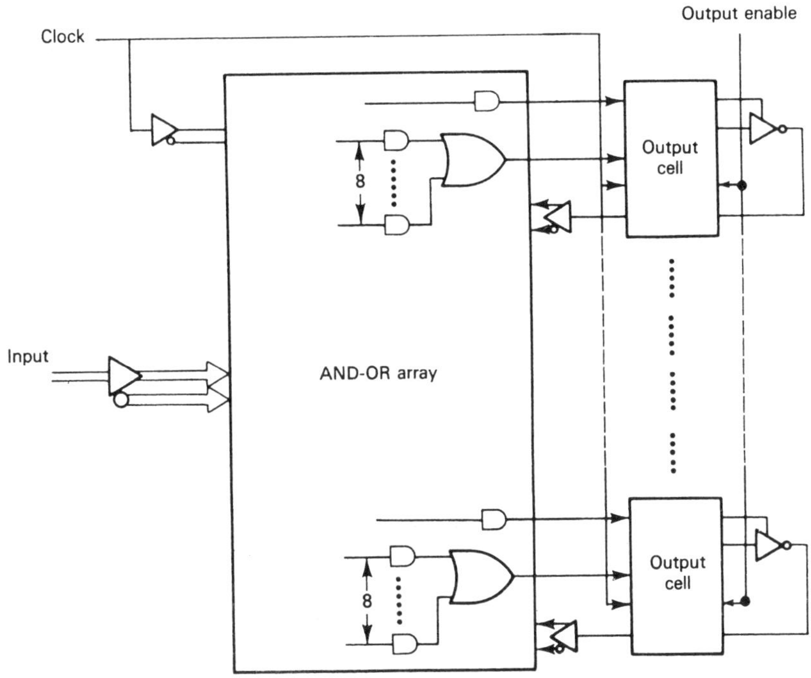

FIGURE 6.14
Block diagram of the PLDC20G10 (Courtesy of Cypress Semiconductors.)

mable CMOS versions of PAL16L8, PAL16R4, PAL16R6, PAL16R8, and PAL22V10 devices.

6.3 ERASABLE PROGRAMMABLE LOGIC ARRAY (EPLA)

There is currently one commercially available EPLA device—PLC473G offered by Signetics. It has 11 dedicated inputs, 2 dedicated outputs, 2 bidirectional I/O lines, and 24 product terms. Figure 6.17 shows the block diagram of the device. The PLC473 is a CMOS device with a maximum delay of 35 ns. As in other EPLD devices, it uses EPROM cells as programmable connections. The device is pin and functional equivalent to the PLHS473 (discussed in Chapter 4).

6.4 GENERIC ARRAY LOGIC (GAL)

This is a family of electrically erasable programmable devices offered by Lattice Semiconductors. The first member of this family is the 20-pin GAL16V8. Figure 6.18 shows the block diagram of the device.

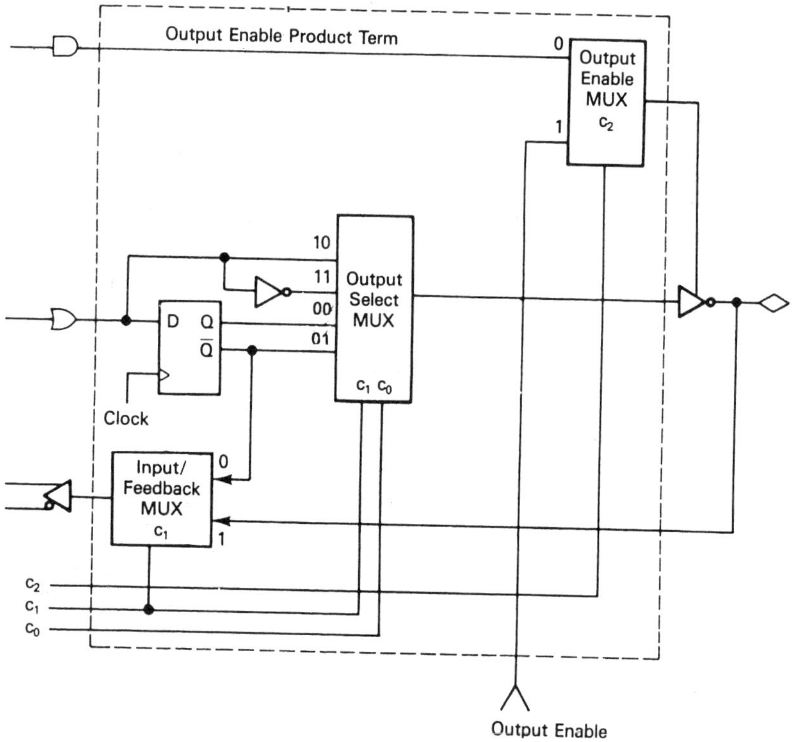

FIGURE 6.15
Structure of output cell array in PLDC20G10

	C_0	C_1	C_2	*Configuration*
Registered	0	0	0	Product term output enable/active-low
	1	0	0	Product term output enable/active-high
	0	0	1	External output enable/active-low
	1	0	1	External output enable/active-high
Combinational	0	1	0	Product term output enable/active-low
	1	1	0	Product term output enable/active-high
	0	1	1	External output enable/active-low
	1	1	1	External output enable/active-high

FIGURE 6.16
Output configurations for PLDC20G10

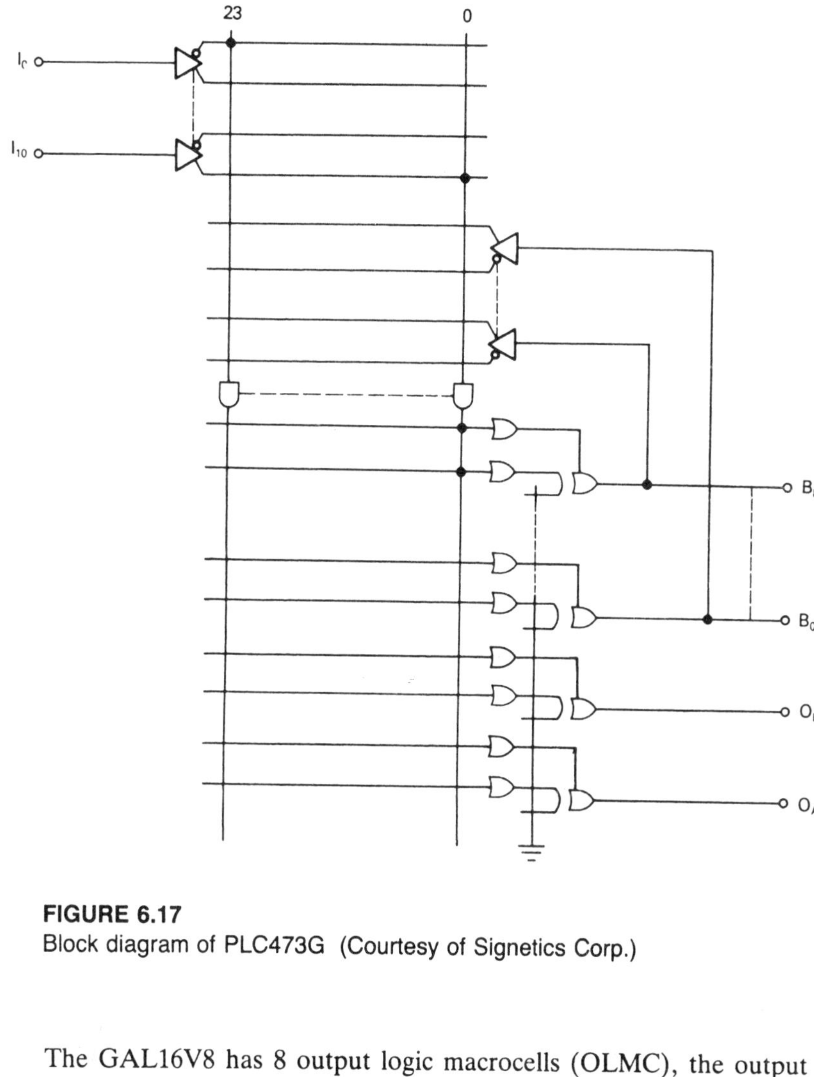

FIGURE 6.17
Block diagram of PLC473G (Courtesy of Signetics Corp.)

The GAL16V8 has 8 output logic macrocells (OLMC), the output of which is user configurable. Figure 6.19 shows the structure of an OLMC. The outputs of AND gates are fed into an OLMC, where they are summed by an OR gate. The output of the OR gate drives 1 input of an EX-OR gate. Each OLMC contains 4 cells, SYN, ACO, AC1(n), and EX-OR(n) which can be programmed to select 1 of the 5 operating modes of the OLMC. The SYN bit determines whether the output of the OLMC will be registered or purely combinational. It replaces the ACO bit in OLMC (12) and OLMC (19). The bit ACO, together with 8 AC1(n), selects 1 of the following output enable configurations:

1. I/O pin in an OLMC is a dedicated output;
2. I/O pin in an OLMC is a dedicated input;
3. the tri-state inverters at the outputs of all OLMCs are enabled by the common output enable OE; or
4. the tri-state inverters can be individually enabled by a product term.

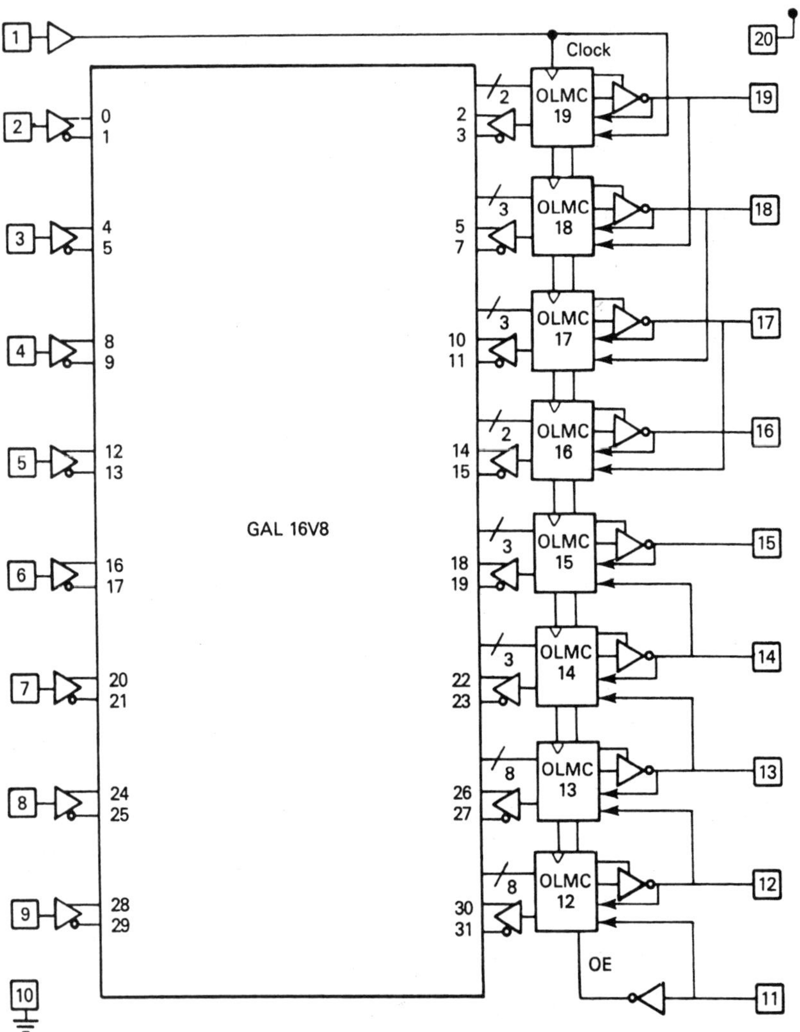

FIGURE 6.18
Block diagram of 16V8 (Copyright © 1988 Lattice Semiconductors Corp.)

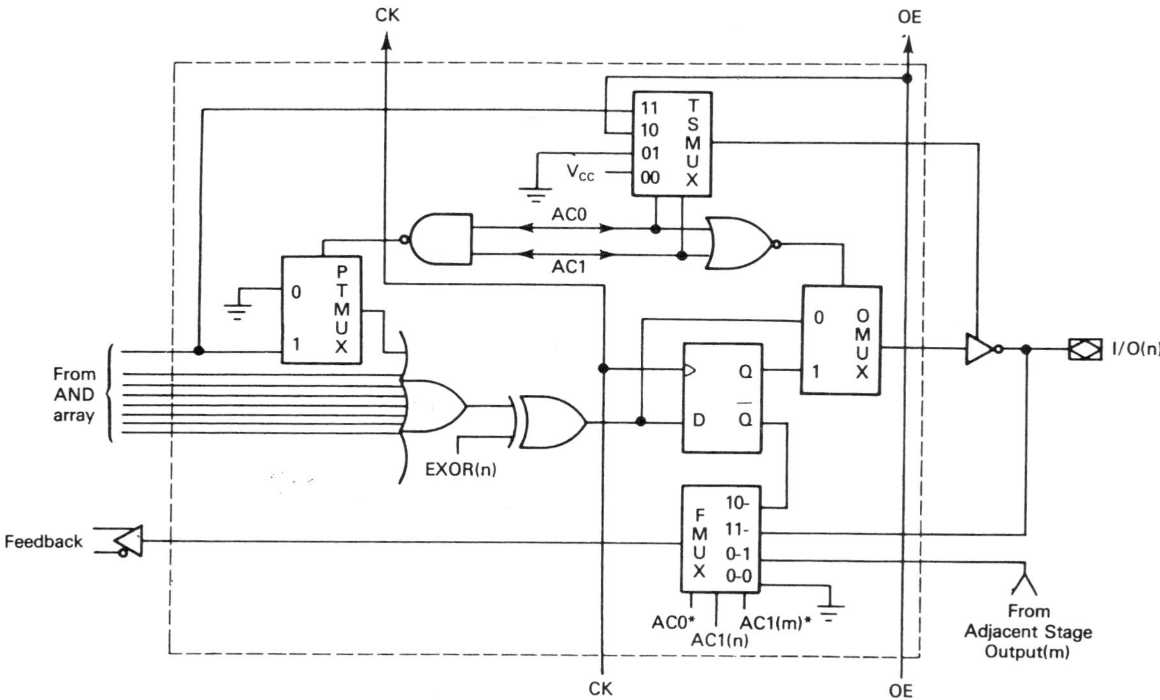

* $\overline{SYN}$ replaces ACO and SYN replaces AC1(m) as an input to the FMUX in OLMC(15) and OLMC(22).

FIGURE 6.19
Output logic macrocell structure. (Copyright © 1988 Lattice Semiconductors Corp.)

The control bits ACO and AC1(n) also determine the source of the feedback term, this term is fed back to the AND array via the multiplexer FMUX. The 5 possible operating modes of the macrocells in the GAL16V8 are explained in Table 6.2 and illustrated in Figure 6.20.

Mode	*SYN*	*ACO*	*AC1(n)*	*EX-OR(n)*	*Function*
1	1	0	1	—	Dedicated input; the output of the adjacent macrocell is fed back to the AND array.
2A	1	0	0	0	Combinational output (active-low); the enable input of the tri-state inverter is connected to V_{CC}.
2B	1	0	0	1	Same as above with active-high output.
3A	1	1	1	0	Combinational output (active-low); the enable input of the tri-state inverter is driven by a dedicated product term and the output is fed back to the AND array. The clock line is disconnected from the macrocell.
3B	1	1	1	1	Same as above with active-high output.
4A	0	1	1	0	Combinational output (active-low); the enable input of the tri-state inverter is driven by a dedicated product term and the output is fed back to the AND array. The clock line is connected to the macrocell.
4B	0	1	1	1	Same as above with active-high output.
5A	0	1	0	0	Registered output (active-low); the tri-state inverter is activated by the enable line.
5B	0	1	0	1	Same as above with active-high output

TABLE 6.2
Operating modes of the OLMCs

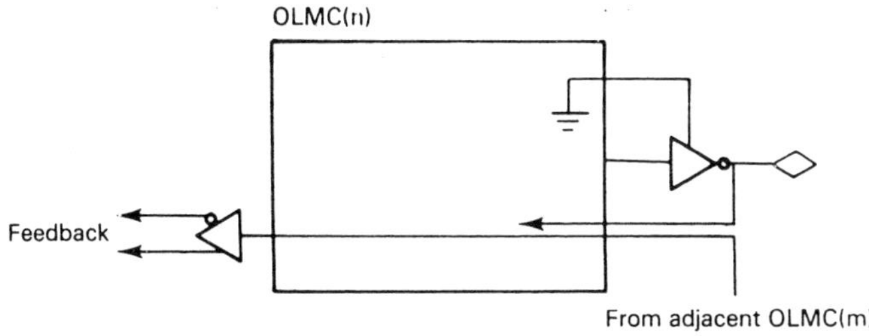

Mode 1

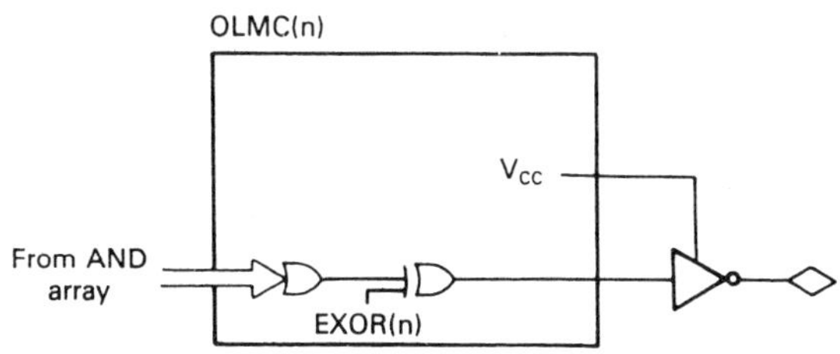

Modes 2A and 2B

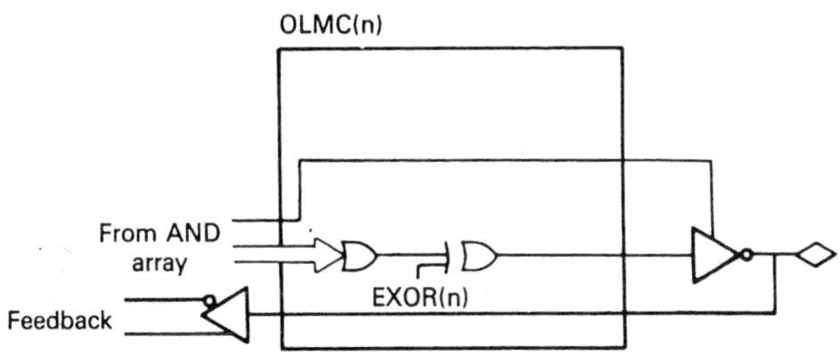

Modes 3A and 3B

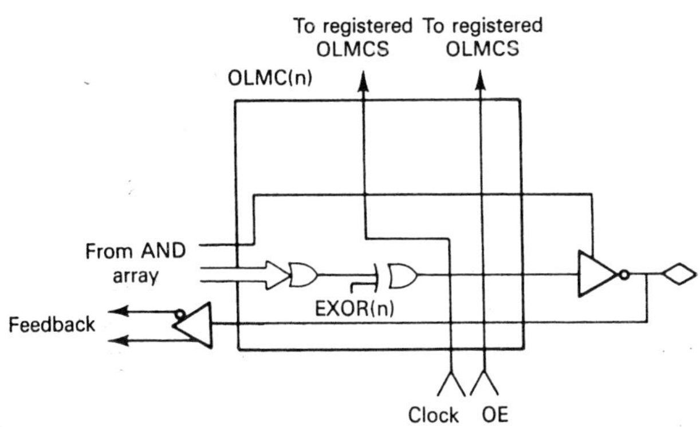

Mode 4A and 4B

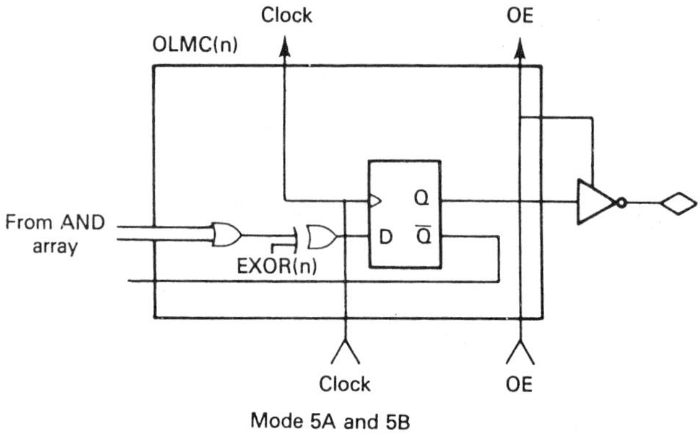

FIGURE 6.20
Macrocell configurations (Copyright © 1988 Lattice Semiconductors Corp.)

By selecting appropriate operating modes for the OLMCs, most of the 20-pin PAL devices can be emulated by the GAL16V8. For example, by making OLMC(19) and OLMC(18) to operate in Mode 1 and the remaining 6 OLMCs operate in Mode 2B, the function of the PAL12H6 can be emulated. Note that except in operating Modes 4 and 5, the CLK and the OE line function as input lines.

The operating modes of the OLMCs are set by programming the cells within an 82-bit control word in location 60. The location of specific bits within the control word is shown in Figure 6.21. The numbers below the EXOR(n) and AC1(n) bits in the control word indicate the output pin numbers of the devices controlled by these bits.

The row address 61 contains the user security cell. If the cell is programmed, any further programming or verification of the configuration pattern cannot be done.

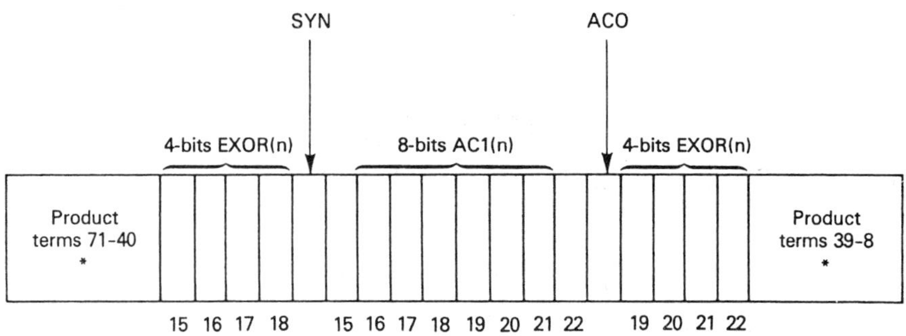

*If a bit is 1, the corresponding product term is enabled, otherwise it is disabled.

FIGURE 6.21
Control word in Row 60 of the GAL16V8 (Copyright © 1988 Lattice Semiconductors Corp.)

To illustrate the application of the device, we design a 4-bit binary counter. The input to the counter is A; the count value is incremented if A = 1, and decremented if A = 0. The counter generates an overflow if the input A is made logic "1" after a count of all 1's (i.e., 15 is reached) and is reset to its initial state (i.e., all 0's), on the next clock pulse. By designating the state variables for the counter as y_1, y_2, y_3 and y_4, we obtain the following design equations for the counter from Karnaugh maps as shown in Figure 6.22.

$$Y_1 = \overline{y}_1 y_2 y_3 y_4 \bullet A + y_1 \bullet \overline{A} + y_1 \overline{y}_2 + y_1 \overline{y}_3 + y_1 \overline{y}_4$$

$$Y_2 = \overline{y}_2 y_3 y_4 A + y_2 \overline{A} + y_2 \overline{y}_3 + y_2 \overline{y}_4$$

$$Y_3 = \overline{y}_3 y_4 A + y_3 \overline{A} + y_3 \overline{y}_4$$

$$Y_4 = \overline{y}_4 A + y_4 \overline{A}$$

$$\text{Overflow} = y_1 y_2 y_3 y_4 A$$

The logic diagram of the GAL16V8 is coded as shown in Figure 6.23 to implement the above expressions. It should be noted that OLMC(18) operates in mode 4B, whereas OLMC(17–14) operate in mode 5B.

GAL20V8. This device offers up to 20 inputs and 8 output logic macrocells in a 24-pin package. The macrocells have identical features to those in GAL16V8. The GAL20V8 can emulate most of the 24-pin PAL chips. Both GAL16V8 and GAL20V8 can operate at very high speed (15 ns from input to output), and are rated at a maximum of 90 mA power dissipation. Furthermore, both devices have **reset** and **preload** capability.

GAL39V18. This is a 24-pin device with a new internal architecture. It contains 10 output logic macrocells (OLMC) whose structures are significantly different from those in the previously discussed GAL devices. In addition, it has 8 **buried** state logic macrocells (SLMC) and 20 input logic macrocells (ILMC). Figure 6.24 shows the block diagram of the device.

The structure of the ILMC, shown in Figure 6.25, is the same irrespective of whether the input to the macrocell is applied via an input pin or via an I/O pin. Each macrocell can be configured to provide direct, latched, or registered input. The latch enable signal is applied via pin 1; the signal, when active-high, makes the latch transparent. For a registered input, the clock signal is also applied through pin 1, which triggers the D flip-flop on the positive edge. An ILMC can be configured to operate in 1 of the 3 modes by properly selecting the control inputs (S_0,S_1) to the multiplexer.

The structure of the SLMC is shown in Figure 6.26. Each cell receives the outputs of two OR gates identified as A and B in the diagram; these gates may generate the sum of any number of product terms. If the flip-flops in all SLMCs are to be clocked simultaneously, then the output of gate B is used as the clock enable input for each flip-flop; all flip-flops are triggered on the positive edge

Y_1

A=0

	$\bar{y}_1\bar{y}_2$	$\bar{y}_1 y_2$	$y_1 y_2$	$y_1\bar{y}_2$
$\bar{y}_3\bar{y}_4$			1	1
$\bar{y}_3 y_4$			1	1
$y_3 y_4$			1	1
$y_3\bar{y}_4$			1	1

A=1

	$\bar{y}_1\bar{y}_2$	$\bar{y}_1 y_2$	$y_1 y_2$	$y_1\bar{y}_2$
$\bar{y}_3\bar{y}_4$			1	1
$\bar{y}_3 y_4$			1	1
$y_3 y_4$		1		1
$y_3\bar{y}_4$			1	1

Y_2

A=0

	$\bar{y}_1\bar{y}_2$	$\bar{y}_1 y_2$	$y_1 y_2$	$y_1\bar{y}_2$
$\bar{y}_3\bar{y}_4$		1	1	
$\bar{y}_3 y_4$		1	1	
$y_3 y_4$		1	1	
$y_3\bar{y}_4$		1	1	

A=1

	$\bar{y}_1\bar{y}_2$	$\bar{y}_1 y_2$	$y_1 y_2$	$y_1\bar{y}_2$
$\bar{y}_3\bar{y}_4$		1	1	
$\bar{y}_3 y_4$		1	1	
$y_3 y_4$	1			1
$y_3\bar{y}_4$		1	1	

Y_3

A=0

	$\bar{y}_1\bar{y}_2$	$\bar{y}_1 y_2$	$y_1 y_2$	$y_1\bar{y}_2$
$\bar{y}_3\bar{y}_4$				
$\bar{y}_3 y_4$				
$y_3 y_4$	1	1	1	1
$y_3\bar{y}_4$	1	1	1	1

A=1

	$\bar{y}_1\bar{y}_2$	$\bar{y}_1 y_2$	$y_1 y_2$	$y_1\bar{y}_2$
$\bar{y}_3\bar{y}_4$				
$\bar{y}_3 y_4$	1	1	1	1
$y_3 y_4$				
$y_3\bar{y}_4$	1	1	1	1

Y_4

A=0

	$\bar{y}_1\bar{y}_2$	$\bar{y}_1 y_2$	$y_1 y_2$	$y_1\bar{y}_2$
$\bar{y}_3\bar{y}_4$				
$\bar{y}_3 y_4$	1	1	1	1
$y_3 y_4$	1	1	1	1
$y_3\bar{y}_4$				

A=1

	$\bar{y}_1\bar{y}_2$	$\bar{y}_1 y_2$	$y_1 y_2$	$y_1\bar{y}_2$
$\bar{y}_3\bar{y}_4$	1	1	1	1
$\bar{y}_3 y_4$				
$y_3 y_4$				
$y_3\bar{y}_4$	1	1	1	1

overflow

A=0

	$\bar{y}_1\bar{y}_2$	$\bar{y}_1 y_2$	$y_1 y_2$	$y_1\bar{y}_2$
$\bar{y}_3\bar{y}_4$				
$\bar{y}_3 y_4$				
$y_3 y_4$				
$y_3\bar{y}_4$				

A=1

	$\bar{y}_1\bar{y}_2$	$\bar{y}_1 y_2$	$y_1 y_2$	$y_1\bar{y}_2$
$\bar{y}_3\bar{y}_4$				
$\bar{y}_3 y_4$				
$y_3 y_4$			1	
$y_3\bar{y}_4$				

FIGURE 6.22
Karnaugh maps for deriving design equations for the 4-bit counter

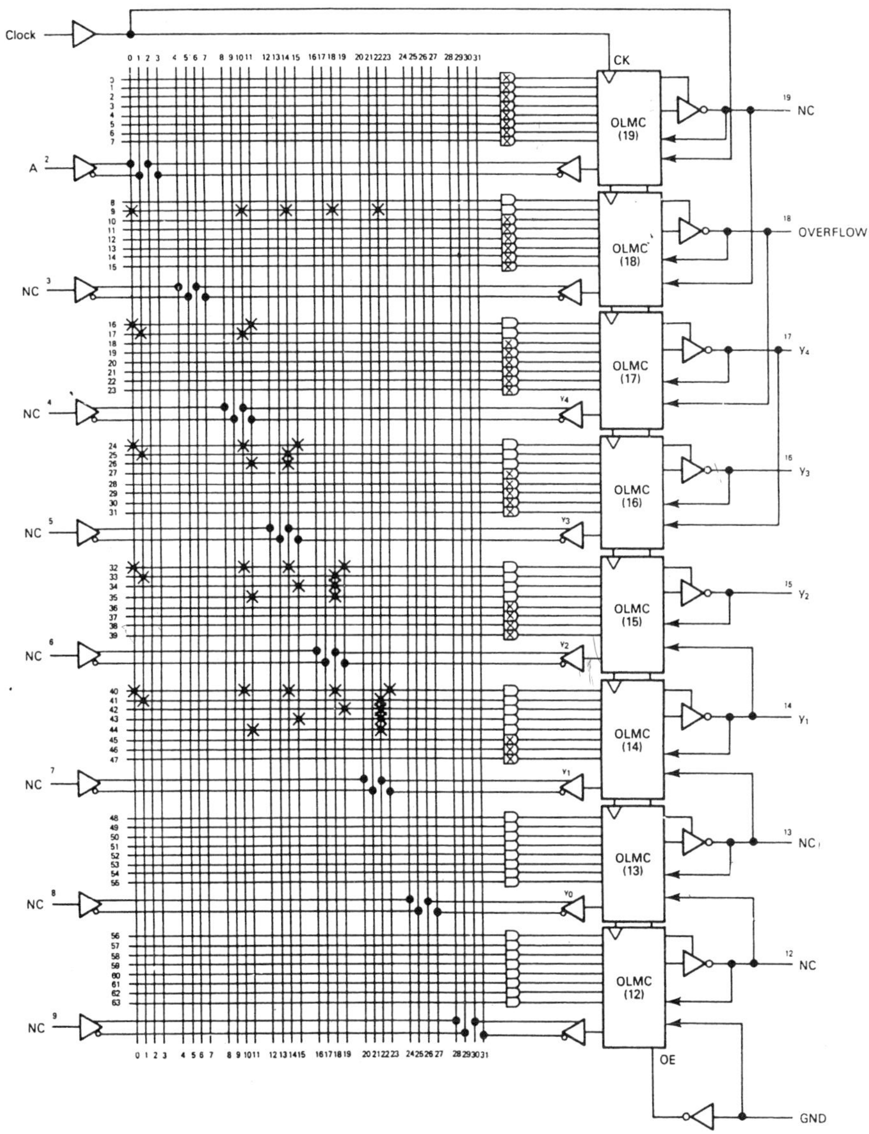

FIGURE 6.23
A 4-bit binary counter

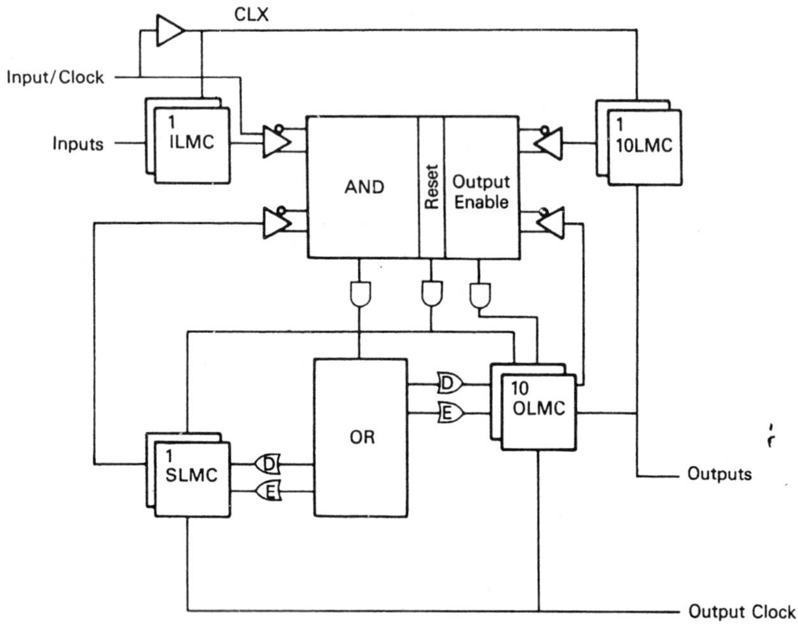

FIGURE 6.24
Block diagram of GAL39V18 (Copyright © 1988 Lattice Semiconductors Corp.)

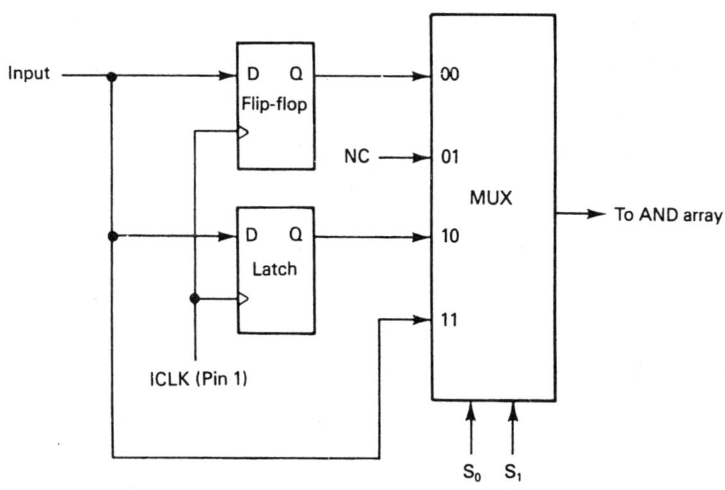

FIGURE 6.25
Input (and I/O) output logic macrocell

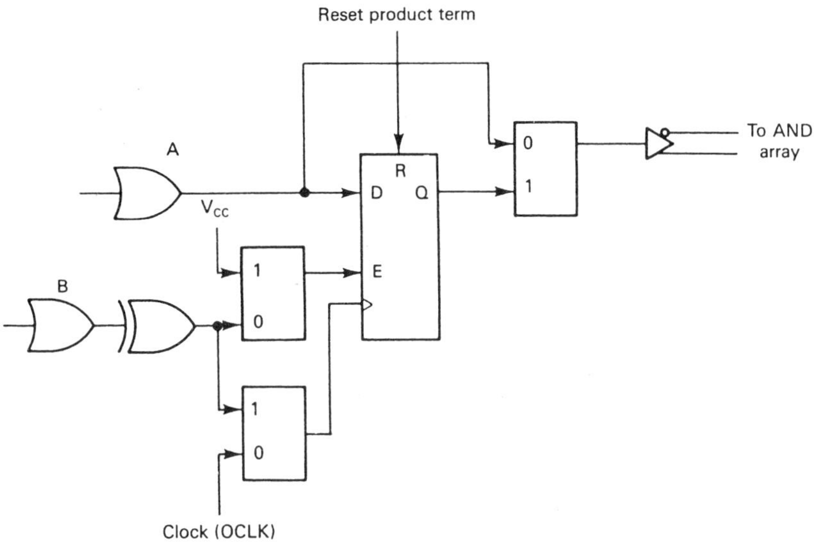

FIGURE 6.26
State logic macrocell

of the clock, OCLK. Alternatively, the flip-flops may be clocked individually, in which case the output of gate B is used as a clock. The output of gate A drives the D input of the flip-flop.

The structure of an OLMC is basically similar to that of an SLMC, except that an additional EXOR gate and a tri-state inverter are incorporated as shown in Figure 6.27. The tri-state inverters are enabled by a set of dedicated AND gates.

The GAL39V8 can emulate the functions of the currently available 24-pin PAL and FPLA devices. The maximum input-to-output delay for the devices is 30 ns, with a typical power consumption of 80 mA. Like all other GAL devices, the 39V8 provides preload feature for all the flip-flops incorporated into the device; a security fuse is also available.

GAL16Z8. EPLDs have a major advantage over other types of PLDs in that they can be reprogrammed. However, it is still necessary to remove such a chip from the system for erasing and reprogramming. Every time a chip is put into or removed from the system, there is the risk of damaging the chip. Lattice Semiconductors introduced an in-circuit reprogrammable version of the GAL16V8, the GAL16Z8, which can be erased and reprogrammed without removal from the system. The GAL16Z8 is a 24-pin device and offers all the functions of the 20-pin GAL16V8 described above. The 4 additional pins are used exclusively for in-system programming and diagnostic testing.

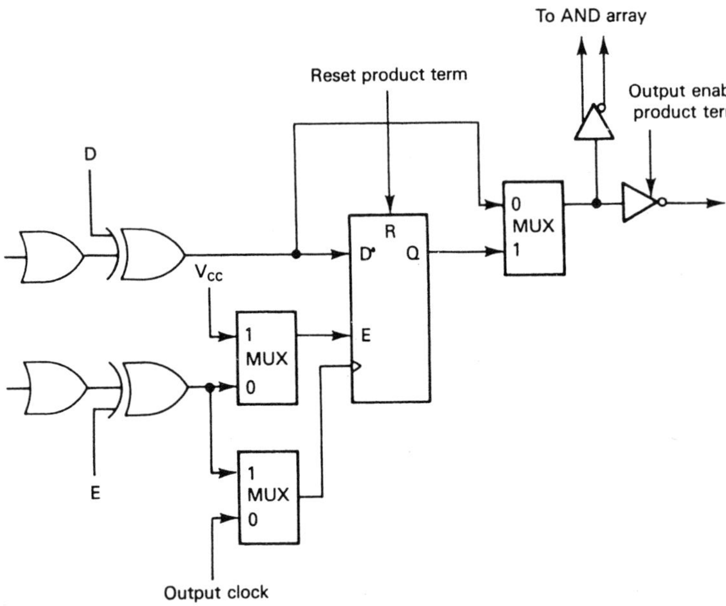

FIGURE 6.27
Output logic macrocell

Like the GAL16V8, the GAL16Z8 has an AND array plane and 8 programmable output logic macrocells. It also has a built-in state machine which controls all programming and testing with information supplied via the 4 pins: SDI (serial data in), Mode, DCLK (diagnostic clock), and SDO (serial data out), as shown in Figure 6.28. When the Mode pin is at logic "0," the address and data bits for programming the AND array is supplied via the SDI pin and is clocked into the shift register latch, on the rising edge of the clock signal at the DCLK pin. When both the Mode and SDI pins are at logic 1, the present states of the macrocells are loaded into the shift register when the clock signal is applied at the DCLK pin, and can be shifted out via the SDO pin for verification. The device moves to its normal state on the rising clock edge at DCLK if the user-controlled reset signal is activated, and the Mode and SDI pins are at logic "1" and logic "0," respectively. In its normal state, GAL16Z8 remembers the last update to its EEPROM cells and functions in the system accordingly.

6.5 PROGRAMMABLE ELECTRICALLY ERASABLE LOGIC (PEEL™) DEVICES

The PEEL devices produced by International CMOS Technology, Inc., like the GAL family of chips, offer electrically erasable reprogrammability. Two

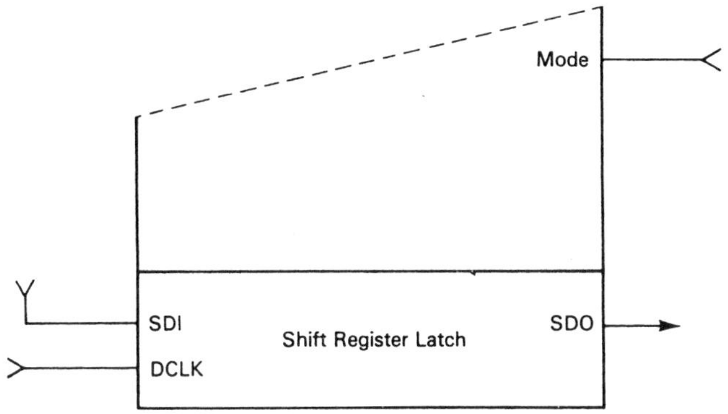

FIGURE 6.28
Special pins in GAL16Z8

of these devices, PEEL18CV8 and PEEL22CV10, can architecturally emulate the 20-pin and 24-pin PAL chips, respectively. Two devices, PEEL153 and PEEL173, can emulate the Signetics' FPLA devices PLS153 and PLS173, respectively. Super-set version of the PLS153 and PLS173, the PEEL253 and PEEL273, respectively, are also available.

PEEL18CV8. It has 9 dedicated inputs, 1 clock/input line and 8 I/O pins which can be configured to be either input, output or bidirectional I/O. Thus, the device can have a maximum of 18 inputs. Figure 6.29 shows the block diagram of PEEL18CV8.

The device has 8 macrocells, each of which consists of a D flip-flop, and 2 multiplexers (Figure 6.30). The multiplexer control bits of each macrocell

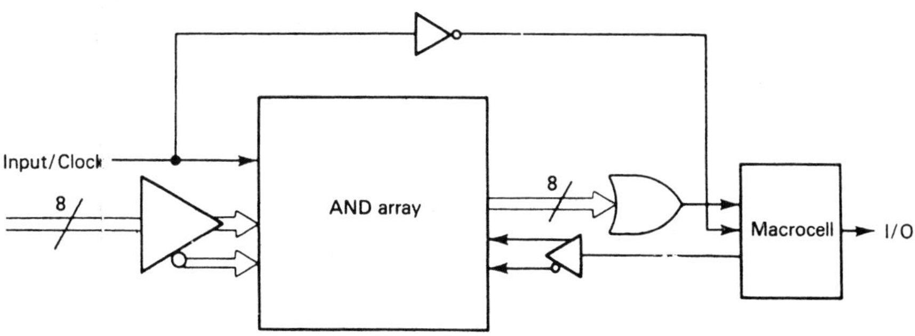

FIGURE 6.29
Block diagram of PEEL18CV8 (Courtesy of International CMOS Technology.)

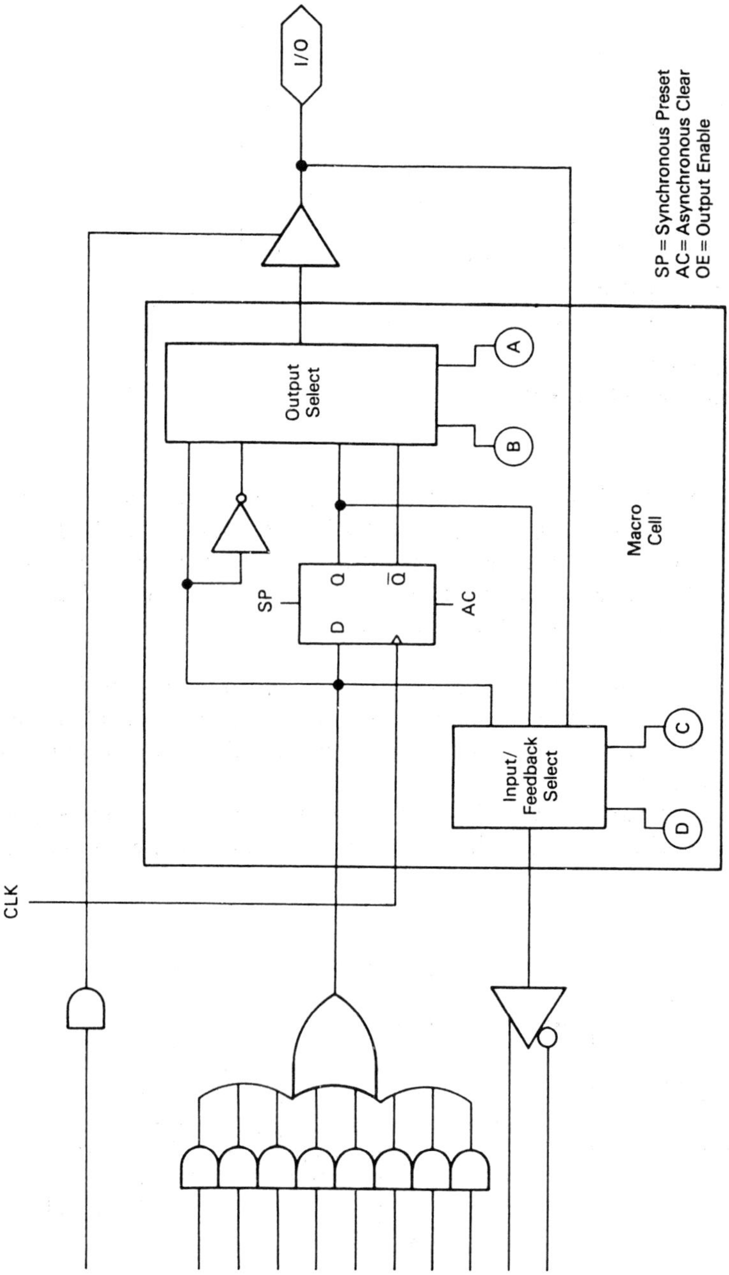

FIGURE 6.30
PEEL18CV8 macrocell (Courtesy of International CMOS Technology.)

(A, B, C, D), can be programmed via 4 electrically erasable memory bits to assume 1 of 12 configurations shown in Figure 6.31.

The data input of the D flip-flop in a macrocell is derived by ORing 8 product terms of the AND array. The flip-flop is triggered on the positive edge of the clock signal applied via the CLK input. The **synchronous preset** (SP) and the **asynchronous clear** (AC) inputs of the flip-flop are each driven by a separate product term. If the SP product term produces a logic high, the output of the D flip-flop will be set to logic "1" on the rising edge of the next clock signal. On the other hand, if the AC product term generates a logic high, the output of the flip-flop changes immediately to logic "0." The SP and AC product terms are common to all the flip-flops in the device. An additional product term is employed to enable the output buffer of each macrocell. Thus, the total number of product terms available in the PEEL18CV8 is 74–64 corresponding to the 8 macrocells, 1 synchronous-preset term, 1 asynchronous reset term, and 8 output enable terms.

Figure 6.32 shows the logic array diagram of PEEL18CV8. At the intersection of an input line and each product term, there is an EEPROM cell which is programmed to connect or disconnect the input line to the corresponding AND gate. In the erased state, all input line and product term intersections in the device are open. The implementation of a particular function is done by programming the appropriate EEPROM cells.

As an example, let us implement the 3-input, 7-state sequential circuit specified in Figure 6.33. Since there are 7 states in the sequential circuit and PEEL18CV8 has 8 macrocells, it is possible to use a state assignment based on the principle of ring-counter operation. Thus only 7 of the 8 macrocells, and 3 dedicated input lines of the PEEL18CV8 are required to implement the sequential circuit. State 1 corresponds to only the output of the macrocell 1 being at logic "1," the output of the remaining macrocells being at logic "0"; State 2 corresponds to only the output of macrocell 2 being at logic "1," and so on. Thus, the truth table of the sequential circuit can be represented as shown in Figure 6.34.

The excitation equations for the flip-flops in the macrocells are:

$$Q1 = A \cdot Q1 + A \cdot Q6 + A \cdot Q7$$

$$Q2 = \overline{A} \cdot Q1$$

$$Q3 = \overline{C} \cdot Q2 + \overline{A} \cdot Q3 + \overline{B}\overline{C} \cdot Q5$$

$$Q4 = A \cdot Q3 + A \cdot Q4$$

$$Q5 = \overline{A} \cdot Q4$$

$$Q6 = \overline{B}C \cdot Q5 + \overline{A} \cdot Q6$$

$$Q7 = C \cdot Q2 + B \cdot Q5 + \overline{A} \cdot Q7$$

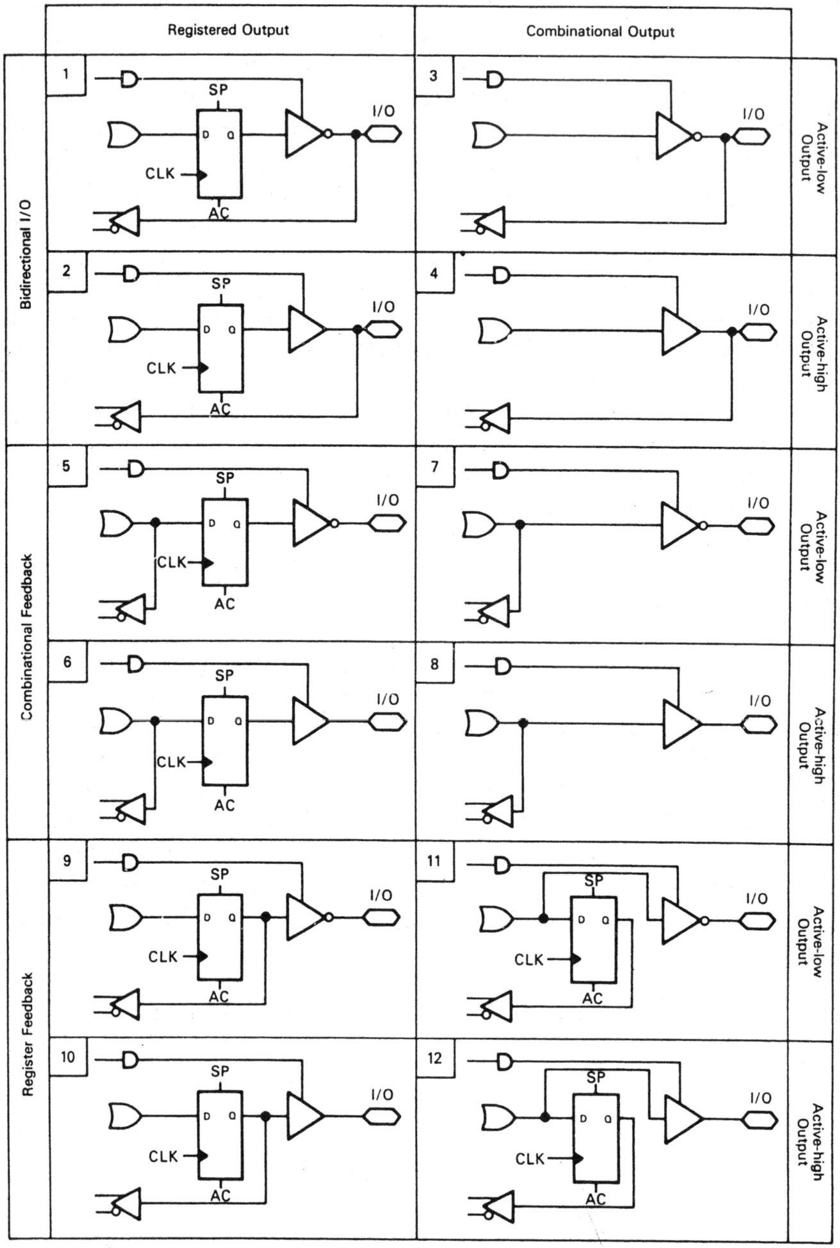

FIGURE 6.31
PEEL18CV8 macrocell configurations (Courtesy of International CMOS Technology.)

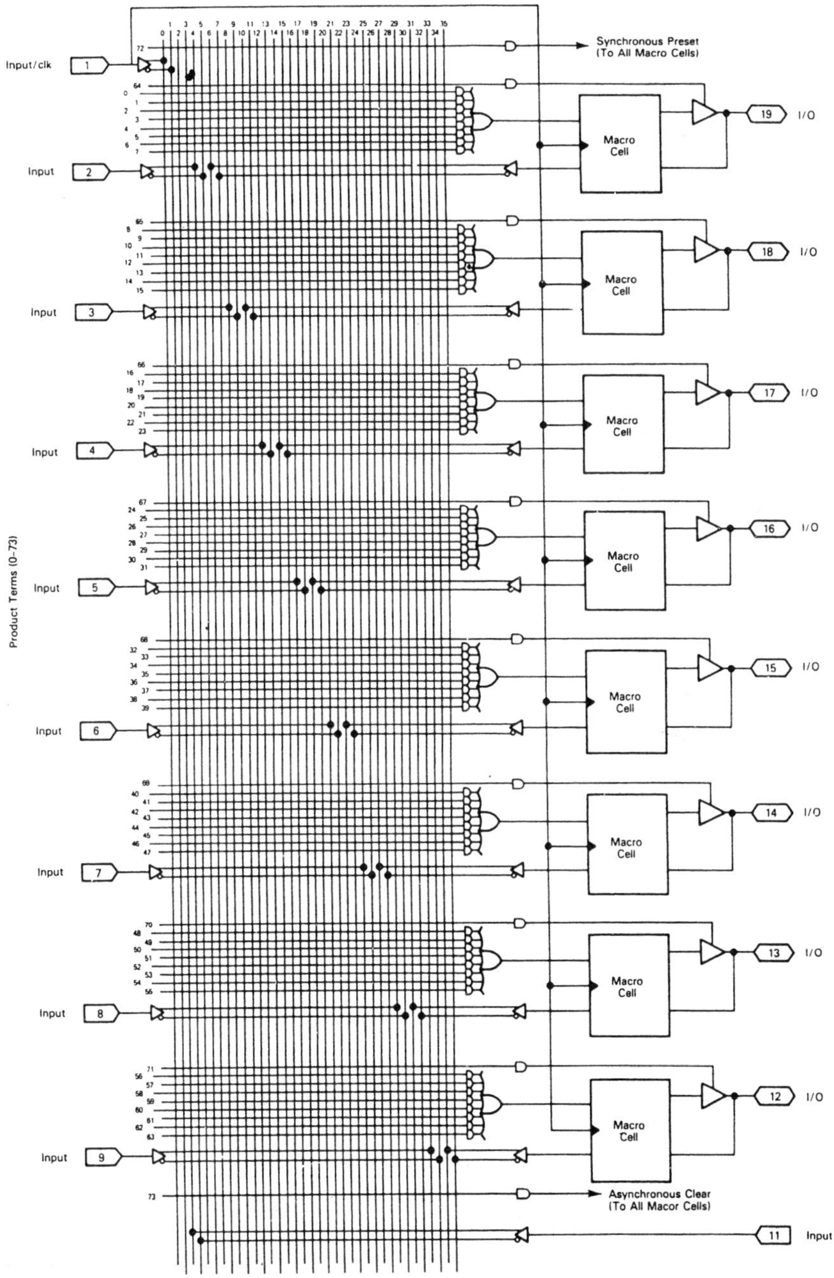

FIGURE 6.32
Logic diagram of PEEL18CV8 (Courtesy of International CMOS Technology.)

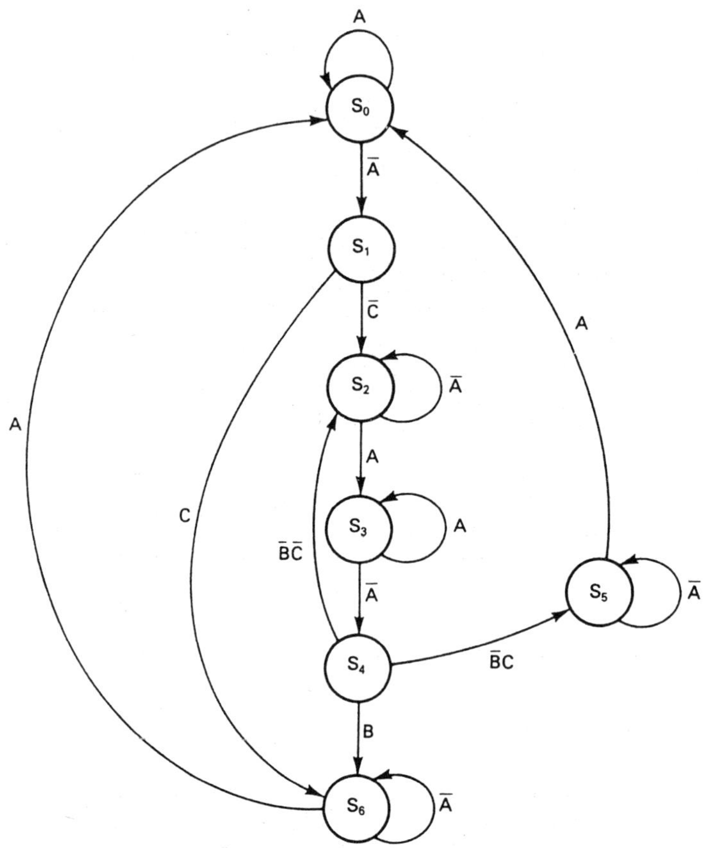

FIGURE 6.33
A state diagram

The ABEL input file for the sequential circuit is derived from the above excitation equations, and is shown in Figure 6.35. The implementation of the circuit on a PEEL18CV8 is shown in Figure 6.36; a dot (•) in the array indicates the presence of a connection. All the macrocells in the programmed device are configured to operate in Mode 10.

PEEL22CV10. This device offers complete functional compatibility with the PAL22V10. It contains 10 macrocells which have similar structures to those in PEEL18CV8. However, this device does not provide the pre-load feature available in the PAL22V10.

Present state (Outputs of macrocells)							Input			Next state (Output of macrocells)						
Q1	*Q2*	*Q3*	*Q4*	*Q5*	*Q6*	*Q7*	*A*	*B*	*C*	*Q1*	*Q2*	*Q3*	*Q4*	*Q5*	*Q6*	*Q7*
1	0	0	0	0	0	0	0	X	X	0	1	0	0	0	0	0
1	0	0	0	0	0	0	1	X	X	1	0	0	0	0	0	0
0	1	0	0	0	0	0	X	X	0	0	0	1	0	0	0	0
0	1	0	0	0	0	0	X	X	1	0	0	0	0	0	0	1
0	0	1	0	0	0	0	0	X	X	0	0	1	0	0	0	0
0	0	1	0	0	0	0	1	X	X	0	0	0	1	0	0	0
0	0	0	1	0	0	0	0	X	X	0	0	0	0	1	0	0
0	0	0	1	0	0	0	1	X	X	0	0	0	1	0	0	0
0	0	0	0	1	0	0	X	0	0	0	0	1	0	0	0	0
0	0	0	0	1	0	0	X	0	1	0	0	0	0	0	1	0
0	0	0	0	1	0	0	X	1	X	0	0	0	0	0	0	1
0	0	0	0	0	1	0	0	X	X	0	0	0	0	0	1	0
0	0	0	0	0	1	0	1	X	X	1	0	0	0	0	0	0
0	0	0	0	0	0	1	0	X	X	0	0	0	0	0	0	1
0	0	0	0	0	0	1	1	X	X	1	0	0	0	0	0	0

FIGURE 6.34
Truth table corresponding to Figure 6.33

PEEL253. This device is a super-set version of PEEL153. As mentioned before the PEEL153 is a direct replacement for the Signetics' Field-programmable logic array, PLS153. The logic array diagram of the PEEL253 is shown in Figure 6.37. It has 42 products compared to 32 in the PEEL153. The enable inputs of the tri-state buffers in these devices are driven by a set of dedicated OR gates, whereas in the PEEL153 a set of dedicated AND gates was used for this purpose. In addition, it provides a user signature word for device identification.

PEEL273. This is a super-set version of PEEL173. It has the same features as the PEEL253, with 4 additional input lines.

PEEL20CG10. This device can provide up to 22 inputs and 10 outputs, and has 12 macrocells. It can directly replace 24-pin PAL devices, without having to modify the existing design.

International CMOS Technology offers 2 PC-based software packages—PEEL evaluation kit and PEEL development system. The evaluation kit is free. It includes the APEEL™ assembler, and a translator which can translate a PLD-JDEC file to a PEEL programming file. The PEEL development system is a low-cost personal work-station providing a word processor for design entry/editing, the APEEL assembler, a PEEL programmer, and an enhanced logic tester.

```
module          moore
title           'sequential circuit
Parag K. Lala          14 November 1988';

      m2               device 'PEEL18CV8';

      Clk,A,B,C             pin 1,2,3,4;
      Q7,Q6,Q5,Q4           pin 13,14,15,16;
      Q3,Q2,Q1              pin 17,18,19;

equations
      Q1 := A & Q1
          # A & Q6
          # A & Q7;

      Q2 := !A & Q1;

      Q3 := !C & Q2
          # !A & Q3
          # !B & !C & Q5;

      Q4 := A & Q3
          # A & Q4;

      Q5 := !A & Q4;

      Q6 := !B & C & Q5
          # !A & Q6;

      Q7 := C & Q2
          # B & Q5
          # !A & Q7;

            •
            •
            •
            •
            •

end
```

FIGURE 6.35
ABEL input file

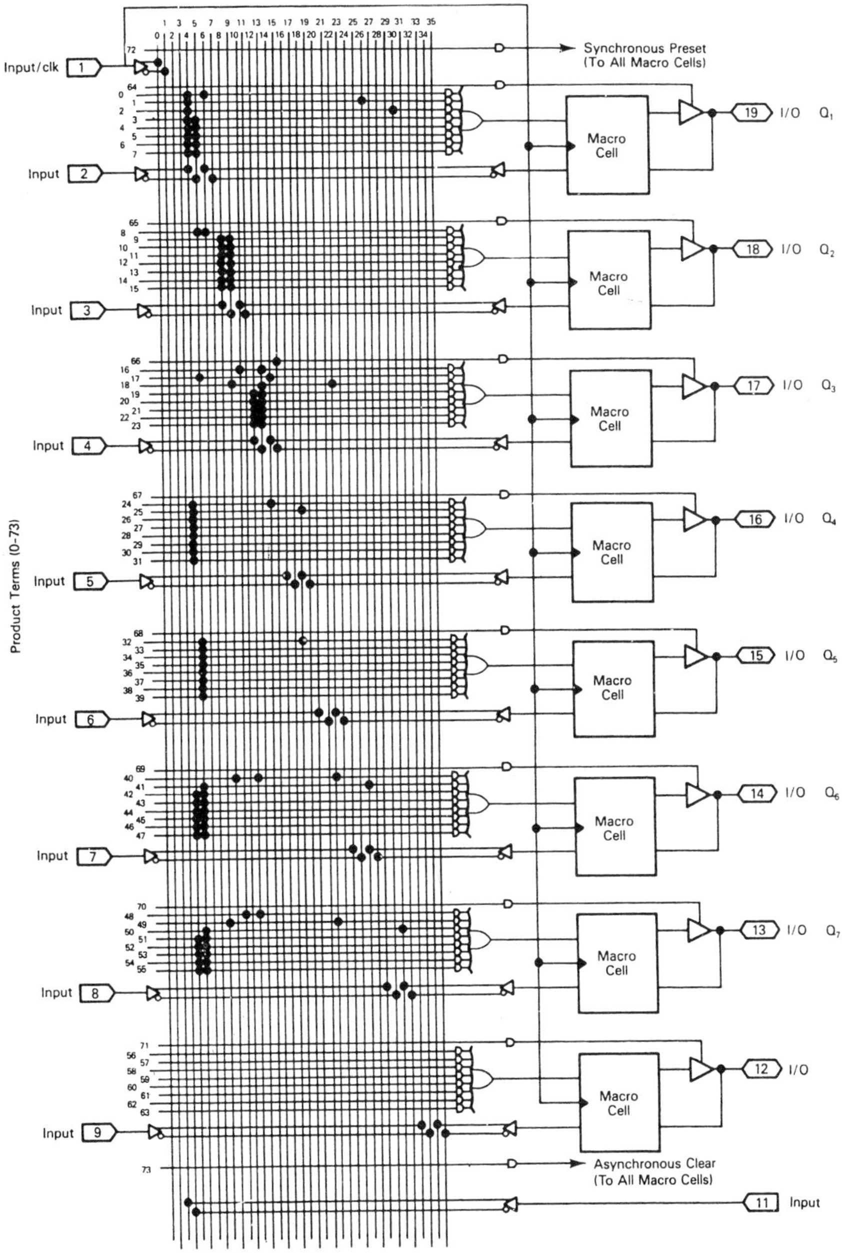

FIGURE 6.36
Implementation of the state machine of Figure 6.33 (Courtesy of International CMOS Technology.)

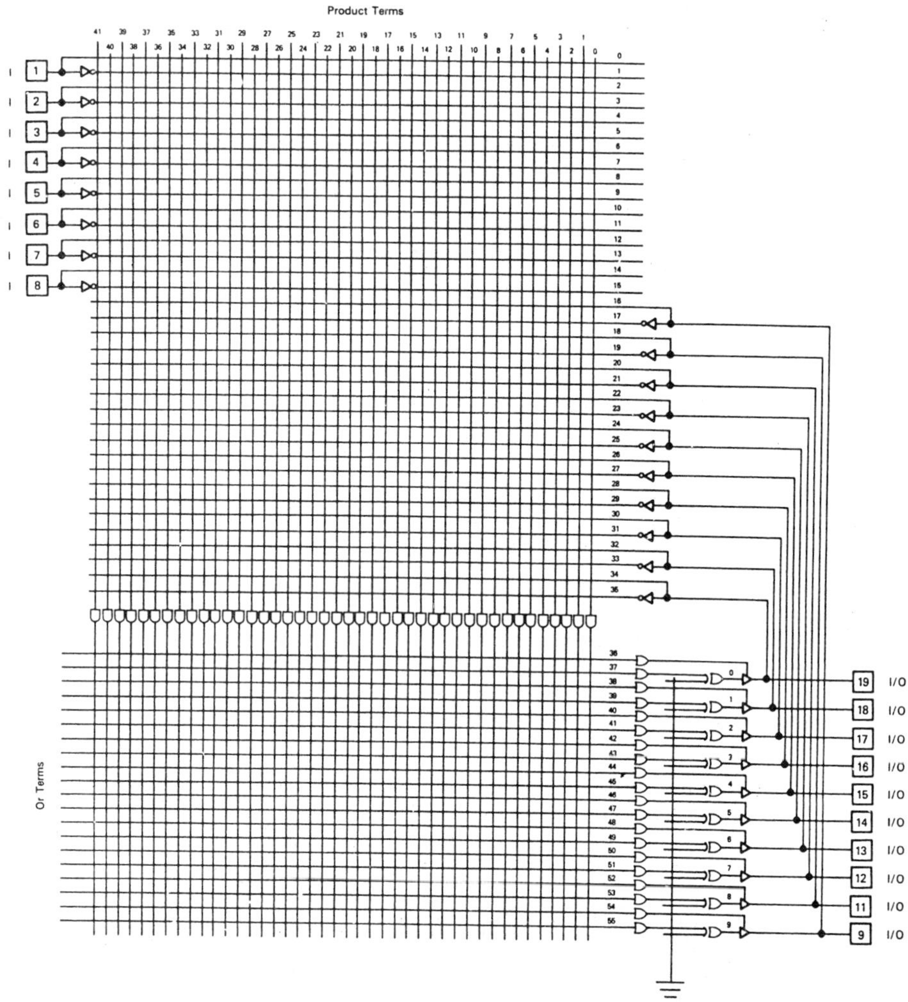

FIGURE 6.37
PEEL 253 Logic Array Diagram (Courtesy of International CMOS Technology.)

6.6 PAL29M16

Currently PAL29M16 is the most complex electrically erasable device available. It features propagation delay of 45 ns and can operate at a maximum clock frequency of 15 MHz; a high-speed version with a propagation delay of 35 ns and 20 MHz operation is also available.

The PAL29M16 is a 24-pin device, and has 3 dedicated inputs and 16

I/O logic macrocells. Each macrocell is user programmable for combinational, registered, or latched operation. Figure 6.38 shows the structure of an I/O macrocell. Eight of the macrocells provide single feedback, while the remaining 8 provide double feedback to the AND array. The configuration of a macrocell is carried out by programming 9 EEPROM cells (S_0–S_8) incorporated into it; macrocells with double feedback to the AND array contain 8 (S_0–S_7) EEPROM cells. All macrocells receive inputs from a dedicated clock/latch enable pin, from an alternate clock/latch enable pin (which can also be used as a dedicated input), as well as from a pin which can be used as a dedicated input or as the output enable control pin.

As in PAL22V10, this device uses variable product term distribution, which allocates 8, 12, or 16 product terms to the macrocells. Four pairs of the 188 product terms available in the device are used for enabling the tri-state inverters in the macrocells. Each of these 4 pairs of dedicated product terms is EX-ORed and the output of the EX-OR gate is made available to a bank of 4 macrocells.

As mentioned previously, a particular macrocell configuration is achieved by appropriately programming the EEPROM cells (S_0–S_8) incorporated into the macrocell. In the unprogrammed or erased state, these cells are all charged (i.e., contain 1s); a cell is discharged (i.e., contains 0) when it is programmed. The functions of the EEPROM cells are explained Table 6.3 on page 212.

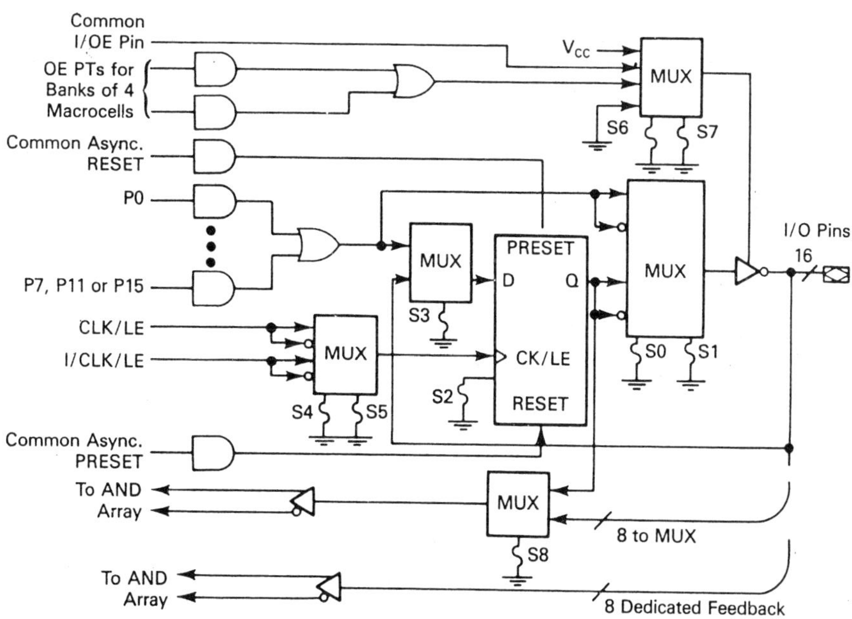

FIGURE 6.38
Structure of I/O logic macrocells in PAL29M16 (Courtesy of AMD, Inc.)

EEPROM Cell(s)	*Function*	*Content*	*Result*
S_0	Controls output polarity	0	Active-high
S_1	Determines output type	1	Active-low
S_2	Selects register or latch as the memory element	0 1	Registered/latched Combinational
S_3	Determines whether the macrocell will be used as an input reg/latch or as an output reg/latch	0 1	Input reg/latch Output reg/latch
S_4,S_5	Select the triggering edge (level) for the clock (latch enable) signal	0 0	Negative edge clock/ active-low latch enable
		0 1	Positive edge clock/ active-high latch enable
		1 0	Negative edge clock/ active-low latch enable
		1 1	Positive edge clock/ active-high latch enable
S_6,S_7	Determine the type of output enable	0 0	Permanently disabled (I/O pin is programmed as input)
		0 1	Permanently enabled (I/O pin is programmed as output).
		1 0	Ex-OR of the dedicated pair of product terms drive the enable input of the tri-state inverter
		1 1	Ouptut enable signal on the dedicated control input drive the enable input of the tri-state inverter
S_8 (for macrocells with single-feed back path only	Selects either the I/O or register/latch feedback	0 1	I/O pin Register/latch

TABLE 6.3
Functions of EEPROM cells in PAL29M16 macrocells

The PAL29M16 can pre-load the registers/latches to any desired state during testing for full logic verification. In addition, it has a dedicated product term called, **the observability product term**. When this product term is activated, the contents of the register/latch in the macrocells are available on the I/O pins. All register/latches in the device are cleared after the power-up.

6.7 PLDs WITH FOLDBACK ARCHITECTURE

One of the major limitations of PLDs using AND-OR structure is that in most of these devices, outputs are fed back to their inputs via registers. Thus, a signal has to pass through two gate levels every time a feedback is needed, resulting in increased delay. Furthermore, in fixed-OR devices the outputs of the registers are tied to the I/O pins even when they are fed back to the AND array. This not only results in the wastage of the I/O pins, but also unnecessary intermediate results are produced at their outputs.

The PML devices offered by Signetics, and the ERASIC chip from Exel Corporation have managed to overcome some of the limitations of the AND-OR with the NAND-NAND and NOR-NOR structure, respectively. The PML devices are bipolar, whereas the ERASIC is CMOS EEPROM-based. Their structures are based on the fundamental property of Boolean algebra, which enables any sum-of-products expression to be implemented by a two-level NAND or NOR logic. For example, the Boolean expression,

$$f(A,B,C) = AB + BC + AC$$

can be rewritten as

$$f(A,B,C) = \overline{\overline{AB} \bullet \overline{BC} \bullet \overline{AC}}$$

or,

$$f(A,B,C) = \overline{\overline{(A + C)} + \overline{(A + B)} + \overline{(B + C)}}$$

The implementation of the NAND-NAND and NOR-NOR expression are shown in Figure 6.39a and b, respectively.

6.7.1 Programmable Macro Logic (PML)

Figure 6.40 shows the basic PML architecture. It consists of a core NAND array surrounded by I/O macros and functional macros. The I/O macros provide paths to the outside world, while the functional macros provide logic processing capability. Macros include various types of flip-flops, EX-OR gates, buffers, counters, shift registers and counters, an ALU unit, and so on. The NAND array can drive the macros directly; alternatively, a logic function

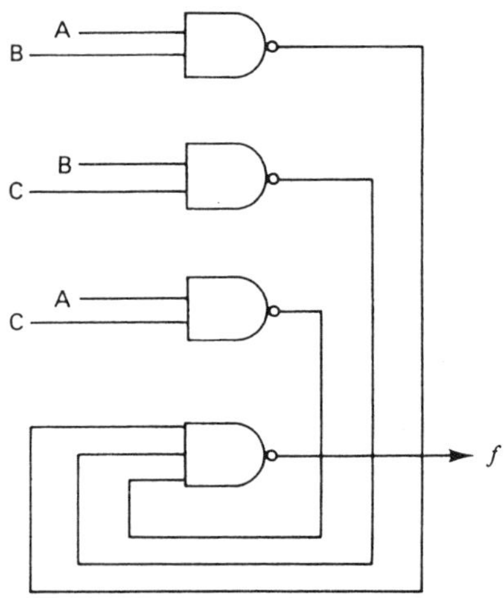

FIGURE 6.39a
Implementation with a single NAND array using feedback

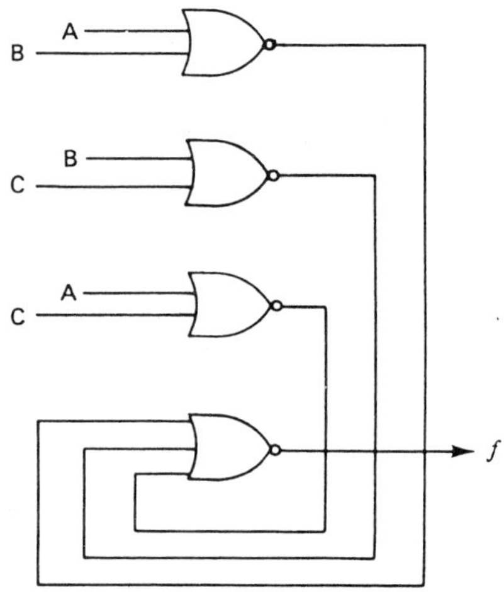

FIGURE 6.39b
Implementation with a single NOR array using feedback

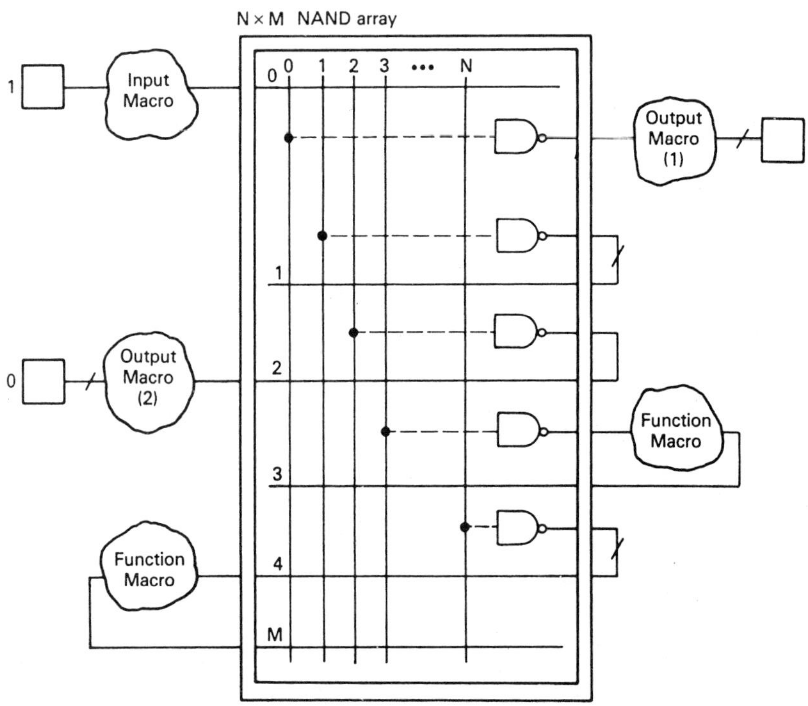

FIGURE 6.40
Programmable macro logic (PML) architecture (Courtesy of Signetics Corp.)

can be created first by looping a path through the NAND array, which is then used to drive a macro.

The main advantage of this architecture is that it allows the creation of multi-level paths through the NAND array without having to take a signal out through an output pin and back through an input pin. Besides, an output macro is not tied to an output pin only, the rest of the logic system can share the macro, if necessary.

Currently, two PML devices are available—PLHS501 and PLHS502. Both devices are supported by AMAZE, Signetics' proprietary PLD design software.

PLHS501. This device is intended primarily to implement combinational functions. It has 24 inputs, 4 active-high, and 4 active-low I/O lines. Figure 6.41 shows the logic diagram of the device. A single level function can be performed in 18 ns using a PLHS501. Additional logic levels require only 8 ns per level. The power consumption of the device is about 1.25 W.

Although primarily a combinational device, PLHS501 is well suited for implementing asynchronous state machines. As an example, we will realize the state table of the machine shown in Figure 6.42.

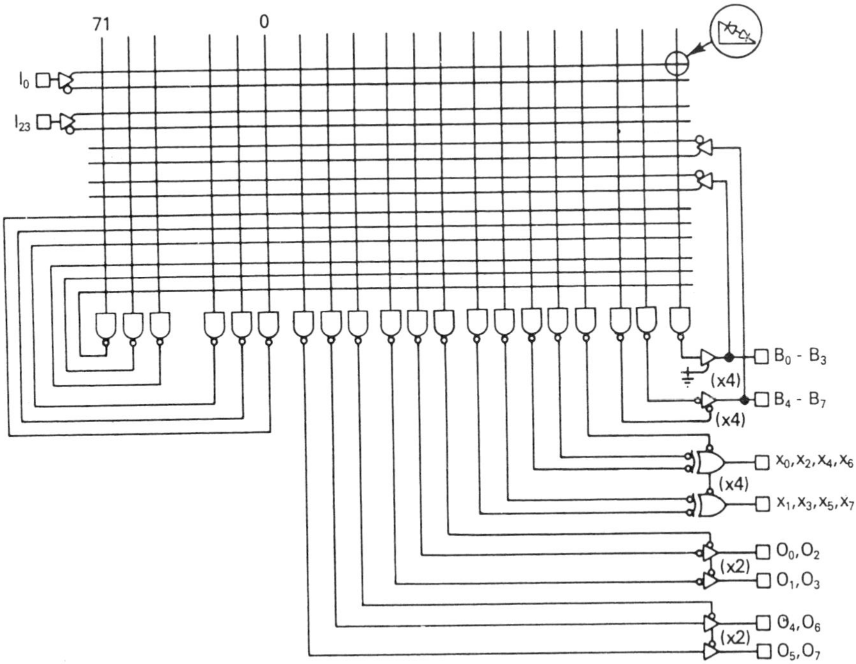

FIGURE 6.41
Logic diagram of PLHS501 (Courtesy of Signetics Corp.)

State	$\bar{x}_1\bar{x}_2$	$\bar{x}_1 x_2$	$x_1 x_2$	$x_1\bar{x}_2$
A	Ⓐ,00	B,01	Ⓐ,00	D,10
B	A,00	Ⓑ,01	Ⓑ,01	C,10
C	D,00	Ⓒ,01	Ⓒ,01	Ⓒ,10
D	Ⓓ,00	D,10	A,10	Ⓓ,10

FIGURE 6.42
State table of an asynchronous state machine

Since there are 4 states, 2 RS latches are needed for the realization. The state assignment and the excitation equations are shown in Figure 6.43.

y_1y_2	$\bar{x}_1\bar{x}_2$		$\bar{x}_1 x_2$		$x_1 x_2$		$x_1\bar{x}_2$	
	S_1R_1	S_2R_2	S_1R_1	S_2R_2	S_1R_1	S_2R_2	S_1R_1	S_2R_2
A → 0 0	0 –	0 –	0 –	1 0	0 –	0 –	1 0	0 –
B → 0 1	0 –	0 1	0 –	– 0	0 –	– 0	1 0	– 0
C → 1 1	– 0	0 1	– 0	– 0	– 0	– 0	– 0	– 0
D → 1 0	– 0	0 –	– 0	0 –	0 1	0 –	– 0	0 –

FIGURE 6.43
State assignment and excitation tables

The excitation equations are found by considering each column separately,

$$S_1 = x_1\bar{x}_2$$

$$R_1 = x_1 x_2 \bar{y}_2$$

$$S_2 = \bar{x}_1 x_2 \bar{y}_1$$

$$R_2 = \bar{x}_1\bar{x}_2$$

$$Z_1 = x_1\bar{x}_2 y_1$$

$$Z_2 = x_2 y_2$$

Figure 6.44 shows the appropriate fuses in the logic diagram of PLHS501 to implement the state machine. Notice that a cross-coupled latch can be formed on-chip without involving any output pins.

PLHS502. It is a sequential device and is intended especially for state machine design. It contains a NAND array, plus 8 SR and 8 D flip-flops (see Figure 6.45). As can be seen from the diagram, the architecture employs buried flip-flops and does not require output pins to implement feedback functions. The device has 20 dedicated inputs, 4 dedicated clock lines which

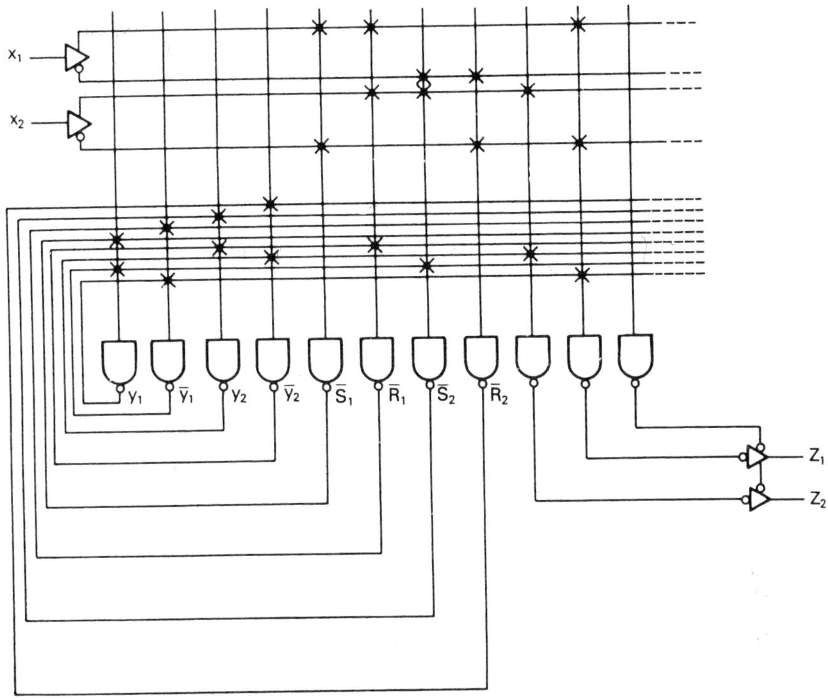

FIGURE 6.44
Implementation of the asynchronous state machine of Figure 6.42

may also be used as input lines, 8 active-high outputs, 4 outputs with polarity control, as well as 4 tri-state outputs with polarity control. The clock signal to each of the registers in PLHS502 can be provided via one of the 4 dedicated clock input lines, or can be derived from the NAND array. The maximum clock frequency is 35 MHz.

The device can be programmed to perform a single-level function in 22 ns; each additional level requires 8 ns. It has the same power consumption as the PLHS501.

We illustrate the application of the device by implementing a 4-bit counter and a polarity generator for a 3-bit number, using the same chip. The design equations for the 4-bit counter were derived in Section 6.4, and are repeated below

$$Y_1 = \bar{y}_1 y_2 y_3 y_4 A + y_1 \bar{A} + y_1 \bar{y}_2 + y_1 \bar{y}_3 + y_1 \bar{y}_4$$

$$Y_2 = \bar{y}_2 y_3 y_4 A + y_2 \bar{A} + y_2 \bar{y}_3 + y_2 \bar{y}_4$$

$$Y_3 = \bar{y}_3 y_4 A + y_3 \bar{A} + y_3 \bar{y}_4$$

$$Y_4 = \bar{y}_4 A + y_4 \bar{A}$$

$$\text{Overflow} = y_1 y_2 y_3 y_4 A$$

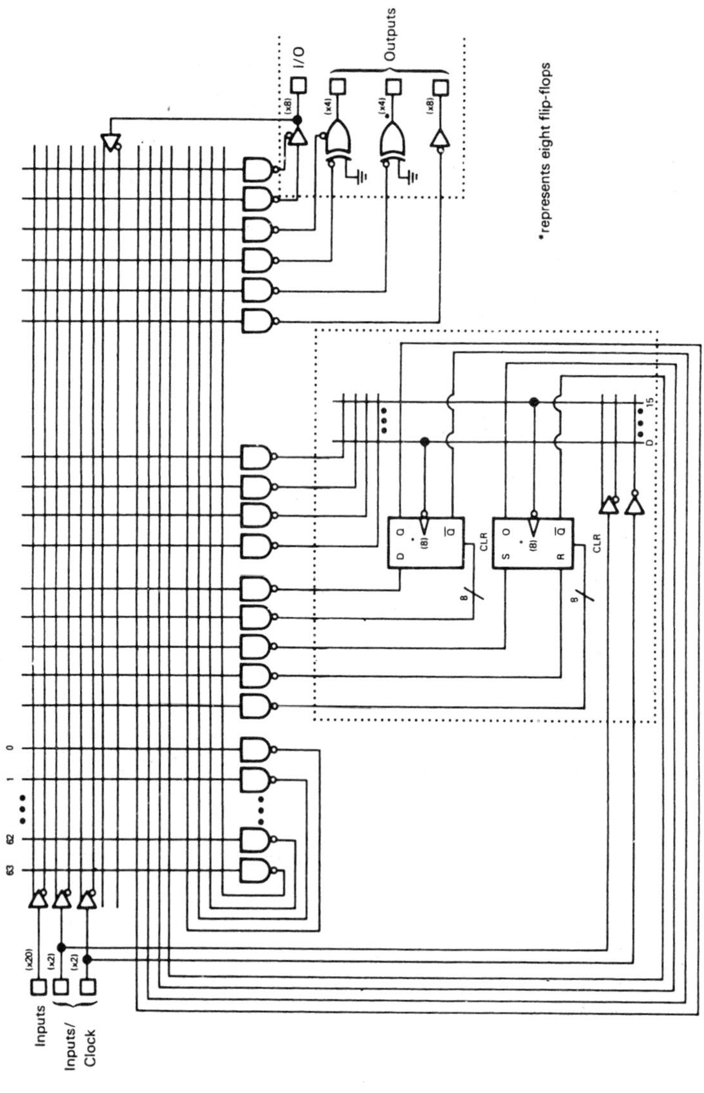

FIGURE 6.45
Logic diagram of PLHS502 (Courtesy of Signetics Corp.)

The polarity generator circuit receives a 3-bit number and produces an output of 1 if the number of 1s in the number is odd. Thus, the output expression for the polarity generator is

$$f(x_1, x_2, x_3) = \overline{x}_1\overline{x}_2x_3 + \overline{x}_1x_2\overline{x}_3 + x_1\overline{x}_2\overline{x}_3 + x_1x_2x_3$$

The logic diagram of the PLHS502 is encoded (as shown in Figure 6.46) to implement the counter and the polarity generator circuit.

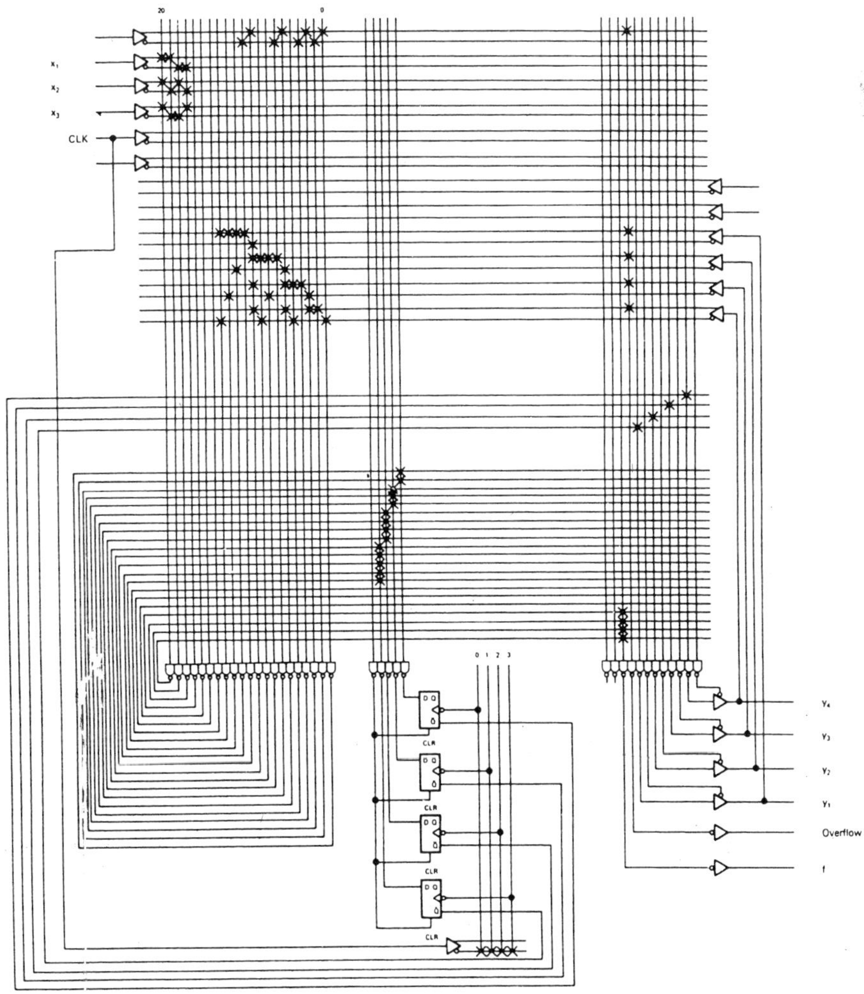

FIGURE 6.46
Implementation of a 4-bit counter and a parity-bit generator using the PLHS502

6.7.2 ERASIC

This is a 24-pin device and is electrically reprogrammable, hence the name **electrically reprogrammable application specific** IC (ERASIC). It can assume a single or a multi-level structure by feeding back the original signals and their complements through a single NOR array. Figure 6.47 shows the block diagram of XL78C800. It has 10 macrocells, each of which contains a JK flip-flop (see Figure 6.48). The output of a flip-flop can be taken out via an I/O pin, or can remain **buried**. Each macrocell is configured by 6 EEPROM cells. The stored bits in 3 of these cells, cells 0–2, are decoded into 4 lines that drive the control lines w, x, y, z of the three multiplexers in the macrocell. The input multiplexer selects either the I/O pin or the output of the NOR gate Ø of the macrocell, as an input to the NOR array. The output multiplexer selects either the output of the flip-flop or the output of the NOR gate Ø, as the output of the macrocell. The 3 remaining EEPROM cells are programmed to set the polarity of the J, K, and output terms. The device has 8 latched-inputs, which are grouped into 2 sections of 4 inputs each. A separate latch enable signal controls each group. A logic "0" on the latch enable line renders the latches transparent, whereas a logic "1" on it latches the input signals.

As mentioned previously, a multi-level function in XL78C800 can be implemented by feeding back terms generated at a lower level to the next higher level. The NOR-array of XL78C800 can generate 66 single-level functions, each of which may contain 96 inputs.

Another advantage of XL78C800 is that unlike other PLDs in which the implementation of SR latches is extremely inefficient, it takes only 2 terms and no I/O pins to realize an SR latch in this device (see Figure 6.49). Thus designers have the freedom to use these latches in system design without sacrificing any I/O pins or any significant amount of internal logic of XL78C800.

The JK flip-flop in a macrocell can be programmed as a D or a T flip-flop. For a D flip-flop, the logic expressions for J and K inputs are comple-

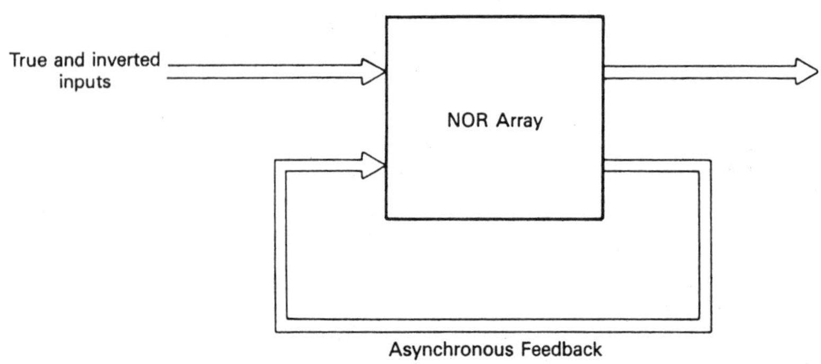

FIGURE 6.47
Block diagram of XL78C800

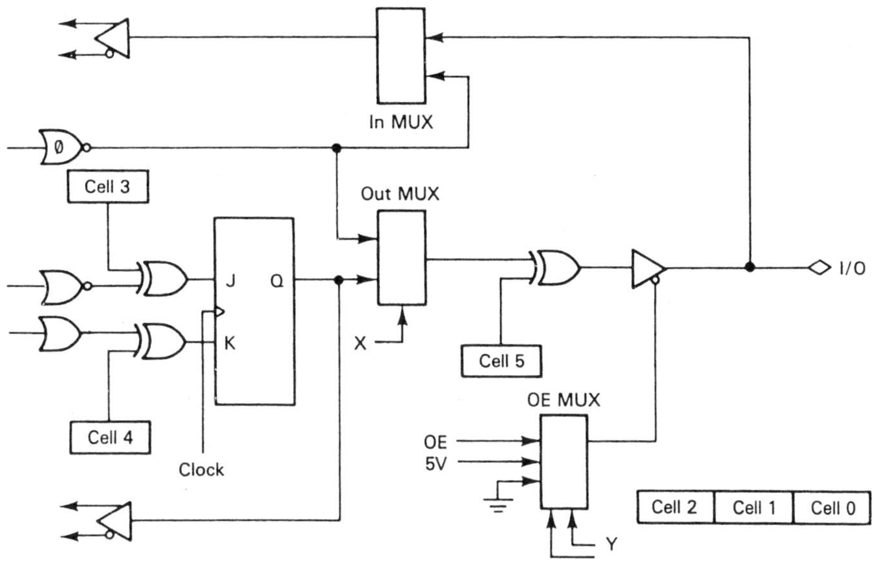

FIGURE 6.48
Macrocell of XL78C800 (Courtesy of Exel Corp.)

ments of each other whereas for a T flip-flop the logic expressions are identical. Unlike most other devices, when the flip-flop in the ERASIC's macrocell is buried, the output portion of the I/O pin can be used as an asynchronous output from the chip or as an asynchronous input to the chip.

The XL78C800 provides the preload feature, as well. This is accomplished by first setting the clock input at 12 V. The desired preload value is then applied to the I/O pins of the macrocells. On the next positive edge of the

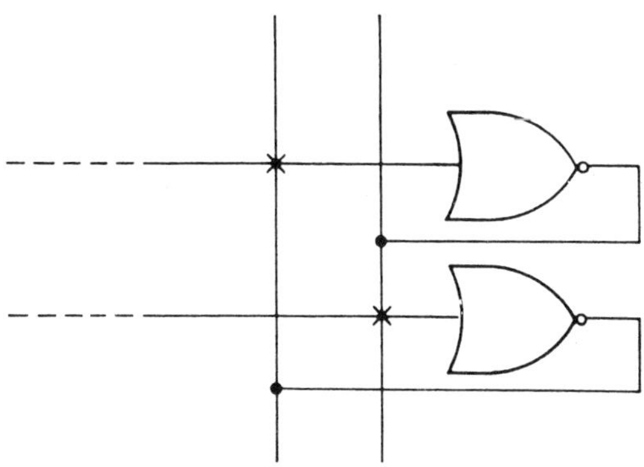

FIGURE 6.49
A SR latch using two NOR terms

clock pulse, the JK flip-flops are loaded with the logic values on the I/O pins. As an example of the application of the device in multi-level logic realization, let us implement a 4-bit comparator circuit. The input to the circuit are two 4-bit binary numbers $a_0 a_1 a_2 a_3$ and $b_0 b_1 b_2 b_3$. If the 2 numbers match then the comparator circuit produces an output of 1, otherwise it produces a 0. Thus, the comparator circuit implements the following Boolean expression:

$$f = (a_0 b_0 + \bar{a}_0 \bar{b}_0)(a_1 b_1 + \bar{a}_1 \bar{b}_1)(a_2 b_2 + \bar{a}_2 \bar{b}_2)(a_3 b_3 + \bar{a}_3 \bar{b}_3)$$

This expression can be expressed in three-level NOR form as below

$$f = \overline{\overline{\overline{(\bar{a}_0 + \bar{b}_0)} + \overline{(a_0 + b_0)}} + \overline{\overline{(\bar{a}_1 + \bar{b}_1)} + \overline{(a_1 + b_1)}} + \overline{\overline{(\bar{a}_2 + \bar{b}_2)} + \overline{(a_2 + b_2)}} + \overline{\overline{(\bar{a}_3 + \bar{b}_3)} + \overline{(a_3 + b_3)}}}$$

Figure 6.50 shows the coded logic diagram of the XL78C800 for the implementation of the comparator.

The ERASIC has 20-ns propagation delay for 1 logic level; each additional level of the NOR logic adds 10 ns to the signal delay. It dissipates less than 20 mW when operating with a 10 MHz clock, which is about 5 times lower than that of PLHS501. Exel, Inc. provides **MultiMap**™ software which, when used with ABEL, supports the ERASIC.

6.8 PROGRAMMABLE STATE MACHINES

State machines are usually designed with discrete logic to minimize circuit delays. They can also be built by adding registered feedback to the combinational PLDs. But due to the fixed OR array, combinational PLDs are somewhat limited for sequencing. Moreover, a number of I/O pins are used up to feed back the register outputs to the device inputs. Some of the newer PLDs have **buried** registers in them, thereby eliminating the need for sending their outputs to the I/O pins. However, state machines built with the buried registers tend to use up the I/O macrocell logic and array product terms, leaving very little logic to implement other system functions. To overcome some of the problems, a number of PLDs, whose architectures are tailored to state machine implementation, have been marketed. In this section, we'll discuss 3 such devices.

PMS14R21. PMS14R21 is the first member of the **PROgrammable SEquencer** (PROSE) family. It incorporates a bipolar PAL and a PROM on the same chip, to form a Moore-type state machine with 128 states. Figure 6.51 shows the block diagram of the device. As can be seen from the diagram, the PAL is a 14H2-type (14 inputs, 2 active-high outputs). The PROM has the

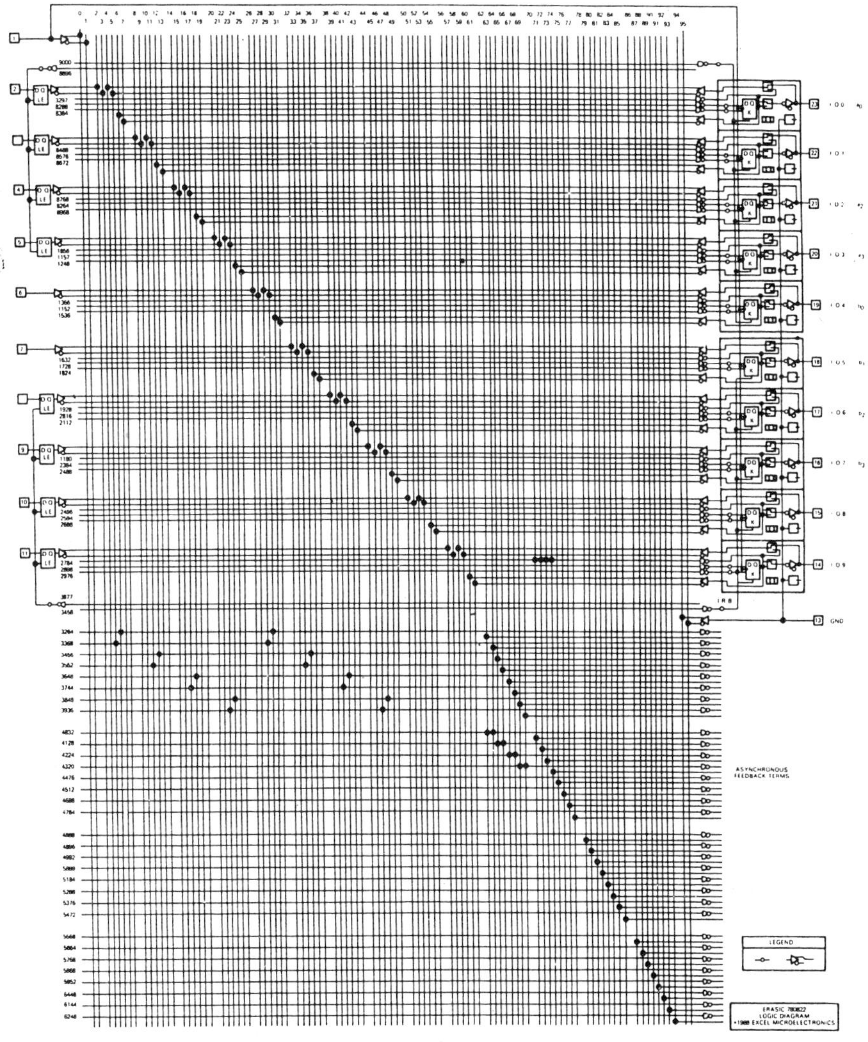

FIGURE 6.50
XL78C800 programmed as a 4-bit comparator (Courtesy of Exel Corp.)

128 × 21 configuration. The contents of an addressed location in the PROM are loaded into the **output register** if the mode input of the **shadow register** is at logic "0." The inputs to the PAL consist of 8 condition code input bits available from the external source, and 6 condition selection bits from the output register. Two bits of the output register are EX-ORed with the 2 outputs of the PAL and form the high-order address bits of the PROM. The 5 remaining input bits of the PROM are derived from the output register.

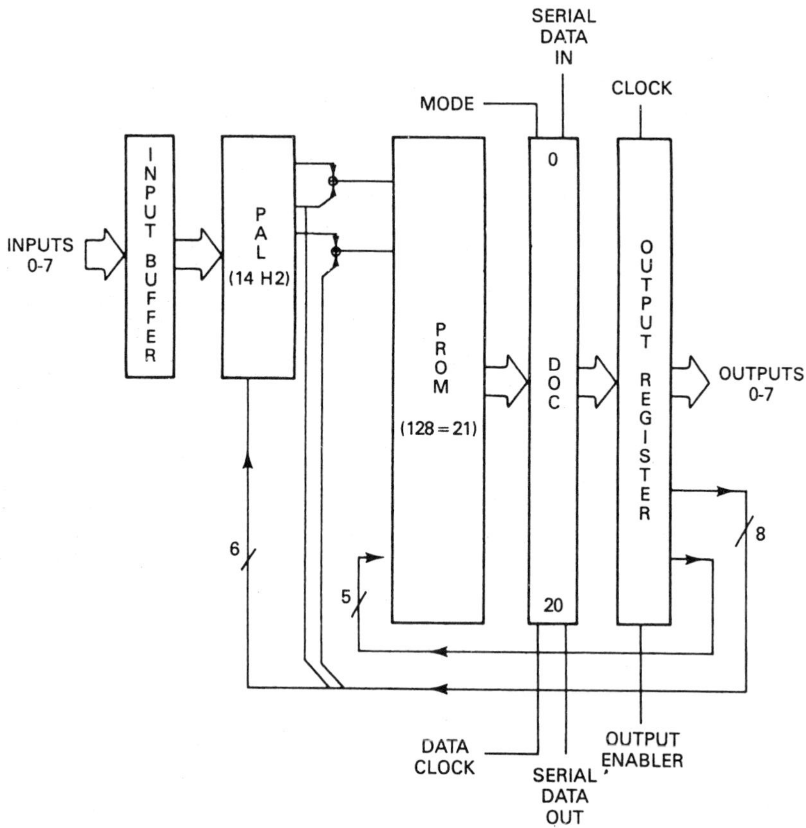

FIGURE 6.51
Block diagram of PMS14R21 (Courtesy of AMD, Inc.)

Each input combination to the PROM constitutes an address for the next state and the output of a state machine. If a state transition does not depend on external conditions (i.e., the outputs of the PAL are low), the high-order address bits for the PROM are obtained from its outputs. On the other hand, for the combinational state transitions the outputs of the PAL in conjunction with the 2 feedback signals from the PROM, determine the two high-order address bits. On power-up, all bits in the output register go high.

The shadow register in the PMS14R21 is included to simplify the testing of state machines designed using this device. The concept of serial shadow register was introduced by Advanced Micro Devices, Inc. to provide sufficient observability and controllability to convert sequential circuits into combinational circuits since they are relatively easy to test. This is accomplished by

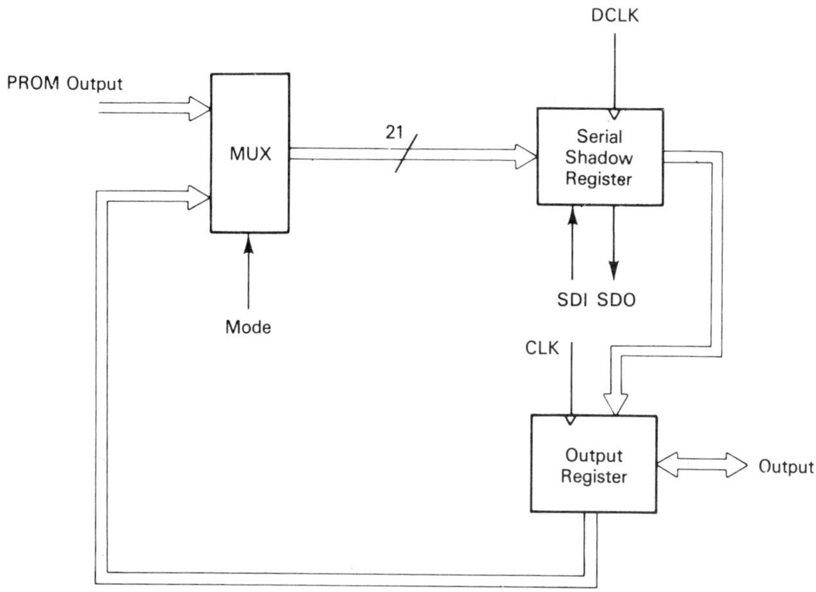

FIGURE 6.52
Incorporation of serial shadow register (Courtesy of AMD, Inc.)

incorporating a multiplexer and an additional register (i.e., the shadow register as shown in Figure 6.52).

The shadow register contains the duplicate of the output register during the normal operation. It can be serially loaded via the SDI (serial data in) input line and its contents can be serially shifted out via the SDO (serial data out) output line. The contents of the shadow register loaded through the SDI line, can be parallel-loaded into the output register by appropriately selecting the MODE control input. In a similar manner, the shadow register can be parallel-loaded with the contents of the output register. As can be seen from the diagram in Figure 6.52, the shadow register has its own clock (DCLK) which is different from the clock (CLK) of the output register. The MODE control signal selects the operation of the shadow register as indicated in Table 6.4.

To illustrate the application of the PMS14R21 to designing state machines, let us consider the control circuit of a small digital device as shown in Figure 6.53a. When the circuit is in state S_i, the control signal y_i is 1, while the other 3 control signals are equal to 0. The state diagram of the control circuit can be translated into an input file for PALASM2 software, as shown in Figure 6.53b. PALASM2 verifies the input file and creates the device programming JDEC format file.

MODE	*SDI*	*CLK*	*DCLK*	Q_{20-0}	S_{20-0}	*SDO*	*Operation*
L	X	$\uparrow$	*	$Q_n \leftarrow$ PROM	No change	S_{20}	Load output registers from PROM
L	X	*	$\uparrow$	No change	$S_n \leftarrow S_{n-1}$ $S_0 \leftarrow$ SDI	S_{20}	Shift shadow register contents
L	X	$\uparrow$	$\uparrow$	$Q_n \leftarrow$ PROM	$S_n \leftarrow S_{n-1}$ $S_0 \leftarrow$ SDI	S_{20}	Load output register from PROM while the contents of shadow register are being shifted
H	X		*	$Q_n \leftarrow S_n$	No change	SDI	Load output register from shadow register
H	L	*	$\uparrow$	No change	$S_n \leftarrow Q_n$	SDI	Load shadow register from output bus and feedback
H	H	*	$\uparrow$	No change	No change	SDI	No operation

TABLE 6.4
Function table for the shadow register in PAL14R21

PSG507. The PSG (Programmable Sequence Generator) is marketed by Texas Instruments and can operate at a maximum clock frequency of 50 MHz. It is a 20-pin device, and incorporates an 8-bit buried register, a 6-bit binary counter, and an 8-bit output register—multiplexer. The block diagram of the device is shown in Figure 6.54.

PSG507 has 13 dedicated inputs, and can generate up to 80 product terms. The outputs of the buried register and the binary counter are fed back

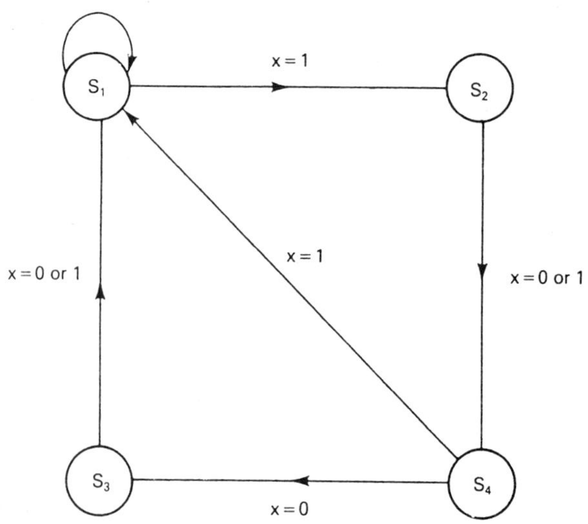

FIGURE 6.53a
Control circuit

```
TITLE          CONTROLLER
AUTHOR         PARAG K. LALA
DATE           NOVEMBER 25, 1988

CHIP      S_MACHINE    PMS14R21

;PINS     1       2      3    4    5    6    7    8    9    10   11     12
          CLK     DCLK   X    NC   NC   NC   NC   NC   NC   NC   SDI    GND

;PINS     13      14     15   16   17   18   19   20   21   22   23     24
          RESET   SDO    NC   NC   NC   NC   Y4   Y3   Y2   Y1   MODE   VCC

STATE

    MOORE-MACHINE                         ;defined as a Moore machine
    MASTER-RESET                          ;initialization
    POWER_UP := VCC→S1                    ;initial state
    POWER_UP.OUTF := Y1*/Y2*/Y3*/Y4       ;initial output

S1 := CO→S2                               ;go to S2 if cond.is true
+ →S1                                     ;otherwise stay in S1

S2 := VCC→S4                              ;jump to S4

S3 := VCC→S1                              ;jump to S3

S4 := CO→S1                               ;go to S1 if cond.is true
+ →S3                                     ;otherwise go to S3

S1.OUTF := Y1*/Y2*/Y3*/Y4;

S2.OUTF := /Y1*Y2*/Y3*/Y4;

S3.OUTF := /Y1*/Y2*Y3*/Y4;

S4.OUTF := /Y1*/Y2*/Y3*Y4;

CONDITION

CO = X                                    ;input x is 1
```

FIGURE 6.53b
PALASM2 input file

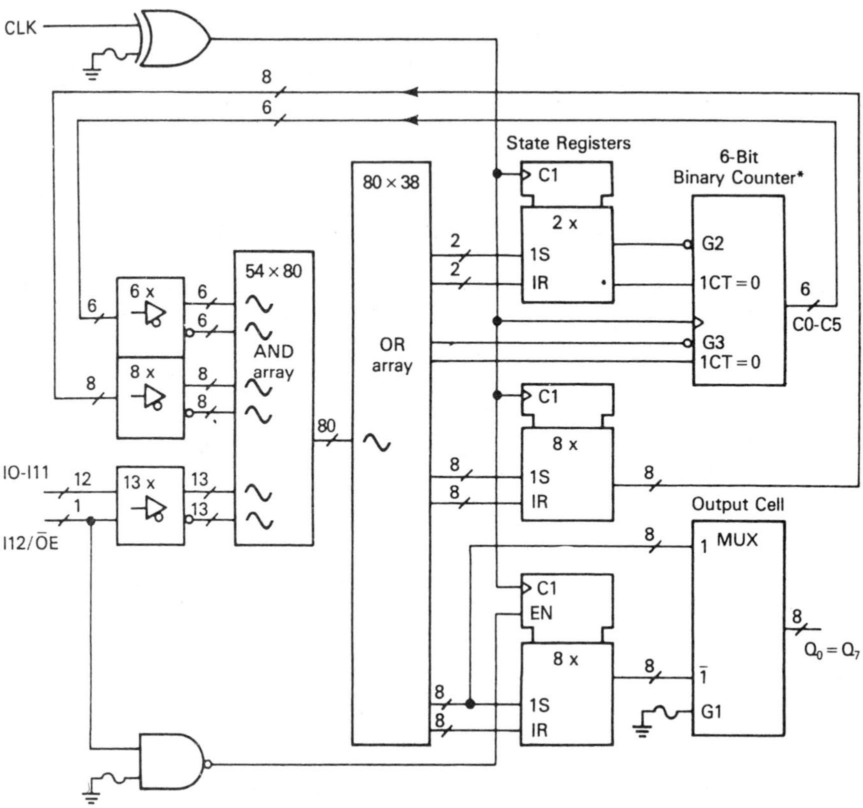

∿denotes fused inputs

*The counter is active when G2 = G3 = 0. If G2 = 1 or G3 = 1, the counter holds its present value. If either of the ICT = 0 inputs is taken to 1, the counter resets on the next clock edge.

FIGURE 6.54
Block diagram of PSG507 (Reprinted by permission of Texas Instruments.)

to the AND array. The output register does not contribute to the dormation of product terms. Its next state is dependent on the device inputs, and the present states of the buried register and the counter. Thus, PSG507 may be considered as a two-level state machine.

Each output of the device can be either registered or combinational. Eight 2-to-1 multiplexers are used to select the outputs of the SR flip-flops in the output register, or the product terms driving their S (Set) inputs. The control bit of each multiplexer is fixed by blowing a fuse or keeping it intact, so that each output of the device is permanently set to either combinational or registered. The outputs of the multiplexers are applied to the I/O pins via tri-state buffers. The enable input of a buffer is controlled by the signal on the 13th input line or permanently set, depending on whether a dedicated fuse is blown or not.

Both the buried and the output registers, as well as the counter use a common clock. The clock signal is applied via an EX-OR gate, the other input of the gate is at a level preset by the status of a fuse. Thus either the positive edge or the negative edge of the clock can be used to trigger the registers and the counter.

The reset input (ICT) of the counter can be driven either by a dedicated output of the OR array or by the output of a dedicated SR flip-flop, whose set and reset inputs are supplied by the OR array. Similarly, the hold input (G2/G3) of the counter is derived either from the OR array or from a dedicated SR flip-flop. The counter is reset or goes on to the hold mode on the next edge of the clock pulse, provided its reset or the hold input is at logic "1" or logic "0," respectively. If both reset and hold inputs are at logic "1" simultaneously, the reset input dominates.

CY7C330. This is a 20-pin device offered by Cypress Semiconductors. Several versions of the device are available with different operating frequency ranging from 25 MHz to 50 MHz. It has 11 dedicated inputs which are applied to an AND array via flip-flops. One of the inputs can be used as a clock input line (C2) as shown in Figure 6.55. There is also a dedicated clock input line C1. Each of the D flip-flops can be triggered by the clock signal applied via C1 or C2. The selection of C1 or C2 as the clock input line is made by appropriately programming the clock multiplexer associated with the D flip-flop. If the control bit A4 in the multiplexer is set to 0, the clock line C1 is selected; alternatively clock line C2 is selected if the control bit is set to 1. The Q and $\overline{Q}$ outputs of the D flip-flops drive the AND array.

The CY7C330 has six macrocells. The logic diagram of a macrocell is shown in Figure 6.56. A macrocell contains four flip-flops, 2 of these drive the I/O pins via tri-state buffers, and are known as **state registers** (FF1 and FF3 in the diagram). These flip-flops can be configured as D, T, JK, or SR; they change state on the positive edge of a clock, known as the **state counter clock.** A product term in the cell array may be used to drive the set (S) inputs of all the state flip-flops in the device. If this product term generates a logic "1," the outputs of all the state flip-flops will settle at logic "1" on the positive edge of the state clock. Similarly, a product term drives the reset (R) inputs of all the state flip-flops. If this product term produces a logic "1," the outputs of the flip-flops will be forced to logic "0" at the next clock pulse.

The other two 1-bit registers in the macrocell (FF2 and FF4 in Figure 6.56) are used to transfer the signal on the I/O pins to the AND array. The control bit A2 on the two clock multiplexers (MUXs 3 and 6) is programmed to select either C1 or C2 as the clock for these flip-flops. Depending on whether A2 = 0 or 1, the clock multiplexer associated with a flip-flop routes the clock signal via C1 or C2, respectively.

The feedback multiplexers (MUXs 2 and 5) can be programmed to feedback the outputs of the state flip-flops or the outputs of flip-flops FF2 and FF4

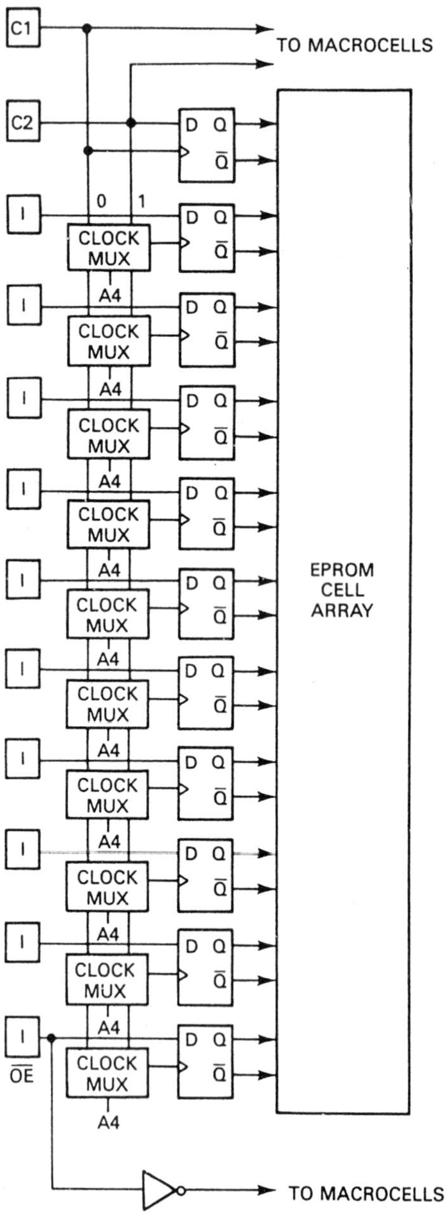

FIGURE 6.55
Input structure of CY7C330 (Courtesy of Cypress Semiconductors.)

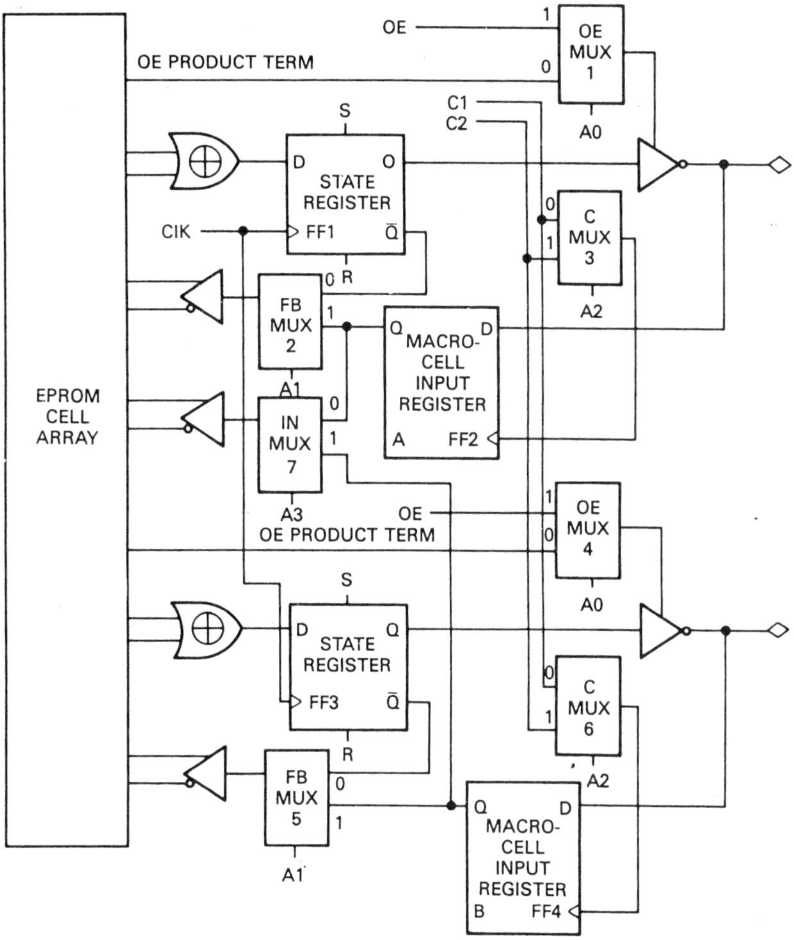

FIGURE 6.56
Structure of macrocells in CY7C330 (Courtesy of Cypress Semiconductors.)

to the AND array. The control bit A1 = 0 selects the outputs of state flip-flops, and A1 = 1 selects the outputs of FF2 and FF4.

The output enable multiplexers (MUXs 1 and 4) can be programmed to select either the $\overline{OE}$ signal on an input pin or the dedicated product term $\overline{OE}$ of the AND array, to drive the enable input of the output buffers. If the control bit A_0 on the multiplexers is equal to 1, the OE from the input pin is selected; and if $A_0 = 0$, OE generated by the dedicated product term is selected. An output buffer is enabled when OE signal is at logic "0" or the OE product term generates a logic "1"; otherwise the corresponding I/O pin can be used as an input pin. There is an additional multiplexer in the macrocell, MUX7. It selects the output of either flip-flop FF2 or FF4 as an input to the AND array, depending on whether the control bit A3 of the multiplexer is 0 or 1, respectively. Thus when one of the I/O pins of the macrocell is used as an input pin (i.e., when FF1 or FF3 remains "buried"), the input signal on the I/O pin can be transferred to the AND array by appropriately programming the control bit of MUX4. Each macrocell contains 32 product terms, out of which 2 are used for enabling the output buffers. The remaining 30 product terms are distributed among the 6 macrocells as shown in Figure 6.57.

In addition, to the two state flip-flops per macrocell, the CY7C330 also contains two pairs of buried flip-flops. These flip-flops are triggered by the same clock used for triggering the state flip-flops in the macrocells. Moreover, like the state flip-flops they have a common set (S) and a common reset (R) input, which are driven by the same product terms used to preset and reset the state flip-flops. Figure 6.58 shows a pair of buried flip-flops. Like the macrocells, a pair of buried flip-flops also contains 32 product terms. Since the outputs of these flip-flops are not taken out of the device, there is no need for output enable product terms; thus all 32 product terms are available for the buried flip-flops. These product terms are distributed as shown in Figure 6.59.

6.9 PROGRAMMABLE GATE ARRAY

This is a new family of CMOS chips introduced by Actel Corporation. These chips combine the design flexibility of gate arrays with the field-programmability of programmable logic devices. Currently, there are 4 devices in the ACT family; the main features of these devices are summarized in Table 6.5.

These chips have a row-and-column module architecture that resembles the layout of a gate-array chip (see Figure 6.60). However, there is a key difference between conventional gate-arrays and ACT devices. In conventional gate-arrays, the routing channels between logic cells are empty areas in which metal lines are arranged for a specific design. In contrast, in the ACT devices there are "segmented" metal tracks of various lengths between logic cells. There are also wiring segments, which run through the channels vertically. A **programmable low impedance circuit element** (PLICE) **antifuse** is placed at each intersection of a horizontal and a vertical segment, and also between adjacent horizontal and vertical segments. Antifuses are so-called, because when a high voltage (18V) is applied across them, their resistance change from high to low; in contrast a conventional fuse, if not blown, provides a low resistance path between connection points. Unlike conventional fuses, the sizes of anti-fuses are extremely small.

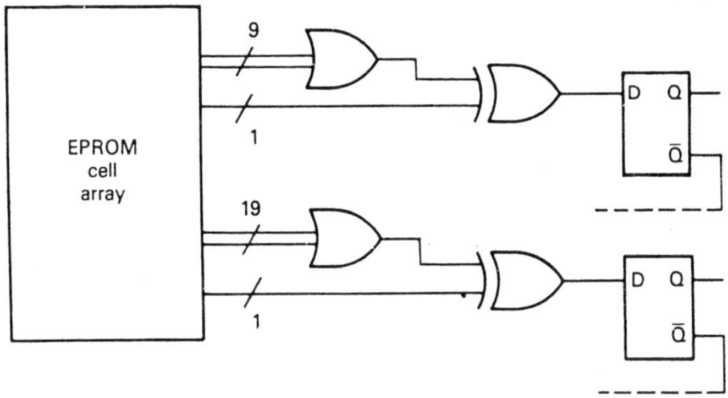

Macrocell 1

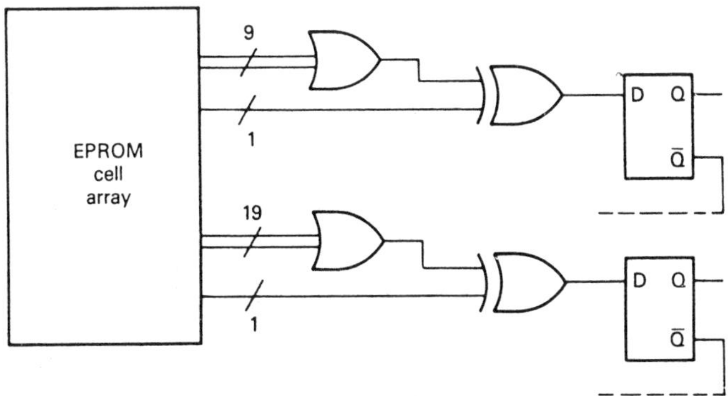

Macrocell 2

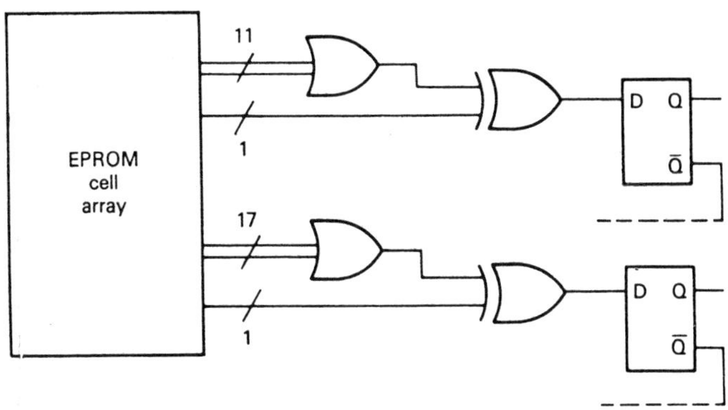

Macrocell 3

FIGURE 6.57
Distribution of product terms in the macrocells

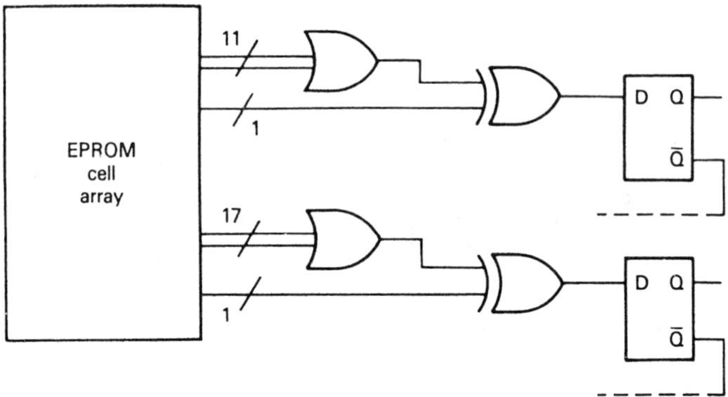

Macrocell 4

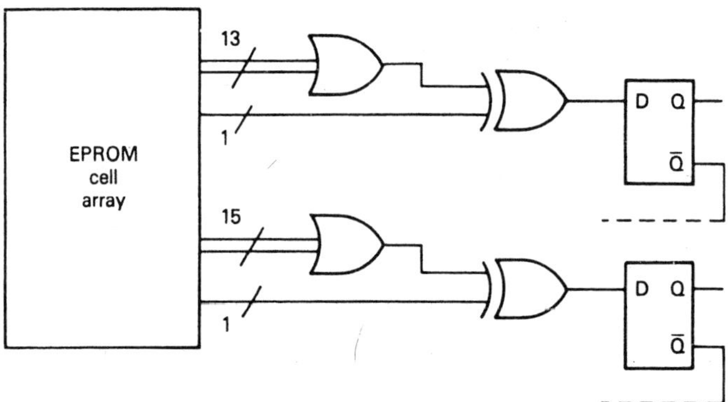

Macrocell 5

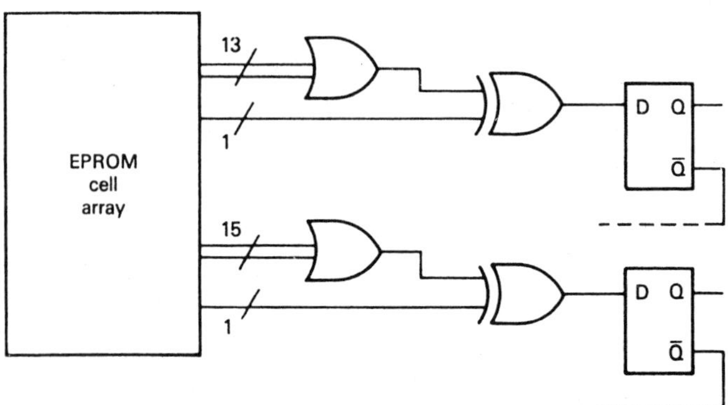

Macrocell 6

FIGURE 6.57 (contd.)
Distribution of product terms in the macrocells

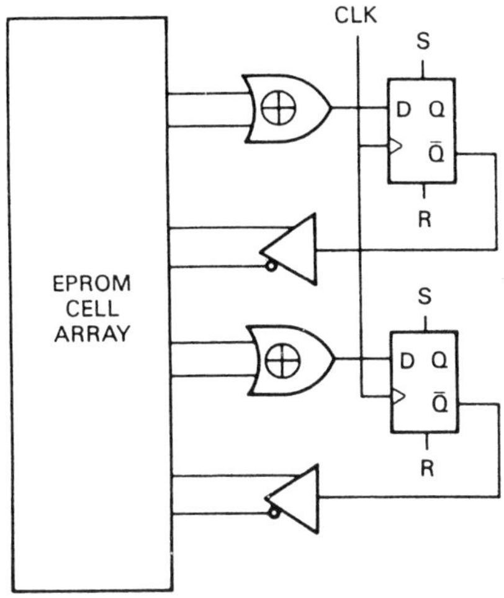

FIGURE 6.58
A pair of buried flip-flops (Courtesy of Cypress Semiconductors.)

The small size allows a large number of them to be included in the device. By "blowing" appropriate anti-fuses, it is possible to increase the lengths of the horizontal and vertical wire segments, as well as choose the number of tracks in each channel. The logic modules in ACT devices have 8 inputs and 1 output. Each module can be configured to implement a logic function selected from Actel's macro library. There are no dedicated flip-flops in ACT devices, they may be implemented from logic modules, anywhere in the array to suit requirement for a particular application.

The output of a module is connected to a vertical segment which covers several channels. Four inputs of a module are connected to 4 vertical segments of the channel immediately above the cell, and the remaining 4 inputs are connected to 4 vertical segments of the channel immediately below the cell. Thus, each input of a module may be accessed from either the channel above or below but not both. The matrix of logic modules in ACT devices is surrounded by a ring of I/O buffers, testability circuits and diagnostic probe circuits providing real-time diagnostic capability.

Each I/O pin in an ACT device may be configured as an input, output, tri-state, or bidirectional buffer by programming the appropriate antifuse elements. Input and output levels are compatible with standard TTL specifications.

The devices in the ACT family are supported by the Action Logic™ system software tools. It includes Viewdraw® schematic capture and Viewsim® simulation software, Actel's logic design system, Activator™ programming tools and diagnostic capability.

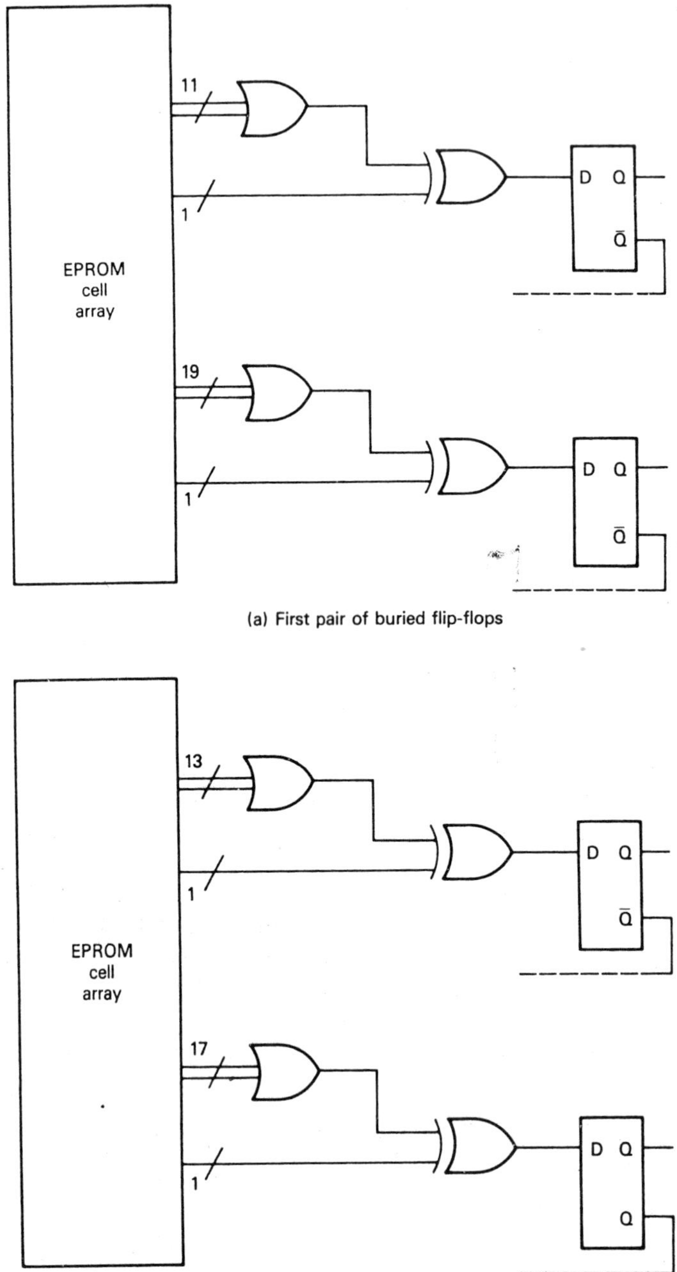

(a) First pair of buried flip-flops

(b) Second pair of buried flip-flops

FIGURE 6.59
Distribution of product terms among buried flip-flops

Device	*No. of gates*	*No. of logic modules*	*No. of I/Os*
ACT 1010	1200	295	57
ACT 1020	2000	546	69
ACT 1130	3000	823	112
ACT 1260	6000	1400	160

TABLE 6.5
Main features of ACT devices

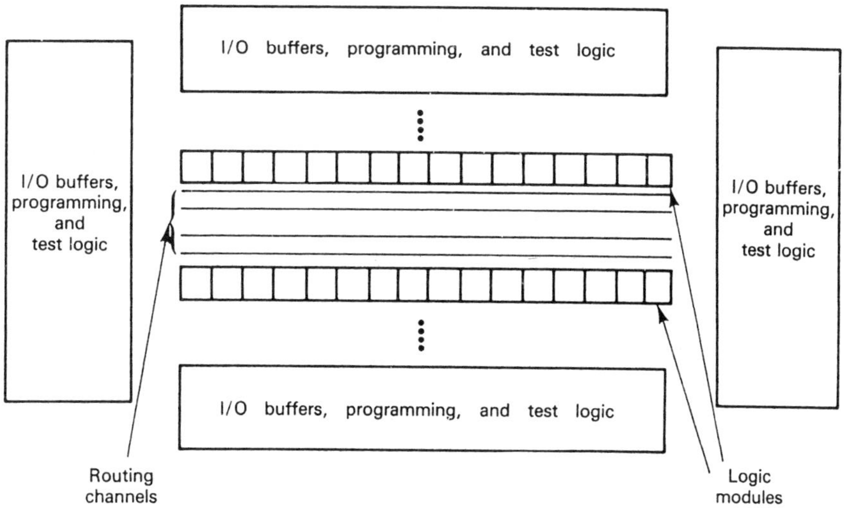

FIGURE 6.60
ACT architecture

PROBLEMS

6-1. A 16-bit up/down counter with built-in left-right shifting facility is to be implemented using an Altera EPLD chip. The counter has three control signals UPDN, SHFTCNT and LTRT. The function table of the counter is shown below

SHFTCNT	*UPDN*	*LTRT*	*Operation*
H	—	H	Shift left
H	—	L	Shift right
L	H	—	Count up
L	L	—	Count down

Select an appropriate Altera EPLD device and write down the design equations for implementing the counter using the device.

6-2. An 8-bit counter is to be implemented using EP600. Assuming that the counter has to be constructed with T flip-flops, write down the appropriate design equations.

6-3. A dual 4-bit comparator is to be implemented using PEEL18CV8. Assume the inputs are organized into 4-bit groups and are labeled w0-3, x0-3, y0-3 and z0-3. The comparison is to be done between inputs w0-3 and y0-3, and inputs x0-3 and z0-3. Code the logic 18CV8 logic diagram to show the implementation. How would you modify the comparator, so that it can act as an 8-bit comparator.

6-4. The block diagram of an 8-bit counter with 4 control inputs is shown below:

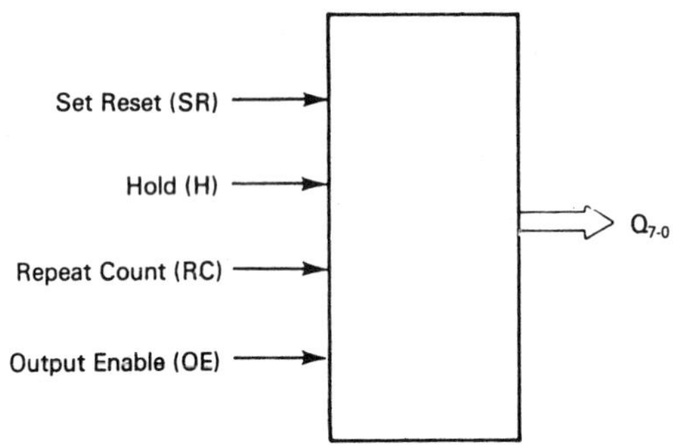

The function of each control input is described in the following table

SR	*H*	*RC*	*OE*	Q_{0-7}
H	—	—	L	00_{HEX} (after the next clock pulse)
L	H	—	L	Hold the current count value
L	L	H	L	Repeat count after FF_{hex} has been reached
L	L	L	L	Stop count after FF_{hex}
—	—	—	H	High impedance

Assuming the counter is to be implemented using PEEL20CV8, write down the design equations for the device.

6-5. A barrel shifter is a specialized shift register used to shift (or rotate) data by any number of bits in a single clock cycle. Figure A and B below show the block diagram and the truth table of an 8-bit barrel shifter. Implement the shifter using PLHS501. Write the appropriate design equations.

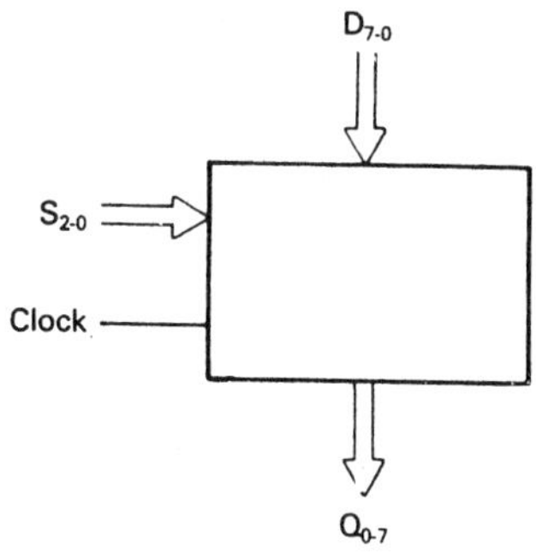

A

S_2	S_1	S_0	Q_7	Q_6	Q_5	Q_4	Q_3	Q_2	Q_1	Q_0
0	0	0	D_7	D_6	D_5	D_4	D_3	D_2	D_1	D_0
0	0	1	D_0	D_7	D_6	D_5	D_4	D_3	D_2	D_1
0	1	0	D_1	D_0	D_7	D_6	D_5	D_4	D_3	D_2
0	1	1	D_2	D_1	D_0	D_7	D_6	D_5	D_4	D_3
1	0	0	D_3	D_2	D_1	D_0	D_7	D_6	D_5	D_4
1	0	1	D_4	D_3	D_2	D_1	D_0	D_7	D_6	D_5
1	1	0	D_5	D_4	D_3	D_2	D_1	D_0	D_7	D_6
1	1	1	D_6	D_5	D_4	D_3	D_2	D_1	D_0	D_7

B

6-6. A 4-bit synchronous counter and a 4-bit register, which have a common clock, is to be implemented using a GAL20V8 device. Data can be loaded into the counter directly from the register. The register can be loaded either from the counter or from the external source under the control of input x. Both the counter and the register can be synchronously cleared. Write down the design equations and indicate the operating modes of the output logic macrocells.

6-7. A certain circuit consists of a 4-bit binary counter, C, and two 4-to-1 multiplexers, X and Y. The operation of the circuit is controlled by 2 inputs, a and b, as specified below:

a	*b*	*Counter*
0	0	Hold
0	1	C←X
1	0	C←Y
1	1	Increment

Assuming the circuit is to be implemented using GAL16V8, write down the design equations for the circuit.

6-8. The following state machine is to be implemented by using PMS 14R21 (PROSE) device. Write down the design equations for the device.

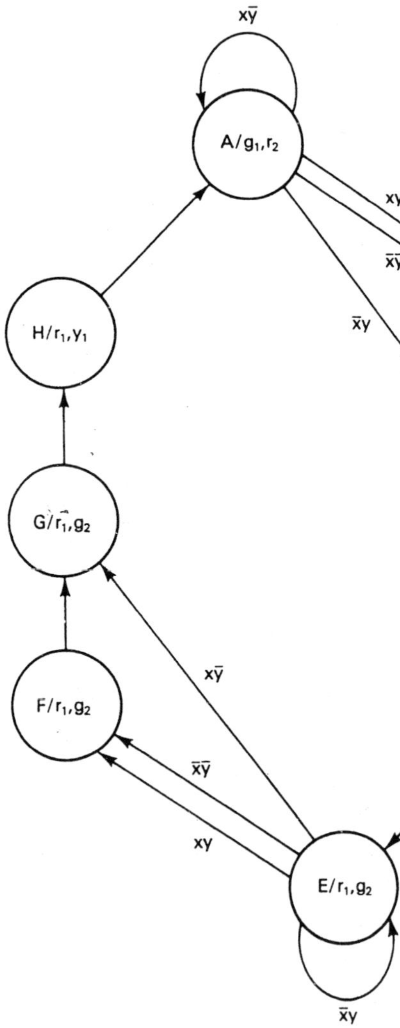

REFERENCES

1. K. Martin, "PLDs Slow Advances of Gate Arrays in Low-end Designs," *Computer Design,* Feb. 1, 1986, pp. 43–54.

2. *Applications Handbook,* Altera Corporation, 1988.
3. *Short Form Catalog,* International CMOS Technology, Inc., June, 1988.
4. *Data Catalog,* Lattice Semiconductors Corp., Fall, 1987.
5. *PAL/PLE Device Programmable Logic Array Handbook,* Monolithic Memories, 1986.
6. *Programmable Logic Data Manual,* Signetics Corp., 1986.
7. *Data Book,* Exel Microelectronics, Inc., April, 1987.
8. *CMOS Data Book,* Cypress Semiconductors Corp., 1987.
9. *ACT1 Family Gate Arrays,* Actel Corp., June, 1988.

Chapter 7

Logic Cell Array

In the previous chapters, we have discussed programmable logic devices in which configuration elements are one of the following types: fuse-link, ultraviolet erasable memory cell, and electrically erasable memory cell. Xilinx, Inc. has taken an alternative approach and developed a series of CMOS cell arrays, known as **Logic Cell Arrays™** (LCA), in which the configuration elements are static memory cells. A cell array is **software programmable**. This means that the personality of an array can be altered by means of a configuration program stored elsewhere in some memory device (e.g., EPROM, EEPROM, floppy disk, or some other non-volatile source).

Figure 7.1 shows the general structure of LCA chips. Inside the chips, there are three categories of elements: configurable logic blocks (CLB), input-output (I/O) blocks, and user-programmable interconnections. Currently, two families of LCA devices are available—XC2000 and XC3000. The XC2000 family was marketed in 1985, and the XC3000, the new generation of LCAs, was introduced in 1987.

One of the advantages of a cell array is that, like a gate array, it has an uncommitted architecture. Moreover, it has a higher logic density than any other programmable logic devices. Thus, the cell array incorporates the advantage of gate-arrays and eliminates the disadvantage of fuse-programmable

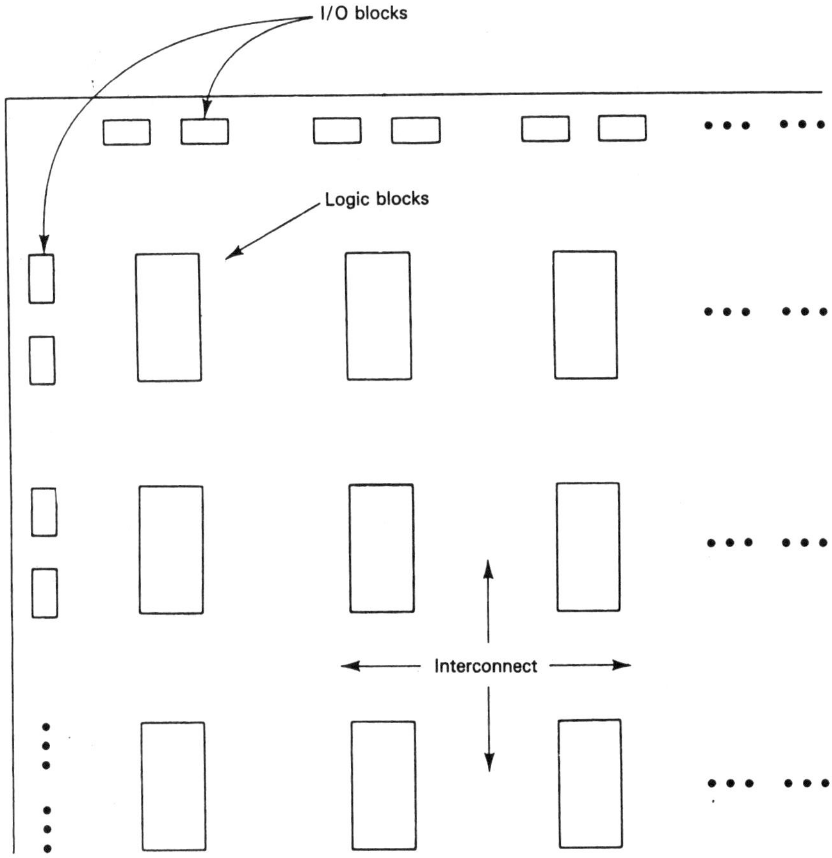

FIGURE 7.1
Structure of logic cell array

devices in many applications. However, the disadvantage of a cell array is that since the programming information is stored in a volatile memory, the device loses its function when the power is removed. Consequently, the configuration program must be booted every time a device is powered up.

7.1 XC2000 SERIES LCA

This series includes devices XC2064 and XC2018. The XC2064 has the equivalent of 1200 two-input gates, and the XC2018 has 1800. The XC2064 has 64 logic blocks surrounded by 58 input/output blocks, whereas the XC2018 packs 100 logic blocks and 74 input/output blocks. The logic blocks are arranged in a 8×8 matrix in XC2064, and in a 10×10 matrix in XC2018.

7.1.1 Logic Block

A logic block has 4 inputs, a clock input, a combinational logic section, 2 outputs, a memory element, and several multiplexers (see Figure 7.2). The combinational logic section uses a RAM look-up table to implement Boolean functions. Since a logic block has 4 inputs, the look-up table can be configured for any 4-variable combinational function; the variables can be chosen from among the 4 inputs (A,B,C,D) of the block and the output (Q) of the memory element.

The memory element in a logic block can be programmed as an edge-triggered D flip-flop or as a level-sensitive latch. The data input of the memory element is supplied by the F output of the combinational logic function (see Figure 7.3). The clock pulse to the flip-flop (level in the case of the latch) can be applied via the clock input line K or input C; alternatively the combinational function can be used to generate the pulse or the level and be applied via the G output. The memory element is also provided with asynchronous **Set** and **Reset** inputs. A logic high signal on the Set or the Reset input of the memory element sets its output to 1 or 0, respectively. The Set signal can be supplied via input A, and the Reset signal via input D; besides the F and G

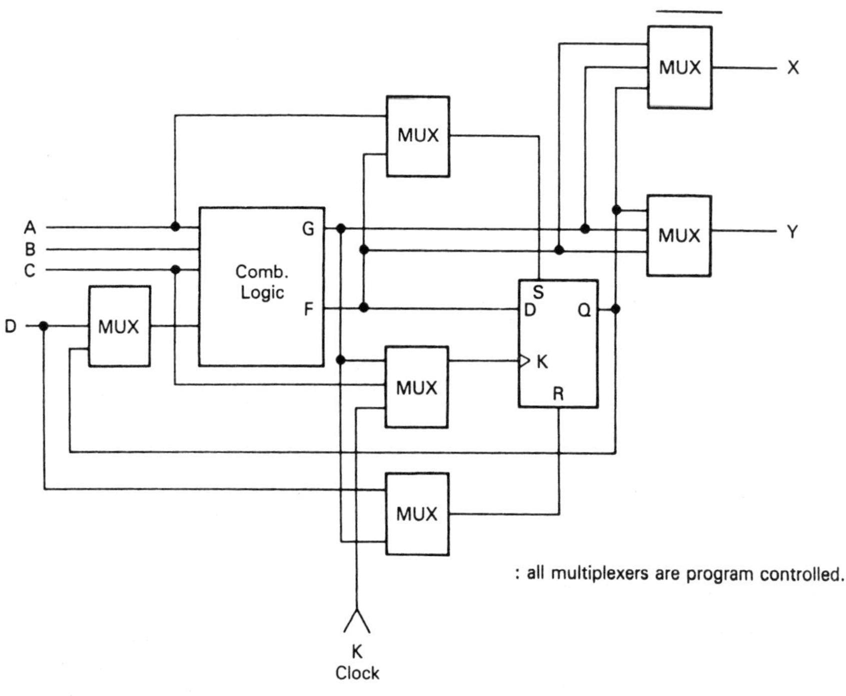

FIGURE 7.2
Logic block in XC2000 series LCA (Courtesy of Xilinx, Inc.)

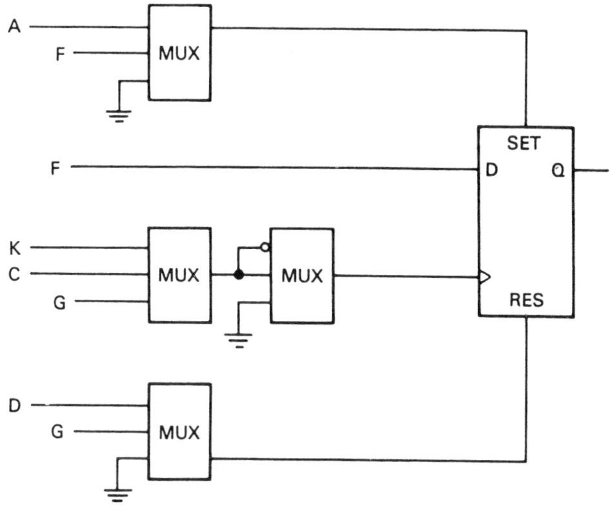

FIGURE 7.3
Memory element of the combinational logic block

of the combinational logic function can generate the Set and the Reset signal, respectively. The memory element can be programmed to be either set-dominant or reset-dominant, when both the set and the reset signal are active-high (see Section 7.4). All memory elements in the logic cell array are reset, if an active-low signal is applied to the $\overline{\text{RESET}}$ pin of the chip.

The F and G outputs can be channeled to either X or Y output of the combinational logic block; besides, the Q output of the memory element can also be routed to either X or Y.

7.1.2 Input/Output Block

The I/O blocks provide an interface between the external pins of a cell-array chip and its internal logic. Each I/O block consists of a D flip-flop, and various buffers and multiplexers to control the routing (see Figure 7.4). It can be programmed to act as an input, output or bidirectional signal path.

When an I/O pin is used as an input, the threshold for the input buffer can be made compatible for either TTL (1.4 V) or CMOS (2.2 V) signal levels. The output of the buffer is connected to the data input of an edge-triggered D flip-flop, as well as to one input of a 2-to-1 multiplexer. The other input of the multiplexer is derived from the output of the flip-flop. Thus, it is possible to apply an input signal directly or via the flip-flop.

When an I/O pin is programmed as an output, the corresponding buffer provides output with sufficient drive for high fan-out CMOS or TTL-compatible signal levels. The buffer is enabled or disabled, depending on the

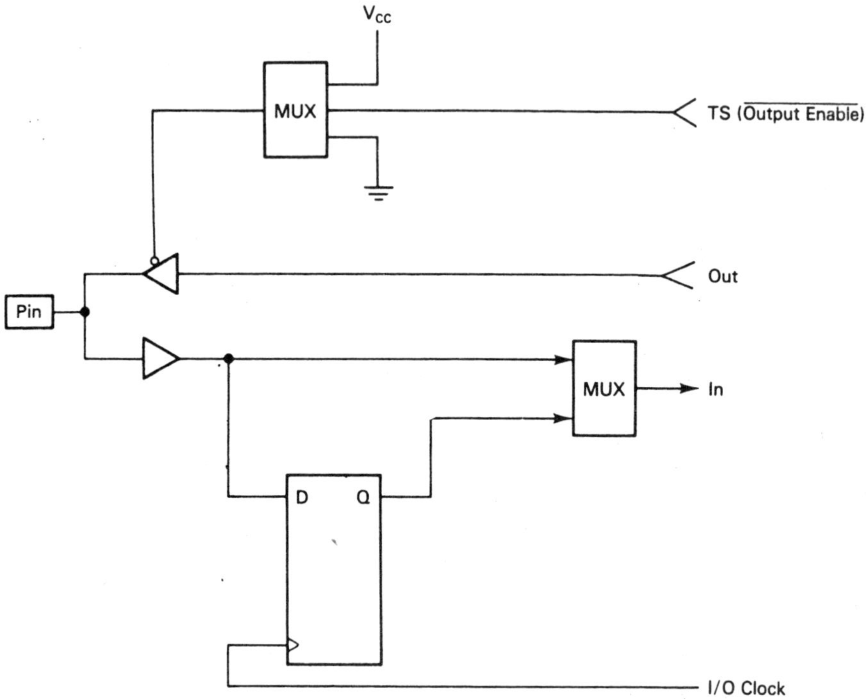

FIGURE 7.4
Input/Output block

contents of 2 configuration memory cells which drive the select inputs of the multiplexer feeding the enable input of the buffer. Moreover, the output pin can be put in a high-impedance state by putting an active-high signal on the TS line.

The clock line for all I/O blocks along the same edge of the die is common and can be externally or internally driven. Like the flip-flops in combinational logic blocks, the flip-flops in the I/O blocks are reset if an active-low signal is applied to the $\overline{\text{RESET}}$ input of the cell array chip.

7.1.3 Programmable Interconnect

The interconnections are used to connect the inputs and outputs of I/O and logic blocks. They are classified into 3 types: general purpose interconnect, direct interconnect, and long lines.

General Purpose Interconnect. General purpose interconnect consists of 4 horizontal metal lines between the rows and 5 vertical metal lines between the columns of the combinational logic blocks. They run through clusters of programmable switches at their intersections. Thus, a signal on a vertical line can be routed to an overlapping horizontal line by enabling the switch at their intersection while still travelling along the vertical line. Figure 7.5 shows the routing of the X output of a combinational logic block to the inputs of three other logic blocks. Each programmable switch is, in fact, a pass transistor and takes about 1 ns to complete a signal routing. Thus, a routing path consisting of several switches will introduce additional delay into the logic system implemented.

Direct Interconnect. Direct interconnect consists of short metal lines that are used to connect adjacent logic or I/O blocks; therefore the switch delays on these interconnect paths are eliminated. As shown in Figure 7.6 the X output of a logic block may be directly connected to the C or D inputs of the logic block above it, and to the A or B input of the logic below it. The Y output of a logic block can be directly connected to the B input of the logic block on its right.

Direct interconnect is also provided from a logic block to the I/O block adjacent to it. For example, the IN line of an I/O block on the left edge of the die is directly connected to an input of the logic block on its right. The OUT

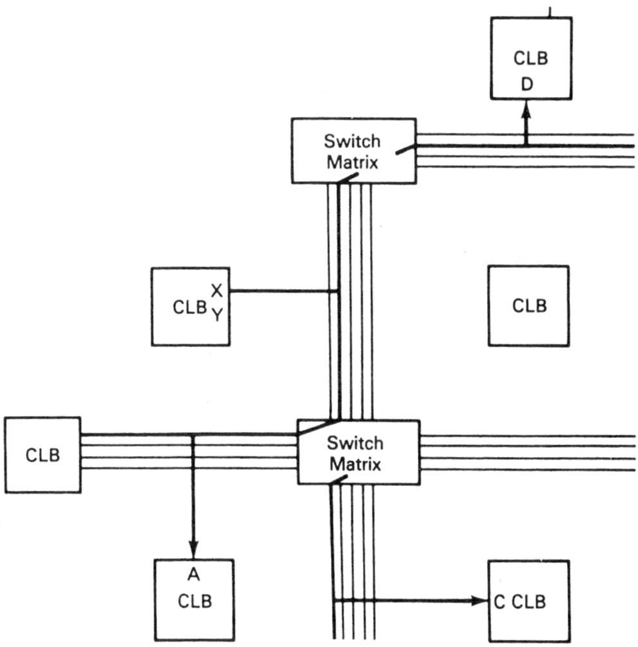

FIGURE 7.5
Routing of a signal from 1 logic block to 3 other blocks

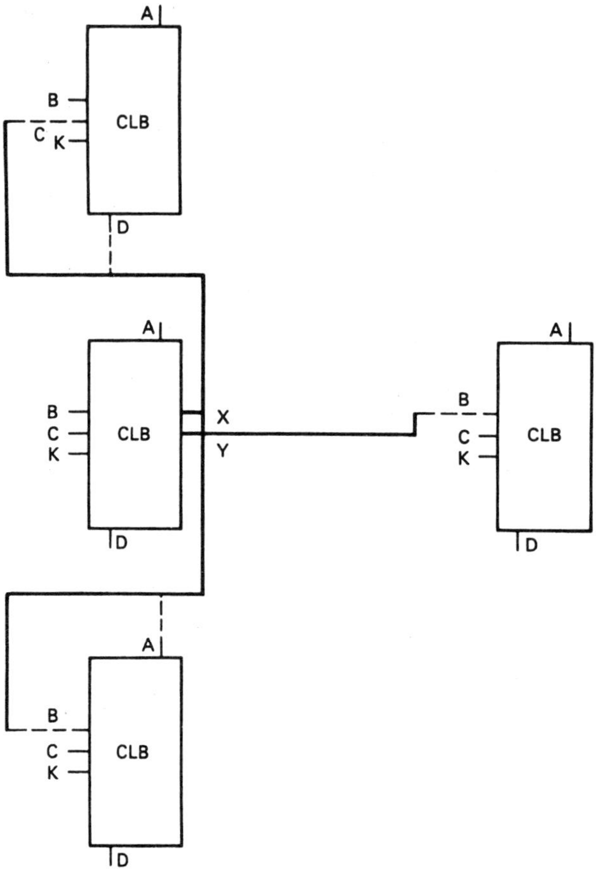

FIGURE 7.6
Direct interconnect between logic blocks

line of an I/O block on the right edge of the die is directly connected to the outputs of the logic block on its left. For I/O blocks at the top and bottom of the die, there are direct interconnects to both IN and OUT lines from the nearest logic blocks. Figure 7.7 shows the direct interconnections of I/O blocks with logic blocks.

Long Lines. Long line interconnect is provided to distribute critical signals (e.g., clock with a minimum propagation delay). Two long lines run between the columns of logic blocks, and one between the rows of the logic blocks as shown in Figure 7.8. These lines bypass the programmable switches and are used to route signals which must have very low skew, thus permitting high-speed reliable operation.

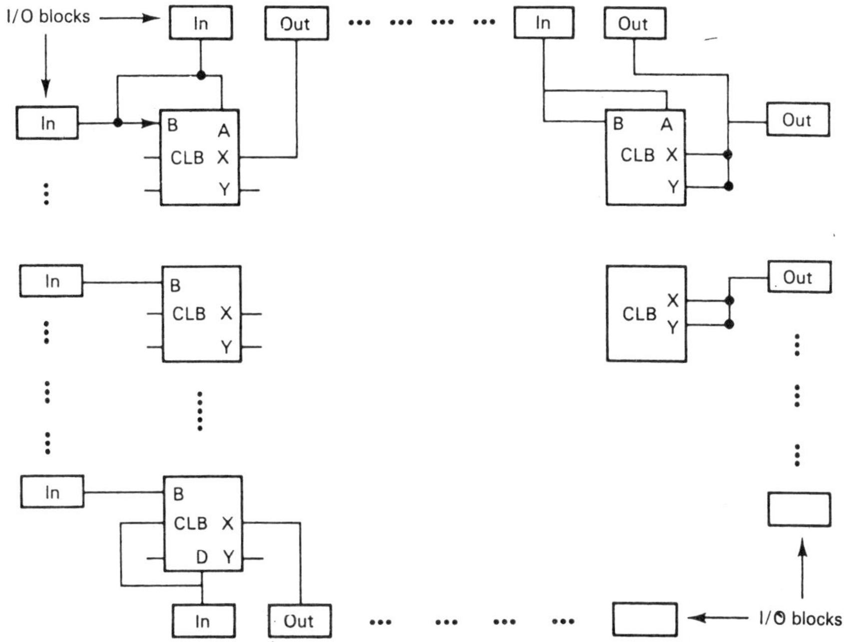

FIGURE 7.7
Direct interconnect between I/O and logic blocks

Two buffers are also provided to drive long lines. One of the buffer drives a single long line, called the **global line**, that is accessible to all B and K inputs of logic blocks. This global line for example may be used to distribute a master clock throughout the chip with minimal skew. The other buffer drives a horizontal long line. The line in turn can drive a vertical long line which may feed the B, C, or K inputs of the logic blocks.

7.1.4 Configuration Memory

The functions and interconnections of a logic cell array are completely defined by a configuration program. This program consists of a series of bits; each bit is stored in a memory cell in the device. A memory cell consists of a pass transistor and 2 CMOS inverters A and B connected in a latch configuration (see Figure 7.9). A data bit can be stored into or read from a memory cell only when the enable line is at logic "1." The pass transistor has been designed in such a way so that the incoming data overrides the output of the feedback inverter B. The output of a memory cell enables or disables an element inside the device.

The reconfiguration program may be loaded into a logic cell array using one of the following modes of operation for the array:

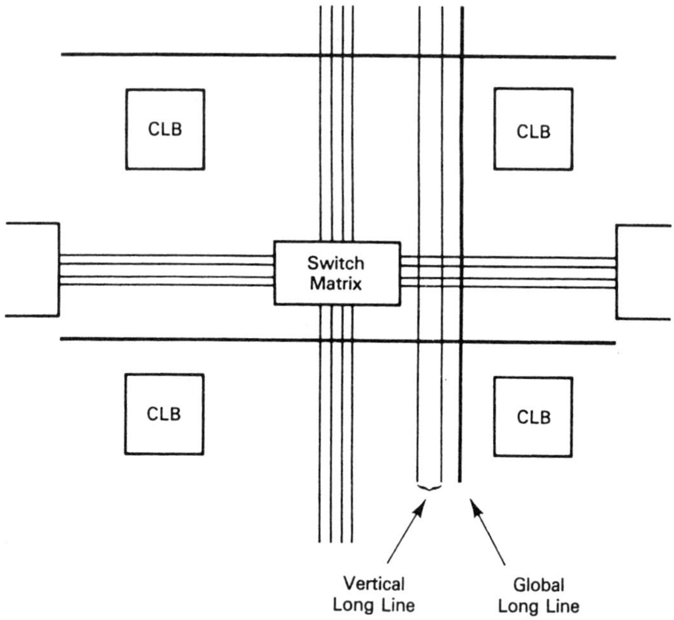

FIGURE 7.8
Long line interconnect

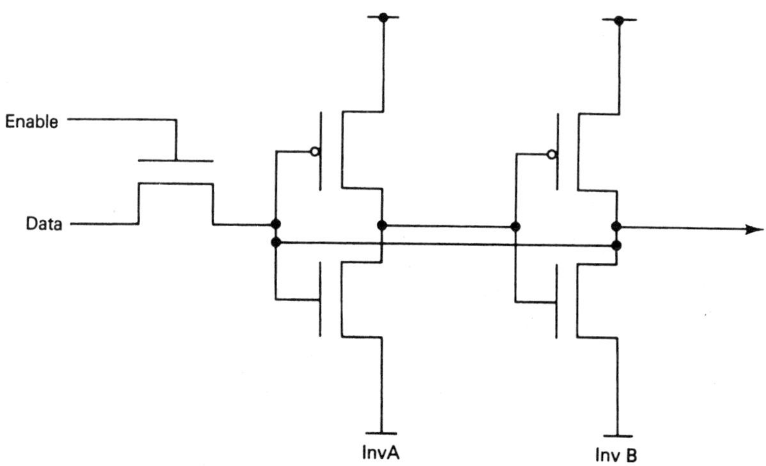

FIGURE 7.9
Memory cell

1. Slave mode.
2. Peripheral mode.
3. Master low mode.
4. Master high mode.

A particular mode of operation is selected by applying an appropriate input combination to the 3-mode select pins M0, M1, and M2 of the cell array chip, as indicated in Figure 7.10; M2 can also be used as a I/O pin after the configuration process has been completed. Irrespective of the mode of operation selected, the cell array has to be initialized first. The initialization process begins when the power is applied to the device. The application of power is detected by an internal circuit, which starts a time-out cycle in order to stabilize the power. At the end of the time-out cycle the mode select pins are sampled and the loading of the configuration program begins. The configuration program is formulated as a serial bit-stream with a bit field at the beginning, this bit field indicates the number of bits which are to be stored in the cell array. When the total number of configuration bits loaded into the device equals the number represented by the bit-field, the loading of the entire configuration program has been completed. The completion of the configuration is indicated by the presence of a logic "1" signal at the DONE/$\overline{\text{PROG}}$ pin of the device.

M0	*M1*	*M2*	*Mode selected*
0	0	0	Master Serial
0	0	1	Master low
0	1	1	Master high
1	0	1	Peripheral
1	1	1	Slave

FIGURE 7.10
Selection of programming mode

The **slave mode** is the simplest among the 4 methods available for loading the configuration data. In this mode, each data bit is serially shifted into a shift register inside the cell array via the DIN pin, on the positive edge of the clock pulse applied to the CCLK pin (see Figure 7.11). When the shift register (71-bit for XC2064, 87-bit for XC2018) is full, its contents are transferred to the internal memory cells as a single word; the XC2064 has 160 words of 71-bits each and the XC2018 has 196 words of 87 bits. After the entire program has been loaded, 3 additional clock pulses are applied in order to load each configuration bit into the appropriate control mode. Note that the CCLK pin is an input only in the slave mode, for all other modes it is an output. Once the program loading process has been started the $\overline{\text{RESET}}$ pin must remain at logic "1"; after the loading is completed it again becomes the master reset control pin. The DONE/$\overline{\text{PROG}}$ pin goes to logic "0" during the loading and

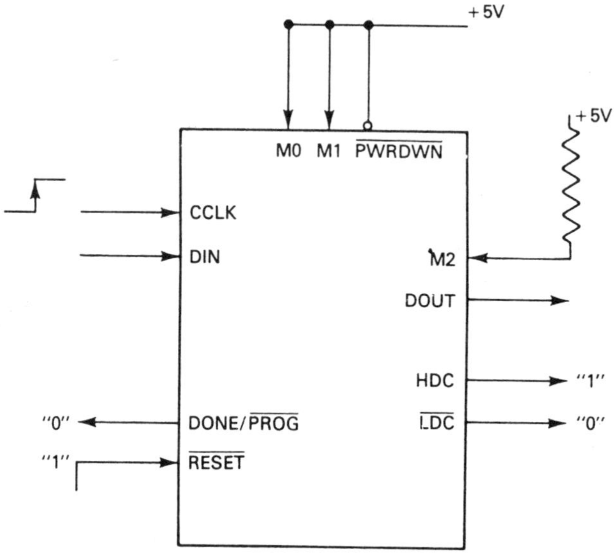

FIGURE 7.11
Slave mode

returns to logic "1" only after the programming has been completed. During the program loading process pins HDC and $\overline{LDC}$ remain at logic "1" and logic "0," respectively, to indicate that the configuration of the device is not complete. All input/output pins not used for programming the device are forced into high-impedance state.

The **peripheral mode** allows data to be loaded directly from a microprocessor bus (see Figure 7.12). The data is serially shifted into the device using the $\overline{WRT}$ (write strobe input) pin, and three chip select signals applied via pins $\overline{CS0}$, $\overline{CS1}$, and CS2. The $\overline{WRT}$ functions in an identical manner as the CCLK does in the slave mode. A pulse on the $\overline{WRT}$ input, while $\overline{CS0}$, $\overline{CS1}$ are at logic "0" and CS2 at logic "1," causes a data bit to be shifted into the device bit via the DIN input pin. As in the slave mode three additional pulses are required to complete the configuration process.

Both slave and peripheral modes permit configuration under the control of an external processor. In the **master-high** and **master-low** modes, on the other hand, the cell array chip itself assumes a more active role in loading the program data. In both cases, the cell array accesses a byte-wide memory chip (e.g., an EPROM or an EEPROM) by using the input/output pins A0–A15 of the device to generate an address bus, and by using input/output pins D0–D7 to form a unidirectional data bus (see Figure 7.13). In the master-low mode, the memory chip is addressed sequentially starting from address zero, whereas in the master high mode addresses are made in a descending order

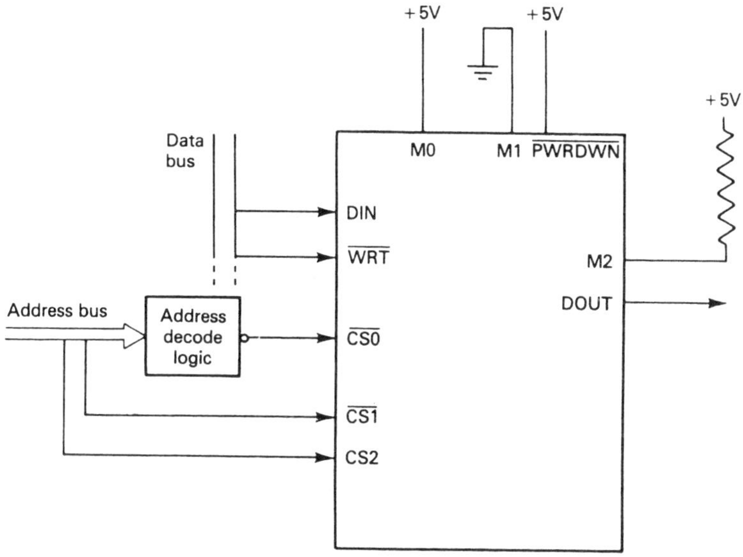

FIGURE 7.12
Peripheral mode

starting from the highest one. The 8-bit parallel data read from the memory is serialized internally and loaded into the memory cells of the cell array chip.

In the **master serial** mode, the $\overline{\text{RCLK}}$ (Read clock) signal of the device is used to synchronize the transfer of serial data corresponding to the configuration program (see Figure 7.14). After the program has been loaded, a logic "1" signal from the DONE/$\overline{\text{PROG}}$ disables the serial memory and the cell array device assumes the specified functionality.

Several cell arrays can also be daisy-chained together by connecting the DOUT pin of one device to the DIN pin of the next device in the chain.

7.2 XC3000 SERIES LCA

The XC3000 family has five devices with densities ranging from 2,000 to 9,000 gates (see Figure 7.15). The devices in this series have about 20 ns worst case propagation delay compared to 25 ns of the XC2000 series. The architecture of the XC3000 series devices is similar to that of XC2000 series, consisting of **configurable logic blocks** (CLB), programmable I/O blocks, and interconnections.

Each CLB has a 5-input combinational logic section and 2 D flip-flops (see Figure 7.16). A block has also a direct data input line D_{in}, which allows a signal to be fed directly to either of the D flip-flops. The outputs of the fip-flops can be fed back as inputs to the combinational logic section.

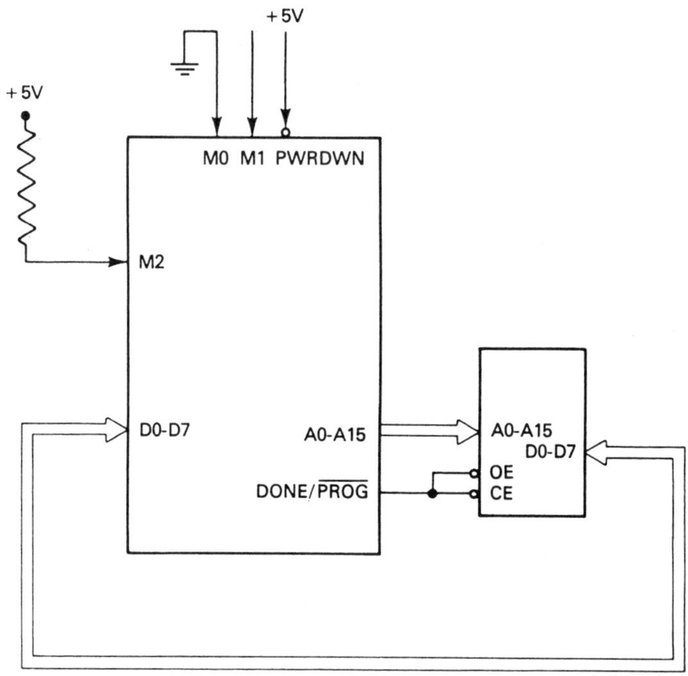

FIGURE 7.13
Master mode

Either of the flip-flop outputs, or the F or G outputs from the combinational logic section can feed the adjacent CLBs in a device. The selection is made by appropriate programming of the output multiplexers. Each CLB has also 3 control lines going into it: **clock**, **clock enable**, and **asynchronous reset**.

A programmable I/O block consists of 2 flip-flops, 1 of which is an edge-triggered D flip-flop, whereas the other can be used either as a D flip-flop or as a transparent latch (see Figure 7.17). The clock signals for each of the flip-flops can be independently selected from 1 of the 2 clock lines feeding an I/O block. The reset inputs of flip-flops in all I/O blocks are tied up to a global reset line. When the dedicated chip reset pin is activated, flip-flops in all I/O blocks are cleared.

The input buffers of the XC3000 series chips can be programmed for TTL or CMOS thresholds. The input signal can be directly fed or latched. The status signal of the output signal can be programmed to be true or inverted. Furthermore, the transient response of the output buffer can be controlled to select a fast or slow slew rate. There is also the provision for connecting an unused I/O pin to V_{cc} via a passive pull-up resistor in order to minimize the power dissipation in a device.

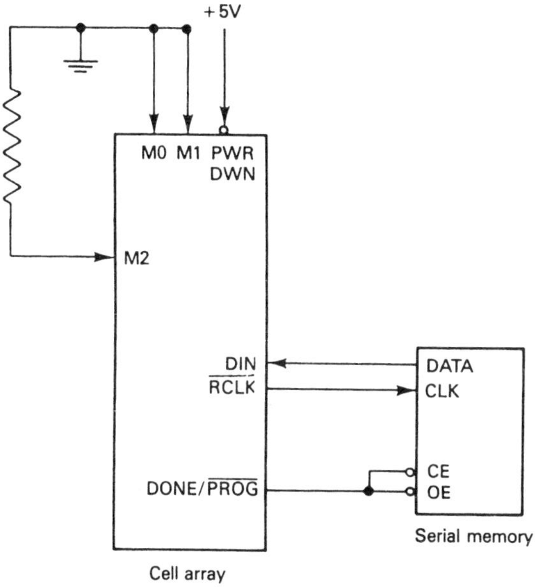

FIGURE 7.14
Master serial mode

As in XC2000 series, 3 levels of programmable interconnections are provided in the XC3000 series devices: **general purpose**, **direct**, and **long line**. In addition, tri-state buffers are embedded in order to set up internal connections from buses; each CLB has 2 tri-state buffers, 1 above and 1 below it (see Figure 7.18a). By applying a logic low signal on the control input of a tri-state buffer, it can be used to drive a horizontal long line. However, the driving of a horizontal line by multiple drivers with opposing logic values should be avoided. The tri-state buffers can be used to build wired-AND logic circuits as shown in Figure 7.18b. If all the buffer control inputs are logic high, their outputs will be in a high impedance state; therefore, the horizontal line will be at logic high because of the pull-up resistor(s).

	XC3020	*XC3030*	*XC3042*	*XC3064*	*XC3090*
Number of gates	2,000	3,000	4,200	6,400	9,000
Number of CLBs	64	100	144	224	320
Number of IOBs	64	80	96	120	144
Latches and flip-flops	256	360	480	688	928

FIGURE 7.15
Features of XC3000 series devices

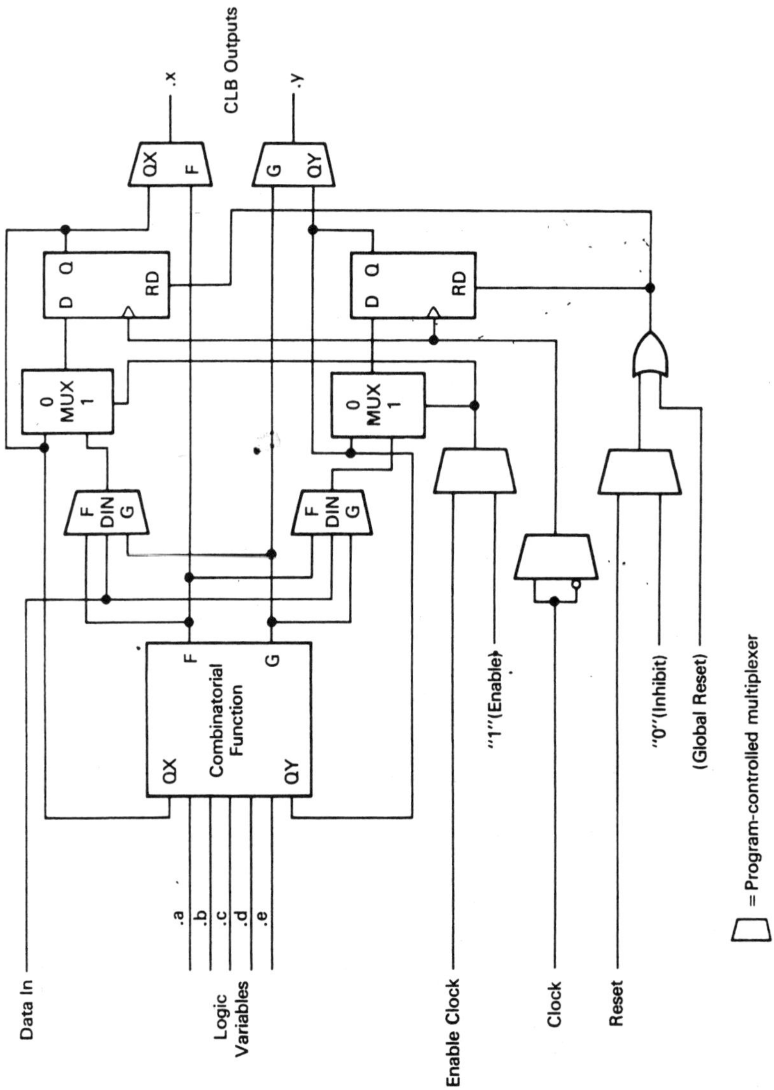

FIGURE 7.16
CLB structure (Courtesy of Xilinx, Inc.)

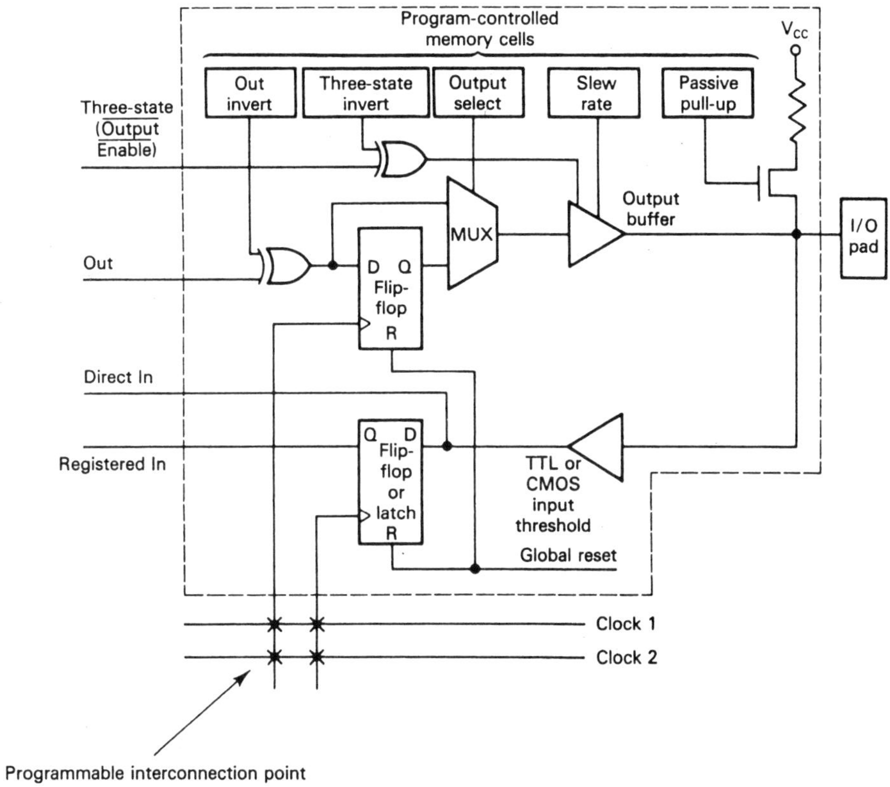

FIGURE 7.17
I/O block in XC3000 family (Courtesy of Xilinx, Inc.)

7.3 LOGIC DESIGN USING CELL ARRAYS

As discussed previously, a combinational function is implemented in the logic block of a cell array by means of a look-up table utilizing a 16-bit RAM. The 1's and 0's stored in the RAM during configuration uniquely define the combinational function a logic block is to perform.

As an example, let us implement a 5-bit Gray code to binary code converter circuit using a logic cell array. The truth table of the converter circuit is shown in Figure 7.19a. The Karnaugh maps for the outputs B1, B2, B3, B4 are plotted as shown in Figure 7.19b. The output equations are:

$$B1 = Z$$

$$B2 = Y\overline{Z} + \overline{Y}Z$$

$$B3 = \overline{X}Y\overline{Z} + \overline{X}\overline{Y}Z + X\overline{Y}\overline{Z} + XYZ$$

$$B4 = W\overline{X}\,\overline{Y}\,\overline{Z} + \overline{W}X\overline{Y}\,\overline{Z} + \overline{W}\,\overline{X}Y\overline{Z} + WXY\overline{Z} + W\overline{X}YZ + \overline{W}XYZ + \overline{W}\,\overline{X}\,\overline{Y}Z + WX\overline{Y}Z$$

$$B5 = \overline{V}\,\overline{W}\,\overline{X}YZ + \overline{V}\,\overline{W}X\overline{Y}\,\overline{Z} + \overline{V}W\overline{X}\,\overline{Y}\,\overline{Z} + \overline{V}WXY\overline{Z} + VW\overline{X}Y\overline{Z} + VWX\overline{Y}\,\overline{Z} + V\overline{W}\,\overline{X}\,\overline{Y}\,\overline{Z} + V\overline{W}XY\overline{Z} + \overline{V}\,\overline{W}\,\overline{X}\,\overline{Y}Z + \overline{V}\,\overline{W}XYZ + \overline{V}W\overline{X}YZ + \overline{V}WX\overline{Y}Z + VW\overline{X}\,\overline{Y}Z + VWXYZ + V\overline{W}\,\overline{X}YZ + V\overline{W}X\overline{Y}Z$$

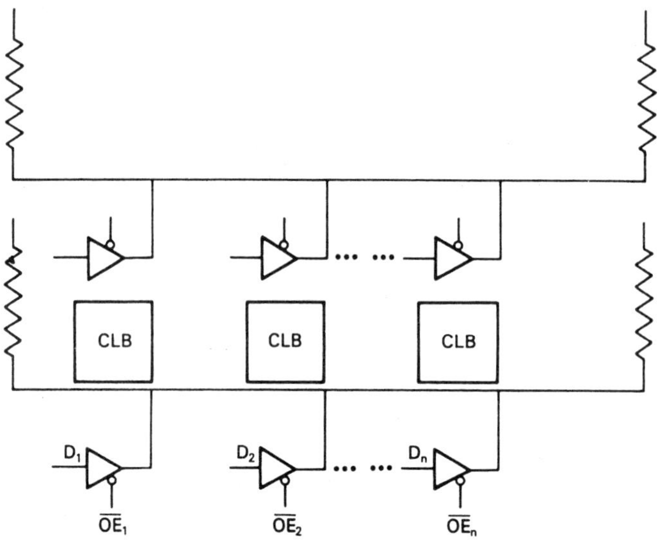

FIGURE 7.18a
Tri-state buffers driving the horizontal long lines

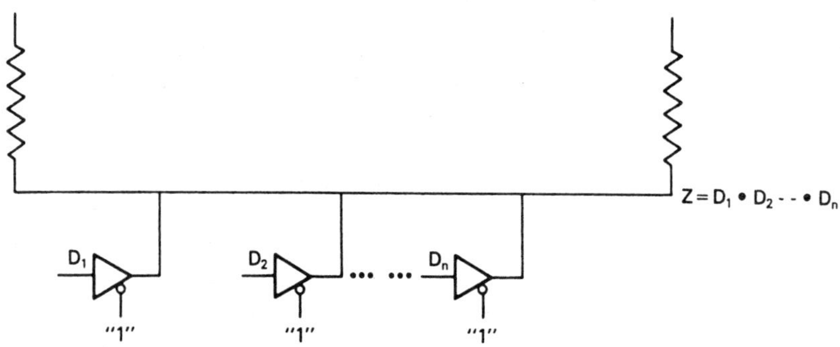

FIGURE 7.18b
Wired-AND function

By factoring B5 we get

$$\begin{aligned} B5 = {} & \overline{V}\{\overline{W}[\overline{X}(Y\overline{Z} + \overline{Y}Z) + X(\overline{Y}\overline{Z} + YZ)] \\ & + W[\overline{X}(\overline{Y}\overline{Z} + YZ) + X(Y\overline{Z} + \overline{Y}Z)]\} \\ & + V\{\overline{W}[\overline{X}(\overline{Y}\overline{Z} + YZ) + X(Y\overline{Z} + \overline{Y}Z)] \\ & + W[\overline{X}(Y\overline{Z} + \overline{Y}Z) + X(\overline{Y}\overline{Z} + YZ)]\} \\ = {} & \overline{V}.B4 + V.\overline{B4} \end{aligned}$$

Gray code					*Pure binary*				
Z	*Y*	*X*	*W*	*V*	*B1*	*B2*	*B3*	*B4*	*B5*
0	0	0	0	0	0	0	0	0	0
0	0	0	0	1	0	0	0	0	1
0	0	0	1	1	0	0	0	1	0
0	0	0	1	0	0	0	0	1	1
0	0	1	1	0	0	0	1	0	0
0	0	1	1	1	0	0	1	0	1
0	0	1	0	1	0	0	1	1	0
0	0	1	0	0	0	0	1	1	1
0	1	1	0	0	0	1	0	0	0
0	1	1	0	1	0	1	0	0	1
0	1	1	1	1	0	1	0	1	0
0	1	1	1	0	0	1	0	1	1
0	1	0	1	0	0	1	1	0	0
0	1	0	1	1	0	1	1	0	1
0	1	0	0	1	0	1	1	1	0
0	1	0	0	0	0	1	1	1	1
1	1	0	0	0	1	0	0	0	0
1	1	0	0	1	1	0	0	0	1
1	1	0	1	1	1	0	0	1	0
1	1	0	1	0	1	0	0	1	1
1	1	1	1	0	1	0	1	0	0
1	1	1	1	1	1	0	1	0	1
1	1	1	0	1	1	0	1	1	0
1	1	1	0	0	1	0	1	1	1
1	0	1	0	0	1	1	0	0	0
1	0	1	0	1	1	1	0	0	1
1	0	1	1	1	1	1	0	1	0
1	0	1	1	0	1	1	0	1	1
1	0	0	1	0	1	1	1	0	0
1	0	0	1	1	1	1	1	0	1
1	0	0	0	1	1	1	1	1	0
1	0	0	0	0	1	1	1	1	1

FIGURE 7.19a
Conversion from Gray code to pure binary

B1

XW \ ZY	00	01	11	10
00			1	1
01			1	1
11			1	1
10			1	1

$\overline{V}$

XW \ ZY	00	01	11	10
00			1	1
01			1	1
11			1	1
10			1	1

V

B2

XW \ ZY	00	01	11	10
00		1		1
01		1		1
11		1		1
10		1		1

$\overline{V}$

XW \ ZY	00	01	11	10
00		1		1
01		1		1
11		1		1
10		1		1

V

B3

XW \ ZY	00	01	11	10
00		1		1
01		1		1
11	1		1	
10	1		1	

$\overline{V}$

XW \ ZY	00	01	11	10
00		1		1
01		1		1
11	1		1	
10	1		1	

V

B4

XW \ ZY	00	01	11	10
00		1		1
01	1		1	
11		1		1
10	1		1	

$\overline{V}$

XW \ ZY	00	01	11	10
00		1		1
01	1		1	
11		1		1
10	1		1	

V

B5

XW \ ZY	00	01	11	10
00		1		1
01	1		1	
11		1		1
10	1		1	

$\overline{V}$

XW \ ZY	00	01	11	10
00	1		1	
01		1		1
11	1		1	
10		1		1

V

FIGURE 7.19b
Kårnaugh maps for the output functions

As can be seen from Figure 7.20a, 3 combinational logic blocks of a cell array chip have been utilized to implement the code converter circuit. Since B1 = Z, it does not need any logic block. B2 and B3 will both fit into CLB1; recall that a logic block can generate two functions of 3 variables. One logic block, CLB2, is needed to realize the expression for B4, since it is a function of 3 variables. B5 is a function of V and B4, hence it needs one half of a logic block, and introduces a second delay. Figure 7.20b shows the truth tables for the 3 logic blocks.

Let us illustrate the implementation of another combinational circuit using the logic blocks of a cell array. The combinational circuit is used to compare the magnitude of two 4-bit binary digits X and Y, and indicates whether a) X > Y, b) X = Y, and c) X < Y. Figure 7.21 shows how a number of combinational logic boxes can be interconnected to realize the comparator circuit.

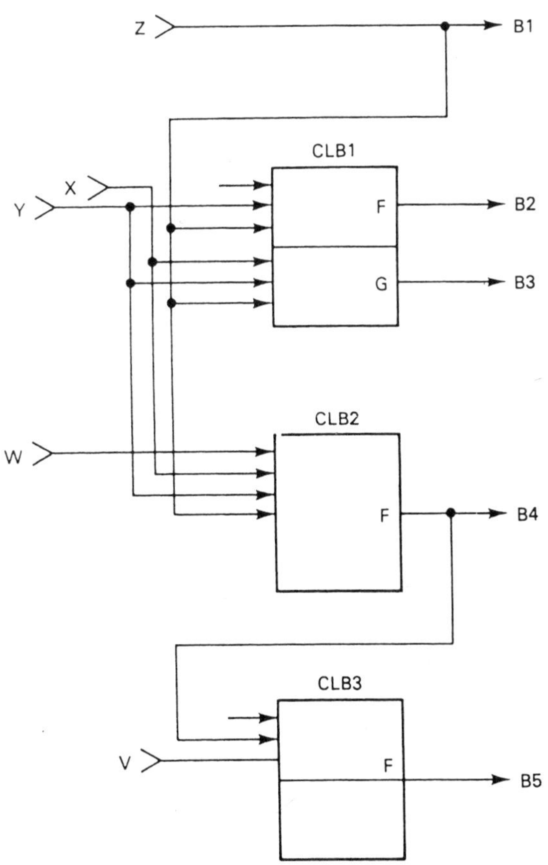

FIGURE 7.20a
Gray-to-binary code converter

CLB1

X	Y	Z	F(B2)	G(B3)
0	0	0	0	0
0	0	1	1	1
0	1	0	1	1
0	1	1	0	0
1	0	0	0	1
1	0	1	1	0
1	1	0	1	0
1	1	1	0	1

CLB3

—	B4	V	F(B5)
x	0	0	0
x	0	1	1
x	1	0	1
x	1	1	0

CLB2

W	X	Y	Z	F(B4)
0	0	0	0	0
0	0	0	1	1
0	0	1	0	1
0	0	1	1	0
0	1	0	0	1
0	1	0	1	0
0	1	1	0	0
0	1	1	1	1
1	0	0	0	1
1	0	0	1	0
1	0	1	0	0
1	0	1	1	1
1	1	0	0	0
1	1	0	1	1
1	1	1	0	1
1	1	1	1	0

FIGURE 7.20b
Truth tables for CLBs

The 2 higher significant bits of X and Y drive the A, B and C, D inputs, respectively, of logic blocks 1 and 2. The two lower significant bits of X and Y are applied to the inputs of logic blocks 3 and 4. The F outputs of the blocks, identified as F_1, F_2, F_3 and F_4 in Figure 7.21a are connected to the inputs of block 5 in such a way so that its F output (O_1) is a function of F_1, F_2 and F_3, and its G output (O_2) is a function of F_1, F_2 and F_4. Finally the outputs of block 5 are used to drive two of the inputs C and D of block 6. The output lines O_1, O_2, O_3 correspond to ">," "<," and "=," respectively. The truth table for each individual block is shown in Figure 7.21b.

7.4 STATE MACHINE DESIGN

In general, state machines are designed using either D flip-flops or J-K flip-flops. The configurable logic blocks of the cell array allow the creation of not only the familiar flip-flop types, but some special purpose variations, as well.

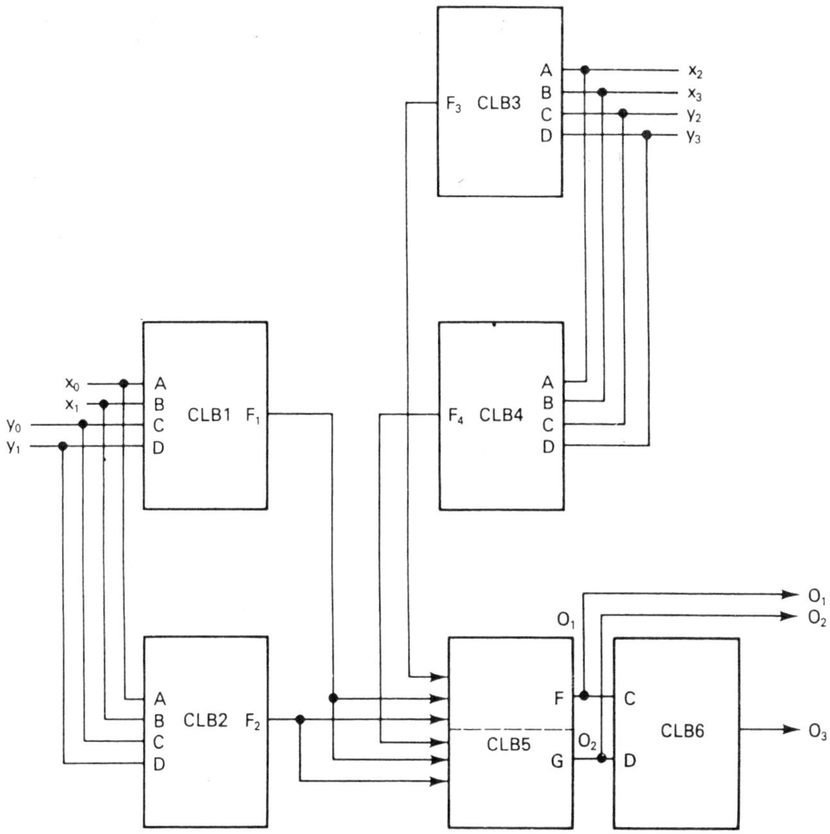

FIGURE 7.21a
4-bit comparator

CLB1					CLB2				
X_0	X_1	Y_0	Y_1	F	X_0	X_1	Y_0	Y_1	F
0	0	0	0	0	0	0	0	0	0
0	0	0	1	0	0	0	0	1	1
0	0	1	0	0	0	0	1	0	1
0	0	1	1	0	0	0	1	1	1
0	1	0	0	1	0	1	0	0	0
0	1	0	1	0	0	1	0	1	0
0	1	1	0	0	0	1	1	0	1
0	1	1	1	0	0	1	1	1	1
1	0	0	0	1	1	0	0	0	0
1	0	0	1	1	1	0	0	1	0
1	0	1	0	0	1	0	1	0	0
1	0	1	1	0	1	0	1	1	1
1	1	0	0	1	1	1	0	0	0
1	1	0	1	1	1	1	0	1	0
1	1	1	0	1	1	1	0	1	0
1	1	1	1	0	1	1	1	1	0

CLB3

X_2	X_3	Y_2	Y_3	F_3
0	0	0	0	0
0	0	0	1	0
0	0	1	0	0
0	0	1	1	0
0	1	0	1	0
0	1	1	0	0
0	1	0	0	1
0	1	1	1	0
1	1	1	0	1
1	1	0	0	1
1	1	0	1	1
1	1	1	1	0
1	0	0	0	1
1	0	0	1	1
1	0	1	0	0
1	0	1	1	0

CLB4

X_2	X_3	Y_2	Y_3	F_4
0	0	0	0	0
0	0	0	1	1
0	0	1	0	1
0	0	1	1	1
0	1	0	0	0
0	1	0	1	0
0	1	1	0	1
0	1	1	1	1
1	1	0	0	0
1	1	0	1	0
1	1	1	0	0
1	1	1	1	0
1	0	0	0	0
1	0	0	1	0
1	0	1	0	0
1	0	1	1	1

CLB5

F_1	F_2	F_3	$F(=O_1)$
1	0	0	1
1	0	1	1
0	0	1	1
0	1	0	0
0	0	0	0
0	1	1	0
1	1	0	x
1	1	1	x

CLB5

F_1	F_2	F_4	$G(=O_2)$
1	0	0	0
1	0	1	0
0	0	0	0
0	0	1	1
0	1	0	1
0	1	1	1
1	1	0	x
1	1	1	x

CLB6

B	$O1$	$O2$	$O3$
0	0	0	1
0	0	1	0
0	1	0	0
0	1	1	0

FIGURE 7.21b
Program for the logic blocks

For example, in conventional flip-flops simultaneous application of set and reset signals results in unpredictable output. However the D flip-flops in the combinational logic blocks of the cell array can be configured to be set- or reset-dominant. In a set-dominant flip-flop the output Q is set to logic "1" when both the S and the R inputs are active, simultaneously. The output of a reset-dominant flip-flop, on the other hand is forced to logic "0" for the same condition. The Karnaugh maps for the set-dominant and the reset-dominant flip-flop are shown in Figure 7.22a and b, respectively; the corresponding Boolean expressions are:

$$Q_{t+1} = S + Q_t\overline{R} \qquad \text{Set-dominant}$$

$$Q_{t+1} = S\overline{R} + Q_t\overline{R} \qquad \text{Reset-dominant}$$

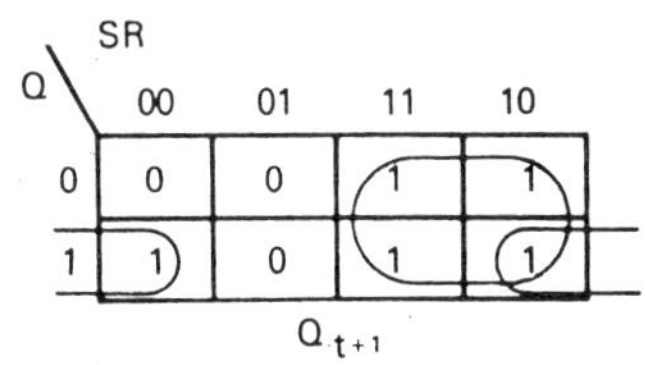

FIGURE 7.22a
Karnaugh maps: Set-dominant

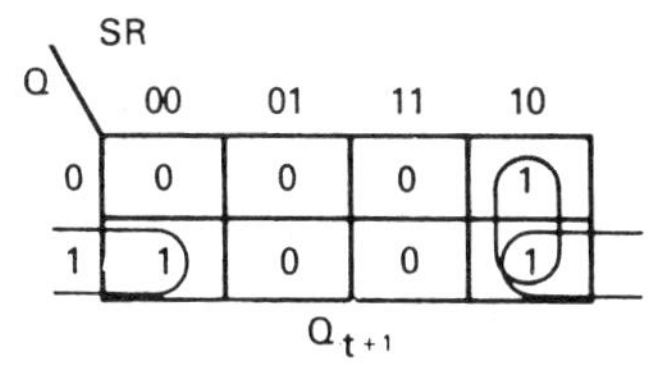

FIGURE 7.22b
Karnaugh maps: Reset-dominant

The implementation of these flip-flops are shown in Figure 7.23.

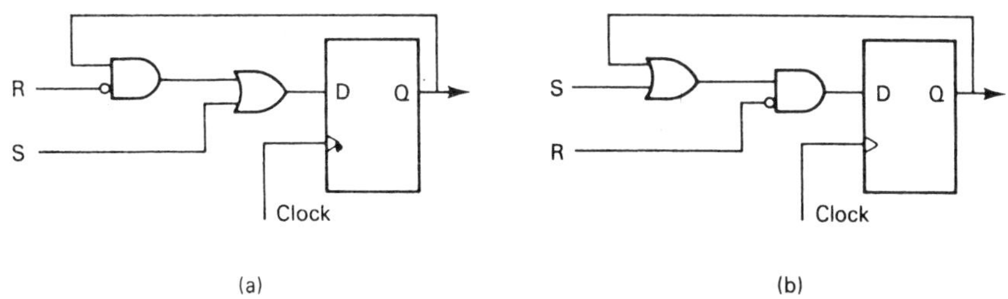

FIGURE 7.23
Implementation of a) set-dominant and b) reset-dominant flip-flop

It is also possible to configure the D flip-flop in a combinational logic block so that its output does not change (i.e., it remains in its present state when S and R are at logic "1").

Alternatively, the output of the D flip-flop may be toggled when logic "1" is simultaneously applied to its set and reset input lines; thus the D flip-flop acts as a JK flip-flop. The Karnaugh maps and the corresponding implementation of these 2 versions of the D flip-flop are shown in Figures 7.24 and 7.25, respectively.

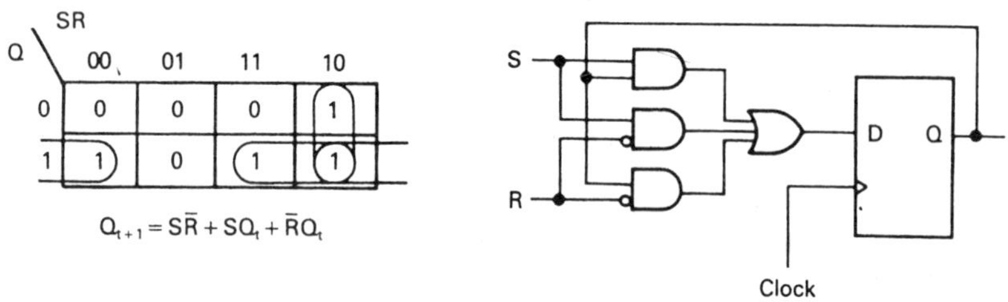

FIGURE 7.24
No change in state when S = R = 1

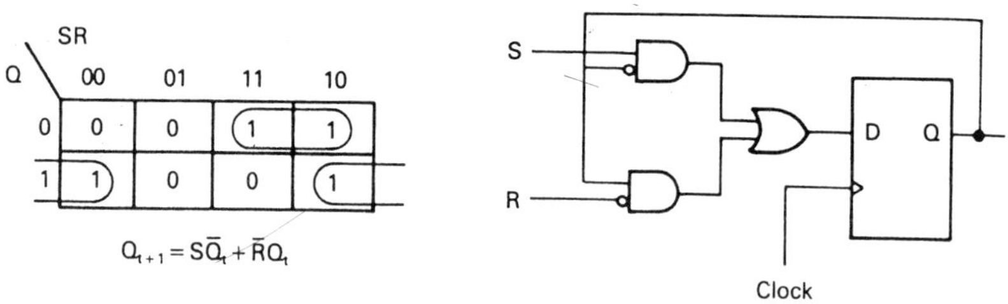

FIGURE 7.25
Toggles when S = R = 1

In addition to the variations on the basic D type flip-flop, a number of other alternatives are available which in many cases may simplify the implementation of control logic in state machine design. Figure 7.26 shows the D flip-flop with its input being driven by a 2-to-1 multiplexer. The next state control expression for the D flip-flop is:

$$Q_{t+1} = \bar{C}D_0 + CD_1$$

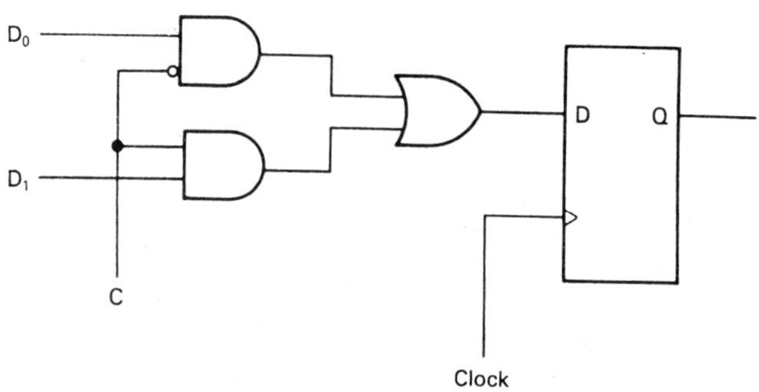

FIGURE 7.26
D flip-flop with multiplexer inputs

Figure 7.27 shows the implementation of a D flip-flop with clock enable, the corresponding next state expression is:

$$Q_{t+1} = CE \bullet D_{in} + \overline{CE} \bullet Q_t$$

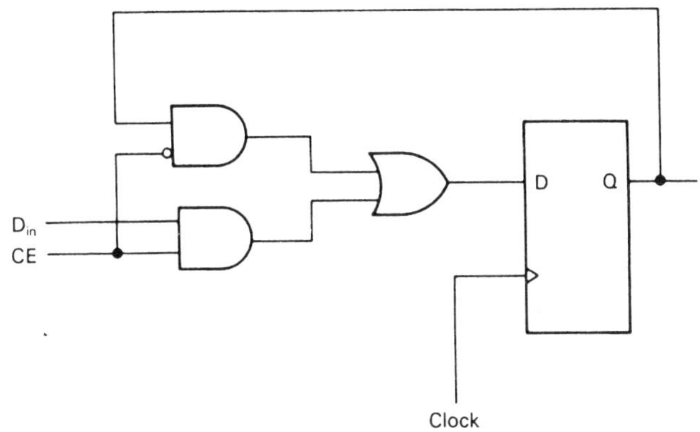

FIGURE 7.27
D flip-flop with clock enable

Let us now illustrate with a design example the use of a logic cell array in implementing a state machine. The state table of a 2-input machine is shown in Figure 7.28.

State \ x_1x_2	*0 0*	*0 1*	*1 1*	*1 0*
A	E,0	B,1	C,1	A,0
B	C,0	B,1	C,1	A,0
C	C,1	E,1	D,1	E,1
D	C,0	A,1	D,1	A,0
E	E,1	E,1	C,1	E,1

FIGURE 7.28
State table of a machine

The state assignment for the machine is selected as follows:

	y_1	y_2	y_3
A	0	0	1
B	1	0	1
C	0	1	0
D	1	1	0
E	0	1	1

The corresponding transition table for the machine, assuming D flip-flop implementation is shown in Figure 7.29.

y_1	y_2	y_3	x_1x_2 = 0 0	0 1	11	10
0	0	1	011,0	101,1	010,1	001,0
1	0	1	010,0	101,1	010,1	001,0
0	1	0	010,1	011,1	110,1	011,1
1	1	0	010,0	001,1	110,1	001,0
0	1	1	011,1	011,1	010,1	011,1

FIGURE 7.29
Transition table for the machine of Figure 7.28

The next state expressions for the flip-flops are:

$$Y_1 = \bar{x}_1\bar{x}_2 y_2 y_3 + \bar{x}_1 x_2 \bar{y}_2 y_3 + x_1 x_2 y_2 \bar{y}_3$$

$$Y_2 = \bar{x}_1\bar{x}_2 + \bar{x}_1 x_2 \bar{y}_1 y_2 + x_1 x_2 + x_1 \bar{x}_2 \bar{y}_1 y_2$$

$$Y_3 = \bar{x}_1\bar{x}_2 \bar{y}_1 y_3 + \bar{x}_1 x_2 + x_1 \bar{x}_2$$

and the output expression is

$$Z = \bar{y}_1 y_2 + x_2$$

These expressions can be implemented by using 4 combinational logic blocks in a cell array, as shown in Figure 7.30. The truth tables for the logic blocks are as shown in Figure 7.31.

Although the primary function of an I/O block in a logic cell array is used to handle inputs and outputs, it can also be configured to perform a variety of other functions. For example, several output pins can be connected together as shown in Figure 7.32 to act as a multiplexer. When the control line TS of the selected I/O block is set to logic "0," the output of the corresponding logic block is propagated to the common output line. The TS line of an I/O block can be driven by a combinational logic block. In Figure 7.32 the G and F outputs of the logic block 1 drive the TS line of the I/O blocks 1 and 2, respectively. Similarly, logic block 2 drives the TS lines of I/O blocks 3 and 4. In other words, logic blocks 1 and 2 are used to generate the control signals for the 4-to-1 multiplexer. The truth tables for logic blocks 1 and 2 are shown in Figure 7.33.

In situations when all the I/O blocks in a cell array are not utilized, the D flip-flops in the unused I/O blocks can be used to create parallel input/parallel output registers or shift registers, as well as certain types of counters (e.g., ring counter and Johnson counter).

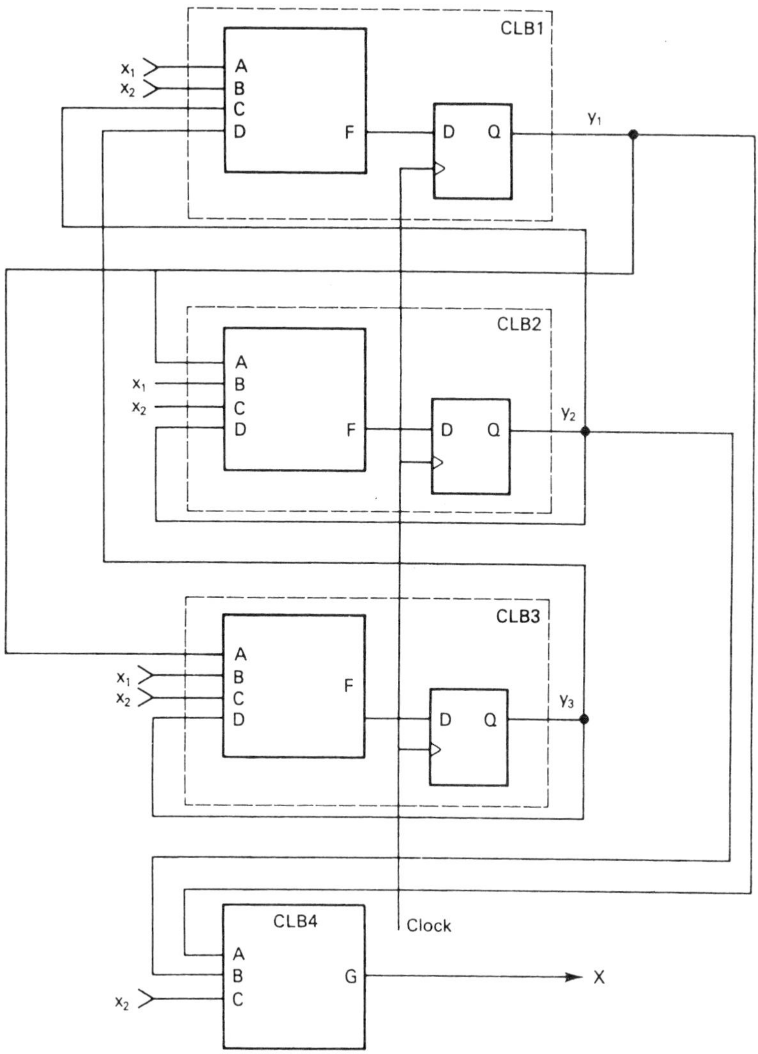

FIGURE 7.30
Implementation of the state table of Figure 7.29

Figure 7.34 shows a 4-bit parallel register built from 4 I/O blocks. A modification of this 4-bit register is shown in Figure 7.35. In this the input and the output line of each I/O block are tied together. The TS lines of all the I/O blocks are also connected together, and is controlled by an external source via another I/O block. When the control line is at logic "0," the contents of the register are available on the I/O pins, and when the control line is set to logic

CLB1

x_1	x_2	y_2	y_3	F,G
0	0	0	0	0
0	0	0	1	0
0	0	1	0	0
0	0	1	1	1
0	1	0	0	0
0	1	0	1	1
0	1	1	0	0
0	1	1	1	0
1	0	0	0	0
1	0	0	1	0
1	0	1	0	0
1	0	1	1	0
1	1	0	0	0
1	1	0	1	0
1	1	1	0	1
1	1	1	0	0

CLB2

x_1	x_2	y_1	y_2	F,G
0	0	0	0	1
0	0	0	1	1
0	0	1	0	1
0	0	1	1	1
0	1	0	0	0
0	1	0	1	1
0	1	1	0	0
0	1	1	1	0
1	0	0	0	0
1	0	0	1	1
1	0	1	0	0
1	0	1	1	0
1	1	0	0	1
1	1	0	1	1
1	1	1	0	1
1	1	1	1	1

CLB3

x_1	x_2	y_1	y_3	F,G
0	0	0	0	0
0	0	0	1	1
0	0	1	0	0
0	0	1	1	0
0	1	0	0	1
0	1	0	1	1
0	1	1	0	1
0	1	1	1	1
1	0	0	0	1
1	0	0	1	1
1	0	1	0	1
1	0	1	1	1
1	1	0	0	0
1	1	0	1	0
1	1	1	0	0
1	1	1	1	0

CLB4

y_1	y_2	x_2	X
0	0	0	0
0	0	1	1
0	1	0	1
0	1	1	1
1	0	0	1
1	0	1	1
1	1	0	0
1	1	1	1

FIGURE 7.31
Truth tables for logic blocks

"1" data from the external source is loaded into the 4-bit register. Since the clock line is common to all the I/O blocks along each edge of the cell array die, it is preferable that only the I/O blocks at one edge be used to form a register.

Shift registers can be constructed from the I/O blocks by connecting the output line of one block to the input of the next block. Figure 7.36 shows a

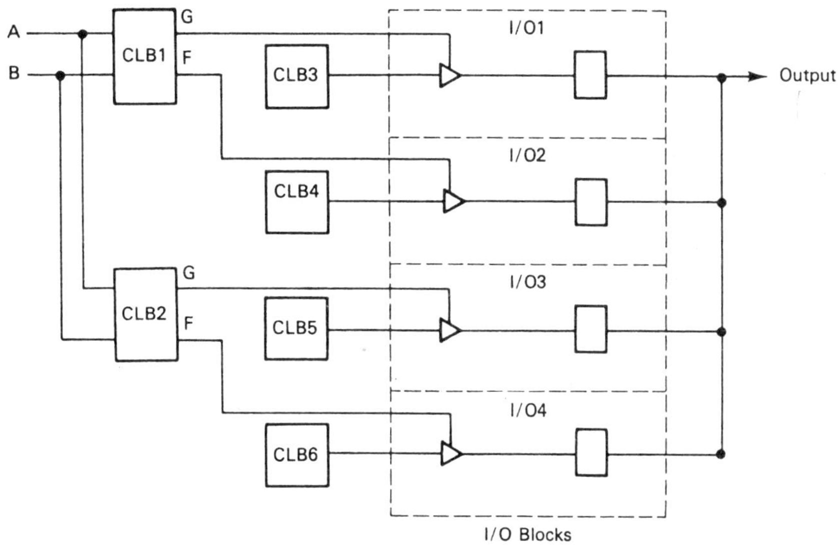

FIGURE 7.32
A 4-to-1 multiplexer

4-bit shift-left register. By changing interconnection of the inputs and outputs the shift-left register can be converted into a 4-bit shift-right register as shown in Figure 7.37.

A conventional shift register can be modified into a **linear feedback shift register** (LFSR), by feeding the outputs of a selected number of stages through EX-OR gates to the input of the shift register. The 4-bit shift register shown in Figure 7.38a feeds the EX-OR of the 2 lower significant stages to the input of the first stage. The complete sequence of states for the LFSR is shown in Figure 7.38b; this sequence repeats after 15 clock pulses and is the maximum number of states a 4-bit LFSR can have, so this sequence is termed the **maximal length sequence.** An all-0 state is not included in this sequence since this state has a next state that is also all 0's. The table in Figure 7.39 gives the

			CLB1		CLB2	
A	*B*	*C*	*F*	*G*	*F*	*G*
0	0	x	0	1	1	1
0	1	x	1	0	1	1
1	0	x	1	1	0	1
1	1	x	1	1	1	0

FIGURE 7.33
Truth tables for logic blocks 1 and 2

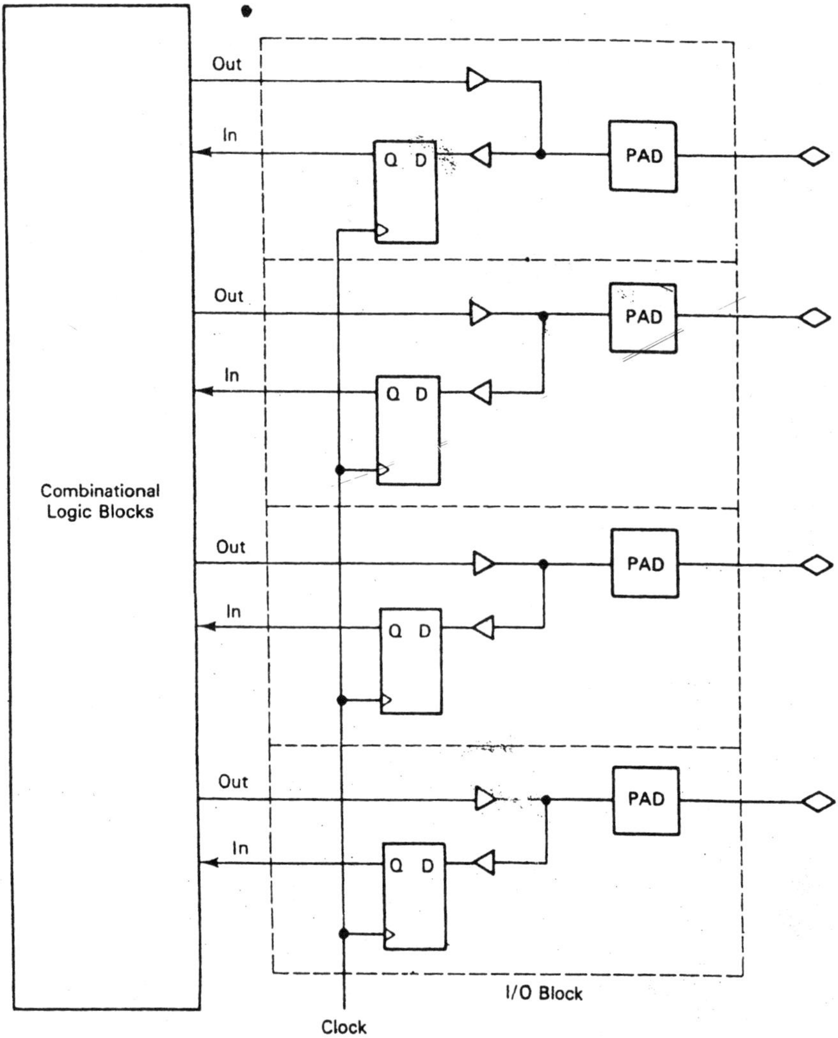

FIGURE 7.34
4-bit parallel in/parallel out register

feedback connections which will result in maximal length sequences for LFSRs of 4 to 16 stages.

The implementation of the 4-bit LFSR of Figure 7.38 using four I/O blocks and a combinational logic block is illustrated in Figure 7.40a. The truth table of the logic block is shown in Figure 7.40b; it performs the EX-OR operation.

It is often economical to implement state machines having a small num-

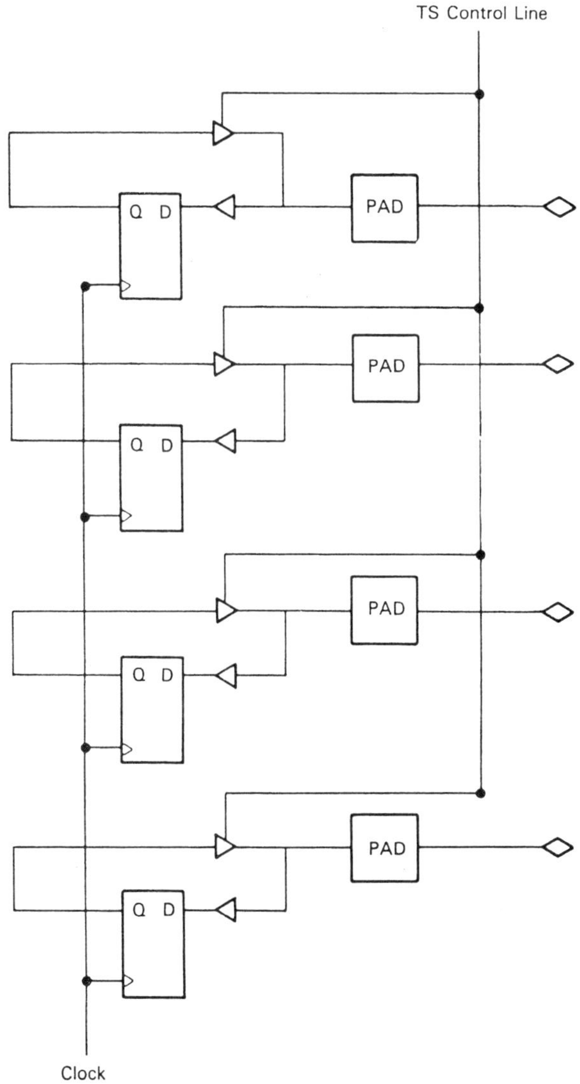

FIGURE 7.35
An externally controllable 4-bit register

ber of states with ring counters rather than using the conventional approach which minimizes the number of flip-flops. In the ring-counter approach the number of stages (i.e., flip-flops in the counter is equal to the number of states in the state machine to be realized). Figure 7.41 shows the sequence of states for the 4-bit ring counter.

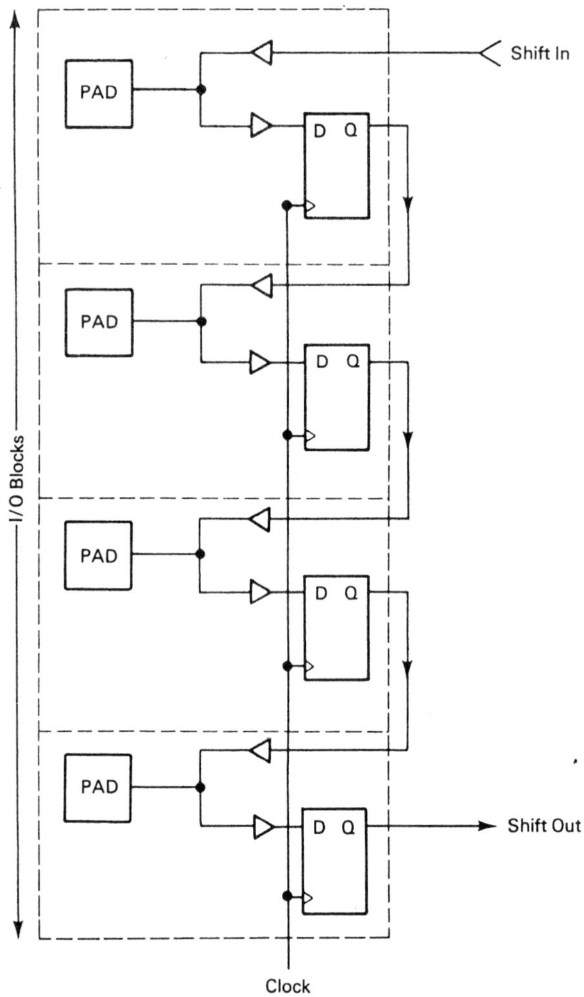

FIGURE 7.36
4-bit shift-left register

One obvious drawback of the ring counter is that if it enters one of the many non-valid states it will sequence through the non-valid states and will never re-enter the valid state sequence. A possible solution is to incorporate a logic network which detects the presence of additional 1's in a state (i.e., a non-valid state) and sets the input of the least significant flip-flop to 0. This will enable an n-bit counter to automatically return to a valid state after at most (n–1) clock pulses. A ring counter having this facility is known as

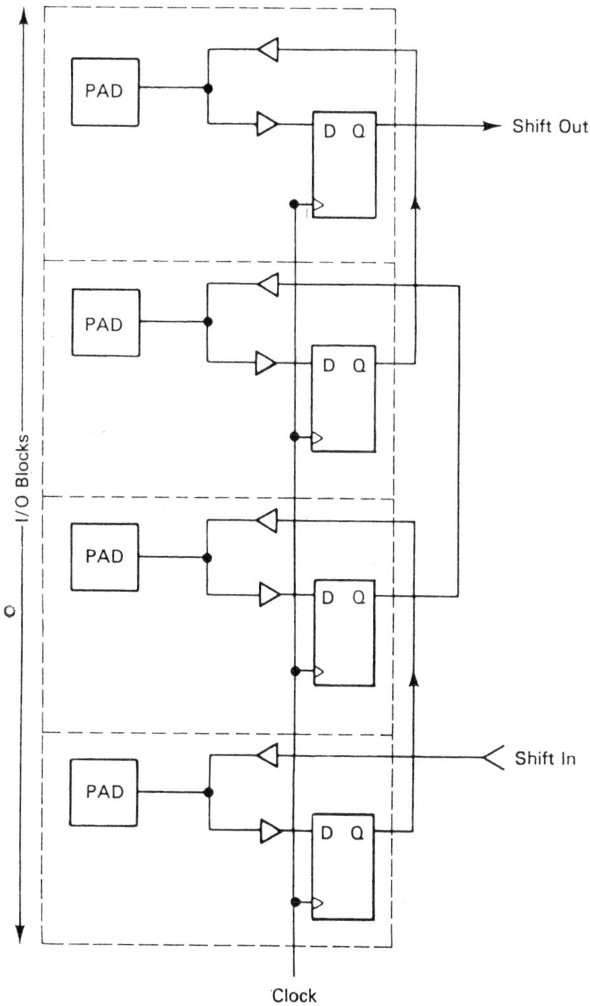

FIGURE 7.37
4-bit shift-right register

self-correcting. In Figure 7.42 combinational logic block is used to make the 4-bit ring counter, constructed from 4 I/O blocks, self-correcting. The self-correcting facility makes the configuration **self-initializing**, since it is not necessary to load the counter with an initial count value. The truth table of the logic block is shown in Figure 7.43, where Q is the output of the memory element in the logic block.

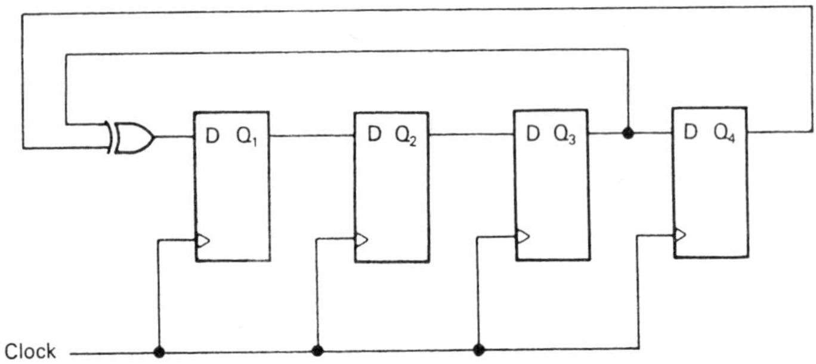

FIGURE 7.38a
A 4-bit LFSR

Q_1	Q_2	Q_3	Q_4
1	0	0	0
0	1	0	0
0	0	1	0
1	0	0	1
1	1	0	0
0	1	1	0
1	0	1	1
0	1	0	1
1	0	1	0
1	1	0	1
1	1	1	0
1	1	1	1
0	1	1	1
0	0	1	1
0	0	0	1

FIGURE 7.38b
Maximal length sequence

No. of stages	*Feedback connection into stage 1*
4	$Q_3 \oplus Q_4$
5	$Q_3 \oplus Q_5$
6	$Q_5 \oplus Q_6$
7	$Q_6 \oplus Q_7$
8	$Q_4 \oplus Q_5 \oplus Q_6 \oplus Q_8$
9	$Q_5 \oplus Q_9$
10	$Q_7 \oplus Q_{10}$
11	$Q_9 \oplus Q_{11}$
12	$Q_6 \oplus Q_8 \oplus Q_{11} \oplus Q_{12}$

FIGURE 7.39
Feedback connections for generating maximal-length sequences

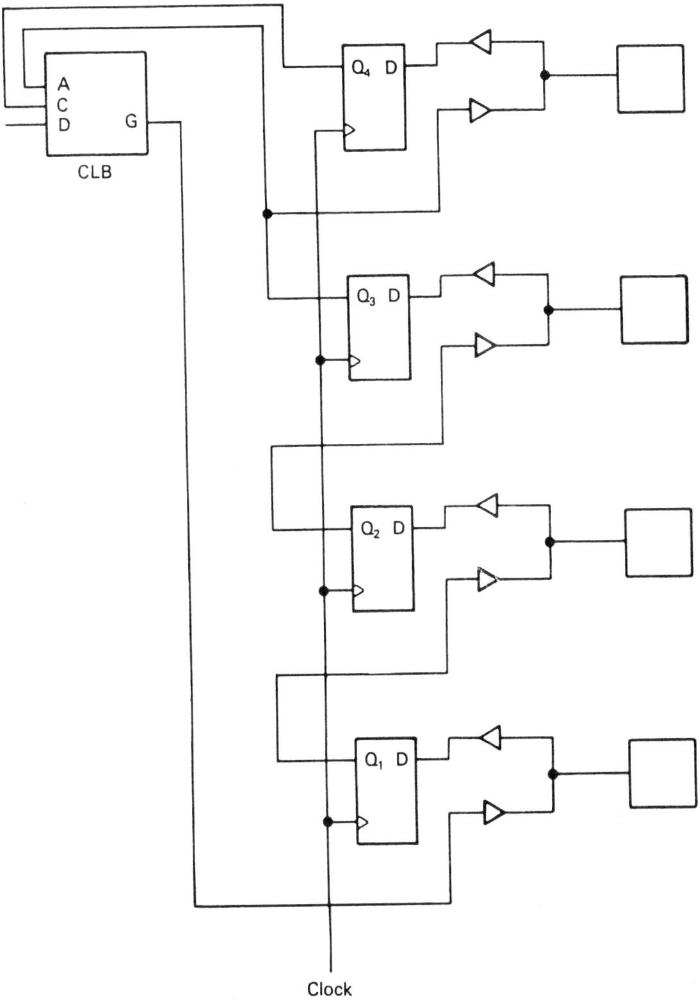

FIGURE 7.40a
4-bit LFSR

A	C	D	G
0	0	x	0
0	1	x	1
1	0	x	1
1	1	x	0

FIGURE 7.40b
Truth table of the CLB

y_4	y_3	y_2	y_1
0	0	0	1
0	0	1	0
0	1	0	0
1	0	0	0

FIGURE 7.41
State sequence for a 4-bit ring counter

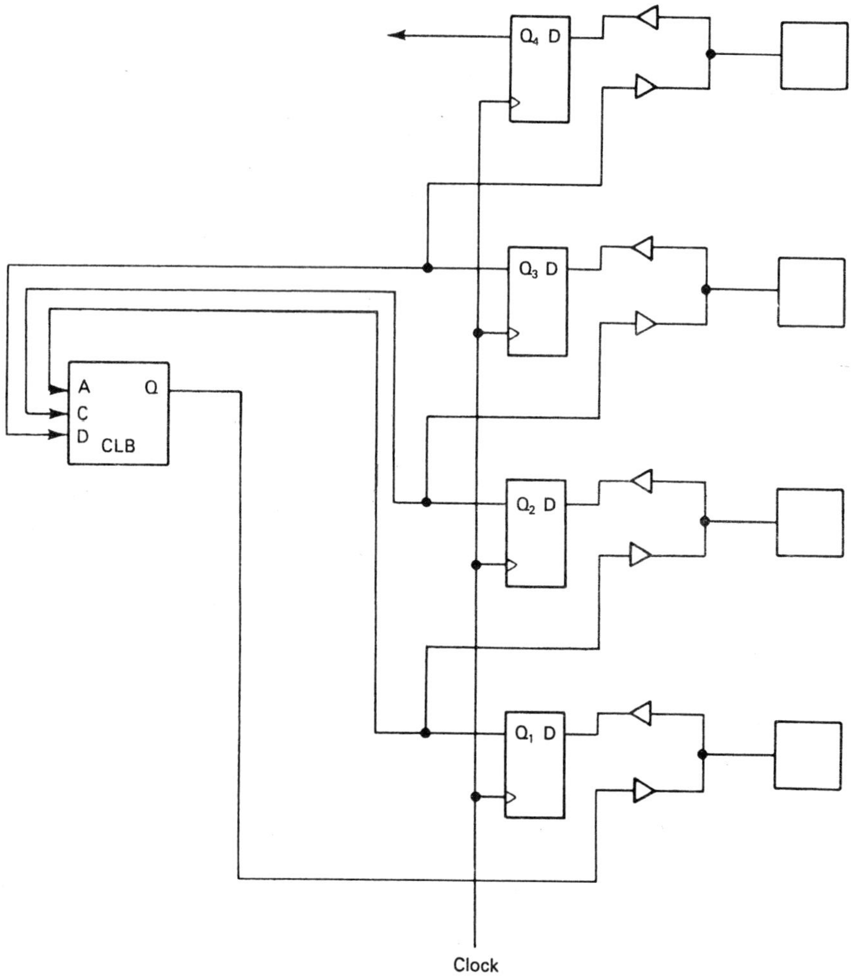

FIGURE 7.42
Self-correcting 4-bit ring counter

D (Q3)	C (Q2)	A (Q1)	Q
0	0	0	1
0	0	1	0
0	1	0	0
0	1	1	0
1	0	0	0
1	0	1	0
1	1	0	0
1	1	1	0

FIGURE 7.43
Truth table of CLB

7.5 DESIGN AIDS

Xilinx offers a design and development system, which permits users to specify and implement logic cell-array based circuits. The design methodology used in this system is similar to that used for conventional gate arrays, and includes design entry, processing and verification. A logic design is entered from its schematic drawing by using a standard schematic editor (such as SchemaII, FutureNet, OrCAD, PCAD, CASE, Viewlogic, Mentor, Daisy, Valid, Cadnetix), running on IBM PC/AT and compatibles or on SUNs, Apollos, and VAXes. The resulting schematic representation is converted into a Xilinx netlist format (XNF) file. Designers can also use PALASM2 or ABEL to enter all or part of a design. The resulting text file is then translated, and then optimized into a XNF file.

A XNF file is partitioned into smaller sub-blocks, each of which can fit into a configurable logic block or an I/O block. The partitioning software also includes optimization software, which eliminates unused and redundant logic. Finally, automatic placement and routing software place the design into configurable logic blocks and I/O blocks of a cell array.

After processing a design, the XACT design editor may be used to interactively edit, if needed, the placement and routing of critical areas. The XACT software package can also perform worstcase timing analysis, and generates the configuration program which defines a cell array's function. A simulator and an in-circuit verifier can be used for debugging and then verifying the design.

PROBLEMS

7-1. Design a circuit to compare a 4-bit serial stream with a preselected 4-bit pattern. The circuit should produce an output of 1 if there is a match between the patterns. Show how the circuit can be implemented using as few CLBs as possible.

7-2. Derive the Boolean expressions for implementing an 8-bit adder with carry-lookahead facility. Implement the expressions using minimum number of CLBs.

7-3. A BCD to binary converter is to be designed using CLBs. Assume the BCD data is shifted in serially, least significant bit first, into the converter; the conversion process begins when a complete BCD word has been shifted in. The binary data is shifted out of the converter with least significant bit first.

7-4. The state table of a sequential circuit is shown below. Determine how many CLBs are needed to implement the circuit. Draw the layout of the circuit and show the program table for each CLB.

State \ xyz	000	001	010	011	100	101	110	111
A	B	B	B	B	A	A	A	A
B	C	G	C	G	C	G	C	G
C	C	C	C	C	D	D	D	D
D	E	E	E	E	D	D	D	D
E	C	F	G	G	C	F	G	G
F	F	F	F	F	A	A	A	A
G	G	G	G	G	A	A	A	A

7-5. The parity of a 25-bit input pattern is to be determined using CLBs in a XC3000 series device. Draw the relevant block diagram and explain your design.

7-6. A 4-bit synchronous Gray code counter is to be incorporated into a XC3000 device. The counter has a clock enable input as well as an asynchronous clear input. Use minimum number of CLBs to implement the counter.

REFERENCES

1. *The Programmable Gate-array Data Book,* Xilinx Inc., 1988

Index

N

O

P

T

U

V

W

X

Z